Programming in Python 3

Developer's Library

ESSENTIAL REFERENCES FOR PROGRAMMING PROFESSIONALS

Developer's Library books are designed to provide practicing programmers with unique, high-quality references and tutorials on the programming languages and technologies they use in their daily work.

All books in the *Developer's Library* are written by expert technology practitioners who are especially skilled at organizing and presenting information in a way that's useful for other programmers.

Key titles include some of the best, most widely acclaimed books within their topic areas:

PHP & MySQL Web Development
Luke Welling & Laura Thomson
ISBN 978-0-672-32916-6

Python Essential Reference
David Beazley
ISBN-13: 978-0-672-32862-6

MySQL
Paul DuBois
ISBN-13: 978-0-672-32938-8

Programming in Objective-C
Stephen G. Kochan
ISBN-13: 978-0-321-56615-7

Linux Kernel Development
Robert Love
ISBN-13: 978-0-672-32946-3

PostgreSQL
Korry Douglas
ISBN-13: 978-0-672-33015-5

Developer's Library books are available at most retail and online bookstores, as well as by subscription from Safari Books Online at **safari.informit.com**

Developer's Library

informit.com/devlibrary

Programming in Python 3

A Complete Introduction to the Python Language

Mark Summerfield

✦✦Addison-Wesley

Upper Saddle River, NJ · Boston · Indianapolis · San Francisco
New York · Toronto · Montreal · London · Munich · Paris · Madrid
Capetown · Sydney · Tokyo · Singapore · Mexico City

The publisher offers excellent discounts on this book when ordered in quantity for bulk purchases or special sales, which may include electronic versions and/or custom covers and content particular to your business, training goals, marketing focus, and branding interests. For more information, please contact:

> U.S. Corporate and Government Sales
> (800) 382-3419
> corpsales@pearsontechgroup.com

For sales outside the United States, please contact:

> International Sales
> international@pearsoned.com

Visit us on the Web: informit.com/aw

Library of Congress Cataloging-in-Publication Data

Summerfield, Mark.
  Programming in Python 3 : a complete introduction to the Python language / Mark Summerfield.
       p. cm.
  Includes index.
  ISBN 978-0-13-712929-4 (pbk. : alk. paper)
1. Python (Computer program language) 2. Object-oriented programming (Computer science)
  I. Title.

  QA76.73.P98S86 2009
  005.1'17—dc22

                                                                          2008038340

ISBN-13: 978-0-13-712929-4

ISBN-10:   0-13-712929-7

Text printed in the United States on recycled paper at Donnelley in Crawfordsville, Indiana.

Second printing, April 2009, with minor corrections

In memory of
Franco Rabaiotti
1961–2001

Contents

ix

List of Tables

Introduction

Python is probably the easiest-to-learn and nicest-to-use programming language in widespread use. Python code is clear to read and write, and it is concise without being cryptic. Python is a very expressive language, which means that we can usually write far fewer lines of Python code than would be required for an equivalent application written in, say, C++ or Java.

Python is a cross-platform language: In general, the same Python program can be run on Windows and Unix-like systems such as Linux, BSD, and Mac OS X, simply by copying the file or files that make up the program to the target machine, with no "building" or compiling necessary. It is possible to create Python programs that use platform-specific functionality, but this is rarely necessary since almost all of Python's standard library and most third-party libraries are fully and transparently cross-platform.

One of Python's great strengths is that it comes with a very complete standard library—this allows us to do such things as download a file from the Internet, unpack a compressed archive file, or create a web server, all with just one or a few lines of code. And in addition to the standard library, thousands of third-party libraries are available, some providing more powerful and sophisticated facilities than the standard library—for example, the Twisted networking library and the NumPy numeric library—while others provide functionality that is too specialized to be included in the standard library—for example, the SimPy simulation package. Most of the third-party libraries are available from the Python Package Index, `pypi.python.org/pypi`.

Python can be used to program in procedural, object-oriented, and to a lesser extent, in functional style, although at heart Python is an object-oriented language. This book shows how to write both procedural and object-oriented programs, and also teaches Python's functional programming features.

The purpose of this book is to show you how to write Python programs in good idiomatic Python 3 style, and to be a useful reference for the Python 3 language after the initial reading. Although Python 3 is an evolutionary rather than revolutionary advance on Python 2, some older practices are no longer appropriate or necessary in Python 3, and new practices have been introduced to take advantage of Python 3 features. Python 3 is a better language than Python 2—it builds on the many years of experience with Python 2 and adds lots of new features (and omits Python 2's misfeatures), to make it even more of a pleasure to use than Python 2, as well as more convenient, easier, and more consistent.

The book's aim is to teach the Python *language*, and although many of the standard Python libraries are used, not all of them are. This is not a problem, because once you have read the book, you will have enough Python knowledge to be able to make use of any of the standard libraries, or any third-party Python library, and be able to create library modules of your own.

The book is designed to be useful to several different audiences, including self-taught and hobbyist programmers, students, scientists, engineers, and others who need to program as part of their work, and of course, computing professionals and computer scientists. To be of use to such a wide range of people without boring the knowledgeable or losing the less-experienced, the book assumes at least some programming experience (in any language). In particular, it assumes a basic knowledge of data types (such as numbers and strings), collection data types (such as sets and lists), control structures (such as if and while statements), and functions. In addition, some examples and exercises assume a basic knowledge of HTML markup, and some of the more specialized chapters at the end assume a basic knowledge of their subject area; for example, the databases chapter assumes a basic knowledge of SQL.

The book is structured in such a way as to make you as productive as possible as quickly as possible. By the end of the first chapter you will be able to write small but useful Python programs. Each successive chapter introduces new topics, and often both broadens and deepens the coverage of topics introduced in earlier chapters. This means that if you read the chapters in sequence, you can stop at any point and you'll be able to write complete programs with what you have learned up to that point, and then, of course, resume reading to learn more advanced and sophisticated techniques when you are ready. For this reason, some topics are introduced in one chapter, and then are explored further in one or more later chapters.

Two key problems arise when teaching a new programming language. The first is that sometimes when it is necessary to teach one particular concept, that concept depends on another concept, which in turn depends either directly or indirectly on the first. The second is that, at the beginning, the reader may know little or nothing of the language, so it is very difficult to present interesting or useful examples and exercises. In this book, we seek to solve both of these problems, first by assuming some prior programming experience, and second by presenting Python's "beautiful heart" in Chapter 1—eight key pieces of Python that are sufficient on their own to write decent programs. One consequence of this approach is that in the early chapters some of the examples are a bit artificial in style, since they use only what has been taught up to the point where they are presented; this effect diminishes chapter by chapter, until by the end of Chapter 7, all the examples are written in completely natural and idiomatic Python 3 style.

The book's approach is wholly practical, and you are encouraged to try out the examples and exercises for yourself to get hands-on experience. Wherever possible, small but complete programs are used as examples to provide realistic use cases. The examples and excercise solutions are available online at www.qtrac.eu/py3book.html—all of them have been tested with Python 3.0 on Windows, Linux, and Mac OS X, and with Python 3.1 alpha on Linux and Mac OS X.

The Structure of the Book

Chapter 1 presents eight key pieces of Python that are sufficient for writing complete programs. It also describes some of the Python programming environments that are available and presents two tiny example programs, both built using the eight key pieces of Python covered earlier in the chapter.

Chapters 2 through 5 introduce Python's procedural programming features, including its basic data types and collection data types, and many useful built-in functions and control structures, as well as very simple text file handling. Chapter 5 shows how to create custom modules and packages and provides an overview of Python's standard library, so that you will have a good idea of the functionality that Python provides out of the box and can avoid reinventing the wheel.

Chapter 6 provides a thorough introduction to object-oriented programming with Python. All of the material on procedural programming that you learned in earlier chapters is still applicable, since object-oriented programming is built on procedural foundations—for example, making use of the same data types, collection data types, and control structures.

Chapter 7 covers writing and reading files. For binary files, the coverage includes compression and random access, and for text files, the coverage includes parsing manually and with regular expressions. This chapter also shows how to write and read XML files, including using element trees, DOM (Document Object Model), and SAX (Simple API for XML).

Chapter 8 revisits material covered in some earlier chapters, exploring many of Python's more advanced features in the areas of data types and collection data types, control structures, functions, and object-oriented programming. This chapter also introduces many new functions, classes, and advanced techniques, including functional-style programming—the material it covers is both challenging and rewarding.

The remaining chapters cover other advanced topics. Chapter 9 shows techniques for spreading a program's workload over multiple processes and over multiple threads. Chapter 10 shows how to write client/server applications using Python's standard networking support. Chapter 11 covers database programming (both simple key–value "DBM" files, and SQL databases). Chapter 12 explains and illustrates Python's regular expression mini-language and covers the regular expressions module, and Chapter 13 introduces GUI (Graphical User Interface) programming.

Most of the book's chapters are quite long to keep all the related material together in one place for ease of reference. However, the chapters are broken down into sections, subsections, and sometimes subsubsections, so it is easy to read at a pace that suits you; for example, by reading one section or subsection at a time.

Obtaining and Installing Python 3

If you have a modern and up-to-date Mac or other Unix-like system you may already have Python 3 installed. You can check by typing python -V (note the capital *V*) in a console (Terminal.app on Mac OS X)—if the version is 3.*x* you've already got Python 3 and don't have to install it yourself. If Python wasn't found at all it may be that it has a name which includes a version number. Try typing python3 -V, and if that does not work try, python3.0 -V, and failing that try, python3.1 -V. If any of these work then you now know that you already have Python installed, what version it is, and what it is called. (In this book we use the name python3, but use whatever name worked for you, for example, python3.1.) If you don't have any verson of Python 3 installed, read on.

For Windows and Mac OS X, easy-to-use graphical installer packages are provided that take you step-by-step through the installation process. These are available from www.python.org/download. For Windows, download the "Windows x86 MSI Installer", unless you know for sure that your machine has a different processor for which a separate installer is suppled—for example, if you have an AMD64, get the "Windows AMD64 MSI Installer". Once you've got the installer, just run it and follow the on-screen instructions.

For Linux, BSD, and other Unixes, the easiest way to install Python is to use your operating system's package management system. In most cases Python is provided in several separate packages. For example, in Ubuntu (from version 8), there is python3.0 for Python, idle-python3.0 for IDLE (a simple development environment), and python3.0-doc for the documentation—as well as many other packages that provide add-ons for even more functionality than that provided by the standard library. (Naturally the package names will start python-3.1 for the Python 3.1 versions, and so on.)

If no Python 3 packages are available for your operating system you will need to download the source from www.python.org/download and build Python from scratch. Get either of the source tarballs and unpack it using tar xvfz Python-3.1.tgz if you got the gzipped tarball or tar xvfj Python-3.1.tar.bz2 if you got the bzip2 tarball. (The version numbers may be different, for example, Python-3.0.1.tgz or Python-3.1.1.bz2, in which case simply replace 3.1 with your actual version number throughout.) The configuration and building are standard. First, change into the newly created Python-3.1 directory and run ./configure. (You can use the --prefix option if you want to do a local install.) Next, run make.

It is possible that you may get some messages at the end saying that not all modules could be built. This normally means that you don't have the required libraries or headers on your machine. For example, if the readline module could not be built, use the package management system to install the corresponding development library; for example, readline-devel on Fedora-based systems and readline-dev on Debian-based systems. (Unfortunately, the relevant package names are not always so obvious.) Once the missing packages are installed, run ./configure and make again.

After successfully making, you could run make test to see that everything is okay, although this is not necessary and can take many minutes to complete.

If you used --prefix to do a local installation, just run make install. You will probably want to add a soft link to the python executable (e.g., ln -s ~/local/python31/bin/python3.1 ~/bin/python3, assuming you used --prefix=$HOME/local/python31 and you have a $HOME/bin directory that is in your PATH). This is the setup we used on Linux and Mac OS X—on Windows we used the binary installer. You might also find it convenient to add a soft link to IDLE (e.g., ln -s ~/local/python31/bin/idle ~/bin/idle3, on the same assumptions as before).

If you did not use --prefix and have root access, log in as root and do make install. On sudo-based systems like Ubuntu, do sudo make install. If Python 2 is on the system, /usr/bin/python won't be changed and Python 3 will be available as python3.0 (or python3.1 depending on the version installed). Python 3's IDLE is installed as idle, so if access to Python 2's IDLE is still required the old IDLE will need to be renamed, for example, to /usr/bin/idle2—*before* doing the install.

Acknowledgments

My first acknowledgments are of the book's technical reviewers, starting with Jasmin Blanchette, a computer scientist, programmer, and writer with whom I have cowritten two C++/Qt books. Jasmin's involvement with chapter planning and his suggestions and criticisms regarding all the examples, as well as his careful reading, have immensely improved the quality of this book.

Georg Brandl is a leading Python developer and documentor responsible for creating Python's new documentation tool chain. Georg spotted many subtle mistakes and very patiently and persistently explained them until they were understood and corrected. He also made many improvements to the examples.

Phil Thompson is a Python expert and the creator of PyQt, probably the best Python GUI library available. Phil's sharp-eyed and sometimes challenging feedback led to many clarifications and corrections.

Trenton Schulz is a senior software engineer at Nokia's Qt Software (fomerly Trolltech) who has been a valuable reviewer of all my previous books, and has once again come to my aid. Trenton's careful reading and the numerous suggestions that he made helped clarify many issues and have led to considerable improvements to the text.

In addition to the aforementioned reviewers, all of whom read the whole book, David Boddie, a senior technical writer at Nokia's Qt Software and an experienced Python practitioner and open source developer, has read and given valuable feedback on portions of it.

Thanks are also due to Guido van Rossum, creator of Python, as well as to the wider Python community who have contributed so much to make Python, and especially its libraries, so useful and enjoyable to use.

As always, thanks to Jeff Kingston, creator of the Lout typesetting language that I have used for more than a decade.

Special thanks to my editor, Debra Williams Cauley, for her support, and for once again making the entire process as smooth as possible. Thanks also to Anna Popick, who managed the production process so well, and to the proofreader, Audrey Doyle, who did such fine work once again.

Last but not least, I want to thank my wife, Andrea, both for putting up with the 4 a.m. wake-ups when book ideas and code corrections often arrived and insisted upon being noted or tested there and then, and for her love, loyalty, and support.

1

- Creating and Running Python Programs
- Python's "Beautiful Heart"

Rapid Introduction to Procedural Programming ||||

This chapter provides enough information to get you started writing Python programs. We strongly recommend that you install Python if you have not already done so, so that you can get hands-on experience to reinforce what you learn here. (The Introduction explains how to obtain and install Python on all major platforms—see page 4.)

This chapter's first section shows you how to create and execute Python programs. You can use your favorite plain text editor to write your Python code, but the IDLE programming environment discussed in this section provides not only a code editor, but also additional functionality, including facilities for experimenting with Python code, and for debugging Python programs.

The second section presents eight key pieces of Python that on their own are sufficient to write useful programs. These pieces are all covered fully in later chapters, and as the book progresses they are supplemented by all of the rest of Python so that by the end of the book, you will have covered the whole language and will be able to use all that it offers in your programs.

The chapter's final section introduces two short programs which use the subset of Python features introduced in the second section so that you can get an immediate taste of Python programming.

Creating and Running Python Programs |||

Python code can be written using any plain text editor that can load and save text using either the ASCII or the UTF-8 Unicode character encoding. By default, Python files are assumed to use the UTF-8 character encoding, a superset of ASCII that can represent pretty well every character in every language. Python files normally have an extension of .py, although on some Unix-like sys-

Character encodings ☞ 85

tems (e.g., Linux and Mac OS X) some Python applications have no extension, and Python GUI (Graphical User Interface) programs usually have an extension of .pyw, particularly on Windows and Mac OS X. In this book we always use an extension of .py for Python console programs and Python modules, and .pyw for GUI programs. All the examples presented in this book run unchanged on all platforms that have Python 3 available.

Just to make sure that everything is set up correctly, and to show the classical first example, create a file called hello.py in a plain text editor (Windows Notepad is fine—we'll use a better editor shortly), with the following contents:

```
#!/usr/bin/env python3

print("Hello", "World!")
```

The first line is a comment. In Python, comments begin with a # and continue to the end of the line. (We will explain the rather cryptic comment in a moment.) The second line is blank—outside quoted strings, Python ignores blank lines, but they are often useful to humans to break up large blocks of code to make them easier to read. The third line is Python code. Here, the print() function is called with two arguments, each of type str (string; i.e., a sequence of characters).

Each statement encountered in a .py file is executed in turn, starting with the first one and progressing line by line. This is different from some other languages, for example, C++ and Java, which have a particular function or method with a special name where they start from. The flow of control can of course be diverted as we will see when we discuss Python's control structures in the next section.

We will assume that Windows users keep their Python code in the C:\py3eg directory and that Unix (i.e., Unix, Linux, and Mac OS X) users keep their code in the $HOME/py3eg directory. Save hello.py into the py3eg directory and close the text editor.

Now that we have a program, we can run it. Python programs are executed by the Python interpreter, and normally this is done inside a console window. On Windows the console is called "Console", or "DOS Prompt", or "MS-DOS Prompt", or something similar, and is usually available from Start→All Programs→Accessories. On Mac OS X the console is provided by the Terminal.app program (located in Applications/Utilities by default), available using Finder, and on other Unixes, we can use an xterm or the console provided by the windowing environment, for example, konsole or gnome-terminal.

Start up a console, and on Windows enter the following commands (which assume that Python is installed in the default location)—the console's output is shown in **bold**; what you type is shown in lightface:

```
C:\>cd c:\py3eg
C:\py3eg\>C:\Python30\python.exe hello.py
```

Since the cd (change directory) command has an absolute path, it doesn't matter which directory you start out from.

Unix users enter this instead (assuming that Python 3 is in the PATH):*

```
$ cd $HOME/py3eg
$ python3 hello.py
```

In both cases the output should be the same:

Hello World!

Note that unless stated otherwise, Python's behavior on Mac OS X is the same as that on any other Unix system. In fact, whenever we refer to "Unix" it can be taken to mean Linux, BSD, Mac OS X, and most other Unixes and Unix-like systems.

Although the program has just one executable statement, by running it we can infer some information about the print() function. For one thing, print() is a built-in part of the Python language—we didn't need to "import" or "include" it from a library to make use of it. Also, it separates each item it prints with a single space, and prints a newline after the last item is printed. These are default behaviors that can be changed, as we will see later. Another thing worth noting about print() is that it can take as many or as few arguments as we care to give it.

print()
☞ 171

Typing such command lines to invoke our Python programs would quickly become tedious. Fortunately, on both Windows and Unix we can use more convenient approaches. Assuming we are in the py3eg directory, on Windows we can simply type:

```
C:\py3eg\>hello.py
```

Windows uses its registry of file associations to automatically call the Python interpreter when a filename with extension .py is entered in a console.

If the output on Windows is:

('Hello', 'World!')

then it means that Python 2 is on the system and is being invoked instead of Python 3. One solution to this is to change the .py file association from Python 2 to Python 3. The other (less convenient, but safer) solution is to put

---

*The Unix prompt may well be different from the $ shown here; it does not matter what it is.

the Python 3 interpreter in the path (assuming it is installed in the default location), and execute it explicitly each time:

```
C:\py3eg\>path=c:\python30;%path%
C:\py3eg\>python hello.py
```

It might be more convenient to create a py3.bat file with the single line path=c:\python30;%path% and to save this file in the C:\Windows directory. Then, whenever you start a console for running Python 3 programs, begin by executing py3.bat. Or alternatively you can have py3.bat executed automatically. To do this, change the console's properties (find the console in the Start menu, then right-click it to pop up its Properties dialog), and in the Shortcut tab's Target string, append the text " /u /k c:\windows\py3.bat" (note the space before, between, and after the "/u" and "/k" options, and be sure to add this at the end after "cmd.exe").

On Unix, we must first make the file executable, and then we can run it:

```
$ chmod +x hello.py
$ ./hello.py
```

We need to run the chmod command only once of course; after that we can simply enter ./hello.py and the program will run.

On Unix, when a program is invoked in the console, the file's first two bytes are read.[*] If these bytes are the ASCII characters #!, the shell assumes that the file is to be executed by an interpreter and that the file's first line specifies which interpreter to use. This line is called the *shebang* (shell execute) line, and if present must be the first line in the file.

The shebang line is commonly written in one of two forms, either:

```
#!/usr/bin/python3
```

or:

```
#!/usr/bin/env python3
```

If written using the first form, the specified interpreter is used. This form may be necessary for Python programs that are to be run by a web server, although the specific path may be different from the one shown. If written using the second form, the first python3 interpreter found in the shell's current environment is used. The second form is more versatile because it allows for the possibility that the Python 3 interpreter is not located in /usr/bin (e.g., it could be in /usr/local/bin or installed under $HOME). The shebang line is not

---

[*]The interaction between the user and the console is handled by a "shell" program. The distinction between the console and the shell does not concern us here, so we use the terms interchangeably.

needed (but is harmless) under Windows; all the examples in this book have a shebang line of the second form, although we won't show it.

Note that for Unix systems we assume that the name of Python 3's executable (or a soft link to it) in the PATH is python3. If this is not the case, you will need to change the shebang line in the examples to use the correct name (or correct name and path if you use the first form), or create a soft link from the Python 3 executable to the name python3 somewhere in the PATH.

Many powerful plain text editors, such as Vim and Emacs, come with built-in support for editing Python programs. This support typically involves providing color syntax highlighting and correctly indenting or unindenting lines. An alternative is to use the IDLE Python programming environment. On Windows and Mac OS X, IDLE is installed by default; on Unixes it is often provided as a separate package as described in the Introduction.

As the screenshot in Figure 1.1 shows, IDLE has a rather retro look that harks back to the days of Motif on Unix and Windows 95. This is because it uses the Tk-based Tkinter GUI library (covered in Chapter 13) rather than one of the more powerful modern GUI libraries such as PyGtk, PyQt, or wxPython. The reasons for the use of Tkinter are a mixture of history, liberal license conditions, and the fact that Tkinter is much smaller than the other GUI libraries. On the plus side, IDLE comes as standard with Python and is very simple to learn and use.

Figure 1.1 *IDLE's Python Shell*

IDLE provides three key facilities: the ability to enter Python expressions and code and to see the results directly in the Python Shell; a code editor that provides Python-specific color syntax highlighting and indentation support; and a debugger that can be used to step through code to help identify and kill bugs. The Python Shell is especially useful for trying out simple algorithms, snippets of code, and regular expressions, and can also be used as a very powerful and flexible calculator.

Several other Python development environments are available, but we recommend that you use IDLE, at least at first. An alternative is to create your programs in the plain text editor of your choice and debug using calls to print().

It is possible to invoke the Python interpreter without specifying a Python program. If this is done the interpreter starts up in interactive mode. In this mode it is possible to enter Python statements and see the results exactly the same as when using IDLE's Python Shell window, and with the same >>> prompts. But IDLE is much easier to use, so we recommend using IDLE for experimenting with code snippets. The short interactive examples we show are all assumed to be entered in an interactive Python interpreter or in IDLE's Python Shell.

We now know how to create and run Python programs, but clearly we won't get very far knowing only a single function. In the next section we will considerably increase our Python knowledge. This will make us able to create short but useful Python programs, something we will do in this chapter's last section.

Python's "Beautiful Heart"

In this section we will learn about eight key pieces of Python, and in the next section we will show how these pieces can be used to write a couple of small but realistic programs. There is much more to say about all of the things covered in this section, so if as you read it you feel that Python is missing something or that things are sometimes done in a long-winded way, peek ahead using the forward references or using the table of contents or index, and you will almost certainly find that Python has the feature you want and often has more concise forms of expression than we show here—and a lot more besides.

Piece #1: Data Types

One fundamental thing that any programming language must be able to do is represent items of data. Python provides several built-in data types, but we will concern ourselves with only two of them for now. Python represents integers (positive and negative whole numbers) using the int type, and it represents strings (sequences of Unicode characters) using the str type. Here are some examples of integer and string literals:

```
-973
210624583337114373395836055367340864637790190800109822250862195072
0
```

```
"Infinitely Demanding"
'Simon Critchley'
'positively αβγ∈÷©'
' '
```

Incidentally, the second number shown is 2^{217}—the size of Python's integers is limited only by machine memory, not by a fixed number of bytes. Strings can be delimited by double or single quotes, as long as the same kind are used at both ends, and since Python uses Unicode, strings are not limited to ASCII characters, as the penultimate string shows. An empty string is simply one with nothing between the delimiters.

Python uses square brackets ([]) to access an item from a sequence such as a string. For example, if we are in a Python Shell (either in the interactive interpreter, or in IDLE) we can enter the following—the Python Shell's output is shown in **bold**; what you type is shown in lightface:

```
>>> "Hard Times"[5]
'T'
>>> "giraffe"[0]
'g'
```

Traditionally, Python Shells use >>> as their prompt, although this can be changed. The square brackets syntax can be used with data items of any data type that is a sequence, such as strings and lists. This consistency of syntax is one of the reasons that Python is so beautiful. Note that all Python index positions start at 0.

In Python, both str and the basic numeric types such as int are *immutable*—that is, once set, their value cannot be changed. At first this appears to be a rather strange limitation, but Python's syntax means that this is a non-issue in practice. The only reason for mentioning it is that although we can use square brackets to retrieve the character at a given index position in a string, we cannot use them to set a new character. (Note that in Python a character is simply a string of length 1.)

To convert a data item from one type to another we can use the syntax *datatype(item)*. For example:

```
>>> int("45")
45
>>> str(912)
'912'
```

The int() conversion is tolerant of leading and trailing whitespace, so int(" 45 ") would have worked just as well. The str() conversion can be applied to almost any data item. We can easily make our own custom data types support str() conversion, and also int() or other conversions if they make sense, as we will see in Chapter 6. If a conversion fails, an exception is raised—we briefly introduce exception-handling in Piece #5, and fully cover exceptions in Chapter 4.

Strings and integers are fully covered in Chapter 2, along with other built-in data types and some data types from Python's standard library. That chapter also covers operations that can be applied to immutable sequences, such as strings.

Piece #2: Object References

Once we have some data types, the next thing we need are variables in which to store them. Python doesn't have variables as such, but instead has *object references*. When it comes to immutable objects like ints and strs, there is no discernable difference between a variable and an object reference. As for mutable objects, there is a difference, but it rarely matters in practice. We will use the terms *variable* and *object reference* interchangeably.

> Shallow and deep copying
> ☞ 136

Let's look at a few tiny examples, and then discuss some of the details.

```
x = "blue"
y = "green"
z = x
```

The syntax is simply *objectReference = value*. There is no need for predeclaration and no need to specify the value's type. When Python executes the first statement it creates a str object with the text "blue", and creates an object reference called x that refers to the str object. For all practical purposes we can say that "variable x has been assigned the 'blue' string". The second statement is similar. The third statement creates a new object reference called z and sets it to refer to the same object that the x object reference refers to (in this case the str containing the text "blue").

The = operator is not the same as the variable assignment operator in some other languages. The = operator binds an object reference to an object in memory. If the object reference already exists, it is simply re-bound to refer to the object on the right of the = operator; if the object reference does not exist it is created by the = operator.

Let's continue with the x, y, z example, and do some rebinding—as noted earlier, comments begin with a # and continue until the end of the line:

```
print(x, y, z) # prints: blue green blue
z = y
print(x, y, z) # prints: blue green green
x = z
print(x, y, z) # prints: green green green
```

After the fourth statement (x = z), all three object references are referring to the same str. Since there are no more object references to the "blue" string, Python is free to garbage-collect it.

Figure 1.2 shows the relationship between objects and object references schematically.

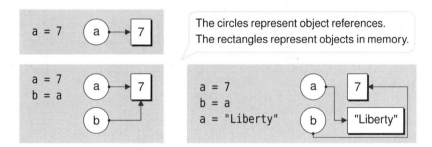

Figure 1.2 *Object references and objects*

The names used for object references (called *identifiers*) have a few restrictions. In particular, they may not be the same as any of Python's keywords, and must start with a letter or an underscore and be followed by zero or more nonwhitespace letter, underscore, or digit characters. There is no length limit, and the letters and digits are those defined by Unicode, that is, they include, but are not limited to, ASCII's letters and digits ("a", "b", ..., "z", "A", "B", ..., "Z", "0", "1", ..., "9"). Python identifiers are case-sensitive, so for example, LIMIT, Limit, and limit are three different identifiers. Further details and some slightly exotic examples are given in Chapter 2.

Identifiers and keywords ☞ 47

Python uses *dynamic typing*, which means that an object reference can be rebound to refer to a different object (which may be of a different data type) at any time. Languages that use strong typing (such as C++ and Java) allow only those operations that are defined for the data types involved to be performed. Python also applies this constraint, but it isn't called strong typing in Python's case because the valid operations can change—for example, if an object reference is re-bound to an object of a different data type. For example:

```
route = 866
print(route, type(route)) # prints: 866 <class 'int'>
route = "North"
print(route, type(route)) # prints: North <class 'str'>
```

Here we create a new object reference called route and set it to refer to a new int of value 866. At this point we could use / with route since division is a valid operation for integers. Then we reuse the route object reference to refer to a new str of value "North", and the int object is scheduled for garbage collection since now no object reference refers to it. At this point using / with `route` would cause a `TypeError` to be raised since / is not a valid operation for a string.

The `type()` function returns the data type (also known as the "class") of the data item it is given—this function can be very useful for testing and debugging, but would not normally appear in production code, since there is a better alternative as we will see in Chapter 6.

isin-
stance()
☞ 232

If we are experimenting with Python code inside the interactive interpreter or in a Python Shell such as the one provided by IDLE, simply typing the name of an object reference is enough to have Python print its value. For example:

```
>>> x = "blue"
>>> y = "green"
>>> z = x
>>> x
'blue'
>>> x, y, z
('blue', 'green', 'blue')
```

This is much more convenient than having to call the `print()` function all the time, but works only when using Python interactively—any programs and modules that we write must use `print()` or similar functions to produce output. Notice that Python displayed the last output in parentheses separated by commas—this signifies a `tuple`, that is, an ordered immutable sequence of objects. We will cover tuples in the next piece.

Piece #3: Collection Data Types

It is often convenient to hold entire collections of data items. Python provides several collection data types that can hold items, including associative arrays and sets. But here we will introduce just two: `tuple` and `list`. Python tuples and lists can be used to hold any number of data items of any data types. Tuples are *immutable*, so once they are created we cannot change them. Lists are *mutable*, so we can easily insert items and remove items whenever we want.

Tuples are created using commas (,), as these examples show:

```
>>> "Denmark", "Norway", "Sweden"
('Denmark', 'Norway', 'Sweden')
>>> "one",
('one',)
```

When Python outputs a tuple it encloses it in parentheses. Many programmers emulate this and always enclose the tuple literals they write in parentheses. If we have a one item tuple and want to use parentheses, we must still use the comma—for example, (1,). An empty tuple is created by using empty parentheses, (). The comma is also used to separate arguments in function

Creat-
ing and
calling
func-
tions
☞ 34

calls, so if we want to pass a tuple literal as an argument we must enclose it in parentheses to avoid confusion.

Here are some example lists:

```
[1, 4, 9, 16, 25, 36, 49]
['alpha', 'bravo', 'charlie', 'delta', 'echo']
['zebra', 49, -879, 'aardvark', 200]
[]
```

Lists can be created using square brackets ([]) as we have done here; later on we will see other ways of creating lists. The fourth list shown is an empty list.

Under the hood, lists and tuples don't store data items at all, but rather object references. When lists and tuples are created (and when items are inserted in the case of lists), they take copies of the object references they are given. In the case of literal items such as integers or strings, an object of the appropriate data type is created in memory and suitably initialized, and then an object reference referring to the object is created, and it is this object reference that is put in the list or tuple.

Like everything else in Python, collection data types are objects, so we can nest collection data types inside other collection data types, for example, to create lists of lists, without formality. In some situations the fact that lists, tuples, and most of Python's other collection data types hold object references rather than objects makes a difference—this is covered in Chapter 3 (starting on page 136).

Shallow and deep copying ☞ 136

In procedural programming we call functions and often pass in data items as arguments. For example, we have already seen the print() function. Another frequently used Python function is len(), which takes a single data item as its argument and returns the "length" of the item as an int. Here are a few calls to len()—we have not used bold for the interpreter's output since we assume you can figure out what you type and what is printed by the interpreter by now:

```
>>> len(("one",))
1
>>> len([3, 5, 1, 2, "pause", 5])
6
>>> len("automatically")
13
```

Tuples, lists, and strings are "sized", that is, they are data types that have a notion of size, and data items of any such data type can be meaningfully passed to the len() function. (An exception is raised if a nonsized data item is passed to len().)

Sized ☞ 373

All Python data items are *objects* (also called *instances*) of a particular data type (also called a *class*). We will use the terms *data type* and *class* interchangeably. One key difference between an object, and the plain items of data that some other languages provide (e.g., C++ or Java's built-in numeric types), is that an object can have *methods*. Essentially, a method is simply a function that is called for a particular object. For example, the list type has an append() method, so we can append an object to a list like this:

```
>>> x = ["zebra", 49, -879, "aardvark", 200]
>>> x.append("more")
>>> x
['zebra', 49, -879, 'aardvark', 200, 'more']
```

The x object knows that it is a list (all Python objects know what their own data type is), so we don't need to specify the data type explicitly. In the implementation of the append() method the first argument will be the x object itself—this is done automatically by Python as part of its syntactic support for methods.

The append() method mutates, that is, changes, the original list. This is possible because lists are mutable. It is also potentially more efficient than creating a new list with the original items and the extra item and then rebinding the object reference to the new list, particularly for very long lists.

In a procedural language the same thing could be achieved by using the list's append() like this (which is perfectly valid Python syntax):

```
>>> list.append(x, "extra")
>>> x
['zebra', 49, -879, 'aardvark', 200, 'more', 'extra']
```

Here we specify the data type and the data type's method, and give as the first argument the data item of the data type we want to call the method on, followed by any additional arguments. (In the face of inheritance there is a subtle semantic difference between the two syntaxes; the first form is the one that is most commonly used in practice. Inheritance is covered in Chapter 6.)

If you are unfamiliar with object-oriented programming this may seem a bit strange at first. For now, just accept that Python has conventional functions called like this: *functionName(arguments)*; and methods which are called like this: *objectName.methodName(arguments)*. (Object-oriented programming is covered in Chapter 6.)

The dot ("access attribute") operator is used to access an object's attributes. An attribute can be any kind of object, although so far we have shown only method attributes. Since an attribute can be an object that has attributes, which in turn can have attributes, and so on, we can use as many dot operators as necessary to access the particular attribute we want.

The list type has many other methods, including insert() which is used to insert an item at a given index position, and remove() which removes an item at a given index position. As noted earlier, Python indexes are always 0-based.

We saw before that we can get characters from strings using the square brackets operator, and noted at the time that this operator could be used with any sequence. Lists are sequences, so we can do things like this:

```
>>> x
['zebra', 49, -879, 'aardvark', 200, 'more', 'extra']
>>> x[0]
'zebra'
>>> x[4]
200
```

Tuples are also sequences, so if x had been a tuple we could retrieve items using square brackets in exactly the same way as we have done for the x list. But since lists are mutable (unlike strings and tuples which are immutable), we can also use the square brackets operator to set list elements. For example:

```
>>> x[1] = "forty nine"
>>> x
['zebra', 'forty nine', -879, 'aardvark', 200, 'more', 'extra']
```

If we give an index position that is out of range, an exception will be raised—we briefly introduce exception-handling in Piece #5, and fully cover exceptions in Chapter 4.

We have used the term *sequence* a few times now, relying on an informal understanding of its meaning, and will continue to do so for the time being. However, Python defines precisely what features a sequence must support, and similarly defines what features a sized object must support, and so on for various other categories that a data type might belong to, as we will see in Chapter 8.

Lists, tuples, and Python's other built-in collection data types are covered in Chapter 3.

Piece #4: Logical Operations

One of the fundamental features of any programming language is its logical operations. Python provides four sets of logical operations, and we will review the fundamentals of all of them here.

The Identity Operator

Since all Python variables are really object references, it sometimes makes sense to ask whether two or more object references are referring to the same object. The is operator is a binary operator that returns True if its left-hand object reference is referring to the same object as its right-hand object reference. Here are some examples:

```
>>> a = ["Retention", 3, None]
>>> b = ["Retention", 3, None]
>>> a is b
False
>>> b = a
>>> a is b
True
```

Note that it usually does not make sense to use is for comparing ints, strs, and most other data types since we almost invariably want to compare their values. In fact, using is to compare data items can lead to unintuitive results, as we can see in the preceding example, where although a and b are initially set to the same list values, the lists themselves are held as separate list objects and so is returns False the first time we use it.

One benefit of identity comparisons is that they are very fast. This is because the objects referred to do not have to be examined themselves. The is operator needs to compare only the memory addresses of the objects—the same address means the same object.

The most common use case for is is to compare a data item with the built-in null object, None, which is often used as a place-marking value to signify "unknown" or "nonexistent":

```
>>> a = "Something"
>>> b = None
>>> a is not None, b is None
(True, True)
```

To invert the identity test we use is not.

The purpose of the identity operator is to see whether two object references refer to the same object, or to see whether an object is None. If we want to compare object values we should use a comparison operator instead.

Comparison Operators

Python provides the standard set of binary comparison operators, with the expected semantics: < less than, <= less than or equal to, == equal to, != not equal to, >= greater than or equal to, and > greater than. These operators compare object values, that is, the objects that the object references used in the comparison refer to. Here are a few examples typed into a Python Shell:

```
>>> a = 2
```

```
>>> b = 6
>>> a == b
False
>>> a < b
True
>>> a <= b, a != b, a >= b, a > b
(True, True, False, False)
```

Everything is as we would expect with integers. Similarly, strings appear to compare properly too:

```
>>> a = "many paths"
>>> b = "many paths"
>>> a is b
False
>>> a == b
True
```

Although a and b are different objects (have different identities), they have the same values, so they compare equal. Be aware, though, that because Python uses Unicode for representing strings, comparing strings that contain non-ASCII characters can be a lot subtler and more complicated than it might at first appear—we will fully discuss this issue in Chapter 2.

Comparing strings
☞ 63

One particularly nice feature of Python's comparison operators is that they can be chained. For example:

```
>>> a = 9
>>> 0 <= a <= 10
True
```

This is a nicer way of testing that a given data item is in range than having to do two separate comparisons joined by logical and, as most other languages require. It also has the additional virtue of evaluating the data item only once (since it appears once only in the expression), something that could make a difference if computing the data item's value is expensive, or if accessing the data item causes side effects.

Thanks to the "strong" aspect of Python's dynamic typing, comparisons that don't make sense will cause an exception to be raised. For example:

```
>>> "three" < 4
Traceback (most recent call last):
...
TypeError: unorderable types: str() < int()
```

When an exception is raised and not handled, Python outputs a traceback along with the exception's error message. For clarity, we have omitted the traceback part of the output, replacing it with an ellipsis.* The same TypeError exception would occur if we wrote "3" < 4 because Python does not try to guess our intentions—the right approach is either to explicitly convert, for example, int("3") < 4, or to use comparable types, that is, both integers or both strings.

Python makes it easy for us to create custom data types that will integrate nicely so that, for example, we could create our own custom numeric type which would be able to participate in comparisons with the built-in int type, and with other built-in or custom numeric types, but not with strings or other non-numeric types.

Alternative Fuzzy- Bool ☞ 246

The Membership Operator

For data types that are sequences or collections such as strings, lists, and tuples, we can test for membership using the in operator, and for nonmembership using the not in operator. For example:

```
>>> p = (4, "frog", 9, -33, 9, 2)
>>> 2 in p
True
>>> "dog" not in p
True
```

For lists and tuples, the in operator uses a linear search which can be slow for very large collections (tens of thousands of items or more). On the other hand, in is very fast when used on a dictionary or a set; both of these collection data types are covered in Chapter 3. Here is how in can be used with a string:

```
>>> phrase = "Peace is no longer permitted during Winterval"
>>> "v" in phrase
True
>>> "ring" in phrase
True
```

Conveniently, in the case of strings, the membership operator can be used to test for substrings of any length. (As noted earlier, a character is just a string of length 1.)

Logical Operators

Python provides three logical operators: and, or, and not. Both and and or use short-circuit logic and return the operand that determined the result—they do

---

*A traceback (sometimes called a backtrace) is a list of all the calls made from the point where the unhandled exception occurred back to the top of the call stack.

not return a Boolean (unless they actually have Boolean operands). Let's see what this means in practice:

```
>>> five = 5
>>> two = 2
>>> zero = 0
>>> five and two
2
>>> two and five
5
>>> five and zero
0
```

If the expression occurs in a Boolean context, the result is evaluated as a Boolean, so the preceding expressions would come out as True, True, and False in, say, an if statement.

```
>>> nought = 0
>>> five or two
5
>>> two or five
2
>>> zero or five
5
>>> zero or nought
0
```

The or operator is similar; here the results in a Boolean context would be True, True, True, and False.

The not unary operator evaluates its argument in a Boolean context and always returns a Boolean result, so to continue the earlier example, not (zero or nought) would produce True, and not two would produce False.

Piece #5: Control Flow Statements

We mentioned earlier that each statement encountered in a .py file is executed in turn, starting with the first one and progressing line by line. The flow of control can be diverted by a function or method call or by a control structure, such as a conditional branch or a loop statement. Control is also diverted when an exception is raised.

In this subsection we will look at Python's if statement and its while and for loops, deferring consideration of functions to Piece #8, and methods to Chapter 6. We will also look at the very basics of exception-handling; we cover the subject fully in Chapter 4. But first we will clarify a couple of items of terminology.

A Boolean expression is anything that can be evaluated to produce a Boolean value (True or False). In Python, such an expression evaluates to False if it is the predefined constant False, the special object None, an empty sequence or collection (e.g., an empty string, list, or tuple), or a numeric data item of value 0; anything else is considered to be True. When we create our own custom data types (e.g., in Chapter 6), we can decide for ourselves what they should return in a Boolean context.

In Python-speak a block of code, that is, a sequence of one or more statements, is called a *suite*. Because some of Python's syntax *requires* that a suite be present, Python provides the keyword pass which is a statement that does nothing and that can be used where a suite is required (or where we want to indicate that we have considered a particular case) but where no processing is necessary.

The if Statement

The general syntax for Python's if statement is this:*

```
if boolean_expression1:
    suite1
elif boolean_expression2:
    suite2
...
elif boolean_expressionN:
    suiteN
else:
    else_suite
```

There can be zero or more elif clauses, and the final else clause is optional. If we want to account for a particular case, but want to do nothing if it occurs, we can use pass as that branch's suite.

The first thing that stands out to programmers used to C++ or Java is that there are no parentheses and no braces. The other thing to notice is the colon: This is part of the syntax and is easy to forget at first. Colons are used with else, elif, and essentially in any other place where a suite is to follow.

Unlike most other programming languages, Python uses indentation to signify its block structure. Some programmers don't like this, especially before they have tried it, and some get quite emotional about the issue. But it takes just a few days to get used to, and after a few weeks or months, brace-free code seems much nicer and less cluttered to read than code that uses braces.

Since suites are indicated using indentation, the question that naturally aris-es is, "What kind of indentation?" The Python style guidelines recommend

---

*In this book, ellipses (...) are used to indicate lines that are not shown.

four spaces per level of indentation, and only spaces (no tabs). Most modern text editors can be set up to handle this automatically (IDLE's editor does of course, and so do most other Python-aware editors). Python will work fine with any number of spaces or with tabs or with a mixture of both, providing that the indentation used is consistent. In this book, we follow the official Python guidelines.

Here is a very simple if statement example:

```
if x:
    print("x is nonzero")
```

In this case, if the condition (x) evaluates to True, the suite (the print() function call) will be executed.

```
if lines < 1000:
    print("small")
elif lines < 10000:
    print("medium")
else:
    print("large")
```

This is a slightly more elaborate if statement that prints a word that describes the value of the lines variable.

The while Statement

The while statement is used to execute a suite zero or more times, the number of times depending on the state of the while loop's Boolean expression. Here's the syntax:

```
while boolean_expression:
    suite
```

Actually, the while loop's full syntax is more sophisticated than this, since both break and continue are supported, and also an optional else clause that we will discuss in Chapter 4. The break statement switches control to the statement following the innermost loop in which the break statement appears—that is, it breaks out of the loop. The continue statement switches control to the start of the loop. Both break and continue are normally used inside if statements to conditionally change a loop's behavior.

```
while True:
    item = get_next_item()
    if not item:
        break
    process_item(item)
```

This while loop has a very typical structure and runs as long as there are items to process. (Both get_next_item() and process_item() are assumed to be custom functions defined elsewhere.) In this example, the while statement's suite contains an if statement, which itself has a suite—as it must—in this case consisting of a single break statement.

The for ... in Statement

Python's for loop reuses the in keyword (which in other contexts is the membership operator), and has the following syntax:

```
for variable in iterable:
    suite
```

Just like the while loop, the for loop supports both break and continue, and also has an optional else clause. The *variable* is set to refer to each object in the *iterable* in turn. An *iterable* is any data type that can be iterated over, and includes strings (where the iteration is character by character), lists, tuples, and Python's other collection data types.

```
for country in ["Denmark", "Finland", "Norway", "Sweden"]:
    print(country)
```

Here we take a very simplistic approach to printing a list of countries. In practice it is much more common to use a variable:

```
countries = ["Denmark", "Finland", "Norway", "Sweden"]
for country in countries:
    print(country)
```

In fact, an entire list (or tuple) can be printed using the print() function directly, for example, print(countries), but we often prefer to print collections using a for loop (or a list comprehension, covered later), to achieve full control over the formatting.

List comprehensions

☞ 110

```
for letter in "ABCDEFGHIJKLMNOPQRSTUVWXYZ":
    if letter in "AEIOU":
        print(letter, "is a vowel")
    else:
        print(letter, "is a consonant")
```

In this snippet the first use of the in keyword is part of a for statement, with the variable letter taking on the values "A", "B", and so on up to "Z", changing at each iteration of the loop. On the snippet's second line we use in again, but this time as the membership testing operator. Notice also that this example shows nested suites. The for loop's suite is the if ... else statement, and both the if and the else branches have their own suites.

Basic Exception Handling

Many of Python's functions and methods indicate errors or other important events by raising an exception. An exception is an object like any other Python object, and when converted to a string (e.g., when printed), the exception produces a message text. A simple form of the syntax for exception handlers is this:

```
try:
    try_suite
except exception1 as variable1:
    exception_suite1
...
except exceptionN as variableN:
    exception_suiteN
```

Note that the as *variable* part is optional; we may care only that a particular exception was raised and not be interested in its message text.

The full syntax is more sophisticated; for example, each except clause can handle multiple exceptions, and there is an optional else clause. All of this is covered in Chapter 4.

The logic works like this. If the statements in the try block's suite all execute without raising an exception, the except blocks are skipped. If an exception is raised inside the try block, control is immediately passed to the suite corresponding to the first matching *exception*—this means that any statements in the suite that follow the one that caused the exception will not be executed. If this occurs and if the as *variable* part is given, then inside the exception-handling suite, *variable* refers to the exception object.

If an exception occurs in the handling except block, or if an exception is raised that does not match any of the except blocks in the first place, Python looks for a matching except block in the next enclosing scope. The search for a suitable exception handler works outward in scope and up the call stack until either a match is found and the exception is handled, or no match is found, in which case the program terminates with an unhandled exception. In the case of an unhandled exception, Python prints a traceback as well as the exception's message text.

Here is an example:

```
s = input("enter an integer: ")
try:
    i = int(s)
    print("valid integer entered:", i)
except ValueError as err:
    print(err)
```

If the user enters "3.5", the output will be:

```
invalid literal for int() with base 10: '3.5'
```

But if they were to enter "13", the output will be:

```
valid integer entered: 13
```

Many books consider exception-handling to be an advanced topic and defer it as late as possible. But raising and especially handling exceptions is fundamental to the way Python works, so we make use of it from the beginning. And as we shall see, using exception handlers can make code much more readable, by separating the "exceptional" cases from the processing we are really interested in.

Piece #6: Arithmetic Operators

Python provides a full set of arithmetic operators, including binary operators for the four basic mathematical operations: + addition, – subtraction, * multiplication, and / division. In addition, many Python data types can be used with augmented assignment operators such as += and *=. The +, –, and * operators all behave as expected when both of their operands are integers:

```
>>> 5 + 6
11
>>> 3 - 7
-4
>>> 4 * 8
32
```

Notice that – can be used both as a unary operator (negation) and as a binary operator (subtraction), as is common in most programming languages. Where Python differs from the crowd is when it comes to division:

```
>>> 12 / 3
4.0
>>> 3 / 2
1.5
```

The division operator produces a floating-point value, not an integer; many other languages will produce an integer, truncating any fractional part. If we need an integer result, we can always convert using int() (or use the truncating division operator //, discussed later).

Numeric operators and functions
☞ 52

```
>>> a = 5
>>> a
5
```

```
>>> a += 8
>>> a
13
```

At first sight the preceding statements are unsurprising, particularly to those familiar with C-like languages. In such languages, augmented assignment is shorthand for assigning the results of an operation—for example, a += 8 is essentially the same as a = a + 8. However, there are two important subtleties here, one Python-specific and one to do with augmented operators in any language.

The first point to remember is that the int data type is immutable—that is, once assigned, an int's value cannot be changed. So, what actually happens behind the scenes when an augmented assignment operator is used on an immutable object is that the operation is performed, and an object holding the result is created; and then the target object reference is re-bound to refer to the result object rather than the object it referred to before. So, in the preceding case when the statement a += 8 is encountered, Python computes a + 8, stores the result in a new int object, and then rebinds a to refer to this new int. (And if the original object a was referring to has no more object references referring to it, it will be scheduled for garbage collection.) Figure 1.3 illustrates this point.

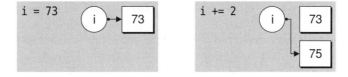

Figure 1.3 *Augmented assignment of an immutable object*

The second subtlety is that a *operator*= b is not quite the same as a = a *operator* b. The augmented version looks up a's value only once, so it is potentially faster. Also, if a is a complex expression (e.g., a list element with an index position calculation such as items[offset + index]), using the augmented version may be less error-prone since if the calculation needs to be changed the maintainer has to change it in only one rather than two expressions.

Python overloads (i.e., reuses for a different data type) the + and += operators for both strings and lists, the former meaning concatenation and the latter meaning append for strings and extend (append another list) for lists:

```
>>> name = "John"
>>> name + "Doe"
'JohnDoe',
>>> name += " Doe"
>>> name
'John Doe'
```

Like integers, strings are immutable, so when += is used a new string is created and the expression's left-hand object reference is re-bound to it, exactly as described earlier for ints. Lists support the same syntax but are different behind the scenes:

```
>>> seeds = ["sesame", "sunflower"]
>>> seeds += ["pumpkin"]
>>> seeds
['sesame', 'sunflower', 'pumpkin']
```

Since lists are mutable, when += is used the original list object is modified, so no rebinding of seeds is necessary. Figure 1.4 shows how this works.

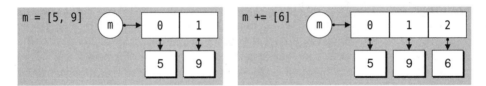

Figure 1.4 *Augmented assignment of a mutable object*

Since Python's syntax cleverly hides the distinction between mutable and immutable data types, why does it need both kinds at all? The reasons are mostly about performance. Immutable types are potentially a lot more efficient to implement (since they never change) than mutable types. Also, some collection data types, for example, sets, can work only with immutable types. On the other hand, mutable types can be more convenient to use. Where the distinction matters, we will discuss it—for example, in Chapter 4 when we discuss setting default arguments for custom functions, in Chapter 3 when we discuss lists, sets, and some other data types, and again in Chapter 6 when we show how to create custom data types.

The right-hand operand for the list += operator must be an iterable; if it is not an exception is raised:

```
>>> seeds += 5
Traceback (most recent call last):
...
TypeError: 'int' object is not iterable
```

The correct way to extend a list is to use an iterable object, such as a list:

```
>>> seeds += [5]
>>> seeds
['sesame', 'sunflower', 'pumpkin', 5]
```

And of course, the iterable object used to extend the list can itself have more than one item:

```
>>> seeds += [9, 1, 5, "poppy"]
>>> seeds
['sesame', 'sunflower', 'pumpkin', 5, 9, 1, 5, 'poppy']
```

Appending a plain string—for example, `"durian"`—rather than a list containing a string, `["durian"]`, leads to a logical but perhaps surprising result:

```
>>> seeds = ["sesame", "sunflower", "pumpkin"]
>>> seeds += "durian"
>>> seeds
['sesame', 'sunflower', 'pumpkin', 'd', 'u', 'r', 'i', 'a', 'n']
```

The list `+=` operator extends the list by appending each item of the iterable it is provided with; and since a string is an iterable, this leads to each character in the string being appended individually. If we use the list `append()` method, the argument is always added as a single item.

Piece #7: Input/Output

To be able to write genuinely useful programs we must be able to read input—for example, from the user at the console, and from files—and produce output, either to the console or to files. We have already made use of Python's built-in `print()` function, although we will defer covering it further until Chapter 4. In this subsection we will concentrate on console I/O, and use shell redirection for reading and writing files.

Python provides the built-in `input()` function to accept input from the user. This function takes an optional string argument (which it prints on the console); it then waits for the user to type in a response and to finish by pressing Enter (or Return). If the user does not type any text but just presses Enter, the `input()` function returns an empty string; otherwise, it returns a string containing what the user typed, without any line terminator.

Here is our first complete "useful" program; it draws on many of the previous pieces—the only new thing it shows is the `input()` function:

```
print("Type integers, each followed by Enter; or just Enter to finish")

total = 0
count = 0

while True:
    line = input("integer: ")
    if line:
        try:
            number = int(line)
        except ValueError as err:
```

```
                print(err)
                continue
            total += number
            count += 1
        else:
            break

    if count:
        print("count =", count, "total =", total, "mean =", total / count)
```

Book's examples

3 ☜

The program (in file `sum1.py` in the book's examples) has just 17 executable lines. Here is what a typical run looks like:

```
Type integers, each followed by Enter; or just Enter to finish
number: 12
number: 7
number: 1x
invalid literal for int() with base 10: '1x'
number: 15
number: 5
number:
count = 4 total = 39 mean = 9.75
```

Although the program is very short, it is fairly robust. If the user enters a string that cannot be converted to an integer, the problem is caught by an exception handler that prints a suitable message and switches control to the start of the loop ("continues the loop"). And the last `if` statement ensures that if the user doesn't enter any numbers at all, the summary isn't output, and division by zero is avoided.

File handling is fully covered in Chapter 7; but right now we can create files simply by redirecting the `print()` functions' output from the console. For example:

```
C:\>test.py > results.txt
```

will cause the output of plain `print()` function calls made in the fictitious `test.py` program to be written to the file `results.txt`. This syntax works in the Windows console and in Unix consoles. For Windows we must write `C:\Python30\python.exe test.py > results.txt` if Python 2 is the machine's default Python version, or `python test.py > results.txt` if Python 3 comes first in the `PATH` (although we won't mention this again), and for Unixes we need to make the program executable (`chmod +x test.py`) and then invoke it by writing `./test.py` unless the directory it is in happens to be in the `PATH`.

Reading data can be achieved by redirecting a file of data as input in an analogous way to redirecting output. However, if we used redirection with `sum1.py`, the program would fail. This is because the `input()` function raises an exception if it receives an EOF (end of file) character. Here is a more robust version (sum2.py) that can accept input from the user typing at the keyboard, or via file redirection:

```
print("Type integers, each followed by Enter; or ^D or ^Z to finish")

total = 0
count = 0

while True:
    try:
        line = input()
        if line:
            number = int(line)
            total += number
            count += 1
    except ValueError as err:
        print(err)
        continue
    except EOFError:
        break

if count:
    print("count =", count, "total =", total, "mean =", total / count)
```

Given the command line sum2.py < data\sum2.dat (where the sum2.dat file contains a list of numbers one per line and is in the examples' data subdirectory), the output to the console is:

```
Type integers, each followed by Enter; or ^D or ^Z to finish
count = 37 total = 1839 mean = 49.7027027027
```

We have made several small changes to make the program more suitable for use both interactively and using redirection. First, we have changed the termination from being a blank line to the EOF character (Ctrl+D on Unix, Ctrl+Z, Enter on Windows). This makes the program more robust when it comes to handling input files that contain blank lines. We have stopped printing a prompt for each number since it doesn't make sense to have one for redirected input. And we have also used a single try block with two exception handlers.

Notice that if an invalid integer is entered (either via the keyboard or due to a "bad" line of data in a redirected input file), the int() conversion will raise a ValueError exception and the flow of control will immediately switch to the relevant except block—this means that neither total nor count will be incremented when invalid data is encountered, which is exactly what we want.

We could just as easily have used two separate exception-handling try blocks instead:

```
while True:
    try:
        line = input()
        if line:
            try:
                number = int(line)
            except ValueError as err:
                print(err)
                continue
            total += number
            count += 1
    except EOFError:
        break
```

But we preferred to group the exceptions together at the end to keep the main processing as uncluttered as possible.

Piece #8: Creating and Calling Functions

It is perfectly possible to write programs using the data types and control structures that we have covered in the preceding pieces. However, very often we want to do essentially the same processing repeatedly, but with a small difference, such as a different starting value. Python provides a means of encapsulating suites as functions which can be parameterized by the arguments they are passed. Here is the general syntax for creating a function:

```
def functionName(arguments):
    suite
```

The *arguments* are optional and multiple arguments must be comma-separated. Every Python function has a return value; this defaults to None unless we return from the function using the syntax return *value*, in which case *value* is returned. The return value can be just one value or a tuple of values. The return value can be ignored by the caller, in which case it is simply thrown away.

return
☞ 163

Note that def is a statement that works in a similar way to the assignment operator. When def is executed a function object is created and an object reference with the specified name is created and set to refer to the function object. Since functions are objects, they can be stored in collection data types and passed as arguments to other functions, as we will see in later chapters.

One frequent need when writing interactive console applications is to obtain an integer from the user. Here is a function that does just that:

```
def get_int(msg):
    while True:
        try:
```

```
        i = int(input(msg))
        return i
    except ValueError as err:
        print(err)
```

This function takes one argument, msg. Inside the while loop the user is prompted to enter an integer. If they enter something invalid a ValueError exception will be raised, the error message will be printed, and the loop will repeat. Once a valid integer is entered, it is returned to the caller. Here is how we would call it:

```
age = get_int("enter your age: ")
```

In this example the single argument is mandatory because we have provided no default value. In fact, Python supports a very sophisticated and flexible syntax for function parameters that supports default argument values and positional and keyword arguments. All of the syntax is covered in Chapter 4.

Although creating our own functions can be very satisfying, in many cases it is not necessary. This is because Python has a lot of functions built in, and a great many more functions in the modules in its standard library, so what we want may well already be available.

A Python module is just a .py file that contains Python code, such as custom function and class (custom data type) definitions, and sometimes variables. To access the functionality in a module we must import it. For example:

```
import sys
```

To import a module we use the import statement followed by the name of the .py file, but omitting the extension.* Once a module has been imported, we can access any functions, classes, or variables that it contains. For example:

```
print(sys.argv)
```

The sys module provides the argv variable—a list whose first item is the name under which the program was invoked and whose second and subsequent items are the program's command-line arguments. The two previously quoted lines constitute the entire echoargs.py program. If the program is invoked with the command line echoargs.py -v, it will print ['echoargs.py', '-v'] on the console. (On Unix the first entry may be './echoargs.py'.)

Dot (.) operator 18 ☜	In general, the syntax for using a function from a module is *moduleName.functionName(arguments)*. It makes use of the dot ("access attribute") operator we introduced in Piece #3. The standard library contains lots of modules, and we

---

*The sys module, some other built-in modules, and modules implemented in C don't necessarily have corresponding .py files—but they are used in just the same way as those that do.

will make use of many of them throughout the book. The standard modules all have lowercase names, so some programmers use title-case names (e.g., My-Module) for their own modules to keep them distinct.

Let us look at just one example, the random module (in the standard library's random.py file), which provides many useful functions:

```
import random
x = random.randint(1, 6)
y = random.choice(["apple", "banana", "cherry", "durian"])
```

After these statements have been executed, x will contain an integer between 1 and 6 inclusive, and y will contain one of the strings from the list passed to the random.choice() function.

It is conventional to put all the import statements at the beginning of .py files, after the shebang line, and after the module's documentation. (Documenting modules is covered in Chapter 5.) We recommend importing standard library modules first, then third-party library modules, and finally your own modules.

shebang
(#!) line

10 ☜

Examples   ‖‖‖

In the preceding section we learned enough Python to write real programs. In this section we will study two complete programs that use only the Python covered earlier. This is both to show what is possible, and to help consolidate what has been learned so far.

In subsequent chapters we will increasingly cover more of Python's language and library, so that we will be able to write programs that are more concise and more robust than those shown here—but first we must have the foundations on which to build.

bigdigits.py   ‖

The first program we will review is quite short, although it has some subtle aspects, including a list of lists. Here is what it does: Given a number on the command line, the program outputs the same number onto the console using "big" digits.

At sites where lots of users share a high-speed line printer, it used to be common practice for each user's print job to be preceded by a cover page that showed their username and some other identifying details printed using this kind of technique.

We will review the code in three parts: the import, the creation of the lists holding the data the program uses, and the processing itself. But first, let's look at a sample run:

```
bigdigits.py 41072819
     *        *      ***    *****   ***     ***     *     ****
    **       **     *   *           *   *   *   *   *  **  *   *
   *  *      *     *         *      *   *   *   *   *   *  *   *
   *  *      *     *         *          *      ***      *  ****
  ******     *     *         *      *       *   *   *         *
     *       *     *   *     *      *       *   *   *         *
     *      ***     ***      *      *****   ***   ***         *
```

We have not shown the console prompt (or the leading `./` for Unix users); we will take them for granted from now on.

```
import sys
```

Since we must read in an argument from the command line (the number to output), we need to access the `sys.argv` list, so we begin by importing the sys module.

We represent each number as a list of strings. For example, here is zero:

```
Zero = ["  ***  ",
        " *   * ",
        "*     *",
        "*     *",
        "*     *",
        " *   * ",
        "  ***  "]
```

One detail to note is that the Zero list of strings is spread over multiple lines. Python statements normally occupy a single line, but they can span multiple lines if they are a parenthesized expression, a list, set, or dictionary literal, a function call argument list, or a multiline statement where every end-of-line character except the last is escaped by preceding it with a backslash (\). In all these cases any number of lines can be spanned and indentation does not matter for the second and subsequent lines.

set type
☞ 112

dict type
☞ 118

Each list representing a number has seven strings, all of uniform width, although what this width is differs from number to number. The lists for the other numbers follow the same pattern as for zero, although they are laid out for compactness rather than for clarity:

```
One = [" * ", "** ", " * ", " * ", " * ", " * ", "***"]
Two = [" *** ", "*   *", "*  * ", "  *  ", " *   ", "*    ", "*****"]
# ...
```

```
Nine = [" ****", "*    *", "*    *", " ****", "     *", "     *", "     *"]
```

The last piece of data we need is a list of all the lists of digits:

```
Digits = [Zero, One, Two, Three, Four, Five, Six, Seven, Eight, Nine]
```

We could have created the Digits lists directly, and avoided creating the extra variables. For example:

```
Digits = [
    [" *** ", " *   * ", "*    *", "*    *", "*    *", "*    *",
     " *   * ", " ***  "], # Zero
    [" * ", "** ", " * ", " * ", " * ", " * ", "***"], # One
    # ...
    [" ****", "*    *", "*    *", " ****", "     *", "     *",
     "     *"] # Nine
    ]
```

We preferred to use a separate variable for each number both for ease of understanding and because it looks neater using the variables.

We will quote the rest of the code in one go so that you can try to figure out how it works before reading the explanation that follows.

```
try:
    digits = sys.argv[1]
    row = 0
    while row < 7:
        line = ""
        column = 0
        while column < len(digits):
            number = int(digits[column])
            digit = Digits[number]
            line += digit[row] + "  "
            column += 1
        print(line)
        row += 1
except IndexError:
    print("usage: bigdigits.py <number>")
except ValueError as err:
    print(err, "in", digits)
```

The whole code is wrapped in an exception handler that can catch the two things that can go wrong. We begin by retrieving the program's command-line argument. The sys.argv list is 0-based like all Python lists; the item at index position 0 is the name the program was invoked as, so in a running program this list always starts out with at least one item. If no argument was given we

will be trying to access the second item in a one-item list and this will cause
an IndexError exception to be raised. If this occurs, the flow of control is immediately switched to the corresponding exception-handling block, and there we
simply print the program's usage. Execution then continues after the end of
the try block; but there is no more code, so the program simply terminates.

If no IndexError occurs, the digits string holds the command-line argument,
which we hope is a sequence of digit characters. (Remember from Piece #2 that
identifiers are case-sensitive, so digits and Digits are different.) Each big digit
is represented by seven strings, and to output the number correctly we must
output the top row of every digit, then the next row, and so on, until all seven
rows have been output. We use a while loop to iterate over each row. We could
just as easily have done this instead: for row in (0, 1, 2, 3, 4, 5, 6): and later
on we will see a much better way using the built-in range() function.

range()
☞ 131

We use the line string to hold the row strings from all the digits involved. Then
we loop by column, that is, by each successive character in the command-line
argument. We retrieve each character with digits[column] and convert the
digit to an integer called number. If the conversion fails a ValueError exception
is raised and the flow of control immediately switches to the corresponding
exception handler. In this case we print an error message, and control resumes
after the try block. As noted earlier, since there is no more code at this point,
the program will simply terminate.

If the conversion succeeds, we use number as an index into the Digits list, from
which we extract the digit list of strings. We then add the row-th string from
this list to the line we are building up, and also append two spaces to give some
horizontal separation between each digit.

Each time the inner while loop finishes, we print the line that has been built
up. The key to understanding this program is where we append each digit's
row string to the current row's line. Try running the program to get a feel for
how it works. We will return to this program in the exercises to improve its
output slightly.

generate_grid.py

One frequently occurring need is the generation of test data. There is no single
generic program for doing this, since test data varies enormously. Python is
often used to produce test data because it is so easy to write and modify Python
programs. In this subsection we will create a program that generates a grid
of random integers; the user can specify how many rows and columns they
want and over what range the integers should span. We'll start by looking at
a sample run:

```
generate_grid.py
rows: 4x
```

```
invalid literal for int() with base 10: '4x'
rows: 4
columns: 7
minimum (or Enter for 0): -100
maximum (or Enter for 1000):
        554      720      550      217      810      649      912
        -24      908      742      -65      -74      724      825
        711      968      824      505      741       55      723
        180      -60      794      173      487        4      -35
```

The program works interactively, and at the beginning we made a typing error
when entering the number of rows. The program responded by printing an
error message and then asking us to enter the number of rows again. For the
maximum we just pressed Enter to accept the default.

We will review the code in four parts: the import, the definition of a get_int()
function (a more sophisticated version than the one shown in Piece #8), the
user interaction to get the values to use, and the processing itself.

```
import random
```

random.
rand-
int()

36 ☜
We need the random module to give us access to the random.randint() function.

```
def get_int(msg, minimum, default):
    while True:
        try:
            line = input(msg)
            if not line and default is not None:
                return default
            i = int(line)
            if i < minimum:
                print("must be >=", minimum)
            else:
                return i
        except ValueError as err:
            print(err)
```

This function requires three arguments: a message string, a minimum value,
and a default value. If the user just presses Enter there are two possibilities. If
default is None, that is, no default value has been given, the flow of control will
drop through to the int() line. There the conversion will fail (since '' cannot
be converted to an integer), and a ValueError exception will be raised. But if
default is not None, then it is returned. Otherwise, the function will attempt
to convert the text the user entered into an integer, and if the conversion is
successful, it will then check that the integer is at least equal to the minimum
that has been specified.

So, the function will always return either default (if the user just pressed Enter), or a valid integer that is greater than or equal to the specified minimum.

```
rows = get_int("rows: ", 1, None)
columns = get_int("columns: ", 1, None)
minimum = get_int("minimum (or Enter for 0): ", -1000000, 0)

default = 1000
if default < minimum:
    default = 2 * minimum
maximum = get_int("maximum (or Enter for " + str(default) + "): ",
                  minimum, default)
```

Our get_int() function makes it easy to obtain the number of rows and columns and the minimum random value that the user wants. For rows and columns we give a default value of None, meaning no default, so the user must enter an integer. In the case of the minimum, we supply a default value of 0, and for the maximum we give a default value of 1 000, or twice the minimum if the minimum is greater than or equal to 1 000.

As we noted in the previous example, function call argument lists can span any number of lines, and indentation is irrelevant for their second and subsequent lines.

Once we know how many rows and columns the user requires and the minimum and maximum values of the random numbers they want, we are ready to do the processing.

```
row = 0
while row < rows:
    line = ""
    column = 0
    while column < columns:
        i = random.randint(minimum, maximum)
        s = str(i)
        while len(s) < 10:
            s = " " + s
        line += s
        column += 1
    print(line)
    row += 1
```

To generate the grid we use three while loops, the outer one working by rows, the middle one by columns, and the inner one by characters. In the middle loop we obtain a random number in the specified range and then convert it to a string. The inner while loop is used to pad the string with leading spaces so that each number is represented by a string 10 characters wide. We use the line string to accumulate the numbers for each row, and print the line after each column's numbers have been added. This completes our second example.

Python provides very sophisticated string formatting functionality, as well as excellent support for for ... in loops, so more realistic versions of both bigdigits.py and generate_grid.py would have used for ... in loops, and generate_grid.py would have used Python's string formatting capabilities rather than crudely padding with spaces. But we have limited ourselves to the eight pieces of Python introduced in this chapter, and they are quite sufficient for writing complete and useful programs. In each subsequent chapter we will learn new Python features, so as we progress through the book the programs we will see and be capable of writing will grow in sophistication.

str.
format()
☞ 74

Summary

In this chapter we learned how to edit and run Python programs and reviewed a few small but complete programs. But most of the chapter's pages were devoted to the eight pieces of Python's "beautiful heart"—enough of Python to write real programs.

We began with two of Python's most basic data types, int and str. Integer literals are written just as they are in most other programming languages. String literals are written using single or double quotes; it doesn't matter which as long as the same kind of quote is used at both ends. We can convert between strings and integers, for example, int("250") and str(125). If an integer conversion fails a ValueError exception is raised; whereas almost anything can be converted to a string.

Strings are sequences, so those functions and operations that can be used with sequences can be used with strings. For example, we can access a particular character using the item access operator ([]), concatenate strings using +, and append one string to another using +=. Since strings are immutable, behind the scenes, appending creates a new string that is the concatenation of the given strings, and rebinds the left-hand string object reference to the resultant string. We can also iterate over a string character by character using a for ... in loop. And we can use the built-in len() function to report how many characters are in a string.

For immutable objects like strings, integers, and tuples, we can write our code as though an object reference is a variable, that is, as though an object reference is the object it refers to. We can also do this for mutable objects, although any change made to a mutable object will affect all occurrences of the object (i.e., all object references to the object); we will cover this issue in Chapter 3.

Python provides several built-in collection data types and has some others in its standard library. We learned about the list and tuple types, and in particular how to create tuples and lists from literals, for example, even = [2, 4, 6, 8]. Lists, like everything else in Python, are objects, so we can call methods on them—for example, even.append(10) will add an extra item to the list. Like strings, lists and tuples are sequences, so we can iterate over them item by item using a for ... in loop, and find out how many items they have using len(). We can also retrieve a particular item in a list or tuple using the item access operator ([ ]), concatenate two lists or tuples using +, and append one to another using +=. If we want to append a single item to a list we must either use list.append() or use += with the item made into a single-item list—for example, even += [12]. Since lists are mutable, we can use [ ] to change individual items, for example, even[1] = 16.

The fast is and is not identity operators can be used to check whether two object references refer to the same thing—this is particularly useful when checking against the unique built-in None object. All the usual comparison operators are available (<, <=, ==, !=, >=, >), but they can be used only with compatible data types, and then only if the operations are supported. The data types we have seen so far—int, str, list, and tuple—all support the complete set of comparison operators. Comparing incompatible types, for example, comparing an int with a str or list, will quite sensibly produce a TypeError exception.

Python supports the standard logical operators and, or, and not. Both and and or are short-circuit operators that return the operand that determined their result—and this may not be a Boolean (although it can be converted to a Boolean); not always returns either True or False.

We can test for membership of sequence types, including strings, lists, and tuples, using the in and not in operators. Membership testing uses a slow linear search on lists and tuples, and a potentially much faster hybrid algorithm for strings, but performance is rarely an issue except for very long strings, lists, and tuples. In Chapter 3 we will learn about Python's associative array and set collection data types, both of which provide very fast membership testing. It is also possible to find out an object variable's type (i.e., the type of object the object reference refers to) using type()—but this function is normally used only for debugging and testing.

Python provides several control structures, including conditional branching with if ... elif ... else, conditional looping with while, looping over sequences with for ... in, and exception-handling with try ... except blocks. Both while and for ... in loops can be prematurely terminated using a break statement, and both can switch control to the beginning using continue.

The usual arithmetic operators are supported, including +, -, *, and /, although Python is unusual in that / always produces a floating-point result even if both its operands are integers. (The truncating division that many other languages use is also available in Python as //.) Python also provides augmented assignment operators such as += and *=; these create new objects and rebind behind the scenes if their left-hand operand is immutable. The arithmetic operators are overloaded by the str and list types as we noted earlier.

Console I/O can be achieved using input() and print(); and using file redirection in the console, we can use these same built-in functions to read and write files.

In addition to Python's rich built-in functionality, its extensive standard library is also available, with modules accessible once they have been imported using the import statement. One commonly imported module is sys, which holds the sys.argv list of command-line arguments. And when Python doesn't have the function we need we can easily create one that does what we want using the def statement.

By making use of the functionality described in this chapter it is possible to write short but useful Python programs. In the following chapter we will learn more about Python's data types, going into more depth for ints and strs and introducing some entirely new data types. In Chapter 3 we will learn more about tuples and lists, and also about some of Python's other collection data types. Then, in Chapter 4 we will cover Python's control structures in much more detail, and will learn how to create our own functions so that we can package up functionality to avoid code duplication and promote code reuse.

Exercises

Book's examples

3 🖘

The purpose of the exercises here, and throughout the book, is to encourage you to experiment with Python, and to get hands-on experience to help you absorb each chapter's material. The examples and exercises cover both numeric and text processing to appeal to as wide an audience as possible, and they are kept fairly small so that the emphasis is on thinking and learning rather than just typing code. Every exercise has a solution provided with the book's examples.

1. One nice variation of the bigdigits.py program is where instead of printing *s, the relevant digit is printed instead. For example:

```
bigdigits_ans.py 719428306
77777   1    9999    4      222    888    333     000     666
    7  11    9   9   44     2   2  8   8  3   3   0   0   6
    7   1    9   9   4 4    2   2  8   8      3   0     0  6
    7   1    9999   4 4       2   888     33   0     0  6666
    7   1       9 444444    2     8   8      3   0     0  6   6
    7   1       9    4     2      8   8  3   3  0   0   6   6
    7  111      9    4    22222   888    333     000     666
```

Two approaches can be taken. The easiest is to simply change the *s in the lists. But this isn't very versatile and is not the approach you should take. Instead, change the processing code so that rather than adding each digit's row string to the line in one go, you add character by character, and whenever a * is encountered you use the relevant digit.

This can be done by copying `bigdigits.py` and changing about five lines. It isn't hard, but it is slightly subtle. A solution is provided as `bigdigits_ans.py`.

2. IDLE can be used as a very powerful and flexible calculator, but sometimes it is useful to have a task-specific calculator. Create a program that prompts the user to enter a number in a `while` loop, gradually building up a list of the numbers entered. When the user has finished (by simply pressing Enter), print out the numbers they entered, the count of numbers, the sum of the numbers, the lowest and highest numbers entered, and the mean of the numbers (sum / count). Here is a sample run:

```
average1_ans.py
enter a number or Enter to finish: 5
enter a number or Enter to finish: 4
enter a number or Enter to finish: 1
enter a number or Enter to finish: 8
enter a number or Enter to finish: 5
enter a number or Enter to finish: 2
enter a number or Enter to finish:
numbers: [5, 4, 1, 8, 5, 2]
count = 6 sum = 25 lowest = 1 highest = 8 mean = 4.16666666667
```

It will take about four lines to initialize the necessary variables (an empty list is simply []), and less than 15 lines for the `while` loop, including basic error handling. Printing out at the end can be done in just a few lines, so the whole program, including blank lines for the sake of clarity, should be about 25 lines.

3. In some situations we need to generate test text—for example, to populate a web site design before the real content is available, or to provide test content when developing a report writer. To this end, write a program that generates awful poems (the kind that would make a Vogon blush).

Create some lists of words, for example, articles ("the", "a", etc.), subjects ("cat", "dog", "man", "woman"), verbs ("sang", "ran", "jumped"), and adverbs ("loudly", "quietly", "well", "badly"). Then loop five times, and on each iteration use the `random.choice()` function to pick an article, subject, verb, and adverb. Use `random.randint()` to choose between two sentence structures: article, subject, verb, and adverb, or just article, subject, and verb, and print the sentence. Here is an example run:

`random.randint()` and `random.choice()`

36 ☜

```
awfulpoetry1_ans.py
her man heard politely
```

```
his boy sang
another woman hoped
her girl sang slowly
the cat heard loudly
```

You will need to import the `random` module. The lists can be done in about 4–10 lines depending on how many words you put in them, and the loop itself requires less than ten lines, so with some blank lines the whole program can be done in about 20 lines of code. A solution is provided as `awfulpoetry1_ans.py`.

4. To make the awful poetry program more versatile, add some code to it so that if the user enters a number on the command line (between 1 and 10 inclusive), the program will output that many lines. If no command-line argument is given, default to printing five lines as before. You'll need to change the main loop (e.g., to a `while` loop). Keep in mind that Python's comparison operators can be chained, so there's no need to use logical and when checking that the argument is in range. The additional functionality can be done by adding about ten lines of code. A solution is provided as `awfulpoetry2_ans.py`.

5. It would be nice to be able to calculate the median (middle value) as well as the mean for the averages program in Exercise 2, but to do this we must sort the list. In Python a list can easily be sorted using the `list.sort()` method, but we haven't covered that yet, so we won't use it here. Extend the averages program with a block of code that sorts the list of numbers—efficiency is of no concern, just use the easiest approach you can think of. Once the list is sorted, the median is the middle value if the list has an odd number of items, or the average of the two middle values if the list has an even number of items. Calculate the median and output that along with the other information.

This is rather tricky, especially for inexperienced programmers. If you have some Python experience, you might still find it challenging, at least if you keep to the constraint of using only the Python we have covered so far. The sorting can be done in about a dozen lines and the median calculation (where you can't use the modulus operator, since it hasn't been covered yet) in four lines. A solution is provided in `average2_ans.py`.

- Identifiers and Keywords
- Integral Types
- Floating-Point Types
- Strings

Data Types

In this chapter we begin to take a much more detailed look at the Python language. We start with a discussion of the rules governing the names we give to object references, and provide a list of Python's keywords. Then we look at all of Python's most important data types—excluding collection data types, which are covered in Chapter 3. The data types considered are all built-in, except for one which comes from the standard library. The only difference between built-in data types and library data types is that in the latter case, we must first import the relevant module and we must qualify the data type's name with the name of the module it comes from—Chapter 5 covers importing in depth.

Identifiers and Keywords

When we create a data item we can either assign it to a variable, or insert it into a collection. (As we noted in the preceding chapter, when we assign in Python, what really happens is that we bind an object reference to refer to the object in memory that holds the data.) The names we give to our object references are called *identifiers* or just plain *names*.

Object references
14

A valid Python identifier is a nonempty sequence of characters of any length that consists of a "start character" and zero or more "continuation characters". Such an identifier must obey a couple of rules and ought to follow certain conventions.

The first rule concerns the start and continuation characters. The start character can be anything that Unicode considers to be a letter, including the ASCII letters ("a", "b", ..., "z", "A", "B", ..., "Z"), the underscore ("_"), as well as the letters from most non-English languages. Each continuation character can be any character that is permitted as a start character, or pretty well any non-whitespace character, including any character that Unicode considers to be a digit, such as ("0", "1", ..., "9"), or the Catalan character "·". Identifiers are case-sensitive, so for example, TAXRATE, Taxrate, TaxRate, taxRate, and taxrate are five different identifiers.

The precise set of characters that are permitted for the start and continuation are described in the documentation (Python language reference, Lexical analysis, Identifiers and keywords section), and in PEP 3131★ (Supporting Non-ASCII Identifiers).

The second rule is that no identifier can have the same name as one of Python's keywords, so we cannot use any of the names shown in Table 2.1.

Table 2.1 *Python's Keywords*

and	continue	except	global	lambda	pass	while
as	def	False	if	None	raise	with
assert	del	finally	import	nonlocal	return	yield
break	elif	for	in	not	True	
class	else	from	is	or	try	

We already met most of these keywords in the preceding chapter, although 11 of them—assert, class, del, finally, from, global, lambda, nonlocal, raise, with, and yield—have yet to be discussed.

The first convention is: Don't use the names of any of Python's predefined identifiers for your own identifiers. So, avoid using NotImplemented and Ellipsis, and the name of any of Python's built-in data types (such as int, float, list, str, and tuple), and any of Python's built-in functions or exceptions. How can we tell whether an identifier falls into one of these categories? Python has a built-in function called dir() that returns a list of an object's attributes. If it is called with no arguments it returns the list of Python's built-in attributes. For example:

```
>>> dir()
['__builtins__', '__doc__', '__name__']
```

The __builtins__ attribute is, in effect, a module that holds all of Python's built-in attributes. We can use it as an argument to the dir() function:

```
>>> dir(__builtins__)
['ArithmeticError', 'AssertionError', 'AttributeError',
...
'sum', 'super', 'tuple', 'type', 'vars', 'zip']
```

★A "PEP" is a Python Enhancement Proposal. If someone wants to change or extend Python, providing they get enough support from the Python community, they submit a PEP with the details of their proposal so that it can be formally considered, and in some cases such as with PEP 3131, accepted and implemented. All the PEPs are accessible from www.python.org/dev/peps/.

There are more than 130 names in the list, so we have omitted most of them. Those that begin with a capital letter are the names of Python's built-in exceptions; the rest are function and data type names.

If remembering or looking up those identifier names that should be avoided is too tedious, an alternative is to use one of the Python code-checking tools such as PyLint (`www.logilab.org/project/name/pylint`). This tool can also help identify many other actual or potential problems in Python programs.

The second convention concerns the use of underscores (_). Names that begin and end with two underscores (such as __lt__) should not be used. Python defines various special methods and variables that use such names (and in the case of special methods, we can reimplement them, that is, make our own versions of them), but we should not introduce new names of this kind ourselves. We will cover such names in Chapter 6. Names that begin with one or two leading underscores (and that don't end with two underscores) are treated specially in some contexts. We will show when to use names with a single leading underscore in Chapter 5, and when to use those with two leading underscores in Chapter 6.

A single underscore on its own can be used as an identifier, and inside an interactive interpreter or Python Shell, _ holds the result of the last expression that was evaluated. In a normal running program no _ exists, unless we use it explicitly in our code. Some programmers like to use _ in for ... in loops when they don't care about the items being looped over. For example:

```
for _ in (0, 1, 2, 3, 4, 5):
    print("Hello")
```

import
35 ☞

Be aware, however, that those who write programs that are internationalized often use _ as the name of their translation function. They do this so that instead of writing gettext.gettext("Translate me"), they can write _("Translate me"). (For this code to work we must have first imported the gettext module so that we can access the module's gettext() function.)

import
☞ 186

Let's look at some valid identifiers in a snippet of code written by a Spanish-speaking programmer. The code assumes we have done import math and that the variables radio and vieja_área have been created earlier in the program:

```
π = math.pi
ε = 0.0000001
nueva_área = π * radio * radio
if abs(nueva_área – vieja_área) < ε:
    print("las áreas han convergido")
```

We've used the math module, set epsilon (ε) to be a very small floating-point number, and used the abs() function to get the absolute value of the difference between the areas—we cover all of these later in this chapter. What we are concerned with here is that we are free to use accented characters and Greek letters for identifiers. We could just as easily create identifiers using Arabic, Chinese, Hebrew, Japanese, and Russian characters, or indeed characters from any other language supported by the Unicode character set.

The easiest way to check whether something is a valid identifier is to try to assign to it in an interactive Python interpreter or in IDLE's Python Shell window. Here are some examples:

```
>>> stretch-factor = 1
SyntaxError: can't assign to operator (...)
>>> 2miles = 2
SyntaxError: invalid syntax (...)
>>> str = 3 # Legal but BAD
>>> l'impôt31 = 4
SyntaxError: EOL while scanning single-quoted string (...)
>>> l_impôt31 = 5
>>>
```

When an invalid identifier is used it causes a SyntaxError exception to be raised. In each case the part of the error message that appears in parentheses varies, so we have replaced it with an ellipsis. The first assignment fails because "–" is not a Unicode letter, digit, or underscore. The second one fails because the start character is not a Unicode letter or underscore; only continuation characters can be digits. No exception is raised if we create an identifier that is valid—even if the identifier is the name of a built-in data type, exception, or function—so the third assignment works, although it is ill-advised. The fourth fails because a quote is not a Unicode letter, digit, or underscore. The fifth is fine.

Integral Types   ▐▐▐

Python provides two built-in integral types, int and bool.* Both integers and Booleans are immutable, but thanks to Python's augmented assignment operators this is rarely noticeable. When used in Boolean expressions, 0 and False are False, and any other integer and True are True. When used in numerical expressions True evaluates to 1 and False to 0. This means that we can write some rather odd things—for example, we can increment an integer, i, using the expression i += True. Naturally, the right way to do this is i += 1.

---

*The standard library also provides the fractions.Fraction type (unlimited precision rationals) which may be useful in some specialized mathematical and scientific contexts.

Integers

The size of an integer is limited only by the machine's memory, so integers hundreds of digits long can easily be created and worked with—although they will be slower to use than integers that can be represented natively by the machine's processor.

Integer literals are written using base 10 (decimal) by default, but other number bases can be used when this is convenient:

```
>>> 14600926                     # decimal
14600926
>>> 0b110111101100101011011110   # binary
14600926
>>> 0o67545336                   # octal
14600926
>>> 0xDECADE                     # hexadecimal
14600926
```

Binary numbers are written with a leading 0b, octal numbers with a leading 0o,* and hexadecimal numbers with a leading 0x. Uppercase letters can also be used.

All the usual mathematical functions and operators can be used with integers, as Table 2.2 shows. Some of the functionality is provided by built-in functions like abs()—for example, abs(i) returns the absolute value of integer i—and other functionality is provided by int operators—for example, i + j returns the sum of integers i and j.

All the binary numeric operators (+, -, /, //, %, and **) have augmented assignment versions (+=, -=, /=, //=, %=, and **=) where x *op*= y is logically equivalent to x = x *op* y in the normal case when reading x's value has no side effects.

Objects can be created by assigning literals to variables, for example, x = 17, or by calling the relevant data type as a function, for example, x = int(17). Some objects (e.g., those of type decimal.Decimal) can be created only by using the data type since they have no literal representation. When an object is created using its data type there are three possible use cases.

The first use case is when a data type is called with no arguments. In this case an object with a default value is created—for example, x = int() creates an integer of value 0. All the built-in types can be called with no arguments.

The second use case is when the data type is called with a single argument. If an argument of the same type is given, a new object which is a shallow copy of

---

*Users of C-style languages note that a single leading 0 is not sufficient to specify an octal number; 0o (zero, letter *o*) must be used in Python.

Table 2.2 *Numeric Operators and Functions*

Syntax	Description
x + y	Adds number x and number y
x − y	Subtracts y from x
x * y	Multiplies x by y
x / y	Divides x by y; always produces a float (or a complex if x or y is complex)
x // y	Divides x by y; truncates any fractional part so always produces an int result; see also the round() function
x % y	Produces the modulus (remainder) of dividing x by y
x ** y	Raises x to the power of y; see also the pow() functions
−x	Negates x; changes x's sign if nonzero, does nothing if zero
+x	Does nothing; is sometimes used to clarify code
abs(x)	Returns the absolute value of x
divmod(x, y)	Returns the quotient and remainder of dividing x by y as a tuple of two ints
pow(x, y)	Raises x to the power of y; the same as the ** operator
pow(x, y, z)	A faster alternative to (x ** y) % z
round(x, n)	Returns the int corresponding to float x rounded to a whole number (or a float to n decimal places if n is given)

Tuples
16 ☜

Tuples
☞ 100

Table 2.3 *Integer Conversion Functions*

Syntax	Description
bin(i)	Returns the binary representation of int i as a string, e.g., bin(1980) == '0b11110111100'
hex(i)	Returns the hexadecimal representation of i as a string, e.g., hex(1980) == '0x7bc'
int(x)	Converts object x to an integer; raises ValueError on failure—or TypeError if x's data type does not support integer conversion. If x is a floating-point number it is truncated.
int(s, base)	Converts str s to an integer; raises ValueError on failure. If the optional base argument is given it should be an integer between 2 and 36 inclusive.
oct(i)	Returns the octal representation of i as a string, e.g., oct(1980) == '0o3674'

Table 2.4 *Integer Bitwise Operators*

Syntax	Description
i | j	Bitwise OR of int i and int j; negative numbers are assumed to be represented using 2's complement
i ^ j	Bitwise XOR (exclusive or) of i and j
i & j	Bitwise AND of i and j
i << j	Shifts i left by j bits; like i * (2 ** j) without overflow checking
i >> j	Shifts i right by j bits; like i // (2 ** j) without overflow checking
~i	Inverts i's bits

the original object is created. (Shallow copying is covered in Chapter 3.) If an argument of a different type is given, a conversion is attempted. This use is shown for the int type in Table 2.3. If the argument is of a type that supports conversions to the given type and the conversion fails, a ValueError exception is raised; otherwise, the resultant object of the given type is returned. If the argument's data type does not support conversion to the given type a TypeError exception is raised. The built-in float and str types both provide integer conversions; it is also possible to provide integer and other conversions for our own custom data types as we will see in Chapter 6.

Copying collections
☞ 136

Type conversions
☞ 242

The third use case is where two or more arguments are given—not all types support this, and for those that do the argument types and their meanings vary. For the int type two arguments are permitted where the first is a string that represents an integer and the second is the number base of the string representation. For example, int("A4", 16) creates an integer of value 164. This use is shown in Table 2.3.

The bitwise operators are shown in Table 2.4. All the binary bitwise operators (|, ^, &, <<, and >>) have augmented assignment versions (|=, ^=, &=, <<=, and >>=) where i *op*= j is logically equivalent to i = i *op* j in the normal case when reading i's value has no side effects.

If many true/false flags need to be held, one possibility is to use a single integer, and to test individual bits using the bitwise operators. The same thing can be achieved less compactly, but more conveniently, using a list of Booleans.

Booleans

There are two built-in Boolean objects: True and False. Like all other Python data types (whether built-in, library, or custom), the bool data type can be called as a function—with no arguments it returns False, with a bool argument it returns a copy of the argument, and with any other argument it attempts to convert the given object to a bool. All the built-in and standard library data types can be converted to produce a Boolean value, and it is easy to provide Boolean conversions for custom data types. Here are a couple of Boolean assignments and a couple of Boolean expressions:

```
>>> t = True
>>> f = False
>>> t and f
False
>>> t and True
True
```

Logical opera-tors
22 ☜

As we noted earlier, Python provides three logical operators: and, or, and not. Both and and or use short-circuit logic and return the operand that determined the result, whereas not always returns either True or False.

Programmers who have been using older versions of Python sometimes use 1 and 0 instead of True and False; this almost always works fine, but new code should use the built-in Boolean objects when a Boolean value is required.

Floating-Point Types

Python provides three kinds of floating-point values: the built-in float and complex types, and the decimal.Decimal type from the standard library. All three are immutable. Type float holds double-precision floating-point numbers whose range depends on the C (or C# or Java) compiler Python was built with; they have limited precision and cannot reliably be compared for equality. Numbers of type float are written with a decimal point, or using exponential notation, for example, 0.0, 4., 5.7, -2.5, -2e9, 8.9e-4.

Computers natively represent floating-point numbers using base 2—this means that some decimals can be represented exactly (such as 0.5), but others only approximately (such as 0.1 and 0.2). Furthermore, the representation uses a fixed number of bits, so there is a limit to the number of digits that can be held. Here is a salutary example typed into IDLE:

```
>>> 0.0, 5.4, -2.5, 8.9e-4
(0.0, 5.4000000000000004, -2.5, 0.00088999999999999995)
```

The inexactness is not a problem specific to Python—all programming languages have this problem with floating-point numbers.

If we need really high precision, Python's decimal.Decimal numbers from the decimal module can be used. These perform calculations that are accurate to the level of precision we specify (by default, to 28 decimal places) and can represent periodic numbers like 0.1 exactly; but processing is a lot slower than with normal floats. Because of their accuracy, decimal.Decimal numbers are suitable for financial calculations.

Mixed mode arithmetic is supported such that using an int and a float produces a float, and using a float and a complex produces a complex. Because decimal.Decimals are of fixed precision they can be used only with other decimal. Decimals and with ints, in the latter case producing a decimal.Decimal result. If an operation is attempted using incompatible types, a TypeError exception is raised.

Floating-Point Numbers

All the numeric operators and functions in Table 2.2 (page 52) can be used with floats, including the augmented assignment versions. The float data type can be called as a function—with no arguments it returns 0.0, with a float argument it returns a copy of the argument, and with any other argument it attempts to convert the given object to a float. When used for conversions a string argument can be given, either using simple decimal notation or using exponential notation. It is possible that NaN ("not a number") or "infinity" may be produced by a calculation involving floats—unfortunately the behavior is not consistent across implementations and may differ depending on the system's underlying math library.

Here is a simple function for comparing floats for equality to the limit of the machine's accuracy:

```
def equal_float(a, b):
    return abs(a - b) <= sys.float_info.epsilon
```

This requires us to import the sys module. The sys.float_info object has many attributes; sys.float_info.epsilon is effectively the smallest difference that the machine can distinguish between two floating-point numbers. On one of the author's 32-bit machines it is just over 0.000 000 000 000 000 2. (Epsilon is the traditional name for this number.) Python floats normally provide reliable accuracy for up to 17 significant digits.

If you type sys.float_info into IDLE, all its attributes will be displayed; these include the minimum and maximum floating-point numbers the machine can represent. And typing help(sys.float_info) will print some information about the sys.float_info object.

Floating-point numbers can be converted to integers using the int() function which returns the whole part and throws away the fractional part, or using round() which accounts for the fractional part, or using math.floor() or math.ceil() which convert down to or up to the nearest integer. The float.is_integer() method returns True if a floating-point number's fractional part is 0, and a float's fractional representation can be obtained using the float.as_integer_ratio() method. For example, given x = 2.75, the call

Table 2.5 *The Math Module's Functions and Constants #1*

Syntax	Description
math.acos(x)	Returns the arc cosine of x in radians
math.acosh(x)	Returns the arc hyperbolic cosine of x in radians
math.asin(x)	Returns the arc sine of x in radians
math.asinh(x)	Returns the arc hyperbolic sine of x in radians
math.atan(x)	Returns the arc tangent of x in radians
math.atan2(y, x)	Returns the arc tangent of y / x in radians
math.atanh(x)	Returns the arc hyperbolic tangent of x in radians
math.ceil(x)	Returns $\lceil x \rceil$, i.e., the smallest integer greater than or equal to x as an int; e.g., math.ceil(5.4) == 6
math.copysign(x,y)	Returns x with y's sign
math.cos(x)	Returns the cosine of x in radians
math.cosh(x)	Returns the hyperbolic cosine of x in radians
math.degrees(r)	Converts float r from radians to degrees
math.e	The constant e; approximately 2.718 281 828 459 045 1
math.exp(x)	Returns e^x, i.e., math.e ** x
math.fabs(x)	Returns $\lvert x \rvert$, i.e., the absolute value of x as a float
math.factorial(x)	Returns $x!$
math.floor(x)	Returns $\lfloor x \rfloor$, i.e., the smallest integer less than or equal to x as an int; e.g., math.floor(5.4) == 5
math.fmod(x, y)	Produces the modulus (remainder) of dividing x by y; this produces better results than % for floats
math.frexp(x)	Returns a 2-tuple with the mantissa (as a float) and the exponent (as an int)
math.fsum(i)	Returns the sum of the values in iterable i as a float
math.hypot(x, y)	Returns $\sqrt{x^2 + y^2}$
math.isinf(x)	Returns True if float x is $\pm$ inf ($\pm\infty$)
math.isnan(x)	Returns True if float x is nan ("not a number")
math.ldexp(m, e)	Returns $m \times 2^e$; effectively the inverse of math.frexp()
math.log(x, *b*)	Returns $\log_b x$; b is optional and defaults to math.e
math.log10(x)	Returns $\log_{10} x$
math.log1p(x)	Returns $\log_e(1 + x)$; accurate even when x is close to 0
math.modf(x)	Returns x's fractional and whole parts as two floats

Tuples

16 ☞

Tuples

☞ 100

Table 2.6 *The Math Module's Functions and Constants #2*

Syntax	Description
math.pi	The constant π; approximately $3.141\,592\,653\,589\,793\,1$
math.pow(x, y)	Returns x^y as a float
math.radians(d)	Converts float d from degrees to radians
math.sin(x)	Returns the sine of x in radians
math.sinh(x)	Returns the hyperbolic sine of x in radians
math.sqrt(x)	Returns $\sqrt{x}$
math.sum(i)	Returns the floating-point sum of iterable i's items
math.tan(x)	Returns the tangent of x in radians
math.tanh(x)	Returns the hyperbolic tangent of x in radians
math.trunc(x)	Returns the whole part of x as an int; same as int(x)

x.as_integer_ratio() returns (11, 4). Integers can be converted to floating-point numbers using float().

Floating-point numbers can also be represented as strings in hexadecimal format using the float.hex() method. The opposite conversion can be done using float.fromhex().* For example:

```
s = 14.25.hex()          # str s == '0x1.c800000000000p+3'
f = float.fromhex(s)     # float f == 14.25
t = f.hex()              # str t == '0x1.c800000000000p+3'
```

The exponent is indicated using p ("power") rather than e since e is a valid hexadecimal digit.

In addition to the built-in floating-point functionality, the math module provides many more functions that operate on floats, as shown in Tables 2.5 and 2.6. Here are some code snippets that show how to make use of the module's functionality:

```
>>> import math
>>> math.pi * (5 ** 2)
78.539816339744831
>>> math.hypot(5, 12)
13.0
>>> math.modf(13.732)
(0.73199999999999932, 13.0)
```

---

*Note for object-oriented programmers: float.fromhex() is a class method.

The math.hypot() function calculates the distance from the origin to the point (x, y) and produces the same result as math.sqrt((x ** 2) + (y ** 2)).

The math module is very dependent on the underlying math library that Python was compiled against. This means that some error conditions and boundary cases may behave differently on different platforms.

Complex Numbers

The complex data type is an immutable type that holds a pair of floats, one representing the real part and the other the imaginary part of a complex number. Literal complex numbers are written with the real and imaginary parts joined by a + or – sign, and with the imaginary part followed by a j.* Here are some examples: 3.5+2j, 0.5j, 4+0j, –1–3.7j. Notice that if the real part is 0, we can omit it entirely.

The separate parts of a complex are available as attributes real and imag. For example:

```
>>> z = -89.5+2.125j
>>> z.real, z.imag
(-89.5, 2.125)
```

Except for //, %, divmod(), and the three-argument pow(), all the numeric operators and functions in Table 2.2 (page 52) can be used with complex numbers, and so can the augmented assignment versions. In addition, complex numbers have a method, conjugate(), which changes the sign of the imaginary part. For example:

```
>>> z.conjugate()
(-89.5-2.125j)
>>> 3-4j.conjugate()
(3+4j)
```

Notice that here we have called a method on a literal complex number. In general, Python allows us to call methods or access attributes on any literal, as long as the literal's data type provides the called method or the attribute—however, this does not apply to special methods, since these always have corresponding operators such as + that should be used instead. For example, 4j.real produces 0.0, 4j.imag produces 4.0, and 4j + 3+2j produces 3+6j.

The complex data type can be called as a function—with no arguments it returns 0j, with a complex argument it returns a copy of the argument, and with any other argument it attempts to convert the given object to a complex. When used for conversions complex() accepts either a single string argument,

---

*Mathematicians use i to signify $\sqrt{-1}$, but Python follows the engineering tradition and uses j.

or one or two floats. If just one float is given, the imaginary part is taken to be 0j.

The functions in the math module do not work with complex numbers. This is a deliberate design decision that ensures that users of the math module get exceptions rather than silently getting complex numbers in some situations.

Users of complex numbers can import the cmath module, which provides complex number versions of most of the trigonometric and logarithmic functions that are in the math module, plus some complex number-specific functions such as cmath.phase(), cmath.polar(), and cmath.rect(), and also the cmath.pi and cmath.e constants which hold the same float values as their math module counterparts.

Decimal Numbers

In many applications the numerical inaccuracies that can occur when using floats don't matter, and in any case are far outweighed by the speed of calculation that floats offer. But in some cases we prefer the opposite trade-off, and want complete accuracy, even at the cost of speed. The decimal module provides immutable Decimal numbers that are as accurate as we specify. Calculations involving Decimals are slower than those involving floats, but whether this is noticeable will depend on the application.

To create a Decimal we must import the decimal module. For example:

```
>>> import decimal
>>> a = decimal.Decimal(9876)
>>> b = decimal.Decimal("54321.012345678987654321")
>>> a + b
Decimal('64197.012345678987654321')
```

Decimal numbers are created using the decimal.Decimal() function. This function can take an integer or a string argument—but not a float, since floats are held inexactly whereas decimals are represented exactly. If a string is used it can use simple decimal notation or exponential notation. In addition to providing accuracy, the exact representation of decimal.Decimals means that they can be reliably compared for equality.

All the numeric operators and functions listed in Table 2.2 (page 52), including the augmented assignment versions, can be used with decimal.Decimals, but with a couple of caveats. If the ** operator has a decimal.Decimal left-hand operand, its right-hand operand must be an integer. Similarly, if the pow() function's first argument is a decimal.Decimal, then its second and optional third arguments must be integers.

The math and cmath modules are not suitable for use with decimal.Decimals, but some of the functions provided by the math module are provided as decimal.Decimal methods. For example, to calculate e^x where x is a float, we write math.exp(x), but where x is a decimal.Decimal, we write x.exp(). From the discussion in Piece #3 (page 18), we can see that x.exp() is, in effect, syntactic sugar for decimal.Decimal.exp(x).

The decimal.Decimal data type also provides ln() which calculates the natural (base *e*) logarithm (just like math.log() with one argument), log10(), and sqrt(), along with many other methods specific to the decimal.Decimal data type.

Numbers of type decimal.Decimal work within the scope of a *context*; the context is a collection of settings that affect how decimal.Decimals behave. The context specifies the precision that should be used (the default is 28 decimal places), the rounding technique, and some other details.

In some situations the difference in accuracy between floats and decimal. Decimals becomes obvious:

```
>>> 23 / 1.05
21.904761904761905
>>> print(23 / 1.05)
21.9047619048
>>> print(decimal.Decimal(23) / decimal.Decimal("1.05"))
21.90476190476190476190476190
>>> decimal.Decimal(23) / decimal.Decimal("1.05")
Decimal('21.90476190476190476190476190')
```

Although the division using decimal.Decimals is more accurate than the one involving floats, in this case (on a 32-bit machine) the difference only shows up in the fifteenth decimal place. In many situations this is insignificant—for example, in this book, all the examples that need floating-point numbers use floats.

One other point to note is that the last two of the preceding examples reveal for the first time that printing an object involves some behind-the-scenes formatting. When we call print() on the result of decimal.Decimal(23) / decimal.Decimal("1.05") the bare number is printed—this output is in *string form*. If we simply enter the expression we get a decimal.Decimal output—this output is in *representational form*. All Python objects have two output forms. String form is designed to be human-readable. Representational form is designed to produce output that if fed to a Python interpreter would (when possible) reproduce the represented object. We will return to this topic in the next section where we discuss strings, and again in Chapter 6 when we discuss providing string and representational forms for our own custom data types.

The Library Reference's decimal module documentation provides all the details that are too obscure or beyond our scope to cover; it also provides more examples, and a FAQ list.

Strings ▌

Strings are represented by the immutable str data type which holds a sequence of Unicode characters. The str data type can be called as a function to create string objects—with no arguments it returns an empty string, with a non-string argument it returns the string form of the argument, and with a string argument it returns a copy of the string. The str() function can also be used as a conversion function, in which case the first argument should be a string or something convertable to a string, with up to two optional string arguments being passed, one specifying the encoding to use and the other specifying how to handle encoding errors.

Character encodings ☞ 85

Earlier we mentioned that string literals are created using quotes, and that we are free to use single or double quotes providing we use the same at both ends. In addition, we can use a *triple quoted string*—this is Python-speak for a string that begins and ends with three quote characters (either three single quotes or three double quotes). For example:

```
text = """A triple quoted string like this can include 'quotes' and
"quotes" without formality. We can also escape newlines \
so this particular string is actually only two lines long."""
```

If we want to use quotes inside a normal quoted string we can do so without formality if they are different from the delimiting quotes; otherwise, we must escape them:

```
a = "Single 'quotes' are fine; \"doubles\" must be escaped."
b = 'Single \'quotes\' must be escaped; "doubles" are fine.'
```

Python uses newline as its statement terminator, except inside parentheses (()), square brackets ([ ]), braces ({}), or triple quoted strings. Newlines can be used without formality in triple quoted strings, and we can include newlines in any string literal using the \n escape sequence. All of Python's escape sequences are shown in Table 2.7. In some situations—for example, when writing regular expressions—we need to create strings with lots of literal backslashes. (Regular expressions are the subject of Chapter 12.) This can be inconvenient since each one must be escaped:

```
import re
phone1 = re.compile("^((?:[(]\\d+[)])?\\s*\\d+(?:-\\d+)?)$")
```

Table 2.7 *Python's String Escapes*

Escape	Meaning
newline	Escape (i.e., ignore) the newline
\\\\	Backslash (\\)
\\'	Single quote (')
\\"	Double quote (")
\\a	ASCII bell (BEL)
\\b	ASCII backspace (BS)
\\f	ASCII formfeed (FF)
\\n	ASCII linefeed (LF)
\\N{*name*}	Unicode character with the given name
ooo	Character with the given octal value
\\r	ASCII carriage return (CR)
\\t	ASCII tab (TAB)
\\u*hhhh*	Unicode character with the given 16-bit hexadecimal value
\\U*hhhhhhhh*	Unicode character with the given 32-bit hexadecimal value
\\v	ASCII vertical tab (VT)
\\x*hh*	Character with the given 8-bit hexadecimal value

The solution is to use *raw* strings. These are quoted or triple quoted strings whose first quote is preceded by the letter *r*. Inside such strings all characters are taken to be literals, so no escaping is necessary. Here is the phone regular expression using a raw string:

```
phone2 = re.compile(r"^((?:[(|]\d+[)])?\s*\d+(?:-\d+)?)$")
```

If we want to write a long string literal spread over two or more lines but without using a triple quoted string there are a couple of approaches we can take:

```
t = "This is not the best way to join two long strings " + \
    "together since it relies on ugly newline escaping"
```

```
s = ("This is the nice way to join two long strings "
     "together; it relies on string literal concatenation.")
```

Notice that in the second case we must use parentheses to create a single expression—without them, s would be assigned only to the first string, and the second string would cause an IndentationError exception to be raised. The Python documentation's "Idioms and Anti-Idioms" HOWTO document recommends always using parentheses to spread statements of any kind over multiple lines rather than escaping newlines; a recommendation we endeavor to follow.

Since .py files default to using the UTF-8 Unicode encoding, we can write any Unicode characters in our string literals without formality. We can also put any Unicode characters inside strings using hexadecimal escape sequences or using Unicode names. For example:

```
>>> euros = "€ \N{euro sign} \u20AC \U000020AC"
>>> print(euros)
€ € € €
```

In this case we could not use a hexadecimal escape because they are limited to two digits, so they cannot exceed 0xFF. Note that Unicode character names are not case-sensitive, and spaces inside them are optional.

If we want to know the Unicode code point (the integer assigned to the character in the Unicode encoding) for a particular character in a string, we can use the built-in ord() function. For example:

```
>>> ord(euros[0])
8364
>>> hex(ord(euros[0]))
'0x20ac'
```

Character encodings

☞ 85

Similarly, we can convert any integer that represents a valid code point into the corresponding Unicode character using the built-in chr() function:

```
>>> s = "anarchists are " + chr(8734) + chr(0x23B7)
>>> s
'anarchists are ∞√'
>>> ascii(s)
"'anarchists are \u221e\u23b7'"
```

If we enter s on its own in IDLE, it is output in its string form, which for strings means the characters are output enclosed in quotes. If we want only ASCII characters, we can use the built-in ascii() function which returns the representational form of its argument using 7-bit ASCII characters where possible, and using the shortest form of \xhh, \uhhhh, or \Uhhhhhhhh escape otherwise. We will see how to achieve precise control of string output later in this chapter.

str.
format()

☞ 74

Comparing Strings

Strings support the usual comparison operators <, <=, ==, !=, >, and >=. These operators compare strings byte by byte in memory. Unfortunately, two problems arise when performing comparisons, such as when sorting lists of strings. Both problems afflict every programming language that uses Unicode strings—neither is specific to Python.

The first problem is that some Unicode characters can be represented by two or more different byte sequences. For example, the character Å (Unicode code point 0x00C5) can be represented in UTF-8 encoded bytes in three different ways: [0xE2, 0x84, 0xAB], [0xC3, 0x85], and [0x41, 0xCC, 0x8A]. Fortunately, we can solve this problem. If we import the unicodedata module and call unicodedata.normalize() with "NFKD" as the first argument (this is the normalization method to use and stands for "Normalization Form Compatibility Decomposition"), and a string containing the Å character using any of its valid byte sequences, the function will return a string that when represented as UTF-8 encoded bytes will always be the byte sequence [0x41, 0xCC, 0x8A].

Character encodings ☞ 85

The second problem is that the sorting of some characters is language-specific. One example is that in Swedish *ä* is sorted after *z*, whereas in German, *ä* is sorted as if though were spelled *ae*. Another example is that although in English we sort *ø* as if it were *o*, in Danish and Norwegian it is sorted after *z*. There are lots of problems along these lines, and they can be complicated by the fact that sometimes the same application is used by people of different nationalities (who therefore expect different sorting orders), and sometimes strings are in a mixture of languages (e.g., some Spanish, others English), and some characters (such as arrows, dingbats, and mathematical symbols) don't really have meaningful sort positions.

As a matter of policy—to prevent subtle mistakes—Python does not make guesses. In the case of string comparisons, it compares using the strings' in-memory byte representation. This gives a sort order based on Unicode code points which gives ASCII sorting for English. Lower- or uppercasing all the strings compared produces a more natural English language ordering. Normalizing is unlikely to be needed unless the strings are from external sources like files or network sockets, but even in these cases it probably shouldn't be done unless there is evidence that it is needed. We can of course customize Python's sort methods as we will see in Chapter 3. The whole issue of sorting Unicode strings is explained in detail in the Unicode Collation Algorithm document (unicode.org/reports/tr10).

Slicing and Striding Strings

Piece #3 16 ☞

We know from Piece #3 that individual items in a sequence, and therefore individual characters in a string, can be extracted using the item access operator ([]). In fact, this operator is much more versatile and can be used to extract not just one item or character, but an entire slice (subsequence) of items or characters, in which context it is referred to as the slice operator.

First we will begin by looking at extracting individual characters. Index positions into a string begin at 0 and go up to the length of the string minus 1. But it is also possible to use negative index positions—these count from the last character back toward the first. Given the assignment s = "Light ray", Figure 2.1 shows all the valid index positions for string s.

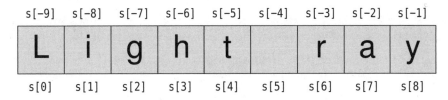

Figure 2.1 *String index positions*

Negative indexes are surprisingly useful, especially -1 which always gives us the last character in a string. Accessing an out-of-range index (or any index in an empty string) will cause an IndexError exception to be raised.

The slice operator has three syntaxes:

    seq[start]
    seq[start:end]
    seq[start:end:step]

The *seq* can be any sequence, such as a list, string, or tuple. The *start*, *end*, and *step* values must all be integers (or variables holding integers). We have used the first syntax already: It extracts the *start*-th item from the sequence. The second syntax extracts a slice from and including the *start*-th item, up to and *excluding* the *end*-th item. We'll discuss the third syntax shortly.

If we use the second (one colon) syntax, we can omit either of the integer indexes. If we omit the start index, it will default to 0. If we omit the end index, it will default to len(*seq*). This means that if we omit both indexes, for example, s[:], it is the same as writing s[0:len(s)], and extracts—that is, copies—the entire sequence.

Given the assignment s = "The waxwork man", Figure 2.2 shows some example slices for string s.

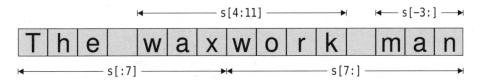

Figure 2.2 *Sequence slicing*

One way of inserting a substring inside a string is to mix slicing with concatenation. For example:

```
>>> s = s[:12] + "wo" + s[12:]
>>> s
'The waxwork woman'
```

In fact, since the text "wo" appears in the original string, we could have achieved the same effect by assigning s[:12] + s[7:9] + s[12:].

Using + to concatenate and += to append is not particularly efficient when many strings are involved. For joining lots of strings it is usually best to use the str.join() method, as we will see in the next subsection.

String operators and methods ☞ 67

The third (two colon) slice syntax is like the second, only instead of extracting every character, every *step*-th character is taken. And like the second syntax, we can omit either of the index integers. If we omit the start index, it will default to 0—unless a negative step is given, in which case the start index defaults to -1. If we omit the end index, it will default to len(*seq*)—unless a negative step is given, in which case the end index effectively defaults to before the beginning of the string. We cannot omit the step and the step cannot be zero; if we don't want a step, we should use the second (one colon) syntax that does not have a step variable.

If we have the assignment s = "he ate camel food", Figure 2.3 shows a couple of example strided slices for string s.

s[::-2] == 'do ea t h'

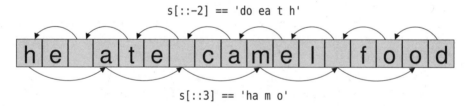

s[::3] == 'ha m o'

Figure 2.3 *Sequence striding*

Here we have used the default start and end indexes, so s[::-2] starts at the last character and extracts every second character counting toward the start of the string. Similarly, s[::3] starts at the first character and extracts every third character counting toward the end.

It is also possible to combine slicing indexes with striding, as Figure 2.4 illustrates.

Striding is most often used with sequence types other than strings, but there is one context in which it is used for strings:

```
>>> s, s[::-1]
('The waxwork woman', 'namow krowxaw ehT')
```

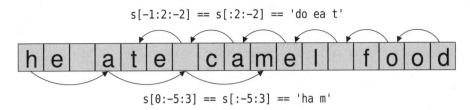

$$s[-1:2:-2] == s[:2:-2] == \text{'do ea t'}$$

$$s[0:-5:3] == s[:-5:3] == \text{'ha m'}$$

Figure 2.4 *Sequence slicing and striding*

Stepping by -1 means that every character is extracted, from the end back to the beginning—and therefore produces the string in reverse.

String Operators and Methods

Since strings are immutable sequences, all the functionality that can be used with immutable sequences can be used with strings. This includes membership testing with in, concatenation with +, appending with +=, replication with *, and augmented assignment replication with *=. We will discuss all of these in the context of strings in this subsection, in addition to discussing many of the string methods. Tables 2.8, 2.9, and 2.10 summarize all the string methods, except for two rather specialized ones (str.maketrans() and str.translate()) that we will briefly discuss further on.

Iterable operators and functions ☞ 130

As strings are sequences they are "sized" objects, and therefore we can call len() with a string as the argument. The length returned is the number of characters in the string (zero for an empty string).

Sized ☞ 373

We have seen that the + operator is overloaded to provide string concatenation. In cases where we want to concatenate lots of strings the str.join() method offers a better solution. The method takes a sequence as an argument (e.g., a list or tuple of strings), and joins them together into a single string with the string the method was called on between each one. For example:

```
>>> treatises = ["Arithmetica", "Conics", "Elements"]
>>> " ".join(treatises)
'Arithmetica Conics Elements'
>>> "-<>-".join(treatises)
'Arithmetica-<>-Conics-<>-Elements'
>>> "".join(treatises)
'ArithmeticaConicsElements'
```

The first example is perhaps the most common, joining with a single character, in this case a space. The third example is pure concatenation thanks to the empty string which means that the sequence of strings are joined with nothing in between.

Table 2.8 *String Methods #1*

Syntax	Description
s.capitalize()	Returns a copy of str s with the first letter capitalized; see also the str.title() method
s.center(width, *char*)	Returns a copy of s centered in a string of length width padded with spaces or optionally with *char* (a string of length 1); see str.ljust(), str.rjust(), and str.format()
s.count(t, *start*, *end*)	Returns the number of occurrences of str t in str s (or in the *start*:*end* slice of s)
s.encode(*encoding*, *err*)	Returns a bytes object that represents the string using the default encoding or using the specified *encoding* and handling errors according to the optional *err* argument
s.endswith(x, *start*, *end*)	Returns True if s (or the *start*:*end* slice of s) ends with str x or with any of the strings in tuple x; otherwise, returns False. See also str.startswith().
s.expandtabs(*size*)	Returns a copy of s with tabs replaced with spaces in multiples of 8 or of *size* if specified
s.find(t, *start*, *end*)	Returns the leftmost position of t in s (or in the *start*:*end* slice of s) or -1 if not found. Use str.rfind() to find the rightmost position. See also str.index().
s.format(...)	Returns a copy of s formatted according to the given arguments. This method and its arguments are covered in the next subsection.
s.index(t, *start*, *end*)	Returns the leftmost position of t in s (or in the *start*:*end* slice of s) or raises ValueError if not found. Use str.rindex() to search from the right. See str.find().
s.isalnum()	Returns True if s is nonempty and every character in s is alphanumeric
s.isalpha()	Returns True if s is nonempty and every character in s is alphabetic
s.isdecimal()	Returns True if s is nonempty and every character in s is a Unicode base 10 digit
s.isdigit()	Returns True if s is nonempty and every character in s is an ASCII digit
s.isidentifier()	Returns True if s is nonempty and is a valid identifier
s.islower()	Returns True if s has at least one lowercaseable character and all its lowercaseable characters are lowercase; see also str.isupper()

bytes type ☞ 286

Character encodings ☞ 85

str.format() ☞ 74

Identifiers and keywords 47 ☜

Table 2.9 *String Methods #2*

Syntax	Description
s.isnumeric()	Returns True if s is nonempty and every character in s is a numeric Unicode character such as a digit or fraction
s.isprintable()	Returns True if s is empty or if every character in s is considered to be printable, including space, but not newline
s.isspace()	Returns True if s is nonempty and every character in s is a whitespace character
s.istitle()	Returns True if s is a nonempty title-cased string; see also str.title()
s.isupper()	Returns True if str s has at least one uppercaseable character and all its uppercaseable characters are uppercase; see also str.islower()
s.join(seq)	Returns the concatenation of every item in the sequence seq, with str s (which may be empty) between each one
s.ljust(width, char)	Returns a copy of s left-aligned in a string of length width padded with spaces or optionally with *char* (a string of length 1). Use str.rjust() to right-align and str.center() to center. See also str.format().
s.lower()	Returns a lowercased copy of s; see also str.upper()
s.maketrans()	Companion of str.translate(); see text for details
s.partition(t)	Returns a tuple of three strings—the part of str s before the leftmost str t, t, and the part of s after t; or if t isn't in s returns s and two empty strings. Use str.rpartition() to partition on the rightmost occurrence of t.
s.replace(t, u, n)	Returns a copy of s with every (or a maximum of *n* if given) occurrences of str t replaced with str u
s.split(*t*, *n*)	Returns a list of strings splitting at most *n* times on str *t*; if *n* isn't given, splits as many times as possible; if *t* isn't given, splits on whitespace. Use str.rsplit() to split from the right—this makes a difference only if *n* is given and is less than the maximum number of splits possible.
s.splitlines(*f*)	Returns the list of lines produced by splitting s on line terminators, stripping the terminators unless *f* is True
s.startswith(x, *start*, *end*)	Returns True if s (or the *start*:*end* slice of s) starts with str x or with any of the strings in tuple x; otherwise, returns False. See also str.endswith().

Table 2.10 *String Methods #3*

Syntax	Description
s.strip(*chars*)	Returns a copy of s with leading and trailing whitespace (or the characters in str *chars*) removed; str.lstrip() strips only at the start, and str.rstrip() strips only at the end
s.swapcase()	Returns a copy of s with uppercase characters lowercased and lowercase characters uppercased; see also str.lower() and str.upper()
s.title()	Returns a copy of s where the first letter of each word is uppercased and all other letters are lowercased; see str.istitle()
s.translate()	Companion of str.maketrans(); see text for details
s.upper()	Returns an uppercased copy of s; see also str.lower()
s.zfill(w)	Returns a copy of s, which if shorter than w is padded with leading zeros to make it w characters long

The str.join() method can also be used with the built-in reversed() function, to reverse a string, for example, "".join(reversed(s)), although the same result can be achieved more concisely by striding, for example, s[::-1].

The * operator provides string replication:

```
>>> s = "=" * 5
>>> print(s)
=====
>>> s *= 10
>>> print(s)
==================================================
```

As the example shows, we can also use the augmented assignment version of the replication operator.*

When applied to strings, the in membership operator returns True if its left-hand string argument is a substring of, or equal to, its right-hand string argument. In cases where we want to find the position of one string inside another, we have two methods to choose from. One is the str.index() method; this returns the index position of the substring, or raises a ValueError exception on failure. The other is the str.find() method; this returns the index position of the substring, or -1 on failure. Both methods take the string to find as their first argument, and can accept a couple of optional arguments. The second argu-

---

*Strings also support the % operator for formatting. This operator is deprecated and provided only to ease conversion from Python 2 to Python 3. It is not used in any of the book's examples.

ment is the start position in the string being searched, and the third argument is the end position in the string being searched.

Which search method we use is purely a matter of taste and circumstance, although if we are looking for multiple index positions, using the str.index() method often produces cleaner code, as the following two equivalent functions illustrate:

```
def extract_from_tag(tag, line):          def extract_from_tag(tag, line):
    opener = "<" + tag + ">"                  opener = "<" + tag + ">"
    closer = "</" + tag + ">"                 closer = "</" + tag + ">"
    try:                                      i = line.find(opener)
        i = line.index(opener)                if i != -1:
        start = i + len(opener)                   start = i + len(opener)
        j = line.index(closer, start)             j = line.find(closer, start)
        return line[start:j]                      if j != -1:
    except ValueError:                                return line[start:j]
        return None                           return None
```

Both versions of the extract_from_tag() function have exactly the same behavior. For example, extract_from_tag("red", "what a <red>rose</red> this is") returns the string "rose". The exception-handling version on the left separates out the code that does what we want from the code that handles errors, and the error return value version on the right intersperses what we want with error handling.

The methods str.count(), str.endswith(), str.find(), str.rfind(), str.index(), str.rindex(), and str.startswith() all accept up to two optional arguments: a start position and an end position. Here are a couple of equivalences to put this in context, assuming that s is a string:

```
s.count("m", 6) == s[6:].count("m")
s.count("m", 5, -3) == s[5:-3].count("m")
```

As we can see, the string methods that accept start and end indexes operate on the slice of the string specified by those indexes.

Now we will look at another equivalence, this time to help clarify the behavior of str.partition():

```
                                          i = s.rfind("/")
                                          if i == -1:
                                              result = s, "", ""
                                          else:
result = s.rpartition("/")                    result = s[:i], s[i], s[i + 1:]
```

The left- and right-hand code snippets are not quite equivalent because the one on the right also creates a new variable, i. Notice that we can assign tuples without formality, and that in both cases we looked for the rightmost occurrence of /. If s is the string "/usr/local/bin/firefox", both snippets produce the same result: ('/usr/local/bin', '/', 'firefox').

We can use str.endswith() (and str.startswith()) with a single string argument, for example, s.startswith("From:"), or with a tuple of strings. Here is a statement that uses both str.endswith() and str.lower() to print a filename if it is a JPEG file:

```
if filename.lower().endswith((".jpg", ".jpeg")):
    print(filename, "is a JPEG image")
```

The is*() methods such as isalpha() and isspace() return True if the string they are called on has at least one character, and every character in the string meets the criterion. For example:

```
>>> "917.5".isdigit(), "".isdigit(), "-2".isdigit(), "203".isdigit()
(False, False, False, True)
```

The is*() methods work on the basis of Unicode character classifications, so for example, calling str.isdigit() on the strings "\N{circled digit two}03" and "②03" returns True for both of them. For this reason we cannot assume that a string can be converted to an integer when isdigit() returns True.

When we receive strings from external sources (other programs, files, network connections, and especially interactive users), the strings may have unwanted leading and trailing whitespace. We can strip whitespace from the left using str.lstrip(), from the right using str.rstrip(), or from both ends using str.strip(). We can also give a string as an argument to the strip methods, in which case every occurrence of every character given will be stripped from the appropriate end or ends. For example:

```
>>> s = "\t no parking "
>>> s.lstrip(), s.rstrip(), s.strip()
('no parking ', '\t no parking', 'no parking')
>>> "<[unbracketed]>".strip("[](){}<>")
'unbracketed'
```

We can also replace strings within strings using the str.replace() method. This method takes two string arguments, and returns a copy of the string it is called on with every occurrence of the first string replaced with the second. If the second argument is an empty string the effect is to delete every occurrence of the first string. We will see examples of str.replace() and some other string methods in the csv2html.py example in the Examples section toward the end of the chapter.

csv2-
html.py
example

☞ 90

One frequent requirement is to split a string into a list of strings. For example, we might have a text file of data with one record per line and each record's fields separated by asterisks. This can be done using the `str.split()` method and passing in the string to split on as its first argument, and optionally the maximum number of splits to make as the second argument. If we don't specify the second argument, as many splits are made as possible. Here is an example:

```
>>> record = "Leo Tolstoy*1828-8-28*1910-11-20"
>>> fields = record.split("*")
>>> fields
['Leo Tolstoy', '1828-8-28', '1910-11-20']
```

Now we can use `str.split()` again on the date of birth and date of death to calculate how long he lived (give or take a year):

```
>>> born = fields[1].split("-")
>>> born
['1828', '8', '28']
>>> died = fields[2].split("-")
>>> print("lived about", int(died[0]) - int(born[0]), "years")
lived about 82 years
```

We had to use `int()` to convert the years from strings to integers, but other than that the snippet is straightforward. We could have gotten the years directly from the `fields` list, for example, `year_born = int(fields[1].split("-")[0])`.

The two methods that we did not summarize in Tables 2.8, 2.9, and 2.10 are `str.maketrans()` and `str.translate()`. The `str.maketrans()` method is used to create a translation table which maps characters to characters. It accepts one, two, or three arguments, but we will show only the simplest (two argument) call where the first argument is a string containing characters to translate from and the second argument is a string containing the characters to translate to. Both arguments must be the same length. The `str.translate()` method takes a translation table as an argument and returns a copy of its string with the characters translated according to the translation table. Here is how we could translate strings that might contain Bengali digits to English digits:

```
table = "".maketrans("\N{bengali digit zero}"
    "\N{bengali digit one}\N{bengali digit two}"
    "\N{bengali digit three}\N{bengali digit four}"
    "\N{bengali digit five}\N{bengali digit six}"
    "\N{bengali digit seven}\N{bengali digit eight}"
    "\N{bengali digit nine}", "0123456789")
print("20749".translate(table))                 # prints: 20749
print("\N{bengali digit two}07\N{bengali digit four}"
    "\N{bengali digit nine}".translate(table))   # prints: 20749
```

Notice that we have taken advantage of Python's string literal concatenation inside the str.maketrans() call and inside the second print() call to spread strings over multiple lines without having to escape newlines or use explicit concatenation.

We called str.maketrans() on an empty string because it doesn't matter what string it is called on; it simply processes its arguments and returns a translation table.* The str.maketrans() and str.translate() methods can also be used to delete characters by passing a string containing the unwanted characters as the third argument to str.maketrans(). If more sophisticated character translations are required, we could create a custom codec—see the codecs module documentation for more about this.

Python has a few other library modules that provide string-related functionality. We've already briefly mentioned the unicodedata module, and we'll show it in use in the next subsection. Other modules worth looking up are difflib which can be used to show differences between files or between strings, the io module's io.StringIO class which allows us to read from or write to strings as though they were files, and the textwrap module which provides facilities for wrapping and filling strings. There is also a string module that has a few useful constants such as ascii_letters and ascii_lowercase. We will see examples of some of these modules in use in Chapter 5. In addition, Python provides excellent support for regular expressions in the re module—Chapter 12 is dedicated to this topic.

String Formatting with the str.format() Method

The str.format() method provides a very flexible and powerful way of creating strings. Using str.format() is easy for simple cases, but for complex formatting we need to learn the formatting syntax the method requires.

The str.format() method returns a new string with the *replacement fields* in its string replaced with its arguments suitably formatted. For example:

```
>>> "The novel '{0}' was published in {1}".format("Hard Times", 1854)
"The novel 'Hard Times' was published in 1854"
```

Each replacement field is identified by a field name in braces. If the field name is a simple integer, it is taken to be the index position of one of the arguments passed to str.format(). So in this case, the field whose name was 0 was replaced by the first argument, and the one with name 1 was replaced by the second argument.

If we need to include braces inside format strings, we can do so by doubling them up. Here is an example:

---

*Note for object-oriented programmers: str.maketrans() is a static method.

```
>>> "{{{0}}} {1} ;-}}".format("I'm in braces", "I'm not")
"{I'm in braces} I'm not ;-}"
```

If we try to concatenate a string and a number, Python will quite rightly raise a TypeError. But we can easily achieve what we want using str.format():

```
>>> "{0}{1}".format("The amount due is $", 200)
'The amount due is $200'
```

We can also concatenate strings using str.format() (although the str.join() method is best for this):

```
>>> x = "three"
>>> s ="{0} {1} {2}"
>>> s = s.format("The", x, "tops")
>>> s
'The three tops'
```

Here we have used a couple of string variables, but in most of this section we'll use string literals for str.format() examples, simply for the sake of convenience—just keep in mind that any example that uses a string literal could use a string variable in exactly the same way.

The replacement field can have any of the following general syntaxes:

```
{field_name}
{field_name!conversion}
{field_name:format_specification}
{field_name!conversion:format_specification}
```

One other point to note is that replacement fields can *contain* replacement fields. Nested replacement fields cannot have any formatting; their purpose is to allow for computed formatting specifications. We will see an example of this when we take a detailed look at format specifications. We will now study each part of the replacement field in turn, starting with field names.

Field Names

A field name can be either an integer corresponding to one of the str.format() method's arguments, or the name of one of the method's keyword arguments. We discuss keyword arguments in Chapter 4, but they are not difficult, so we will provide a couple of examples here for completeness:

```
>>> "{who} turned {age} this year".format(who="She", age=88)
'She turned 88 this year'
>>> "The {who} was {0} last week".format(12, who="boy")
'The boy was 12 last week'
```

The first example uses two keyword arguments, who and age, and the second example uses one positional argument (the only kind we have used up to now) and one keyword argument. Notice that in an argument list, keyword arguments always come after positional arguments; and of course we can make use of any arguments in any order inside the format string.

Field names may refer to collection data types—for example, lists. In such cases we can include an index (not a slice!) to identify a particular item:

```
>>> stock = ["paper", "envelopes", "notepads", "pens", "paper clips"]
>>> "We have {0[1]} and {0[2]} in stock".format(stock)
'We have envelopes and notepads in stock'
```

The 0 refers to the positional argument, so {0[1]} is the stock list argument's second item, and {0[2]} is the stock list argument's third item.

Later on we will learn about Python dictionaries. These store key–value items, and since they can be used with str.format(), we'll just show a quick example here. Don't worry if it doesn't make sense; it will once you've read Chapter 3.

dict type
☞ 118

```
>>> d = dict(animal="elephant", weight=12000)
>>> "The {0[animal]} weighs {0[weight]}kg".format(d)
'The elephant weighs 12000kg'
```

Just as we access list and tuple items using an integer position index, we access dictionary items using a key.

We can also access named attributes. Assuming we have imported the math and sys modules, we can do this:

```
>>> "math.pi=={0.pi} sys.maxunicode=={1.maxunicode}".format(math, sys)
'math.pi==3.14159265359 sys.maxunicode==65535'
```

So in summary, the field name syntax allows us to refer to positional and keyword arguments that are passed to the str.format() method. If the arguments are collection data types like lists or dictionaries, or have attributes, we can access the part we want using [] or . notation. This is illustrated in Figure 2.5.

Conversions

Decimal numbers
59 ☜

When we discussed decimal.Decimal numbers we noticed that such numbers are output in one of two ways. For example:

```
>>> decimal.Decimal("3.4084")
Decimal('3.4084')
>>> print(decimal.Decimal("3.4084"))
3.4084
```

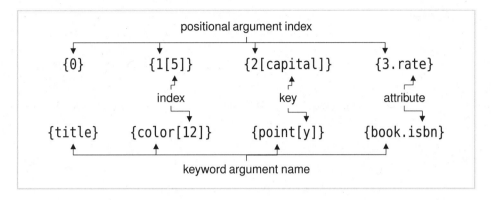

Figure 2.5 *Annotated format specifier field name examples*

The first way that the decimal.Decimal is shown is in its representational form. The purpose of this form is to provide a string which if interpreted by Python would re-create the object it represents. Python programs can evaluate snippets of Python code or entire programs, so this facility can be useful in some situations. Not all objects can provide a reproducing representation, in which case they provide a string enclosed in angle brackets. For example, the representational form of the sys module is the string "<module 'sys' (built-in)>".

eval()
☞ 334

The second way that decimal.Decimal is shown is in its string form. This form is aimed at human readers, so the concern is to show something that makes sense to people. If a data type doesn't have a string form and a string is required, Python will use the representational form.

Python's built-in data types know about str.format(), and when passed as an argument to this method they return a suitable string to display themselves. It is also straightforward to add str.format() support to custom data types as we will see in Chapter 6. In addition, it is possible to override the data type's normal behavior and force it to provide either its string or its representational form. This is done by adding a conversion specifier to the field. Currently there are three such specifiers: *s* to force string form, *r* to force representational form, and *a* to force representational form but only using ASCII characters. Here is an example:

```
>>> "{0} {0!s} {0!r} {0!a}".format(decimal.Decimal("93.4"))
"93.4 93.4 Decimal('93.4') Decimal('93.4')"
```

In this case, decimal.Decimal's string form produces the same string as the string it provides for str.format() which is what commonly happens. Also, in this particular example, there is no difference between the representational and ASCII representational forms since both use only ASCII characters.

Here is another example, this time concerning a string that contains the title of a movie, "翻訳で失われる", held in the variable movie. If we print the string using `"{0}".format(movie)` the string will be output unchanged, but if we want to avoid non-ASCII characters we can use either `ascii(movie)` or `"{0!a}".format(movie)`, both of which will produce the string `'\u7ffb\u8a33 \u3067\u5931\u308f\u308c\u308b'`.

So far we have seen how to put the values of variables into a format string, and how to force string or representational forms to be used. Now we are ready to consider the formatting of the values themselves.

Format Specifications

The default formatting of integers, floating-point numbers, and strings is often perfectly satisfactory. But if we want to exercise fine control, we can easily do so using format specifications. We will deal separately with formatting strings, integers, and floating-point numbers, to make learning the details easier. The the general syntax that covers all of them is shown in Figure 2.6.

:	*fill*	*align*	*sign*	#	0	*width*	. *precision*	*type*
	Any character except }	< left > right ^ center = pad between sign and digits for numbers	+ force sign; − sign if needed; " " space or − as appropriate	prefix ints with 0b, 0o, or 0x	0-pad numbers	Minimum field width	Maximum field width for strings; number of decimal places for floating-point numbers	ints b, c, d, n, o, x, X; floats e, E, f, g, G, n, %

Figure 2.6 *The general form of a format specification*

For strings, the things that we can control are the fill character, the alignment within the field, and the minimum and maximum field widths.

A string format specification is introduced with a colon (:) and this is followed by an optional pair of characters—a fill character (which may not be }) and an alignment character (< for left align, ^ for center, > for right align). Then comes an optional minimum width integer, and if we want to specify a maximum width, this comes last as a period followed by an integer.

Note that if we specify a fill character we must also specify an alignment. We omit the sign and type parts of the format specification because they have no effect on strings. It is harmless (but pointless) to have a colon without any of the optional elements.

Let's see some examples:

```
>>> s = "The sword of truth"
>>> "{0}".format(s)        # default formatting
'The sword of truth'
>>> "{0:25}".format(s)    # minimum width 25
'The sword of truth       '
>>> "{0:>25}".format(s)   # right align, minimum width 25
'       The sword of truth'
>>> "{0:^25}".format(s)   # center align, minimum width 25
'   The sword of truth    '
>>> "{0:-^25}".format(s)  # - fill, center align, minimum width 25
'---The sword of truth----'
>>> "{0:.<25}".format(s)  # . fill, left align, minimum width 25
'The sword of truth.......'
>>> "{0:.10}".format(s)   # maximum width 10
'The sword '
```

In the penultimate example we had to specify the left alignment (even though this is the default). If we left out the <, we would have :.25, and this simply means a maximum field width of 25 characters.

As we noted earlier, it is possible to have replacement fields inside format specifications. This makes it possible to have computed formats. Here, for example, are two ways of setting a string's maximum width using a maxwidth variable:

```
>>> maxwidth = 12
>>> "{0}".format(s[:maxwidth])
'The sword of'
>>> "{0:.{1}}".format(s, maxwidth)
'The sword of'
```

The first approach uses standard string slicing; the second uses an inner replacement field.

For integers, the format specification allows us to control the fill character, the alignment within the field, the sign, the minimum field width, and the number base.

An integer format specification begins with a colon, after which we can have an optional pair of characters—a fill character (which may not be }) and an alignment character (< for left align, ^ for center, > for right align, and = for the filling to be done between the sign and the number). Next is an optional sign character: + forces the output of the sign, - outputs the sign only for negative numbers, and a space outputs a space for positive numbers and a - sign for negative numbers. Then comes an optional minimum width integer—this can be preceded by a # character to get the base prefix output (for binary, octal, and hexadecimal numbers), and by a 0 to get 0-padding. If we want the output in a base other than decimal we must add a type character—b for binary, o for octal, x for lowercase hexadecimal, and X for uppercase hexadecimal, although

for completeness, d for decimal integer is also allowed. There are two other
type characters: c, which means that the Unicode character corresponding to
the integer should be output, and n, which outputs numbers in a locale-sensi-
tive way.

We can get 0-padding in two different ways:

```
>>> "{0:0=12}".format(8749203)  # 0 fill, minimum width 12
'000008749203'
>>> "{0:0=12}".format(-8749203) # 0 fill, minimum width 12
'-00008749203'
>>> "{0:012}".format(8749203)   # 0-pad and minimum width 12
'000008749203'
>>> "{0:012}".format(-8749203)  # 0-pad and minimum width 12
'-00008749203'
```

The first two examples have a fill character of 0 and fill between the sign and
the number itself (=). The second two examples have a minimum width of 12
and 0-padding.

Here are some alignment examples:

```
>>> "{0:*<15}".format(18340427)  # * fill, left align, min width 15
'18340427*******'
>>> "{0:*>15}".format(18340427)  # * fill, right align, min width 15
'*******18340427'
>>> "{0:*^15}".format(18340427)  # * fill, center align, min width 15
'***18340427****'
>>> "{0:*^15}".format(-18340427) # * fill, center align, min width 15
'***-18340427***'
```

Here are some examples that show the effects of the sign characters:

```
>>> "[{0: }] [{1: }]".format(539802, -539802) # space or - sign
'[ 539802] [-539802]'
>>> "[{0:+}] [{1:+}]".format(539802, -539802) # force sign
'[+539802] [-539802]'
>>> "[{0:-}] [{1:-}]".format(539802, -539802) # - sign if needed
'[539802] [-539802]'
```

And here are two examples that use some of the type characters:

```
>>> "{0:b} {0:o} {0:x} {0:X}".format(14613198)
'110111101111101011001110 67575316 deface DEFACE'
>>> "{0:#b} {0:#o} {0:#x} {0:#X}".format(14613198)
'0b110111101111101011001110 0o67575316 0xdeface 0XDEFACE'
```

It is not possible to specify a maximum field width for integers. This is because doing so might require digits to be chopped off, thereby rendering the integer meaningless.

The last format character available for integers (and which is also available for floating-point numbers) is n. This has the same effect as d when given an integer and the same effect as g when given a floating-point number. What makes n special is that it respects the current locale, and will use the locale-specific decimal character and grouping character in the output it produces. The default locale is called the C locale, and for this the decimal and grouping characters are a period and an empty string. We can respect the user's locale by starting our programs with the following two lines as the first executable statements:[*]

```
import locale
locale.setlocale(locale.LC_ALL, "")
```

Passing an empty string as the locale tells Python to try to automatically determine the user's locale (e.g., by examining the LANG environment variable), with a fallback of the C locale. Here are some examples that show the effects of different locales on an integer and a floating-point number:

```
x, y = (1234567890, 1234.56)
locale.setlocale(locale.LC_ALL, "C")
c = "{0:n} {1:n}".format(x, y)      # c == "1234567890  1234.56"
locale.setlocale(locale.LC_ALL, "en_US.UTF-8")
en = "{0:n} {1:n}".format(x, y)     # en == "1,234,567,890  1,234.56"
locale.setlocale(locale.LC_ALL, "de_DE.UTF-8")
de = "{0:n} {1:n}".format(x, y)     # de == "1.234.567.890  1.234,56"
```

Although n is very useful for integers, it is of more limited use with floating-point numbers because as soon as they become large they are output using exponential form.

For floating-point numbers, the format specification gives us control over the fill character, the alignment within the field, the sign, the minimum field width, the number of digits after the decimal place, and whether to present the number in standard or exponential form, or as a percentage.

The format specification for floating-point numbers is the same as for integers, except for two differences at the end. After the optional minimum width, we can specify the number of digits after the decimal place by writing a period followed by an integer. We can also add a type character at the end: e for exponential form with a lowercase *e*, E for exponential form with an uppercase *E*, f for standard floating-point form, g for "general" form—this is the same as f unless the number is very large in which case it is the same as e—and G which

---

[*]In multithreaded programs it is best to call locale.setlocale() only once, at program start-up, and before any additional threads have been started, since the function is not usually thread-safe.

is almost the same as g, but uses either f or E. Also avaliable is %—this results in the number being multiplied by 100 with the resultant number output in f format with a % symbol appended.

Here are a few examples that show exponential and standard forms:

```
>>> amount = (10 ** 3) * math.pi
>>> "[{0:12.2e}] [{0:12.2f}]".format(amount)
'[    3.14e+03] [     3141.59]'
>>> "[{0:*>12.2e}] [{0:*>12.2f}]".format(amount)
'[****3.14e+03] [*****3141.59]'
>>> "[{0:*>+12.2e}] [{0:*>+12.2f}]".format(amount)
'[***+3.14e+03] [****+3141.59]'
```

The first example has a minimum width of 12 characters and has 2 digits after the decimal point. The second example builds on the first, and adds a * fill character. If we use a fill character we must also have an alignment character, so we have specified align right (even though that is the default for numbers). The third example builds on the previous two, and adds the + sign character to force the output of the sign.

At the time of this writing, Python does not have direct support for formatting complex numbers. However, we can easily solve this by formatting the real and imaginary parts as individual floating-point numbers. For example:

```
>>> "{0.real:.3f}{0.imag:+.3f}j".format(4.75917+1.2042j)
'4.759+1.204j'
>>> "{0.real:.3f}{0.imag:+.3f}j".format(4.75917-1.2042j)
'4.759-1.204j'
```

We access each attribute of the complex number individually, and format them both as floating-point numbers with three digits after the decimal place. We also force the sign to be output for the imaginary part, and add on the *j*.

Example: print_unicode.py

In the preceding subsubsections we closely examined the str.format() method's format specifications, and we have seen many code snippets that show particular aspects. In this subsubsection we will review a small yet useful example that makes use of str.format() so that we can see format specifications in a realistic context. The example also uses some of the string methods we saw in the previous section, and introduces a function from the unicodedata module.*

---

*This program assumes that the console uses the Unicode UTF-8 encoding. Unfortunately, the Windows console has poor UTF-8 support, and the Mac OS X console uses the Apple Roman encoding by default. As a workaround, the examples include print_unicode_uni.py, a version of the program that writes its output to a file which can then be opened using a UTF-8-savvy editor, such as IDLE.

Chapter 7 (File Handling)

☞ 277

The program has just 25 lines of executable code. It imports two modules, sys and unicodedata, and defines one custom function, print_unicode_table(). We'll begin by looking at a sample run to see what it does, then we will look at the code at the end of the program where processing really starts, and finally we will look at the custom function.

```
print_unicode.py spoked
decimal   hex   chr                      name
-------   ---   ---   ----------------------------------------------
  10018   2722   ✢   Four Teardrop-Spoked Asterisk
  10019   2723   ✣   Four Balloon-Spoked Asterisk
  10020   2724   ✤   Heavy Four Balloon-Spoked Asterisk
  10021   2725   ✥   Four Club-Spoked Asterisk
  10035   2733   ✳   Eight Spoked Asterisk
  10043   273B   ✻   Teardrop-Spoked Asterisk
  10044   273C   ✼   Open Centre Teardrop-Spoked Asterisk
  10045   273D   ✽   Heavy Teardrop-Spoked Asterisk
  10051   2743   ❃   Heavy Teardrop-Spoked Pinwheel Asterisk
  10057   2749   ❉   Balloon-Spoked Asterisk
  10058   274A   ❊   Eight Teardrop-Spoked Propeller Asterisk
  10059   274B   ❋   Heavy Eight Teardrop-Spoked Propeller Asterisk
```

If run with no arguments, the program produces a table of every Unicode character, starting from the space character and going up to the character with the highest available code point. If an argument is given, as in the example, only those rows in the table where the lowercased Unicode character name contains the argument are printed.

```
word = None
if len(sys.argv) > 1:
    if sys.argv[1] in ("-h", "--help"):
        print("usage: {0} [string]".format(sys.argv[0]))
        word = 0
    else:
        word = sys.argv[1].lower()
if word != 0:
    print_unicode_table(word)
```

After the imports and the creation of the print_unicode_table() function, execution reaches the code shown here. We begin by assuming that the user has not given a word to match on the command line. If a command-line argument is given and is –h or --help, we print the program's usage information and set word to 0 as a flag to indicate that we are finished. Otherwise, we set the word to a lowercase copy of the argument the user typed in. If the word is not 0, then we print the table.

When we print the usage information we use a format specification that just has the format name—in this case, the position number of the argument. We could have written the line like this instead:

```
print("usage: {0[0]} [string]".format(sys.argv))
```

Using this approach the first 0 is the index position of the argument we want to use, and [0] is the index *within* the argument, and it works because sys.argv is a list.

```
def print_unicode_table(word):
    print("decimal   hex   chr  {0:^40}".format("name"))
    print("-------  -----  ---  {0:-<40}".format(""))

    code = ord(" ")
    end = sys.maxunicode

    while code < end:
        c = chr(code)
        name = unicodedata.name(c, "*** unknown ***")
        if word is None or word in name.lower():
            print("{0:7} {0:5X} {0:^3c} {1}".format(
                    code, name.title()))
        code += 1
```

We've used a couple of blank lines for the sake of clarity. The first two lines of the function's suite print the title lines. The first str.format() prints the text "name" centered in a field 40 characters wide, whereas the second one prints an empty string in a field 40 characters wide, using a fill character of "-", and aligned left. (We must give an alignment if we specify a fill character.) An alternative approach for the second line is this:

```
print("-------  -----  ---  {0}".format("-" * 40))
```

Here we have used the string replication operator (*) to create a suitable string, and simply inserted it into the format string. A third alternative would be to simply type in 40 "-"s and use a literal string.

We keep track of Unicode code points in the code variable, initializing it to the code point for a space (0x20). We set the end variable to be the highest Unicode code point available—this will vary depending on whether Python was compiled to use the UCS-2 or the UCS-4 character encoding.

Charac-
ter
encod-
ings

☞ 85

Inside the while loop we get the Unicode character that corresponds to the code point using the chr() function. The unicodedata.name() function returns the Unicode character name for the given Unicode character; its optional second argument is the name to use if no character name is defined.

If the user didn't specify a word (word is None), or if they did and it is in a low-ercased copy of the Unicode character name, then we print the corresponding row.

Although we pass the code variable to the str.format() method only once, it is used three times in the format string, first to print the code as an integer in a field 7 characters wide (the fill character defaults to space, so we did not need to specify it), second to print the code as an uppercase hexadecimal number in a field 5 characters wide, and third to print the Unicode character that corresponds to the code—using the "c" format specifier, and centered in a field with a minimum width of three characters. Notice that we did not have to specify the type "d" in the first format specification; this is because it is the default for integer arguments. The second argument is the character's Unicode character name, printed using "title" case, that is, with the first letter of each word uppercased, and all other letters lowercased.

Now that we are familiar with the versatile str.format() method, we will make great use of it throughout the rest of the book.

Character Encodings

Ultimately, computers can store only bytes, that is, 8-bit values which if un-signed, range from 0x00 to 0xFF. Every character must somehow be represented in terms of bytes. In the early days of computing the pioneers devised encoding schemes that assigned a particular character to a particular byte. For example, using the ASCII encoding, *A* is represented by 0x41, *B* by 0x42, and so on. In Western Europe the Latin-1 encoding was often used; its first 127 characters are the same as 7-bit ASCII, but the rest are used for accented characters and other symbols needed by Europeans. Many other encodings have been devised over the years, and now there are lots of them in use.

Unfortunately, having all these different encodings has proved very inconve-nient, especially when writing internationalized software. One solution that has been almost universally adopted is the Unicode encoding. Unicode assigns every character to an integer, that is, to a code point, just like the earlier encod-ings, but Unicode is not limited to using one byte per character, and is therefore able to represent every character in every language in a single encoding. And as an aid to compatibility, the first 127 Unicode characters are identical to the first 127 characters of 7-bit ASCII.

But how is Unicode stored? Currently slightly more than 1 million Unicode characters are defined, so even using signed numbers, a 32-bit integer is more than adequate to store any Unicode code point. So the simplest way to store Unicode characters is as a sequence of 32-bit integers, one integer per charac-ter. In memory this is very convenient because we can have arrays of 32-bit integers with a one-to-one correspondence with an array element and a character. But for files or for sending text over network connections, especially if our text is all or mostly just 7-bit ASCII, up to three out of every four bytes used for each integer will be 0x00. To avoid such waste, Unicode itself has several representations.

In memory, Unicode is usually stored in either UCS-2 format (essentially 16-bit unsigned integers) able to represent the first 65 535 code points, or in USC-4 format (32-bit integers) able to represent all code points, of which there are 1 114 111 at the time of this writing. When Python is compiled it is set to use one of these. (If sys.maxunicode is 65 535, then Python was compiled to use UCS-2.)

For data held in files or passed over network connections the story is much more complicated. If Unicode is used, the code points could be encoded using UTF-8—this uses one byte per character for the first 127 code points, and two or more bytes per character for the other code points. UTF-8 is very compact for English text, and if only 7-bit ASCII characters are used a UTF-8 file is indistinguishable from an ASCII file. Another popular Unicode encoding is UTF-16; this uses two bytes for most characters, and four bytes for some. It is more compact for some Asian languages than UTF-8, but unlike UTF-8, UTF-16 text ought to begin with a byte order mark so that the reading code can tell whether the pairs of bytes are big- or little-endian. In addition, all the old encodings, such as GB2312, ISO-8859-5, Latin-1, and so on, are still in regular use.

The str.encode() method returns a sequence of bytes—actually a bytes object, covered in Chapter 7—encoded according to the encoding argument we supply. Using this method we can get some insight into the difference between encodings, and why making incorrect encoding assumptions can lead to errors:

```
>>> artist = "Tage Åsén"
>>> artist.encode("Latin1")
b'Tage \xc5s\xe9n'
>>> artist.encode("CP850")
b'Tage \x8fs\x82n'
>>> artist.encode("utf8")
b'Tage \xc3\x85s\xc3\xa9n'
>>> artist.encode("utf16")
b'\xff\xfeT\x00a\x00g\x00e\x00 \x00\xc5\x00s\x00\xe9\x00n\x00'
```

A *b* before an opening quote signifies a bytes literal rather than a string literal. As a convenience, when creating bytes literals we can use a mixture of printable ASCII characters and hexadecimal escapes.

We cannot encode Tage Åsén's name using the ASCII encoding because it does not have the Å character or any accented characters, so attempting to do so will result in a UnicodeEncodeError exception being raised. The Latin-1 encoding (also known as ISO-8859-1) is an 8-bit encoding that has all the necessary characters for this name. On the other hand, artist Ernő Bánk would be less fortunate since the ő character is not a Latin-1 character and so could not be successfully encoded. Both names can be successfully encoded using Unicode encodings, of course. Notice, though, that for UTF-16, the first two bytes are the byte order mark—these are used by the decoding function to detect whether the data is big- or little-endian so that it can adapt accordingly.

It is worth noting a couple more points about the str.encode() method. The first argument (the encoding name) is case-insensitive, and hyphens and underscores in the name are treated as equivalent, so "us-ascii" and "US_ASCII" are considered the same. There are also many aliases—for example, "latin", "latin1", "latin_1", "ISO-8859-1", "CP819", and some others are all "Latin-1". The method can also accept an optional second argument which is used to tell it how to handle errors. For example, we can encode any string into ASCII if we pass a second argument of "ignore" or "replace"—at the price of losing data, of course—or losslessly if we use "backslashreplace" which replaces non-ASCII characters with \x, \u, and \U escapes. For example, artist.encode("ascii", "ignore") will produce b'Tage sn' and artist.encode("ascii", "replace") will produce b'Tage ?s?n', whereas artist.encode("ascii", "backslashreplace") will produce b'Tage \xc5s\xe9n'. (We can also get an ASCII string using "{0!a}".format(artist), which produces 'Tage \xc5s\xe9n'.)

The complement of str.encode() is bytes.decode() (and bytearray.decode()) which returns a string with the bytes decoded using the given encoding. For example:

```
>>> print(b"Tage \xc3\x85s\xc3\xa9n".decode("utf8"))
Tage Åsén
>>> print(b"Tage \xc5s\xe9n".decode("latin1"))
Tage Åsén
```

The differences between the 8-bit Latin-1, CP850 (an IBM PC encoding), and UTF-8 encodings make it clear that guessing encodings is not likely to be a successful strategy. Fortunately, UTF-8 is becoming the de facto standard for plain text files, so later generations may not even know that other encodings ever existed.

Python .py files use UTF-8, so Python always knows the encoding to use with string literals. This means that we can type any Unicode characters into our strings—providing our editor supports this.[*]

When Python reads data from external sources such as sockets, it cannot know what encoding is used, so it returns bytes which we can then decode accordingly. For text files Python takes a softer approach, using the local encoding unless we specify an encoding explicitly.

---

[*]It is possible to use other encodings. See the Python Tutorial's "Source Code Encoding" topic.

Fortunately, some file formats specify their encoding. For example, we can assume that an XML file uses UTF-8, unless the `<?xml?>` directive explicitly specifies a different encoding. So when reading XML we might extract, say, the first 1 000 bytes, look for an encoding specification, and if found, decode the file using the specified encoding, otherwise falling back to decoding using UTF-8. This approach should work for any XML or plain text file that uses any of the single byte encodings supported by Python, except for EBCDIC-based encodings (CP424, CP500) and a few others (CP037, CP864, CP865, CP1026, CP1140, HZ, SHIFT-JIS-2004, SHIFT-JISX0213). Unfortunately, this approach won't work for multibyte encodings (such as UTF-16 and UTF-32). At least two Python packages for automatically detecting a file's encoding are available from the Python Package Index, `pypi.python.org/pypi`.

Examples

In this section we will draw on what we have covered in this chapter and the one before, to present two small but complete programs to help consolidate what we have learned so far. The first program is a bit mathematical, but it is quite short at around 35 lines. The second is concerned with text processing and is more substantial, with seven functions in around 80 lines of code.

quadratic.py

Quadratic equations are equations of the form $ax^2 + bx + c = 0$ where $a \neq 0$ describe parabolas. The roots of such equations are derived from the formula $x = \frac{-b \pm \sqrt{b^2 - 4ac}}{2a}$. The $b^2 - 4ac$ part of the formula is called the *discriminant*—if it is positive there are two real roots, if it is zero there is one real root, and if it is negative there are two complex roots. We will write a program that accepts the a, b, and c factors from the user (with the b and c factors allowed to be 0), and then calculates and outputs the root or roots.[*]

First we will look at a sample run, and then we will review the code.

```
quadratic.py
ax² + bx + c = 0
enter a: 2.5
enter b: 0
enter c: -7.25
2.5x² + 0.0x + -7.25 = 0 → x = 1.70293863659 or x = -1.70293863659
```

---

[*]Since the Windows console has poor UTF-8 support and since the Mac OS X console defaults to the Apple Roman encoding, there are problems with a couple of the characters (² and →) that `quadratic.py` uses. We have provided `quadratic_uni.py` which displays the correct symbols on Linux consoles, and alternatives (^2 and ->) on other consoles.

With factors 1.5, -3, and 6, the output (with some digits trimmed) is:

```
1.5x² + -3.0x + 6.0 = 0 → x = (1+1.7320508j) or x = (1-1.7320508j)
```

The output isn't quite as tidy as we'd like—for example, rather than + -3.0x it would be nicer to have - 3.0x, and we would prefer not to have any 0 factors shown at all. You will get the chance to fix these problems in the exercises.

Now we will turn to the code, which begins with three imports:

```
import cmath
import math
import sys
```

We need both the float and the complex math libraries since the square root functions for real and complex numbers are different, and we need sys for sys.float_info.epsilon which we need to compare floating-point numbers with 0.

We also need a function that can get a floating-point number from the user:

```
def get_float(msg, allow_zero):
    x = None
    while x is None:
        try:
            x = float(input(msg))
            if not allow_zero and abs(x) < sys.float_info.epsilon:
                print("zero is not allowed")
                x = None
        except ValueError as err:
            print(err)
    return x
```

This function will loop until the user enters a valid floating-point number (such as 0.5, -9, 21, 4.92), and will accept 0 only if allow_zero is True.

Once the get_float() function is defined, the rest of the code is executed. We'll look at it in three parts, starting with the user interaction:

```
print("ax\N{SUPERSCRIPT TWO} + bx + c = 0")
a = get_float("enter a: ", False)
b = get_float("enter b: ", True)
c = get_float("enter c: ", True)
```

Thanks to the get_float() function, getting the a, b, and c factors is simple. The Boolean second argument says whether 0 is acceptable.

```
x1 = None
x2 = None
```

```
discriminant = (b ** 2) - (4 * a * c)
if discriminant == 0:
    x1 = -(b / (2 * a))
else:
    if discriminant > 0:
        root = math.sqrt(discriminant)
    else: # discriminant < 0
        root = cmath.sqrt(discriminant)
    x1 = (-b + root) / (2 * a)
    x2 = (-b - root) / (2 * a)
```

The code looks a bit different to the formula because we begin by calculating the discriminant. If the discriminant is 0, we know that we have one real solution and so we calculate it directly. Otherwise, we take the real or complex square root of the discriminant and calculate the two roots.

```
equation = ("{0}x\N{SUPERSCRIPT TWO} + {1}x + {2} = 0"
            " \N{RIGHTWARDS ARROW} x = {3}").format(a, b, c, x1)
if x2 is not None:
    equation += " or x = {0}".format(x2)
print(equation)
```

We haven't done any fancy formatting since Python's defaults for floating-point numbers are fine for this example, but we have used Unicode character names for a couple of special characters.

csv2html.py

One common requirement is to take a data set and present it using HTML. In this subsection we will develop a program that reads a file that uses a simple CSV (Comma Separated Value) format and outputs an HTML table containing the file's data. Python comes with a powerful and sophisticated module for handling CSV and similar formats—the csv module—but here we will write all the code by hand.

The CSV format we will support has one record per line, with each record divided into fields by commas. Each field can be either a string or a number. Strings must be enclosed in single or double quotes and numbers should be unquoted unless they contain commas. Commas are allowed inside strings, and must not be treated as field separators. We assume that the first record contains field labels. The output we will produce is an HTML table with text left-aligned (the default in HTML) and numbers right-aligned, with one row per record and one cell per field.

The program must output the HTML table's opening tag, then read each line of data and for each one output an HTML row, and at the end output the HTML table's closing tag. We want the background color of the first row (which will display the field labels) to be light green, and the background of the data rows to alternate between white and light yellow. We must also make sure that the special HTML characters ("&", "<", and ">") are properly escaped, and we want strings to be tidied up a bit.

Here's a tiny piece of sample data:

```
"COUNTRY","2000","2001",2002,2003,2004
"ANTIGUA AND BARBUDA",0,0,0,0,0
"ARGENTINA",37,35,33,36,39
"BAHAMAS, THE",1,1,1,1,1
"BAHRAIN",5,6,6,6,6
```

Assuming the sample data is in the file data/co2-sample.csv, and given the command csv2html.py < data/co2-sample.csv > co2-sample.html, the file co2-sample.html will have contents similar to this:

```
<table border='1'><tr bgcolor='lightgreen'>
<td>Country</td><td align='right'>2000</td><td align='right'>2001</td>
<td align='right'>2002</td><td align='right'>2003</td>
<td align='right'>2004</td></tr>
...
<tr bgcolor='lightyellow'><td>Argentina</td>
<td align='right'>37</td><td align='right'>35</td>
<td align='right'>33</td><td align='right'>36</td>
<td align='right'>39</td></tr>
...
</table>
```

We've tidied the output slightly and omitted some lines where indicated by ellipses. We have used a very simple version of HTML—HTML 4 transitional, with no style sheet. Figure 2.7 shows what the output looks like in a web browser.

Country	2000	2001	2002	2003	2004
Antigua and Barbuda	0	0	0	0	0
Argentina	37	35	33	36	39
Bahamas, The	1	1	1	1	1
Bahrain	5	6	6	6	6

Figure 2.7 *A csv2html.py table in a web browser*

Now that we've seen how the program is used and what it does, we are ready to review the code. The program begins with the import of the sys module; we won't show this, or any other imports from now on, unless they are unusual or warrant discussion. And the last statement in the program is a single function call:

```
main()
```

Although Python does not need an entry point as some languages require, it is quite common in Python programs to create a function called main() and to call it to start off processing. Since no function can be called before it has been created, we must make sure we call main() after the functions it relies on have been defined. The order in which the functions appear in the file (i.e., the order in which they are created) does not matter.

In the csv2html.py program, the first function we call is main() which in turn calls print_start() and then print_line(). And print_line() calls extract_fields() and escape_html(). The program structure we have used is shown in Figure 2.8.

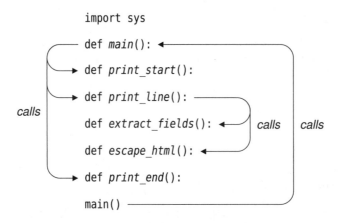

Figure 2.8 *The csv2html.py program's structure*

When Python reads a file it begins at the top. So for this example, it starts by performing the import, then it creates the main() function, and then it creates the other functions in the order in which they appear in the file. When Python finally reaches the call to main() at the end of the file, all the functions that main() will call (and all the functions that those functions will call) now exist. Execution as we normally think of it begins where the call to main() is made.

We will look at each function in turn, starting with main().

```
def main():
    maxwidth = 100
    print_start()
    count = 0
    while True:
```

```
        try:
            line = input()
            if count == 0:
                color = "lightgreen"
            elif count % 2:
                color = "white"
            else:
                color = "lightyellow"
            print_line(line, color, maxwidth)
            count += 1
        except EOFError:
            break
    print_end()
```

The `maxwidth` variable is used to constrain the number of characters in a cell—if a field is bigger than this we will truncate it and signify this by adding an ellipsis to the truncated text. We'll look at the `print_start()`, `print_line()`, and `print_end()` functions in a moment. The `while` loop iterates over each line of input—this could come from the user typing at the keyboard, but we expect it to be a redirected file. We set the color we want to use and call `print_line()` to output the line as an HTML table row.

```
def print_start():
    print("<table border='1'>")

def print_end():
    print("</table>")
```

We could have avoided creating these two functions and simply put the relevant `print()` function calls in `main()`. But we prefer to separate out the logic since this is more flexible, even though it doesn't really matter in this small example.

```
def print_line(line, color, maxwidth):
    print("<tr bgcolor='{0}'>".format(color))
    fields = extract_fields(line)
    for field in fields:
        if not field:
            print("<td></td>")
        else:
            number = field.replace(",", "")
            try:
                x = float(number)
                print("<td align='right'>{0:d}</td>".format(round(x)))
            except ValueError:
                field = field.title()
                field = field.replace(" And ", " and ")
```

```
        field = escape_html(field)
        if len(field) <= maxwidth:
            print("<td>{0}</td>".format(field))
        else:
            print("<td>{0:.{1}} ...</td>".format(field,
                                                    maxwidth))
    print("</tr>")
```

We cannot use str.split(",") to split each line into fields because commas
can occur inside quoted strings. So we have farmed this work out to the
extract_fields() function. Once we have a list of the fields (as strings, with no
surrounding quotes), we iterate over them, creating a table cell for each one.

If a field is empty, we output an empty cell. If a field is quoted it could be
a string or it could be a number that has been quoted to allow for internal
commas, for example, "1,566". To account for this, we make a copy of the field
with commas removed and try to convert the field to a float. If the conversion is
successful we output a right-aligned cell with the field rounded to the nearest
whole number and output it as an integer. If the conversion fails we output the
field as a string. In this case we use str.title() to neaten the case of the letters
and we replace the word *And* with *and* as a correction to str.title()'s effect.
We then escape any special HTML characters and either print the whole field,
or print the first maxwidth characters of it plus an ellipsis. A simpler alternative
to using an inner replacement field is to use string slicing, for example:

```
print("<td>{0} ...</td>".format(field[:maxwidth]))
```

Another advantage of this approach is that it requires slightly less typing.

```
def extract_fields(line):
    fields = []
    field = ""
    quote = None
    for c in line:
        if c in "\"'":
            if quote is None: # start of quoted string
                quote = c
            elif quote == c:  # end of quoted string
                quote = None
            else:
                field += c    # other quote inside quoted string
            continue
        if quote is None and c == ",": # end of a field
            fields.append(field)
            field = ""
        else:
```

```
        field += c          # accumulating a field
    if field:
        fields.append(field)  # adding the last field
    return fields
```

This function reads the line it is given character by character, accumulating a list of fields—each one a string without any enclosing quotes. The function copes with fields that are unquoted, and with fields that are quoted with single or double quotes, and correctly handles commas and quotes (single quotes in double quoted strings, double quotes in single quoted strings).

```
def escape_html(text):
    text = text.replace("&", "&amp;")
    text = text.replace("<", "&lt;")
    text = text.replace(">", "&gt;")
    return text
```

This function straightforwardly replaces each special HTML character with the appropriate HTML entity. We must of course replace ampersands first, although the order doesn't matter for the angle brackets. Python's standard library includes a slightly more sophisticated version of this function—you'll get the chance to use it in the exercises, and will see it again in Chapter 7.

Summary

This chapter began by showing the list of Python's keywords and described the rules that Python applies to identifiers. Thanks to Python's Unicode support, identifiers are not limited to a subset of characters from a small character set like ASCII or Latin-1.

We also described Python's int data type, which differs from similar types in most other languages in that it has no intrinsic size limitation. Python integers can be as large as the machine's memory will allow, and it is perfectly feasible to work with numbers that are hundreds of digits long. All of Python's most basic data types are immutable, but this is rarely noticeable since the augmented assignment operators (+=, *=, -=, /=, and others) means that we can use a very natural syntax while behind the scenes Python creates result objects and rebinds our variables to them. Literal integers are usually written as decimal numbers, but we can write binary literals using the 0b prefix, octal literals using the 0o prefix, and hexadecimal literals using the 0x prefix.

When two integers are divided using /, the result is always a float. This is different from many other widely used languages, but helps to avoid some quite subtle bugs that can occur when division silently truncates. (And if we want integer division we can use the // operator.)

Python has a bool data type which can hold either True or False. Python has three logical operators, and, or, and not, of which the two binary operators (and and or) use short-circuit logic.

Three kinds of floating-point numbers are available: float, complex, and decimal.Decimal. The most commonly used is float; this is a double-precision floating-point number whose exact numerical characteristics depend on the underlying C, C#, or Java library that Python was built with. Complex numbers are represented as two floats, one holding the real value and the other the imaginary value. The decimal.Decimal type is provided by the decimal module. These numbers default to having 28 decimal places of accuracy, but this can be increased or decreased to suit our needs.

All three floating-point types can be used with the appropriate built-in mathematical operators and functions. And in addition, the math module provides a variety of trigonometric, hyperbolic, and logarithmic functions that can be used with floats, and the cmath module provides a similar set of functions for complex numbers.

Most of the chapter was devoted to strings. Python string literals can be created using single quotes or double quotes, or using a triple quoted string if we want to include newlines and quotes without formality. Various escape sequences can be used to insert special characters such as tab (\t) and newline (\n), and Unicode characters both using hexadecimal escapes and Unicode character names. Although strings support the same comparison operators as other Python types, we noted that sorting strings that contain non-English characters can be problematic.

Since strings are sequences, the slicing operator ([]) can be used to slice and stride strings with a very simple yet powerful syntax. Strings can also be concatenated with the + operator and replicated with the * operator, and we can also use the augmented assignment versions of these operators (+= and *=), although the str.join() method is more commonly used for concatenation. Strings have many other methods, including some for testing string properties (e.g., str.isspace() and str.isalpha()), some for changing case (e.g., str.lower() and str.title()), some for searching (e.g., str.find() and str.index()), and many others.

Python's string support is really excellent, enabling us to easily find and extract or compare whole strings or parts of strings, to replace characters or substrings, and to split strings into a list of substrings and to join lists of strings into a single string.

Probably the most versatile string method is str.format(). This method is used to create strings using replacement fields and variables to go in those fields, and format specifications to precisely define the characteristics of each field which is replaced with a value. The replacement field name syntax allows us to access the method's arguments by position or by name (for keyword arguments), and to use an index, key, or attribute name to access an argument item or attribute. The format specifications allow us to specify the fill character, the alignment, and the minimum field width. Furthermore, for numbers we can also control how the sign is output, and for floating-point numbers we can specify the number of digits after the decimal point and whether to use standard or exponential notation.

We also discussed the thorny issue of character encodings. Python .py files use the Unicode UTF-8 encoding by default and so can have comments, identifiers, and data written in just about any human language. We can convert a string into a sequence of bytes using a particular encoding using the str.encode() method, and we can convert a sequence of bytes that use a particular encoding back to a string using the bytes.decode() method. The wide variety of character encodings currently in use can be very inconvenient, but UTF-8 is fast becoming the de facto standard for plain text files (and is already the default for XML files), so this problem should diminish in the coming years.

In addition to the data types covered in this chapter, Python provides two other built-in data types, bytes and bytearray, both of which are covered in Chapter 7. Python also provides several collection data types, some built-in and others in the standard library. In the next chapter we will look at Python's most important collection data types.

Exercises

1. Modify the print_unicode.py program so that the user can enter several separate words on the command line, and print rows only where the Unicode character name contains all the words the user has specified. This means that we can type commands like this:

   ```
   print_unicode_ans.py greek symbol
   ```

   One way of doing this is to replace the word variable (which held 0, None, or a string), with a words list. Don't forget to update the usage information as well as the code. The changes involve adding less than ten lines of code, and changing less than ten more. A solution is provided in file print_unicode_ans.py. (Windows and cross-platform users should modify print_unicode_uni.py; a solution is provided in print_unicode_uni_ans.py.)

2. Modify quadratic.py so that 0.0 factors are not output, and so that negative factors are output as − *n* rather than as + −*n*. This involves replacing the last five lines with about fifteen lines. A solution is provided in quadratic_ans.py. (Windows and cross-platform users should modify quadratic_uni.py; a solution is provided in quadratic_uni_ans.py.)

3. Delete the escape_html() function from csv2html.py, and use the xml.sax.saxutils.escape() function from the xml.sax.saxutils module instead. This

is easy, requiring one new line (the import), five deleted lines (the unwanted function), and one changed line (to use `xml.sax.saxutils.escape()` instead of `escape_html()`). A solution is provided in `csv2html1_ans.py`.

4. Modify `csv2html.py` again, this time adding a new function called `process_options()`. This function should be called from `main()` and should return a tuple of two values: `maxwidth` (an `int`) and `format` (a `str`). When `process_options()` is called it should set a default `maxwidth` of 100, and a default `format` of ".0f"—this will be used as the format specifier when outputting numbers.

   If the user has typed "-h" or "--help" on the command line, a usage message should be output and (`None`, `None`) returned. (In this case `main()` should do nothing.) Otherwise, the function should read any command-line arguments that are given and perform the appropriate assignments. For example, setting `maxwidth` if "maxwidth=n" is given, and similarly setting `format` if "format=s" is given. Here is a run showing the usage output:

```
csv2html2_ans.py -h
usage:
csv2html.py [maxwidth=int] [format=str] < infile.csv > outfile.html

maxwidth is an optional integer; if specified, it sets the maximum
number of characters that can be output for string fields,
otherwise a default of 100 characters is used.

format is the format to use for numbers; if not specified it
defaults to ".0f".
```

   And here is a command line with both options set:

```
csv2html2_ans.py maxwidth=20 format=0.2f < mydata.csv > mydata.html
```

   Don't forget to modify `print_line()` to make use of the `format` for outputting numbers—you'll need to pass in an extra argument, add one line, and modify another line. And this will slightly affect `main()` too. The `process_options()` function should be about twenty-five lines (including about nine for the usage message). This excersise may prove challenging for inexperienced programmers.

   Two files of test data are provided: `data/co2-sample.csv` and `data/co2-from-fossilfuels.csv`. A solution is provided in `csv2html2_ans.py`. In Chapter 5 we will see how to use Python's `optparse` module to simplify command-line processing.

3

- Sequence Types
- Set Types
- Mapping Types
- Iterating and Copying Collections

Collection Data Types

In the preceding chapter we learned about Python's most important fundamental data types. In this chapter we will extend our programming options by learning how to gather data items together using Python's collection data types. We will cover tuples and lists, and also introduce new collection data types, including sets and dictionaries, and cover all of them in depth.*

In addition to collections, we will also see how to create data items that are aggregates of other data items (like C or C++ structs or Pascal records)—such items can be treated as a single unit when this is convenient for us, while the items they contain remain individually accessible. Naturally, we can put aggregated items in collections just like any other items.

Having data items in collections makes it much easier to perform operations that must be applied to all of the items, and also makes it easier to handle collections of items read in from files. We'll cover the very basics of text file handling in this chapter as we need them, deferring most of the detail (including error handling) to Chapter 7.

After covering the individual collection data types, we will look at how to iterate over collections, since the same syntax is used for all of Python's collections, and we will also explore the issues and techniques involved in copying collections.

Sequence Types

A *sequence* type is one that supports the membership operator (in), the size function (len()), slices ([]), and is iterable. Python provides five built-in sequence types: bytearray, bytes, list, str, and tuple—the first two are covered

---

*The definitions of what constitutes a sequence type, a set type, or a mapping type given in this chapter are practical but informal. More formal definitions are given in Chapter 8.

separately in Chapter 7. Some other sequence types are provided in the standard library, most notably, `collections.namedtuple`. When iterated, all of these sequences provide their items in order.

Strings
61 ☜

We covered strings in the preceding chapter. In this section we will cover tuples, named tuples, and lists.

Tuples

String
slicing
and
striding
64 ☜

A tuple is an ordered sequence of zero or more object references. Tuples support the same slicing and striding syntax as strings. This makes it easy to extract items from a tuple. Like strings, tuples are immutable, so we cannot replace or delete any of their items. If we want to be able to modify an ordered sequence, we simply use a list instead of a tuple; or if we already have a tuple but want to modify it, we can convert it to a list using the `list()` conversion function and then apply the changes to the resultant list.

The `tuple` data type can be called as a function, `tuple()`—with no arguments it returns an empty tuple, with a `tuple` argument it returns a shallow copy of the argument, and with any other argument it attempts to convert the given object to a `tuple`. It does not accept more than one argument. Tuples can also be created without using the `tuple()` function. An empty tuple is created using empty parentheses, `()`, and a tuple of one or more items can be created by using commas. Sometimes tuples must be enclosed in parentheses to avoid syntactic ambiguity. For example, to pass the tuple 1, 2, 3 to a function, we would write `function((1, 2, 3))`.

Shallow
and
deep
copying
☞ 136

Figure 3.1 shows the tuple `t = "venus", -28, "green", "21", 19.74`, and the index positions of the items inside the tuple. Strings are indexed in the same way, but whereas strings have a character at every position, tuples have an object reference at each position.

t[-5]	t[-4]	t[-3]	t[-2]	t[-1]
'venus'	-28	'green'	'21'	19.74
t[0]	t[1]	t[2]	t[3]	t[4]

Figure 3.1 *Tuple index positions*

Tuples provide just two methods, `t.count(x)`, which returns the number of times object *x* occurs in tuple *t*, and `t.index(x)`, which returns the index position of the leftmost occurrence of object *x* in tuple *t*—or raises a `ValueError` exception if there is no *x* in the tuple. (These methods are also available for lists.)

In addition, tuples can be used with the operators + (concatenation), * (replication), and [] (slice), and with `in` and `not in` to test for membership. The += and *= augmented assignment operators can be used even though tuples are immutable—behind the scenes Python creates a new tuple to hold the result and sets the left-hand object reference to refer to it; the same technique is used when these operators are applied to strings. Tuples can be compared using the standard comparison operators (<, <=, ==, !=, >=, >), with the comparisons being applied item by item (and recursively for nested items such as tuples inside tuples).

Let's look at a few slicing examples, starting with extracting one item, and a slice of items:

```
>>> hair = "black", "brown", "blonde", "red"
>>> hair[2]
'blonde'
>>> hair[-3:]  # same as: hair[1:]
('brown', 'blonde', 'red')
```

These work the same for strings, lists, and any other sequence type.

```
>>> hair[:2], "gray", hair[2:]
(('black', 'brown'), 'gray', ('blonde', 'red'))
```

Here we tried to create a new 5-tuple, but ended up with a 3-tuple that contains two 2-tuples. This happened because we used the comma operator with three items (a tuple, a string, and a tuple). To get a single tuple with all the items we must concatenate tuples:

```
>>> hair[:2] + ("gray",) + hair[2:]
('black', 'brown', 'gray', 'blonde', 'red')
```

To make a 1-tuple the comma is essential, but in this case, if we had just put in the comma we would get a TypeError (since Python would think we were trying to concatenate a string and a tuple), so here we must have the comma *and* parentheses.

In this book (from this point on), we will use a particular coding style when writing tuples. When we have tuples on the left-hand side of a binary operator or on the right-hand side of a unary statement, we will omit the parentheses, and in all other cases we will use parentheses. Here are a few examples:

```
a, b = (1, 2)          # left of binary operator

del a, b               # right of unary statement

def f(x):
    return x, x ** 2   # right of unary statement

for x, y in ((1, 1), (2, 4), (3, 9)): # left of binary operator
    print(x, y)
```

There is no obligation to follow this coding style; some programmers prefer to always use parentheses—which is the same as the tuple representational form, whereas others use them only if they are strictly necessary.

```
>>> eyes = ("brown", "hazel", "amber", "green", "blue", "gray")
>>> colors = (hair, eyes)
>>> colors[1][3:-1]
('green', 'blue')
```

Here we have nested two tuples inside another tuple. Nested collections to any level of depth can be created like this without formality. The slice operator [] can be applied to a slice, with as many used as necessary. For example:

```
>>> things = (1, -7.5, ("pea", (5, "Xyz"), "queue"))
>>> things[2][1][1][2]
'z'
```

Let's look at this piece by piece, beginning with things[2] which gives us the third item in the tuple (since the first item has index 0), which is itself a tuple, ("pea", (5, "Xyz"), "queue"). The expression things[2][1] gives us the second item in the things[2] tuple, which is again a tuple, (5, "Xyz"). And things[2][1][1] gives us the second item in this tuple, which is the string "Xyz". Finally, things[2][1][1][2] gives us the third item (character) in the string, that is, "z".

Tuples are able to hold any items of any data type, including collection types such as tuples and lists, since what they really hold are object references. Using complex nested data structures like this can easily become confusing. One solution is to give names to particular index positions. For example:

```
>>> MANUFACTURER, MODEL, SEATING = (0, 1, 2)
>>> MINIMUM, MAXIMUM = (0, 1)
>>> aircraft = ("Airbus", "A320-200", (100, 220))
>>> aircraft[SEATING][MAXIMUM]
220
```

This is certainly more meaningful than writing aircraft[2][1], but it involves creating lots of variables and is rather ugly. We will see an alternative in the next subsection.

In the first two lines of the "aircraft" code snippet, we assigned to tuples in both statements. When we have a sequence on the right-hand side of an assignment (here we have tuples), and we have a tuple on the left-hand side, we say that the right-hand side has been *unpacked*. Sequence unpacking can be used to swap values, for example:

```
a, b = (b, a)
```

Strictly speaking, the parentheses are not needed on the right, but as we noted earlier, the coding style used in this book is to omit parentheses for left-hand operands of binary operators and right-hand operands of unary statements, but to use parentheses in all other cases.

We have already seen examples of sequence unpacking in the context of for ... in loops. Here is a reminder:

```
for x, y in ((-3, 4), (5, 12), (28, -45)):
    print(math.hypot(x, y))
```

Here we loop over a tuple of 2-tuples, unpacking each 2-tuple into variables x and y.

Named Tuples

A named tuple behaves just like a plain tuple, and has the same performance characteristics. What it adds is the ability to refer to items in the tuple by name as well as by index position, and this allows us to create aggregates of data items.

The collections module provides the namedtuple() function. This function is used to create custom tuple data types. For example:

```
Sale = collections.namedtuple("Sale",
            "productid customerid date quantity price")
```

The first argument to collections.namedtuple() is the name of the custom tuple data type that we want to be created. The second argument is a string of space-separated names, one for each item that our custom tuples will take. The first argument, and the names in the second argument, must all be valid Python identifiers. The function returns a custom class (data type) that can be used to create named tuples. So, in this case, we can treat Sale just like any other Python class (such as tuple), and create objects of type Sale.* For example:

```
sales = []
sales.append(Sale(432, 921, "2008-09-14", 3, 7.99))
sales.append(Sale(419, 874, "2008-09-15", 1, 18.49))
```

Here we have created a list of two Sale items, that is, of two custom tuples. We can refer to items in the tuples using index positions—for example, the price of the first sale item is sales[0][-1] (i.e., 7.99)—but we can also use names, which makes things much clearer:

---

*Note for object-oriented programmers: Each class created this way is a subclass of tuple.

```
total = 0
for sale in sales:
    total += sale.quantity * sale.price
print("Total ${0:.2f}".format(total))  # prints: Total $42.46
```

The clarity and convenience that named tuples provide are often useful. For example, here is the "aircraft" example from the previous subsection (page 102) done the nice way:

```
>>> Aircraft = collections.namedtuple("Aircraft",
...                                   "manufacturer model seating")
>>> Seating = collections.namedtuple("Seating", "minimum maximum")
>>> aircraft = Aircraft("Airbus", "A320-200", Seating(100, 220))
>>> aircraft.seating.maximum
220
```

Although named tuples can be very convenient, in Chapter 6 we introduce object-oriented programming, and there we will go beyond simple named tuples and learn how to create custom data types that hold data items and that also have their own custom methods.

Lists

String slicing and striding

64 ☜

A list is an ordered sequence of zero or more object references. Lists support the same slicing and striding syntax as strings and tuples. This makes it easy to extract items from a list. Unlike strings and tuples, lists are mutable, so we can replace and delete any of their items. It is also possible to insert, replace, and delete slices of lists.

Shallow and deep copying

☞ 136

List comprehensions

☞ 110

The list data type can be called as a function, list()—with no arguments it returns an empty list, with a list argument it returns a shallow copy of the argument, and with any other argument it attempts to convert the given object to a list. It does not accept more than one argument. Lists can also be created without using the list() function. An empty list is created using empty brackets, [], and a list of one or more items can be created by using a comma-separated sequence of items inside brackets. Another way of creating lists is to use a list comprehension—a topic we will cover later in this subsection.

Since all the items in a list are really object references, lists, like tuples, can hold items of any data type, including collection types such as lists and tuples. Lists can be compared using the standard comparison operators (<, <=, ==, !=, >=, >), with the comparisons being applied item by item (and recursively for nested items such as lists or tuples inside lists).

Given the assignment L = [-17.5, "kilo", 49, "V", ["ram", 5, "echo"], 7], we get the list shown in Figure 3.2.

L[-6]	L[-5]	L[-4]	L[-3]	L[-2]	L[-1]
-17.5	'kilo'	49	'V'	['ram', 5, 'echo']	7
L[0]	L[1]	L[2]	L[3]	L[4]	L[5]

Figure 3.2 *List index positions*

And given this list, L, we can use the slice operator—repeatedly if necessary—to access items in the list, as the following equalities show:

```
L[0] == L[-6] == -17.5
L[1] == L[-5] == 'kilo'
L[1][0] == L[-5][0] == 'k'
L[4][2] == L[4][-1] == L[-2][2] == L[-2][-1] == 'echo'
L[4][2][1] == L[4][2][-3] == L[-2][-1][1] == L[-2][-1][-3] == 'c'
```

Lists can be nested, iterated over, and sliced, the same as tuples. In fact, all the tuple examples presented in the preceding subsection would work exactly the same if we used lists instead of tuples. Lists support membership testing with in and not in, concatenation with +, extending with += (i.e., the appending of all the items in the right-hand operand), and replication with * and *=. Lists can also be used with the built-in len() function, and with the del statement discussed here and described in the "Deleting Items Using the del Statement" sidebar (page 107). In addition, lists provide the methods shown in Table 3.1.

Although we can use the slice operator to access items in a list, in some situations we want to take two or more pieces of a list in one go. This can be done by sequence unpacking. Any iterable (lists, tuples, etc.) can be unpacked using the sequence unpacking operator, an asterisk or star (*). When used with two or more variables on the left-hand side of an assignment, one of which is preceded by *, items are assigned to the variables, with all those left over assigned to the starred variable. Here are some examples:

```
>>> first, *rest = [9, 2, -4, 8, 7]
>>> first, rest
(9, [2, -4, 8, 7])
>>> first, *mid, last = "Charles Philip Arthur George Windsor".split()
>>> first, mid, last
('Charles', ['Philip', 'Arthur', 'George'], 'Windsor')
>>> *directories, executable = "/usr/local/bin/gvim".split("/")
>>> directories, executable
(['', 'usr', 'local', 'bin'], 'gvim')
```

When the sequence unpacking operator is used like this, the expression *rest, and similar expressions, are called *starred expressions*.

Table 3.1 *List Methods*

Syntax	Description
`L.append(x)`	Appends item x to the end of `list` L
`L.count(x)`	Returns the number of times item x occurs in `list` L
`L.extend(m)` `L += m`	Appends all of iterable m's items to the end of `list` L; the operator += does the same thing

`L.index(x,`
    start,
    end`)`
	Returns the index position of the leftmost occurrence of item x in `list` L (or in the *start*:*end* slice of L); otherwise, raises a `ValueError` exception

`L.insert(i, x)`	Inserts item x into `list` L at index position int i
`L.pop()`	Returns and removes the rightmost item of `list` L
`L.pop(i)`	Returns and removes the item at index position int i in L
`L.remove(x)`	Removes the leftmost occurrence of item x from `list` L, or raises a `ValueError` exception if x is not found
`L.reverse()`	Reverses `list` L in-place
`L.sort(...)`	Sorts `list` L in-place; this method accepts the same *key* and *reverse* optional arguments as the built-in `sorted()`

`sorted()`

☞130, 134

Python also has a related concept called *starred arguments*. For example, if we have the following function that requires three arguments:

```
def product(a, b, c):
    return a * b * c  # here, * is the multiplication operator
```

we can call it with three arguments, or by using starred arguments:

```
>>> product(2, 3, 5)
30
>>> L = [2, 3, 5]
>>> product(*L)
30
>>> product(2, *L[1:])
30
```

In the first call we provide the three arguments normally. In the second call we use a starred argument—what happens here is that the three-item list is unpacked by the * operator, so as far as the function is concerned it has received the three arguments it is expecting. We could have achieved the same thing using a 3-tuple. And in the third call we pass the first argument conventionally, and the other two arguments by unpacking a two-item slice of the L list. Functions and argument passing are covered fully in Chapter 4.

Deleting Items Using the del Statement

Although the name of the del statement is reminiscent of the word *delete*, it does not necessarily delete any data. When applied to an object reference that refers to a data item that is not a collection, the del statement unbinds the object reference from the data item and deletes the *object reference*. For example:

```
>>> x = 8143 # object ref. 'x' created; int of value 8143 created
>>> x
8143
>>> del x # object ref. 'x' deleted; int ready for garbage collection
>>> x
Traceback (most recent call last):
...
NameError: name 'x' is not defined
```

When an object reference is deleted, Python schedules the data item to which it referred to be garbage-collected if no other object references refer to the data item. When, or even if, garbage collection takes place may be nondeterministic (depending on the Python implementation), so if any cleanup is required we must handle it ourselves. Python provides two solutions to the nondeterminism. One is to use a try … finally block to ensure that cleanup is done, and another is to use a with statement as we will see in Chapter 8.

When del is used on a collection data type such as a tuple or a list, only the object reference to the collection is deleted. The collection and its items (and for those items that are themselves collections, for their items, recursively) are scheduled for garbage collection if no other object references refer to the collection.

For mutable collections such as lists, del can be applied to individual items or slices—in both cases using the slice operator, [ ]. If the item or items referred to are removed from the collection, and if there are no other object references referring to them, they are scheduled for garbage collection.

There is never any syntactic ambiguity regarding whether operator * is the multiplication or the sequence unpacking operator. When it appears on the left-hand side of an assignment it is the unpacking operator, and when it appears elsewhere (e.g., in a function call) it is the unpacking operator when used as a unary operator and the multiplication operator when used as a binary operator.

We have already seen that we can iterate over the items in a list using the syntax for *item* in *L*:. If we want to change the items in a list the idiom to use is:

```
for i in range(len(L)):
    L[i] = process(L[i])
```

The built-in range() function returns an iterator that provides integers. With one integer argument, *n*, the iterator range() returns, producing 0, 1, ..., *n* - 1.

range()
☞ 131

We could use this technique to increment all the numbers in a list of integers. For example:

```
for i in range(len(numbers)):
    numbers[i] += 1
```

Since lists support slicing, in several cases the same effect can be achieved using either slicing or one of the list methods. For example, given the list woods = ["Cedar", "Yew", "Fir"], we can extend the list in either of two ways:

```
woods += ["Kauri", "Larch"]    |    woods.extend(["Kauri", "Larch"])
```

In either case the result is the list ['Cedar', 'Yew', 'Fir', 'Kauri', 'Larch'].

Individual items can be added at the end of a list using list.append(). Items can be inserted at any index position within the list using list.insert(), or by assigning to a slice of length 0. For example, given the list woods = ["Cedar", "Yew", "Fir", "Spruce"], we can insert a new item at index position 2 (i.e., as the list's third item) in either of two ways:

```
woods[2:2] = ["Pine"]          |    woods.insert(2, "Pine")
```

In both cases the result is the list ['Cedar', 'Yew', 'Pine', 'Fir', 'Spruce'].

Individual items can be replaced in a list by assigning to a particular index position, for example, woods[2] = "Redwood". Entire slices can be replaced by assigning an iterable to a slice, for example, woods[1:3] = ["Spruce", "Sugi", "Rimu"]. The slice and the iterable don't have to be the same length. In all cases, the slice's items are removed and the iterable's items are inserted. This makes the list shorter if the iterable has fewer items than the slice it replaces, and longer if the iterable has more items than the slice.

To make what happens when assigning an iterable to a slice really clear, we will consider one further example. Imagine that we have the list L = ["A", "B", "C", "D", "E", "F"], and that we assign an iterable (in this case, a list) to a slice of it with the code L[2:5] = ["X", "Y"]. First, the slice is removed, so behind the scenes the list becomes ['A', 'B', 'F']. And then all the iterable's items are inserted at the slice's start position, so the resultant list is ['A', 'B', 'X', 'Y', 'F'].

Items can be removed in a number of other ways. We can use list.pop() with no arguments to remove the rightmost item in a list—the removed item is also returned. Similarly we can use list.pop() with an integer index argument to remove (and return) an item at a particular index position. Another way of removing an item is to call list.remove() with the item to be removed as the argument. The del statement can also be used to remove individual items—for example, del woods[4]—or to remove slices of items. Slices can also be removed by assigning an empty list to a slice, so these two snippets are equivalent:

```
woods[2:4] = []                    del woods[2:4]
```

In the left-hand snippet we have assigned an iterable (an empty list) to a slice, so first the slice is removed, and since the iterable to insert is empty, no insertion takes place.

Slicing
and
striding

64 ☞

When we first covered slicing and striding, we did so in the context of strings where striding wasn't very interesting. But in the case of lists, striding allows us to access every *n*-th item which can often be useful. For example, suppose we have the list, x = [1, 2, 3, 4, 5, 6, 7, 8, 9, 10], and we want to set every odd-indexed item (i.e., x[1], x[3], etc.) to 0. We can access every second item by striding, for example, x[::2]. But this will give us the items at index positions 0, 2, 4, and so on. We can fix this by giving an initial starting index, so now we have x[1::2], and this gives us a slice of the items we want. To set each item in the slice to 0, we need a list of 0s, and this list must have exactly the same number of 0s as there are items in the slice.

Here is the complete solution: x[1::2] = [0] * len(x[1::2]). Now list x is [1, 0, 3, 0, 5, 0, 7, 0, 9, 0]. We used the replication operator *, to produce a list consisting of the number of 0s we needed based on the length (i.e., the number of items) of the slice. The interesting aspect is that when we assign the list [0, 0, 0, 0, 0] to the *strided* slice, Python correctly replaces x[1]'s value with the first 0, x[3]'s value with the second 0, and so on.

Lists can be reversed and sorted in the same way as any other iterable using the built-in reversed() and sorted() functions covered in the Iterators and Iterable Operations and Functions subsection (page 128). Lists also have equivalent methods, list.reverse() and list.sort(), both of which work in-place (so they don't return anything), the latter accepting the same optional arguments as sorted(). One common idiom is to case-insensitively sort a list of strings—for example, we could sort the woods list like this: woods.sort(key=str.lower). The key argument is used to specify a function which is applied to each item, and whose return value is used to perform the comparisons used when sorting. As we noted in the previous chapter's section on string comparisons (page 63), for languages other than English, sorting strings in a way that is meaningful to humans can be quite challenging.

sorted()

☞130,
134

For inserting items, lists perform best when items are added or removed at the end (list.append(), list.pop()). The worst performance occurs when we search for items in a list, for example, using list.remove() or list.index(), or using in for membership testing. If fast searching or membership testing is required, a set or a dict (both covered later in this chapter) may be a more suitable collection choice. Alternatively, lists can provide fast searching if they are kept in order by sorting them—Python's sort algorithm is especially well optimized for sorting partially sorted lists—and using a binary search (provided by the bisect module), to find items. (In Chapter 6 we will create an intrinsically sorted custom list class.)

List Comprehensions

Small lists are often created using list literals, but longer lists are usually created programmatically. For a list of integers we can use list(range(*n*)), or if we just need an integer iterator, range() is sufficient, but for other lists using a for ... in loop is very common. Suppose, for example, that we wanted to produce a list of the leap years in a given range. We might start out like this:

```
leaps = []
for year in range(1900, 1940):
    if (year % 4 == 0 and year % 100 != 0) or (year % 400 == 0):
        leaps.append(year)
```

When the built-in range() function is given two integer arguments, *n* and *m*, the iterator it returns produces the integers $n, n + 1, ..., m - 1$.

range()
☞ 131

Of course, if we knew the exact range beforehand we could use a list literal, for example, leaps = [1904, 1908, 1912, 1916, 1920, 1924, 1928, 1932, 1936].

A *list comprehension* is an expression and a loop with an optional condition enclosed in brackets where the loop is used to generate items for the list, and where the condition can filter out unwanted items. The simplest form of a list comprehension is this:

```
[item for item in iterable]
```

This will return a list of every item in the iterable, and is semantically no different from list(*iterable*). Two things that make list comprehensions more interesting and powerful are that we can use expressions, and we can attach a condition—this takes us to the two general syntaxes for list comprehensions:

```
[expression for item in iterable]
[expression for item in iterable if condition]
```

The second syntax is equivalent to:

```
temp = []
for item in iterable:
    if condition:
        temp.append(expression)
```

Normally, the *expression* will either be or involve the *item*. Of course, the list comprehension does not need the temp variable needed by the for ... in loop version.

Now we can rewrite the code to generate the leaps list using a list comprehension. We will develop the code in three stages. First we will generate a list that has all the years in the given range:

```
leaps = [y for y in range(1900, 1940)]
```

This could also be done using leaps = list(range(1900, 1940)). Now we'll add a simple condition to get every fourth year:

```
leaps = [y for y in range(1900, 1940) if y % 4 == 0]
```

Finally, we have the complete version:

```
leaps = [y for y in range(1900, 1940)
         if (y % 4 == 0 and y % 100 != 0) or (y % 400 == 0)]
```

Using a list comprehension in this case reduced the code from four lines to two—a small savings, but one that can add up quite a lot in large projects.

Since list comprehensions produce lists, that is, iterables, and since the syntax for list comprehensions requires an iterable, it is possible to nest list comprehensions. This is the equivalent of having nested for ... in loops. For example, if we wanted to generate all the possible clothing label codes for given sets of sexes, sizes, and colors, but excluding labels for the full-figured females whom the fashion industry routinely ignores, we could do so using nested for ... in loops:

```
codes = []
for sex in "MF":              # Male, Female
    for size in "SMLX":       # Small, Medium, Large, eXtra large
        if sex == "F" and size == "X":
            continue
        for color in "BGW":   # Black, Gray, White
            codes.append(sex + size + color)
```

This produces the 21 item list, ['MSB', 'MSG', ..., 'FLW']. The same thing can be achieved in just a couple of lines using a list comprehension:

```
codes = [s + z + c for s in "MF" for z in "SMLX" for c in "BGW"
         if not (s == "F" and z == "X")]
```

Here, each item in the list is produced by the expression s + z + c. Also, we have used subtly different logic for the list comprehension where we skip invalid sex/size combinations in the innermost loop, whereas the nested for ... in loops version skips invalid combinations in its middle loop. Any list comprehension can be rewritten using one or more for ... in loops.

If the generated list is very large, it may be more efficient to generate each item as it is needed rather than produce the whole list at once. This can be achieved by using a generator rather than a list comprehension. We discuss this later, in Chapter 8.

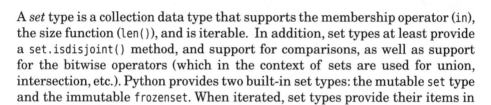

Genera-
tors

☞ 331

Set Types

A *set* type is a collection data type that supports the membership operator (in), the size function (len()), and is iterable. In addition, set types at least provide a set.isdisjoint() method, and support for comparisons, as well as support for the bitwise operators (which in the context of sets are used for union, intersection, etc.). Python provides two built-in set types: the mutable set type and the immutable frozenset. When iterated, set types provide their items in an arbitrary order.

Only *hashable* objects may be added to a set. Hashable objects are objects which have a __hash__() special method whose return value is always the same throughout the object's lifetime, and which can be compared for equality using the __eq__() special method. (Special methods—methods whose name begins and ends with two underscores—are covered in Chapter 6.)

All the built-in immutable data types, such as float, frozenset, int, str, and tuple, are hashable and can be added to sets. The built-in mutable data types, such as dict, list, and set, are not hashable since their hash value changes depending on the items they contain, so they cannot be added to sets.

Set types can be compared using the standard comparison operators (<, <=, ==, !=, >=, >). Note that although == and != have their usual meanings, with the comparisons being applied item by item (and recursively for nested items such as tuples or frozen sets inside sets), the other comparison operators perform subset and superset comparisons, as we will see shortly.

Sets

A set is an unordered collection of zero or more object references that refer to hashable objects. Sets are mutable, so we can easily add or remove items, but since they are unordered they have no notion of index position and so cannot be sliced or strided. Figure 3.3 illustrates the set created by the following code snippet:

```
S = {7, "veil", 0, -29, ("x", 11), "sun", frozenset({8, 4, 7}), 913}
```

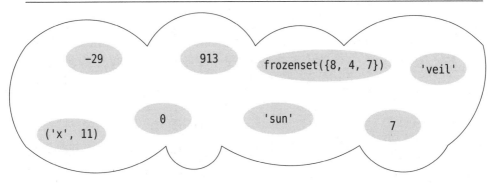

Figure 3.3 *A set is an unordered collection of unique items.*

The set data type can be called as a function, set()—with no arguments it returns an empty set, with a set argument it returns a shallow copy of the argument, and with any other argument it attempts to convert the given object to a set. It does not accept more than one argument. Nonempty sets can also be created without using the set() function, but the empty set must be created using set(), *not* using empty braces.* A set of one or more items can be created by using a comma-separated sequence of items inside braces. Another way of creating sets is to use a set comprehension—a topic we will cover later in this subsection.

Shallow and deep copying ☞ 136

Set com-prehen-sions ☞ 116

Sets always contain unique items—adding duplicate items is safe but pointless. For example, these three sets are the same: set("apple"), set("aple"), and {'e', 'p', 'a', 'l'}. In view of this, sets are often used to eliminate duplicates. For example, if x is a list of strings, after executing x = list(set(x)), all of x's strings will be unique—and in an arbitrary order.

Sets support the built-in len() function, and fast membership testing with in and not in. They also provide the usual set operators, as Figure 3.4 illustrates. The complete list of set methods and operators is given in Table 3.2. All the "update" methods (set.update(), set.intersection_update(), etc.) accept any iterable as their argument—but the equivalent operator versions (|=, &=, etc.) require both of their operands to be sets.

One common use case for sets is when we want fast membership testing. For example, we might want to give the user a usage message if they don't enter any command-line arguments, or if they enter an argument of "-h" or "--help":

```
if len(sys.argv) == 1 or sys.argv[1] in {"-h", "--help"}:
```

Another common use case for sets is to ensure that we don't process duplicate data. For example, suppose we had an iterable (such as a list), containing the IP addresses from a web server's log files, and we wanted to perform some

---

*Empty braces, {}, are used to create an empty dict as we will see in the next section.

processing, once for each unique address. Assuming that the IP addresses are hashable and are in iterable ips, and that the function we want called for each one is called process_ip() and is already defined, the following code snippets will do what we want, although with subtly different behavior:

```
seen = set()
for ip in ips:
    if ip not in seen:
        seen.add(ip)                   for ip in set(ips):
        process_ip(ip)                     process_ip(ip)
```

For the left-hand snippet, if we haven't processed the IP address before, we add it to the seen set and process it; otherwise, we ignore it. For the right-hand snippet, we only ever get each unique IP address to process in the first place. The differences between the snippets are first that the left-hand snippet creates the seen set which the right-hand snippet doesn't need, and second that the left-hand snippet processes the IP addresses in the order they are encountered in the ips iterable while the right-hand snippet processes them in an arbitrary order.

The right-hand approach is easier to code, but if the ordering of the ips iterable is important we must either use the left-hand approach or change the right-hand snippet's first line to something like for ip in sorted(set(ips)): if this is sufficient to get the required order. In theory the right-hand approach might be slower if the number of items in ips is very large, since it creates the set in one go rather than incrementally.

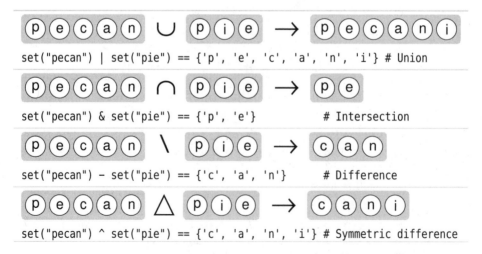

Figure 3.4 *The standard set operators*

Table 3.2 *Set Methods and Operators*

Syntax	Description
s.add(x)	Adds item x to set s if it is not already in s
s.clear()	Removes all the items from set s
s.copy()	Returns a shallow copy of set s[*]
s.difference(t) s – t	Returns a new set that has every item that is in set s that is not in set t[*]
s.difference_update(t) s –= t	Removes every item that is in set t from set s
s.discard(x)	Removes item x from set s if it is in s; see also set.remove()
s.intersection(t) s & t	Returns a new set that has each item that is in both set s and set t[*]
s.intersection_update(t) s &= t	Makes set s contain the intersection of itself and set t
s.isdisjoint(t)	Returns True if sets s and t have no items in common[*]
s.issubset(t) s <= t	Returns True if set s is equal to or a subset of set t; use s < t to test whether s is a proper subset of t[*]
s.issuperset(t) s >= t	Returns True if set s is equal to or a superset of set t; use s > t to test whether s is a proper superset of t[*]
s.pop()	Returns and removes a random item from set s, or raises a KeyError exception if s is empty
s.remove(x)	Removes item x from set s, or raises a KeyError exception if x is not in s; see also set.discard()
s.symmetric_ difference(t) s ^ t	Returns a new set that has every item that is in set s and every item that is in set t, but excluding items that are in both sets[*]
s.symmetric_ difference_update(t) s ^= t	Makes set s contain the symmetric difference of itself and set t
s.union(t) s | t	Returns a new set that has all the items in set s and all the items in set t that are not in set s[*]
s.update(t) s |= t	Adds every item in set t that is not in set s, to set s

Shallow and deep copying

☞ 136

---

[*]This method and its operator (if it has one) can also be used with frozensets.

Sets are also used to eliminate unwanted items. For example, if we have a list of filenames but don't want any makefiles included (perhaps because they are generated rather than handwritten), we might write:

```
filenames = set(filenames)
for makefile in {"MAKEFILE", "Makefile", "makefile"}:
    filenames.discard(makefile)
```

This code will remove any makefile that is in the list using any of the standard capitalizations. It will do nothing if no makefile is in the filenames list. The same thing can be achieved in one line using the set difference (–) operator:

```
filenames = set(filenames) - {"MAKEFILE", "Makefile", "makefile"}
```

We can also use set.remove() to remove items, although this method raises a KeyError exception if the item it is asked to remove is not in the set.

Set Comprehensions

In addition to creating sets by calling set(), or by using a set literal, we can also create sets using *set comprehensions*. A set comprehension is an expression and a loop with an optional condition enclosed in braces. Like list comprehensions, two syntaxes are supported:

```
{expression for item in iterable}
{expression for item in iterable if condition}
```

We can use these to achieve a filtering effect (providing the order doesn't matter). Here is an example:

```
html = {x for x in files if x.lower().endswith((".htm", ".html"))}
```

Given a list of filenames in files, this set comprehension makes the set html hold only those filenames that end in .htm or .html, regardless of case.

Just like list comprehensions, the iterable used in a set comprehension can itself be a set comprehension (or any other kind of comprehension), so quite sophisticated set comprehensions can be created.

Frozen Sets

A frozen set is a set that, once created, cannot be changed. We can of course rebind the variable that refers to a frozen set to refer to something else, though. Frozen sets can only be created using the frozenset data type called as a function. With no arguments, frozenset() returns an empty frozen set, with a frozenset argument it returns a shallow copy of the argument, and with any

Shallow
and
deep
copying

☞ 136

other argument it attempts to convert the given object to a frozenset. It does not accept more than one argument.

Since frozen sets are immutable, they support only those methods and operators that produce a result without affecting the frozen set or sets to which they are applied. Table 3.2 (page 115) lists all the set methods—frozen sets support frozenset.copy(), frozenset.difference() (–), frozenset.intersection() (&), frozenset.isdisjoint(), frozenset.issubset() (<=; also < for proper subsets), frozenset.issuperset() (>=; also > for proper supersets), frozenset.union() (|), and frozenset.symmetric_difference() (^), all of which are indicated by a * in the table.

If a binary operator is used with a set and a frozen set, the data type of the result is the same as the left-hand operand's data type. So if f is a frozen set and s is a set, f & s will produce a frozen set and s & f will produce a set. In the case of the == and != operators, the order of the operands does not matter, and f == s will produce True if both sets contain the same items.

Another consequence of the immutability of frozen sets is that they meet the hashable criterion for set items, so sets and frozen sets can contain frozen sets.

We will see more examples of set use in the next section, and also in the chapter's Examples section.

Mapping Types

A *mapping* type is one that supports the membership operator (in), the size function (len()), and is iterable. Mappings are collections of key–value items and provide methods for accessing items and their keys and values. When iterated, mapping types provide their items in an arbitrary order. Python provides two mapping types, the built-in dict type and the standard library's collections.defaultdict type. We will use the term *dictionary* to refer to either of these types when the difference doesn't matter.

Hash-
able
objects
112 ☞

Only hashable objects may be used as dictionary keys, so immutable data types such as float, frozenset, int, str, and tuple can be used as dictionary keys, but mutable types such as dict, list, and set cannot. On the other hand, each key's associated value can be an object reference referring to an object of any type, including numbers, strings, lists, sets, dictionaries, functions, and so on.

Dictionary types can be compared using the standard comparison operators (<, <=, ==, !=, >=, >), with the comparisons being applied item by item (and recursively for nested items such as tuples or dictionaries inside dictionaries). Arguably, the only comparison operators that are meaningful for dictionaries are == and !=.

Dictionaries   ‖

A dict is an unordered collection of zero or more key–value pairs whose keys
are object references that refer to hashable objects, and whose values are object
references referring to objects of any type. Dictionaries are mutable, so we can
easily add or remove items, but since they are unordered they have no notion
of index position and so cannot be sliced or strided.

The dict data type can be called as a function, dict()—with no arguments it
returns an empty dictionary, and with a mapping argument it returns a dictionary based on the argument; for example, returning a shallow copy if the
argument is a dictionary. It is also possible to use a sequence argument, providing that each item in the sequence is itself a sequence of two objects, the
first of which is used as a key and the second of which is used as a value.
Alternatively, for dictionaries where the keys are valid Python identifiers, keyword arguments can be used, with the key as the keyword and the value as the
key's value. Dictionaries can also be created using braces—empty braces, {},
create an empty dictionary; nonempty braces must contain one or more comma-
separated items, each of which consists of a key, a literal colon, and a value.
Another way of creating dictionaries is to use a dictionary comprehension—a
topic we will cover later in this subsection.

Shallow
and
deep
copying
☞ 136

Key-
word
argu-
ments
☞ 164

Dic-
tionary
com-
prehen-
sions
☞ 125

Here are some examples to illustrate the various syntaxes—they all produce
the same dictionary:

```
d1 = dict({"id": 1948, "name": "Washer", "size": 3})
d2 = dict(id=1948, name="Washer", size=3)
d3 = dict([("id", 1948), ("name", "Washer"), ("size", 3)])
d4 = dict(zip(("id", "name", "size"), (1948, "Washer", 3)))
d5 = {"id": 1948, "name": "Washer", "size": 3}
```

Dictionary d1 is created using a dictionary literal. Dictionary d2 is created using keyword arguments. Dictionaries d3 and d4 are created from sequences,
and dictionary d5 is created from a dictionary literal. The built-in zip() function that is used to create dictionary d4 returns a list of tuples, the first of which
has the first items of each of the zip() function's iterable arguments, the second
of which has the second items, and so on. The keyword argument syntax (used
to create dictionary d2) is usually the most compact and convenient, providing
the keys are valid identifiers.

zip()
☞ 132

Figure 3.5 illustrates the dictionary created by the following code snippet:

```
d = {"root": 18, "blue": [75, "R", 2], 21: "venus", -14: None,
     "mars": "rover", (4, 11): 18, 0: 45}
```

Dictionary keys are unique, so if we add a key–value item whose key is the
same as an existing key, the effect is to replace that key's value with a new val-

ue. Brackets are used to access individual values—for example, d["root"] returns 18, d[21] returns the string "venus", and d[91] causes a KeyError exception to be raised, given the dictionary shown in Figure 3.5.

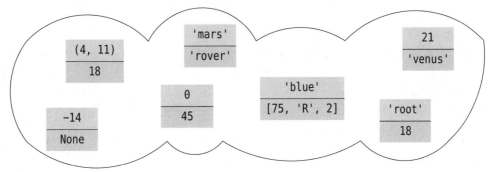

Figure 3.5 *A dictionary is an unsorted collection of (key, value) items with unique keys.*

Brackets can also be used to add and delete dictionary items. To add an item we use the = operator, for example, d["X"] = 59. And to delete an item we use the del statement—for example, del d["mars"] will delete the item whose key is "mars" from the dictionary, or raise a KeyError exception if no item has that key. Items can also be removed (and returned) from the dictionary using the dict.pop() method.

Dictionaries support the built-in len() function, and for their keys, fast membership testing with in and not in. All the dictionary methods are listed in Table 3.3.

Because dictionaries have both keys and values, we might want to iterate over a dictionary by (key, value) items, by values, or by keys. For example, here are two equivalent approaches to iterating by (key, value) pairs:

```
for item in d.items():              for key, value in d.items():
    print(item[0], item[1])             print(key, value)
```

Iterating over a dictionary's values is very similar:

```
for value in d.values():
    print(value)
```

To iterate over a dictionary's keys we can use dict.keys(), or we can simply treat the dictionary as an iterable that iterates over its keys, as these two equivalent code snippets illustrate:

```
for key in d:                       for key in d.keys():
    print(key)                          print(key)
```

Table 3.3 *Dictionary Methods*

Syntax	Description
d.clear()	Removes all items from dict d
d.copy()	Returns a shallow copy of dict d
d.fromkeys(s, v)	Returns a dict whose keys are the items in sequence s and whose values are None or v if v is given
d.get(k)	Returns key k's associated value, or None if k isn't in dict d
d.get(k, v)	Returns key k's associated value, or v if k isn't in dict d
d.items()	Returns a view* of all the (key, value) pairs in dict d
d.keys()	Returns a view* of all the keys in dict d
d.pop(k)	Returns key k's associated value and removes the item whose key is k, or raises a KeyError exception if k isn't in d
d.pop(k, v)	Returns key k's associated value and removes the item whose key is k, or returns v if k isn't in dict d
d.popitem()	Returns and removes an arbitrary (key, value) pair from dict d, or raises a KeyError exception if d is empty
d.setdefault(k, v)	The same as the dict.get() method, except that if the key is not in dict d, a new item is inserted with the key k, and with a value of None or of v if v is given
d.update(a)	Adds every (key, value) pair from a that isn't in dict d to d, and for every key that is in both d and a, replaces the corresponding value in d with the one in a—a can be a dictionary, an iterable of (key, value) pairs, or keyword arguments
d.values()	Returns a view* of all the values in dict d

> Shallow and deep copying
>
> ☞ 136

If we want to change the values in a dictionary, the idiom to use is to iterate over the keys and change the values using the brackets operator. For example, here is how we would increment every value in dictionary d, assuming that all the values are numbers:

```
for key in d:
    d[key] += 1
```

The dict.items(), dict.keys(), and dict.values() methods all return *dictionary views*. A dictionary view is in effect a read-only iterable object that appears to hold the dictionary's items or keys or values, depending on the view we have asked for.

---

*Dictionary views can be thought of—and used as—iterables; they are discussed in the text.

In general, we can simply treat views as iterables. However, two things make a view different from a normal iterable. One is that if the dictionary the view refers to is changed, the view reflects the change. The other is that key and item views support some set-like operations. Given dictionary view *v* and set or dictionary view *x*, the supported operations are:

```
v & x    # Intersection
v | x    # Union
v - x    # Difference
v ^ x    # Symmetric difference
```

We can use the membership operator, in, to see whether a particular key is in a dictionary, for example, *x* in *d*. And we can use the union operator to see which keys from a given set are in a dictionary. For example:

```
d = {}.fromkeys("ABCD", 3)    # d == {'A': 3, 'B': 3, 'C': 3, 'D': 3}
s = set("ACX")                # s == {'A', 'C', 'X'}
matches = d.keys() & s        # matches == {'A', 'C'}
```

Note that in the snippet's comments we have used alphabetical order—this is purely for ease of reading since dictionaries and sets are unordered.

Dictionaries are often used to keep counts of unique items. One such example of this is counting the number of occurrences of each unique word in a file. Here is a complete program (uniquewords1.py) that lists every word and the number of times it occurs in alphabetical order for all the files listed on the command line:

```
import string
import sys

words = {}
strip = string.whitespace + string.punctuation + string.digits + "\"'"
for filename in sys.argv[1:]:
    for line in open(filename):
        for word in line.lower().split():
            word = word.strip(strip)
            if len(word) > 2:
                words[word] = words.get(word, 0) + 1
for word in sorted(words):
    print("'{0}' occurs {1} times".format(word, words[word]))
```

We begin by creating an empty dictionary called words. Then we create a string that contains all those characters that we want to ignore, by concatenating some useful strings provided by the string module. We iterate over each filename given on the command line, and over each line in each file. See the "Reading and Writing Text Files" sidebar (page 122) for an explanation of the

Reading and Writing Text Files

Files are opened using the built-in `open()` function, which returns a "file object" (of type `io.TextIOWrapper` for text files). The `open()` function takes one mandatory argument—the filename, which may include a path—and up to six optional arguments, two of which we briefly cover here. The second argument is the *mode*—this is used to specify whether the file is to be treated as a text file or as a binary file, and whether the file is to be opened for reading, writing, appending, or a combination of these.

Chapter 7 (File Handling) ☞ 277

Character encodings 85 ☞

For text files, Python uses an encoding that is platform-dependent. Where possible it is best to specify the encoding using `open()`'s `encoding` argument, so the syntaxes we normally use for opening files are these:

```
fin  = open(filename, encoding="utf8")       # for reading text
fout = open(filename, "w", encoding="utf8")  # for writing text
```

Because `open()`'s mode defaults to "read text", and by using a keyword rather than a positional argument for the `encoding` argument, we can omit the other optional positional arguments when opening for reading. And similarly, when opening to write we need to give only the arguments we actually want to use. (Argument passing is covered in depth in Chapter 4.)

Once a file is opened for reading in text mode, we can read the whole file into a single string using the file object's `read()` method, or into a list of strings using the file object's `readlines()` method. A very common idiom for reading line by line is to treat the file object as an iterator:

```
for line in open(filename, encoding="utf8"):
    process(line)
```

This works because a file object can be iterated over, just like a sequence, with each successive item being a string containing the next line from the file. The lines we get back include the line termination character, `\n`.

If we specify a mode of "w", the file is opened in "write text" mode. We write to a file using the file object's `write()` method, which takes a single string as its argument. Each line written should end with a `\n`. Python automatically translates between `\n` and the underlying platform's line termination characters when reading and writing.

Once we have finished using a file object we can call its `close()` method—this will cause any outstanding writes to be flushed. In small Python programs it is very common not to bother calling `close()`, since Python does this automatically when the file object goes out of scope. If a problem occurs, it will be indicated by an exception being raised.

open() function. We don't specify an encoding (because we don't know what each file's encoding will be), so we let Python open each file using the default local encoding. We split each lowercased line into words, and then strip off the characters that we want to ignore from both ends of each word. If the resultant word is at least three characters long we need to update the dictionary.

We cannot use the syntax words[word] += 1 because this will raise a KeyError exception the first time a new word is encountered—after all, we can't increment the value of an item that does not yet exist in the dictionary. So we use a subtler approach. We call dict.get() with a default value of 0. If the word is already in the dictionary, dict.get() will return the associated number, and this value plus 1 will be set as the item's new value. If the word is not in the dictionary, dict.get() will return the supplied default of 0, and this value plus 1 (i.e., 1) will be set as the value of a new item whose key is the string held by word. To clarify, here are two code snippets that do the same thing, although the code using dict.get() is more efficient:

```
                                            if word not in words:
                                                words[word] = 0
words[word] = words.get(word, 0) + 1        words[word] += 1
```

In the next subsection where we cover default dictionaries, we will see an alternative solution.

Once we have accumulated the dictionary of words, we iterate over its keys (the words) in sorted order, and print each word and the number of times it occurs.

Using dict.get() allows us to easily update dictionary values, providing the values are single items like numbers or strings. But what if each value is itself a collection? To demonstrate how to handle this we will look at a program that reads HTML files given on the command line and prints a list of each unique Web site that is referred to in the files with a list of the referring files listed indented below the name of each Web site. Structurally, the program (external_sites.py) is very similar to the unique words program we have just reviewed. Here is the main part of the code:

```
sites = {}
for filename in sys.argv[1:]:
    for line in open(filename):
        i = 0
        while True:
            site = None
            i = line.find("http://", i)
            if i > -1:
                i += len("http://")
                for j in range(i, len(line)):
```

```
                    if not (line[j].isalnum() or line[j] in ".-"):
                        site = line[i:j].lower()
                        break
                if site and "." in site:
                    sites.setdefault(site, set()).add(filename)
                i = j
            else:
                break
```

We begin by creating an empty dictionary. Then we iterate over each file listed on the command line and each line within each file. We must account for the fact that each line may refer to any number of Web sites, which is why we keep calling str.find() until it fails. If we find the string "http://", we increment i (our starting index position) by the length of "http://", and then we look at each succeeding character until we reach one that isn't valid for a Web site's name. If we find a site (and as a simply sanity check, only if it contains a period), we add it to the dictionary.

We cannot use the syntax sites[site].add(filename) because this will raise a KeyError exception the first time a new site is encountered—after all, we can't add to a set that is the value of an item that does not yet exist in the dictionary. So we must use a different approach. The dict.setdefault() method returns an object reference to the item in the dictionary that has the given key (the first argument). If there is no such item, the method creates a new item with the key and sets its value either to None, or to the given default value (the second argument). In this case we pass a default value of set(), that is, an empty set. So the call to dict.setdefault() always returns an object reference to a value, either one that existed before or a new one. (Of course, if the given key is not hashable a TypeError exception will be raised.)

In this example, the returned object reference always refers to a set (an empty set the first time any particular key, that is, site, is encountered), and we then add the filename that refers to the site to the site's set of filenames. By using a set we ensure that even if a file refers to a site repeatedly, we record the filename only once for the site.

To make the dict.setdefault() method's functionality clear, here are two equivalent code snippets:

```
                                          if site not in sites:
                                              sites[site] = set()
sites.setdefault(site, set()).add(fname)  sites[site].add(fname)
```

For the sake of completeness, here is the rest of the program:

```
for site in sorted(sites):
    print("{0} is referred to in:".format(site))
```

```
for filename in sorted(sites[site], key=str.lower):
    print("    {0}".format(filename))
```

Each Web site is printed with the files that refer to it printed indented underneath. The sorted() call in the outer for ... in loop sorts all the dictionary's keys—whenever a dictionary is used in a context that requires an iterable it is the keys that are used. If we want the iterable to be the (key, value) items or the values, we can use dict.items() or dict.values(). The inner for ... in loop iterates over the sorted filenames from the current site's set of filenames.

sorted()
☞130, 134

Dictionary Comprehensions

A *dictionary comprehension* is an expression and a loop with an optional condition enclosed in braces, very similar to a set comprehension. Like list and set comprehensions, two syntaxes are supported:

{*keyexpression*: *valueexpression* for *key, value* in *iterable*}
{*keyexpression*: *valueexpression* for *key, value* in *iterable* if *condition*}

Here is how we could use a dictionary comprehension to create a dictionary where each key is the name of a file in the current directory and each value is the size of the file in bytes:

```
file_sizes = {name: os.path.getsize(name) for name in os.listdir(".")}
```

The os ("operating system") module's os.listdir() function returns a list of the files and directories in the path it is passed, although it never includes "." or ".." in the list. The os.path.getsize() function returns the size of the given file in bytes. We can avoid directories and other nonfile entries by adding a condition:

os and os.path modules
☞ 213

```
file_sizes = {name: os.path.getsize(name) for name in os.listdir(".")
              if os.path.isfile(name)}
```

The os.path module's os.path.isfile() function returns True if the path passed to it is that of a file, and False otherwise—that is, for directories, links, and so on.

A dictionary comprehension can also be used to create an inverted dictionary. For example, given dictionary d, we can produce a new dictionary whose keys are d's values and whose values are d's keys:

```
inverted_d = {v: k for k, v in d.items()}
```

The resultant dictionary can be inverted back to the original dictionary if all the original dictionary's values are unique—but the inversion will fail with a TypeError being raised if any value is not hashable.

Just like list and set comprehensions, the iterable in a dictionary comprehension can be another comprehension, so all kinds of nested comprehensions are possible.

Default Dictionaries

Default dictionaries are dictionaries—they have all the operators and methods that dictionaries provide.* What makes default dictionaries different from plain dictionaries is the way they handle missing keys; in all other respects they behave identically to dictionaries.

If we use a nonexistent ("missing") key when accessing a dictionary, a KeyError is raised. This is useful because we often want to know whether a key that we expected to be present is absent. But in some cases we want every key we use to be present, even if it means that an item with the key is inserted into the dictionary at the time we first access it.

For example, if we have a dictionary d which does *not* have an item with key m, the code x = d[m] will raise a KeyError exception. But if d is a suitably created default dictionary, if an item with key m is in the default dictionary, the corresponding value is returned the same as for a dictionary—but if m is not a key in the default dictionary, a new item with key m is created with a default value, and the newly created item's value is returned.

unique-
words1.
py
121 ☜

Earlier we wrote a small program that counted the unique words in the files it was given on the command line. The dictionary of words was created like this:

```
words = {}
```

Each key in the words dictionary was a word and each value an integer holding the number of times the word had occurred in all the files that were read. Here's how we incremented whenever a suitable word was encountered:

```
words[word] = words.get(word, 0) + 1
```

We had to use dict.get() to account for when the word was encountered the first time (where we needed to create a new item with a count of 1) and for when the word was encountered subsequently (where we needed to add 1 to the word's existing count).

When a default dictionary is created, we can pass in a *factory function.* A factory function is a function that, when called, returns an object of a particular type. All of Python's built-in data types can be used as factory functions, for example, data type str can be called as str()—and with no argument it returns an emp-

---

*Note for object-oriented programmers: defaultdict is a subclass of dict.

ty string object. The factory function passed to a default dictionary is used to create default values for missing keys.

Note that the *name* of a function is an object reference to the function—so when we want to pass functions as parameters, we just pass the name. When we use a function with parentheses, the parentheses tell Python that the function should be called.

The program `uniquewords2.py` has one more line than the original `unique-words1.py` program (`import collections`), and the lines for creating and updating the dictionary are written differently. Here is how the default dictionary is created:

```
words = collections.defaultdict(int)
```

The `words` default dictionary will never raise a `KeyError`. If we were to write `x = words["xyz"]` and there was no item with key `"xyz"`, when the access is attempted and the key isn't found, the default dictionary will immediately create a new item with key `"xyz"` and value 0 (by calling `int()`), and this value is what will be assigned to `x`.

```
words[word] += 1
```

Now we no longer need to use `dict.get()`; instead we can simply increment the item's value. The very first time a word is encountered, a new item is created with value 0 (to which 1 is immediately added), and on every subsequent access, 1 is added to whatever the current value happens to be.

We have now completed our review of all of Python's built-in collection data types, and a couple of the standard library's collection data types. In the next section we will look at some issues that are common to all of the collection data types.

Iterating and Copying Collections

Once we have collections of data items, it is natural to want to iterate over all the items they contain. In this section's first subsection we will introduce some of Python's iterators and the operators and functions that involve iterators.

Another common requirement is to copy a collection. There are some subtleties involved here because of Python's use of object references (for the sake of efficiency), so in this section's second subsection, we will examine how to copy collections and get the behavior we want.

Iterators and Iterable Operations and Functions

An *iterable* data type is one that can return each of its items one at a time. Any object that has an __iter__() method, or any sequence (i.e., an object that has a __getitem__() method taking integer arguments starting from 0) is an iterable and can provide an *iterator*. An iterator is an object that provides a __next__() method which returns each successive item in turn, and raises a StopIteration exception when there are no more items. Table 3.4 lists the operators and functions that can be used with iterables.

__it-
er__()
☞ 263

The order in which items are returned depends on the underlying iterable. In the case of lists and tuples, items are normally returned in sequential order starting from the first item (index position 0), but some iterators return the items in an arbitrary order—for example, dictionary and set iterators.

The built-in iter() function has two quite different behaviors. When given a collection data type or a sequence it returns an iterator for the object it is passed—or raises a TypeError if the object cannot be iterated. This use arises when creating custom collection data types, but is rarely needed in other contexts. The second iter() behavior occurs when the function is passed a callable (a function or method), and a sentinel value. In this case the function passed in is called once at each iteration, returning the function's return value each time, or raising a StopIteration exception if the return value equals the sentinel.

When we use a for *item* in *iterable* loop, Python in effect calls iter(*iterable*) to get an iterator. This iterator's __next__() method is then called at each loop iteration to get the next item, and when the StopIteration exception is raised, it is caught and the loop is terminated. Another way to get an iterator's next item is to call the built-in next() function. Here are two equivalent pieces of code (multiplying the values in a list), one using a for ... in loop and the other using an explicit iterator:

```
                                    product = 1
                                    i = iter([1, 2, 4, 8])
                                    while True:
                                        try:
    product = 1                             product *= next(i)
    for i in [1, 2, 4, 8]:              except StopIteration:
        product *= i                        break
    print(product)  # prints: 64   print(product)  # prints: 64
```

Any (finite) iterable, *i*, can be converted into a tuple by calling tuple(*i*), or can be converted into a list by calling list(*i*).

The all() and any() functions can be used on iterators and are often used in functional-style programming. Here are a couple of usage examples that show all(), any(), len(), min(), max(), and sum():

```
>>> x = [-2, 9, 7, -4, 3]
>>> all(x), any(x), len(x), min(x), max(x), sum(x)
(True, True, 5, -4, 9, 13)
>>> x.append(0)
>>> all(x), any(x), len(x), min(x), max(x), sum(x)
(False, True, 6, -4, 9, 13)
```

Func-
tional-
style
pro-
gram-
ming
☞ 384

Of these little functions, len() is probably the most frequently used.

The enumerate() function takes an iterator and returns an enumerator object. This object can be treated like an iterator, and at each iteration it returns a 2-tuple with the tuple's first item the iteration number (by default starting from 0), and the second item the next item from the iterator enumerate() was called on. Let's look at enumerate()'s use in the context of a tiny but complete program.

The grepword.py program takes a word and one or more filenames on the command line and outputs the filename, line number, and line whenever the line contains the given word.* Here's a sample run:

```
grepword.py Dom data/forenames.txt
data/forenames.txt:615:Dominykas
data/forenames.txt:1435:Dominik
data/forenames.txt:1611:Domhnall
data/forenames.txt:3314:Dominic
```

Data files data/forenames.txt and data/surnames.txt contain unsorted lists of names, one per line.

Apart from the sys import, the program is just ten lines long:

```
if len(sys.argv) < 3:
    print("usage: grepword.py word infile1 [infile2 [... infileN]]")
    sys.exit()

word = sys.argv[1]
for filename in sys.argv[2:]:
    for lino, line in enumerate(open(filename), start=1):
        if word in line:
            print("{0}:{1}:{2:.40}".format(filename, lino,
                                          line.rstrip()))
```

---

*In Chapter 9 will see two other implementations of this program, grepword-p.py and grepword-t.py, which spread the work over multiple processes and multiple threads.

Table 3.4 *Common Iterable Operators and Functions*

Syntax	Description
s + t	Returns a sequence that is the concatenation of sequences s and t
s * n	Returns a sequence that is int n concatenations of sequence s
x in i	Returns True if item x is in iterable i; use not in to reverse the test
all(i)	Returns True if every item in iterable i evaluates to True
any(i)	Returns True if any item in iterable i evaluates to True
enumerate(i, start)	Normally used in for ... in loops to provide a sequence of (*index*, *item*) tuples with indexes starting at 0 or *start*; see text
len(x)	Returns the "length" of x. If x is a collection it is the number of items; if x is a string it is the number of characters.
max(i, *key*)	Returns the biggest item in iterable i or the item with the biggest *key*(*item*) value if a *key* function is given
min(i, *key*)	Returns the smallest item in iterable i or the item with the smallest *key*(*item*) value if a *key* function is given
range(start, stop, step)	Returns an integer iterator. With one argument (stop), the iterator goes from 0 to stop - 1; with two arguments (*start*, stop) the iterator goes from *start* to stop - 1; with three arguments it goes from *start* to stop - 1 in steps of *step*.
reversed(i)	Returns an iterator that returns the items from iterator i in reverse order
sorted(i, key, reverse)	Returns a list of the items from iterator i in sorted order; *key* is used to provide DSU (Decorate, Sort, Undecorate) sorting. If *reverse* is True the sorting is done in reverse order.
sum(i, start)	Returns the sum of the items in iterable i plus *start* (which defaults to 0); i may not contain strings
zip(i1, ..., i*N*)	Returns an iterator of tuples using the iterators i1 to i*N*; see text

We begin by checking that there are at least two command-line arguments. If there are not, we print a usage message and terminate the program. The sys.exit() function performs an immediate clean termination, closing any open files. It accepts an optional int argument which is passed to the calling shell.

Read-
ing and
writing
text files
sidebar
122 ☞
We assume that the first argument is the word the user is looking for and that the other arguments are the names of the files to look in. We have deliberately called open() without specifying an encoding—the user might use wildcards to specify any number of files, each potentially with a different encoding, so in this case we leave Python to use the platform-dependent encoding.

The file object returned by the open() function in text mode can be used as an iterator, returning one line of the file on each iteration. By passing the iterator to enumerate(), we get an enumerator iterator that returns the iteration number (in variable lino, "line number") and a line from the file, on each iteration. If the word the user is looking for is in the line, we print the filename, line number, and the first 40 characters of the line with trailing whitespace (e.g., \n) stripped. The enumerate() function accepts an optional keyword argument, start, which defaults to 0; we have used this argument set to 1, since by convention, text file line numbers are counted from 1.

Quite often we don't need an enumerator, but rather an iterator that returns successive integers. This is exactly what the range() function provides. If we need a list or tuple of integers, we can convert the iterator returned by range() by using the appropriate conversion function. Here are a few examples:

```
>>> list(range(5)), list(range(9, 14)), tuple(range(10, -11, -5))
([0, 1, 2, 3, 4], [9, 10, 11, 12, 13], (10, 5, 0, -5, -10))
```

The range() function is most commonly used for two purposes: to create lists or tuples of integers, and to provide loop counting in for … in loops. For example, these two equivalent examples ensure that list x's items are all positive:

```
                                       i = 0
                                       while i < len(x):
for i in range(len(x)):                    x[i] = abs(x[i])
    x[i] = abs(x[i])                       i += 1
```

In both cases, if list x was originally, say, [11, -3, -12, 8, -1], afterward it will be [11, 3, 12, 8, 1].

Since we can unpack an iterable using the * operator, we can unpack the iterator returned by the range() function. For example, if we have a function called calculate() that takes four arguments, here are some ways we could call it with arguments, 1, 2, 3, and 4:

```
calculate(1, 2, 3, 4)
t = (1, 2, 3, 4)
calculate(*t)
calculate(*range(1, 5))
```

In all three calls, four arguments are passed. The second call unpacks a 4-tuple, and the third call unpacks the iterator returned by the range() function.

We will now look at a small but complete program to consolidate some of the things we have covered so far, and for the first time to explicitly write to a file. The generate_test_names1.py program reads in a file of forenames and a file of surnames, creating two lists, and then creates the file test-names1.txt and writes 100 random names into it.

We will use the `random.choice()` function which takes a random item from a sequence, so it is possible that some duplicate names might occur. First we'll look at the function that returns the lists of names, and then we will look at the rest of the program.

```
def get_forenames_and_surnames():
    forenames = []
    surnames = []
    for names, filename in ((forenames, "data/forenames.txt"),
                            (surnames, "data/surnames.txt")):
        for name in open(filename, encoding="utf8"):
            names.append(name.rstrip())
    return forenames, surnames
```

Tuple
unpack-
ing

102 ☞

In the outer for ... in loop, we iterate over two 2-tuples, unpacking each 2-tuple into two variables. Even though the two lists might be quite large, returning them from a function is efficient because Python uses object references, so the only thing that is really returned is a tuple of two object references.

Inside Python programs it is convenient to always use Unix-style paths, since they can be typed without the need for escaping, and they work on all platforms (including Windows). If we have a path we want to present to the user in, say, variable path, we can always import the os module and call `path.replace("/", os.sep)` to replace forward slashes with the platform-specific directory separator.

```
forenames, surnames = get_forenames_and_surnames()
fh = open("test-names1.txt", "w", encoding="utf8")
for i in range(100):
    line = "{0} {1}\n".format(random.choice(forenames),
                              random.choice(surnames))
    fh.write(line)
```

Read-
ing and
writing
text files
sidebar

122 ☞

Having retrieved the two lists we open the output file for writing, and keep the file object in variable fh ("file handle"). We then loop 100 times, and in each iteration we create a line to be written to the file, remembering to include a newline at the end of every line. We make no use of the loop variable i; it is needed purely to satisfy the for ... in loop's syntax. The preceding code snippet, the `get_forenames_and_surnames()` function, and an import statement constitute the entire program.

In the `generate_test_names1.py` program we paired items from two separate lists together into strings. Another way of combining items from two or more lists (or other iterables) is to use the `zip()` function. The `zip()` function takes one or more iterables and returns an iterator that returns tuples. The first tuple has the first item from every iterable, the second tuple the second item from every iterable, and so on, stopping as soon as one of the iterables is exhausted. Here is an example:

```
>>> for t in zip(range(4), range(0, 10, 2), range(1, 10, 2)):
...     print(t)
(0, 0, 1)
(1, 2, 3)
(2, 4, 5)
(3, 6, 7)
```

Although the iterators returned by the second and third range() calls can produce five items each, the first can produce only four, so that limits the number of items zip() can return to four tuples.

Here is a modified version of the program to generate test names, this time with each name occupying 25 characters and followed by a random year. The program is called generate_test_names2.py and outputs the file test-names2.txt. We have not shown the get_forenames_and_surnames() function or the open() call since, apart from the output filename, they are the same as before.

```
limit = 100
years = list(range(1970, 2013)) * 3
for year, forename, surname in zip(
        random.sample(years, limit),
        random.sample(forenames, limit),
        random.sample(surnames, limit)):
    name = "{0} {1}".format(forename, surname)
    fh.write("{0:.<25}.{1}\n".format(name, year))
```

We begin by setting a limit on how many names we want to generate. Then we create a list of years by making a list of the years from 1970 to 2012 inclusive, and then replicating this list three times so that the final list has three occurrences of each year. This is necessary because the random.sample() function that we are using (instead of random.choice()) takes both an iterable and how many items it is to produce—a number that cannot be less than the number of items the iterable can return. The random.sample() function returns an iterator that will produce up to the specified number of items from the iterable it is given—with no repeats. So this version of the program will always produce unique names.

In the for ... in loop we unpack each tuple returned by the zip() function. We want to limit the length of each name to 25 characters, and to do this we must first create a string with the complete name, and then set the maximum width for that string when we call str.format() the second time. We left-align each name, and for names shorter than 25 characters we fill with periods. The extra period ensures that names that occupy the full field width are still separated from the year by a period.

Tuple unpacking

102 ☞

str. format()

74 ☞

We will conclude this subsection by mentioning two other iterable-related functions, sorted() and reversed(). The sorted() function returns a list with the items sorted, and the reversed() function simply returns an iterator that iterates in the reverse order to the iterator it is given as its argument. Here is an example of reversed():

```
>>> list(range(6))
[0, 1, 2, 3, 4, 5]
>>> list(reversed(range(6)))
[5, 4, 3, 2, 1, 0]
```

The sorted() function is more sophisticated, as these examples show:

```
>>> x = []
>>> for t in zip(range(-10, 0, 1), range(0, 10, 2), range(1, 10, 2)):
...     x += t
>>> x
[-10, 0, 1, -9, 2, 3, -8, 4, 5, -7, 6, 7, -6, 8, 9]
>>> sorted(x)
[-10, -9, -8, -7, -6, 0, 1, 2, 3, 4, 5, 6, 7, 8, 9]
>>> sorted(x, reverse=True)
[9, 8, 7, 6, 5, 4, 3, 2, 1, 0, -6, -7, -8, -9, -10]
>>> sorted(x, key=abs)
[0, 1, 2, 3, 4, 5, 6, -6, -7, 7, -8, 8, -9, 9, -10]
```

In the preceding snippet, the zip() function returns 3-tuples, (-10, 0, 1), (-9, 2, 3), and so on. The += operator extends a list, that is, it appends each item in the sequence it is given to the list.

The first call to sorted() returns a copy of the list using the conventional sort order. The second call returns a copy of the list in the reverse of the conventional sort order. The last call to sorted() specifies a "key" function which we will come back to in a moment.

Notice that since Python functions are objects like any other, they can be passed as arguments to other functions, and stored in collections without formality. Recall that a function's name is an object reference to the function; it is the parentheses that follow the name that tell Python to call the function.

When a key function is passed (in this case the abs() function), it is called once for every item in the list (with the item passed as the function's sole parameter), to create a "decorated" list. Then the decorated list is sorted, and the sorted list without the decoration is returned as the result. We are free to use our own custom function as the key function, as we will see shortly.

For example, we can case-insensitively sort a list of strings by passing the str.lower() method as a key. If we have the list, x, of ["Sloop", "Yawl", "Cutter", "schooner", "ketch"], we can sort it case-insensitively using DSU

(Decorate, Sort, Undecorate) with a single line of code by passing a key function, or do the DSU explicitly, as these two equivalent code snippets show:

```
temp = []
for item in x:
    temp.append((item.lower(), item))
x = []
for key, value in sorted(temp):
    x.append(value)
```

```
x = sorted(x, key=str.lower)
```

Both snippets produce a new list: `["Cutter", "ketch", "schooner", "Sloop", "Yawl"]`, although the computations they perform are not identical because the right-hand snippet creates the `temp` list variable.

Python's sort algorithm is an adaptive stable mergesort that is both fast and smart, and it is especially well optimized for partially sorted lists—a very common case.* The "adaptive" part means that the sort algorithm adapts to circumstances—for example, taking advantage of partially sorted data. The "stable" part means that items that sort equally are not moved in relation to each other (after all, there is no need), and the "mergesort" part is the generic name for the sorting algorithm used. When sorting collections of integers, strings, or other simple types their "less than" operator (<) is used. Python can sort collections that contain collections, working recursively to any depth. For example:

```
>>> x = list(zip((1, 3, 1, 3), ("pram", "dorie", "kayak", "canoe")))
>>> x
[(1, 'pram'), (3, 'dorie'), (1, 'kayak'), (3, 'canoe')]
>>> sorted(x)
[(1, 'kayak'), (1, 'pram'), (3, 'canoe'), (3, 'dorie')]
```

Python has sorted the list of tuples by comparing the first item of each tuple, and when these are the same, by comparing the second item. This gives a sort order based on the integers, with the strings being tiebreakers. We can force the sort to be based on the strings and use the integers as tiebreakers by defining a simple key function:

```
def swap(t):
    return t[1], t[0]
```

The `swap()` function takes a 2-tuple and returns a new 2-tuple with the arguments swapped. Assuming that we have entered the `swap()` function in IDLE, we can now do this:

---

* The algorithm was created by Tim Peters. An interesting explanation and discussion of the algorithm is in the file `listsort.txt` which comes with Python's source code.

```
>>> sorted(x, key=swap)
[(3, 'canoe'), (3, 'dorie'), (1, 'kayak'), (1, 'pram')]
```

Lists can also be sorted in-place using the list.sort() method, which takes the same optional arguments as sorted().

Sorting can be applied only to collections where all the items can be compared with each other:

```
sorted([3, 8, -7.5, 0, 1.3])            # returns: [-7.5, 0, 1.3, 3, 8]
sorted([3, "spanner", -7.5, 0, 1.3])    # raises a TypeError
```

Although the first list has numbers of different types (int and float), these types can be compared with each other so that sorting a list containing them works fine. But the second list has a string and this cannot be sensibly compared with a number, and so a TypeError exception is raised. If we want to sort a list that has integers, floating-point numbers, and strings that contain numbers, we can give float() as the key function:

```
sorted(["1.3", -7.5, "5", 4, "-2.4", 1], key=float)
```

This returns the list [-7.3, '-2.4', 1, '1.3', 4, '5']. Notice that the list's values are not changed, so strings remain strings. If any of the strings cannot be converted to a number (e.g., "spanner"), a TypeError exception will be raised.

Copying Collections

Object references

14 ✍

Since Python uses object references, when we use the assignment operator (=), no copying takes place. If the right-hand operand is a literal such as a string or a number, the left-hand operand is set to be an object reference that refers to the in-memory object that holds the literal's value. If the right-hand operand is an object reference, the left-hand operand is set to be an object reference that refers to the same object as the right-hand operand. One consequence of this is that assignment is very efficient.

When we assign large collections, such as long lists, the savings are very apparent. Here is an example:

```
>>> songs = ["Because", "Boys", "Carol"]
>>> beatles = songs
>>> beatles, songs
(['Because', 'Boys', 'Carol'], ['Because', 'Boys', 'Carol'])
```

Here, a new object reference (beatles) has been created, and both object references refer to the same list—no copying has taken place.

Since lists are mutable, we can apply a change. For example:

```
>>> beatles[2] = "Cayenne"
>>> beatles, songs
(['Because', 'Boys', 'Cayenne'], ['Because', 'Boys', 'Cayenne'])
```

We applied the change using the beatles variable—but this is an object reference referring to the same list as songs refers to. So any change made through either object reference is visible to the other. This is most often the behavior we want, since copying large collections is potentially expensive. It also means, for example, that we can pass a list or other mutable collection data type as an argument to a function, modify the collection in the function, and know that the modified collection will be accessible after the function call has completed.

However, in some situations, we really do want a separate copy of the collection (or other mutable object). For sequences, when we take a slice—for example, songs[:2]—the slice is always an independent copy of the items copied. So to copy an entire sequence we can do this:

```
>>> songs = ["Because", "Boys", "Carol"]
>>> beatles = songs[:]
>>> beatles[2] = "Cayenne"
>>> beatles, songs
(['Because', 'Boys', 'Cayenne'], ['Because', 'Boys', 'Carol'])
```

For dictionaries and sets, copying can be achieved using dict.copy() and set.copy(). In addition, the copy module provides the copy.copy() function that returns a copy of the object it is given. Another way to copy the built-in collection types is to use the type as a function with the collection to be copied as its argument. Here are some examples:

```
copy_of_dict_d = dict(d)
copy_of_list_L = list(L)
copy_of_set_s = set(s)
```

Note, though, that all of these copying techniques are *shallow*—that is, only object references are copied and not the objects themselves. For immutable data types like numbers and strings this has the same effect as copying (except that it is more efficient), but for mutable data types such as nested collections this means that the objects they refer to are referred to both by the original collection and by the copied collection. The following snippet illustrates this:

```
>>> x = [53, 68, ["A", "B", "C"]]
>>> y = x[:]  # shallow copy
>>> x, y
([53, 68, ['A', 'B', 'C']], [53, 68, ['A', 'B', 'C']])
>>> y[1] = 40
>>> x[2][0] = 'Q'
>>> x, y
```

```
([53, 68, ['Q', 'B', 'C']], [53, 40, ['Q', 'B', 'C']])
```

When list x is shallow-copied, the reference to the nested list ["A", "B", "C"] is copied. This means that both x and y have as their third item an object reference that refers to this list, so any changes to the nested list are seen by both x and y. If we really need independent copies of arbitrarily nested collections, we can deep-copy:

```
>>> import copy
>>> x = [53, 68, ["A", "B", "C"]]
>>> y = copy.deepcopy(x)
>>> y[1] = 40
>>> x[2][0] = 'Q'
>>> x, y
([53, 68, ['Q', 'B', 'C']], [53, 40, ['A', 'B', 'C']])
```

Here, lists x and y, and the list items they contain, are completely independent.

Note that from now on we will use the terms *copy* and *shallow copy* interchangeably—if we mean *deep copy*, we will say so explicitly.

Examples

We have now completed our review of Python's built-in collection data types, and two of the standard library collection types (collections.namedtuple and collections.defaultdict). Python also provides the collections.deque type, a double-ended queue, and many other collection types are available from third parties and from the Python Package Index, pypi.python.org/pypi. But now we will look at a couple of slightly longer examples that draw together many of the things covered in this chapter, and in the preceding one.

The first program is about seventy lines long and involves text processing. The second program is around ninety lines long and is mathematical in flavor. Between them, the programs make use of dictionaries, lists, named tuples, and sets, and both make great use of the str.format() method from the preceding chapter.

generate_usernames.py

Imagine we are setting up a new computer system and need to generate usernames for all of our organization's staff. We have a plain text data file (UTF-8 encoding) where each line represents a record and fields are colon-delimited. Each record concerns one member of the staff and the fields are their unique staff ID, forename, middle name (which may be an empty field), surname,

and department name. Here is an extract of a few lines from an example
data/users.txt data file:

```
1601:Albert:Lukas:Montgomery:Legal
3702:Albert:Lukas:Montgomery:Sales
4730:Nadelle::Landale:Warehousing
```

The program must read in all the data files given on the command line, and for
every line (record) must extract the fields and return the data with a suitable
username. Each username must be unique and based on the person's name.
The output must be text sent to the console, sorted alphabetically by surname
and forename, for example:

```
Name                               ID     Username
--------------------------------- ------ ----------
Landale, Nadelle................ (4730) nlandale
Montgomery, Albert L............ (1601) almontgo
Montgomery, Albert L............ (3702) almontgo1
```

Each record has exactly five fields, and although we could refer to them by
number, we prefer to use names to keep our code clear:

```
ID, FORENAME, MIDDLENAME, SURNAME, DEPARTMENT = range(5)
```

It is a Python convention that identifiers written in all uppercase characters
are to be treated as constants.

We also need to create a named tuple type for holding the data on each user:

```
User = collections.namedtuple("User",
            "username forename middlename surname id")
```

We will see how the constants and the User named tuple are used when we look
at the rest of the code.

The program's overall logic is captured in the main() function:

```
def main():
    if len(sys.argv) == 1 or sys.argv[1] in {"-h", "--help"}:
        print("usage: {0} file1 [file2 [... fileN]]".format(
                sys.argv[0]))
        sys.exit()

    usernames = set()
    users = {}
    for filename in sys.argv[1:]:
        for line in open(filename, encoding="utf8"):
            line = line.rstrip()
            if line:
```

```
                    user = process_line(line, usernames)
                    users[(user.surname.lower(), user.forename.lower(),
                            user.id)] = user
            print_users(users)
```

If the user doesn't provide any filenames on the command line, or if they type "-h" or "–help" on the command line, we simply print a usage message and terminate the program.

For each line read, we strip off any trailing whitespace (e.g., \n) and process only nonempty lines. This means that if the data file contains blank lines they will be safely ignored.

We keep track of all the allocated usernames in the usernames set to ensure that we don't create any duplicates. The data itself is held in the users dictionary, with each user (member of the staff) stored as a dictionary item whose key is a tuple of the user's surname, forename, and ID, and whose value is a named tuple of type User. Using a tuple of the user's surname, forename, and ID for the dictionary's keys means that if we call sorted() on the dictionary, the iterable returned will be in the order we want (i.e., surname, forename, ID), without us having to provide a key function.

```
    def process_line(line, usernames):
        fields = line.split(":")
        username = generate_username(fields, usernames)
        user = User(username, fields[FORENAME], fields[MIDDLENAME],
                    fields[SURNAME], fields[ID])
        return user
```

Since the data format for each record is so simple, and because we've already stripped the trailing whitespace from the line, we can extract the fields simply by splitting on the colons. We pass the fields and the usernames set to the generate_username() function, and then we create an instance of the User named tuple type which we then return to the caller (main()), which inserts the user into the users dictionary, ready for printing.

If we had not created suitable constants to hold the index positions, we would be reduced to using numeric indexes, for example:

```
    user = User(username, fields[1], fields[2], fields[3], fields[0])
```

Although this is certainly shorter, it is poor practice. First it isn't clear to future maintainers what each field is, and second it is vulnerable to data file format changes—if the order or number of fields in a record changes, this code will break everywhere it is used. But by using named constants in the face of changes to the record struture, we would have to change only the values of the constants, and all uses of the constants would continue to work.

```
def generate_username(fields, usernames):
    username = ((fields[FORENAME][0] + fields[MIDDLENAME][:1] +
                fields[SURNAME]).replace("-", "").replace("'", ""))
    username = original_name = username[:8].lower()
    count = 1
    while username in usernames:
        username = "{0}{1}".format(original_name, count)
        count += 1
    usernames.add(username)
    return username
```

We make a first attempt at creating a username by concatenating the first letter of the forename, the first letter of the middle name, and the whole surname, and deleting any hyphens or single quotes from the resultant string. The code for getting the first letter of the middle name is quite subtle. If we had used `fields[MIDDLENAME][0]` we would get an IndexError exception for empty middle names. But by using a slice we get the first letter if there is one, or an empty string otherwise.

Next we make the username lowercase and no more than eight characters long. If the username is in use (i.e., it is in the `usernames` set), we try the username with a "1" tacked on at the end, and if that is in use we try with a "2", and so on until we get one that isn't in use. Then we add the username to the set of usernames and return the username to the caller.

```
def print_users(users):
    namewidth = 32
    usernamewidth = 9

    print("{0:<{nw}} {1:^6} {2:{uw}}".format(
        "Name", "ID", "Username", nw=namewidth, uw=usernamewidth))
    print("{0:-<{nw}} {0:-<6} {0:-<{uw}}".format(
        "", nw=namewidth, uw=usernamewidth))

    for key in sorted(users):
        user = users[key]
        initial = ""
        if user.middlename:
            initial = " " + user.middlename[0]
        name = "{0.surname}, {0.forename}{1}".format(user, initial)
        print("{0:.<{nw}} ({1.id:4}) {1.username:{uw}}".format(
            name, user, nw=namewidth, uw=usernamewidth))
```

Once all the records have been processed, the `print_users()` function is called, with the `users` dictionary passed as its parameter.

The first `print()` statement prints the column titles, and the second `print()` statement prints hyphens under each title. This second statement's str.

format() call is slightly subtle. The string we give to be printed is "", that is, the empty string—we get the hyphens by printing the empty string padded with hyphens to the given widths.

Next we use a for ... in loop to print the details of each user, extracting the key for each user's dictionary item in sorted order. For convenience we create the user variable so that we don't have to keep writing users[key] throughout the rest of the function. In the loop's first call to str.format() we set the name variable to the user's name in surname, forename (and optional initial) form. We access items in the user named tuple by name. Once we have the user's name as a single string we print the user's details, constraining each column, (name, ID, username) to the widths we want.

The complete program (which differs from what we have reviewed only in that it has some initial comment lines and some imports) is in generate_usernames.py. The program's structure—read in a data file, process each record, write output—is one that is very frequently used, and we will meet it again in the next example.

statistics.py

Suppose we have a bunch of data files containing numbers relating to some processing we have done, and we want to produce some basic statistics to give us some kind of overview of the data. Each file uses plain text (ASCII encoding) with one or more numbers per line (whitespace-separated).

Here is an example of the kind of output we want to produce:

```
count     =     183
mean      =     130.56
median    =      43.00
mode      = [5.00, 7.00, 50.00]
std. dev. =     235.01
```

Here, we read 183 numbers, with 5, 7, and 50 occurring most frequently, and with a sample standard deviation of 235.01.

The statistics themselves are held in a named tuple called Statistics:

```
Statistics = collections.namedtuple("Statistics",
                            "mean mode median std_dev")
```

The main() function also serves as an overview of the program's structure:

```
def main():
    if len(sys.argv) == 1 or sys.argv[1] in {"-h", "--help"}:
        print("usage: {0} file1 [file2 [... fileN]]".format(
            sys.argv[0]))
```

```
            sys.exit()

numbers = []
frequencies = collections.defaultdict(int)
for filename in sys.argv[1:]:
    read_data(filename, numbers, frequencies)
if numbers:
    statistics = calculate_statistics(numbers, frequencies)
    print_results(len(numbers), statistics)
else:
    print("no numbers found")
```

We store all the numbers from all the files in the numbers list. To calculate the mode ("most frequently occurring") numbers, we need to know how many times each number occurs, so we create a default dictionary using the int() factory function, to keep track of the counts.

We iterate over each filename and read in its data. We pass the list and default dictionary as additional parameters so that the read_data() function can update them. Once we have read all the data, assuming some numbers were successfully read, we call calculate_statistics(). This returns a named tuple of type Statistics which we then use to print the results.

```
def read_data(filename, numbers, frequencies):
    for lino, line in enumerate(open(filename, encoding="ascii"),
                                start=1):
        for x in line.split():
            try:
                number = float(x)
                numbers.append(number)
                frequencies[number] += 1
            except ValueError as err:
                print("{0}:{1}: skipping {2}: {3}".format(
                        filename, lino, x, err))
```

We split every line on whitespace, and for each item we attempt to convert it to a float. If a conversion succeeds—as it will for integers and for floating-point numbers in both decimal and exponential notations—we add the number to the numbers list and update the frequencies default dictionary. (If we had used a plain dict, the update code would have been frequencies[number] = frequencies.get(number, 0) + 1.) If a conversion fails, we output the line number (starting from line 1 as is traditional for text files), the text we attempted to convert, and the ValueError exception's error text.

```
def calculate_statistics(numbers, frequencies):
    mean = sum(numbers) / len(numbers)
    mode = calculate_mode(frequencies, 3)
```

```
    median = calculate_median(numbers)
    std_dev = calculate_std_dev(numbers, mean)
    return Statistics(mean, mode, median, std_dev)
```

This function is used to gather all the statistics together. Because the mean ("average") is so easy to calculate, we do so directly here. For the other statistics we call dedicated functions, and at the end we return a `Statistics` named tuple object that contains the four statistics we have calculated.

```
def calculate_mode(frequencies, maximum_modes):
    highest_frequency = max(frequencies.values())
    mode = [number for number, frequency in frequencies.items()
            if math.fabs(frequency - highest_frequency) <=
                sys.float_info.epsilon]
    if not (1 <= len(mode) <= maximum_modes):
        mode = None
    else:
        mode.sort()
    return mode
```

There may be more than one most-frequently-occurring number, so in addition to the dictionary of frequencies, this function also requires the caller to specify the maximum number of modes that are acceptable. (The `calculate_statistics()` function is the caller, and it specified a maximum of three modes.)

The `max()` function is used to find the highest value in the frequencies dictionary. Then, we use a list comprehension to create a list of those modes whose frequency equals the highest value. Since the numbers may be floating-point we compare the difference in absolute values (using `math.fabs()` since it gives better results than `abs()`) with the smallest number the machine can measure.

If the number of modes is 0 or greater than the maximum modes that are acceptable, a mode of `None` is returned; otherwise, a sorted list of the modes is returned.

```
def calculate_median(numbers):
    numbers = sorted(numbers)
    middle = len(numbers) // 2
    median = numbers[middle]
    if len(numbers) % 2 == 0:
        median = (median + numbers[middle - 1]) / 2
    return median
```

The median ("middle value") is the value that occurs in the middle if the numbers are arranged in order—except when the number of numbers is even, in which case the middle falls between two numbers, so in that case the median is the mean of the two middle numbers.

We begin by sorting the numbers into ascending order. Then we use truncating (integer) division to find the index position of the middle number, which we extract and store as the median. If the number of numbers is even, we make the median the mean of the two middle numbers.

```python
def calculate_std_dev(numbers, mean):
    total = 0
    for number in numbers:
        total += ((number - mean) ** 2)
    variance = total / (len(numbers) - 1)
    return math.sqrt(variance)
```

The sample standard deviation is a measure of dispersion, that is, how far the numbers differ from the mean. This function calculates the sample standard deviation using the formula $s = \sqrt{\frac{\sum(x - \bar{x})^2}{n-1}}$, where x is each number, $\bar{x}$ is the mean, and n is the number of numbers.

```python
def print_results(count, statistics):
    real = "9.2f"

    if statistics.mode is None:
        modeline = ""
    elif len(statistics.mode) == 1:
        modeline = "mode      = {0:{fmt}}\n".format(
                statistics.mode[0], fmt=real)
    else:
        modeline = ("mode      = [" +
                ", ".join(["{0:.2f}".format(m)
                for m in statistics.mode]) + "]\n")

    print("""\
count      = {0:6}
mean      = {1.mean:{fmt}}
median    = {1.median:{fmt}}
{2}\
std. dev. = {1.std_dev:{fmt}}""".format(
        count, statistics, modeline, fmt=real))
```

str. format() 74 ☜ Most of this function is concerned with formatting the modes list into the modeline string. If there are no modes, the mode line is not printed at all. If there is one mode, the mode list has just one item (mode[0]) which is printed using the same format as is used for the other statistics. If there are several modes, we print them as a list with each one formatted appropriately. This is done by using a list comprehension to produce a list of mode strings, and then joining all the strings in the list together with ", " in between each one. The printing at the end is easy thanks to our use of a named tuple. This lets us access the statistics in the statistics object using names rather than numeric indexes, and thanks to Python's triple-quoted strings we can lay out the text to be printed in an understandable way.

There is one subtle point to note. The modes are printed as format item {2}, which is followed by a backslash. The backslash escapes the newline, so if the mode is the empty string no blank line will appear. And it is because we have escaped the newline that we must put \n at the end of the modeline string if it is not empty.

Summary

In this chapter we covered all of Python's built-in collection types, and also a couple of collection types from the standard library. We covered the collection sequence types, tuple, collections.namedtuple, and list, which support the same slicing and striding syntax as strings. The use of the sequence unpacking operator (*) was also covered, and brief mention was made of starred arguments in function calls. We also covered the set types, set and frozenset, and the mapping types, dict and collections.defaultdict.

We saw how to use the named tuples provided by Python's standard library to create simple custom tuple data types whose items can be accessed by index position, or more conveniently, by name. We also saw how to create "constants" by using variables with all uppercase names.

In the coverage of lists we saw that everything that can be done to tuples can be done to lists. And thanks to lists being mutable they offer considerably more functionality than tuples. This includes methods that modify the list (e.g., list.pop()), and the ability to have slices on the left-hand side of an assignment, to provide insertion, replacement, and deletion of slices. Lists are ideal for holding sequences of items, especially if we need fast access by index position.

When we discussed the set and frozenset types, we noted that they may contain only hashable items. Sets provide fast membership testing and are useful for filtering out duplicate data.

Dictionaries are in some ways similar to sets—for example, their keys must be hashable and are unique just like the items in a set. But dictionaries hold key–value pairs, whose values can be of any type. The dictionary coverage included the dict.get() and dict.setdefault() methods, and the coverage of default dictionaries showed an alternative to using these methods. Like sets, dictionaries provide very fast membership testing and fast access by key.

Lists, sets, and dictionaries all offer compact comprehension syntaxes that can be used to create collections of these types from iterables (which themselves can be comprehensions), and with conditions attached if required. The range() and zip() functions are frequently used in the creation of collections, both in conventional for … in loops and in comprehensions.

Items can be deleted from the mutable collection types using the relevant methods, such as list.pop() and set.discard(), or using del, for example, del d[k] to delete an item with key k from dictionary d.

Python's use of object references makes assignment extremely efficient, but it also means that objects are not copied when the assignment operator (=) is used. We saw the differences between shallow and deep copying, and later on saw how lists can be shallow-copied using a slice of the entire list, L[:], and how dictionaries can be shallow-copied using the dict.copy() method. Any copyable object can be copied using functions from the copy module, with copy.copy() performing a shallow copy, and copy.deepcopy() performing a deep copy.

We introduced Python's highly optimized sorted() function. This function is used a lot in Python programming, since Python doesn't provide any intrinsically ordered collection data types, so when we need to iterate over collections in sorted order, we use sorted().

Python's built-in collection data types—tuples, lists, sets, frozen sets, and dictionaries—are sufficient in themselves for all purposes. Nonetheless, a few additional collection types are available in the standard library, and many more are available from third parties.

We often need to read in collections from files, or write collections to files. In this chapter we focused just on reading and writing lines of text in our very brief coverage of text file handling. Full coverage of file handling is given in Chapter 7, and additional means of providing data persistence is covered in Chapter 11.

In the next chapter, we will look more closely at Python's control structures, and introduce one that we have not seen before. We will also look in more depth at exception-handling and at some additional statements, such as assert, that we have not yet covered. In addition, we will cover the creation of custom functions, and in particular we will look at Python's incredibly versatile argument-handling facilities.

Exercises

1. Modify the external_sites.py program to use a default dictionary. This is an easy change requiring an additional import, and changes to just two other lines. A solution is provided in external_sites_ans.py.

2. Modify the `uniquewords2.py` program so that it outputs the words in frequency of occurrence order rather than in alphabetical order. You'll need to iterate over the dictionary's items and create a tiny two-line function to extract each item's value and pass this function as `sorted()`'s key function. Also, the call to `print()` will need to be changed appropriately. This isn't difficult, but it is slightly subtle. A solution is provided in `uniquewords_ans.py`.

3. Modify the `generate_usernames.py` program so that it prints the details of two users per line, limiting names to 17 characters and outputting a form feed character after every 64 lines, with the column titles printed at the start of every page. Here's a sample of the expected output:

```
Name                ID   Username  Name                ID   Username
------------------  ----  --------  ------------------  ----  --------

Aitkin, Shatha...  (2370) saitkin   Alderson, Nicole. (8429) nalderso
Allison, Karma...  (8621) kallison  Alwood, Kole E...  (2095) kealwood
Annie, Neervana..  (2633) nannie    Apperson, Lucyann  (7282) leappers
```

This is challenging. You'll need to keep the column titles in variables so that they can be printed when needed, and you'll need to tweak the format specifications to accommodate the narrower names. One way to achieve pagination is to write all the output items to a list and then iterate over the list using striding to get the left- and right-hand items, and using `zip()` to pair them up. A solution is provided in `generate_usernames_ans.py` and a longer sample data file is provided in `data/users2.txt`.

4

- Control Structures
- Exception Handling
- Custom Functions

Control Structures and Functions

This chapter's first two sections cover Python's control structures, with the first section dealing with branching and looping and the second section covering exception-handling. Most of the control structures and the basics of exception-handling were introduced in Chapter 1, but here we give more complete coverage, including additional control structure syntaxes, and how to raise exceptions and create custom exceptions.

The third and largest section is devoted to creating custom functions, with detailed coverage of Python's extremely versatile argument handling. Custom functions allow us to package up and parameterize functionality—this reduces the size of our code by eliminating code duplication and provides code reuse. (In the following chapter we will see how to create custom modules so that we can make use of our custom functions in multiple programs.)

Control Structures

Python provides conditional branching with `if` statements and looping with `while` and `for ... in` statements. Python also has a *conditional expression*—this is a kind of `if` statement that is Python's answer to the ternary operator (?:) used in C-style languages.

Conditional Branching

As we saw in Chapter 1, this is the general syntax for Python's conditional branch statement:

```
if boolean_expression1:
    suite1
```

```
elif boolean_expression2:
    suite2
...
elif boolean_expressionN:
    suiteN
else:
    else_suite
```

There can be zero or more elif clauses, and the final else clause is optional. If we want to account for a particular case, but want to do nothing if it occurs, we can use pass (which serves as a "do nothing" place holder) as that branch's suite.

In some cases, we can reduce an if ... else statement down to a single *conditional expression*. The syntax for a conditional expression is:

```
expression1 if boolean_expression else expression2
```

If the boolean_expression evaluates to True, the result of the conditional expression is expression1; otherwise, the result is expression2.

One common programming pattern is to set a variable to a default value, and then change the value if necessary, for example, due to a request by the user, or to account for the platform on which the program is being run. Here is the pattern using a conventional if statement:

```
offset = 20
if not sys.platform.startswith("win"):
    offset = 10
```

The sys.platform variable holds the name of the current platform, for example, "win32" or "linux2". The same thing can be achieved in just one line using a conditional expression:

```
offset = 20 if sys.platform.startswith("win") else 10
```

No parentheses are necessary here, but using them avoids a subtle trap. For example, suppose we want to set a width variable to 100 plus an extra 10 if margin is True. We might code the expression like this:

```
width = 100 + 10 if margin else 0    # WRONG!
```

 What is particularly nasty about this, is that it works correctly if margin is True, setting width to 110. But if margin is False, width is wrongly set to 0 instead of 100. This is because Python sees 100 + 10 as the expression1 part of the conditional expression. The solution is to use parentheses:

```
width = 100 + (10 if margin else 0)
```

The parentheses also make things clearer for human readers.

Conditional expressions can be used to improve messages printed for users. For example, when reporting the number of files processed, instead of printing "0 file(s)", "1 file(s)", and similar, we could use a couple of conditional expressions:

```
print("{0} file{1}".format((count if count != 0 else "no"),
                           ("s" if count != 1 else "")))
```

This will print "no files", "1 file", "2 files", and similar, which gives a much more professional impression.

Looping

Python provides a while loop and a for ... in loop, both of which have a more sophisticated syntax than the basics we showed in Chapter 1.

while Loops

Here is the complete general syntax of the while loop:

```
while boolean_expression:
    while_suite
else:
    else_suite
```

The else clause is optional. As long as the *boolean_expression* is True, the while block's suite is executed. If the *boolean_expression* is or becomes False, the loop terminates, and if the optional else clause is present, its suite is executed. Inside the while block's suite, if a continue statement is executed, control is immediately returned to the top of the loop, and the *boolean_expression* is evaluated again. If the loop does not terminate normally, any optional else clause's suite is skipped.

The optional else clause is rather confusingly named since the else clause's suite is always executed if the loop terminates normally. If the loop is broken out of due to a break statement, or a return statement (if the loop is in a function or method), or if an exception is raised, the else clause's suite is *not* executed. (If an exception occurs, Python skips the else clause and looks for a suitable exception handler—this is covered in the next section.) On the plus side, the behavior of the else clause is the same for while loops, for ... in loops, and try ... except blocks.

Let's look at an example of the else clause in action. The str.index() and list.index() methods return the index position of a given string or item, or raise a ValueError exception if the string or item is not found. The str.find()

method does the same thing, but on failure, instead of raising an exception it returns an index of -1. There is no equivalent method for lists, but if we wanted a function that did this, we could create one using a while loop:

```
def list_find(lst, target):
    index = 0
    while index < len(lst):
        if lst[index] == target:
            break
        index += 1
    else:
        index = -1
    return index
```

This function searches the given list looking for the target. If the target is found, the break statement terminates the loop, causing the appropriate index position to be returned. If the target is not found, the loop runs to completion and terminates normally. After normal termination, the else suite is executed, and the index position is set to -1 and returned.

for Loops

Like a while loop, the full syntax of the for ... in loop also includes an optional else clause:

```
for expression in iterable:
    for_suite
else:
    else_suite
```

The *expression* is normally either a single variable or a sequence of variables, usually in the form of a tuple. If a tuple or list is used for the *expression*, each item is unpacked into the *expression*'s items.

If a continue statement is executed inside the for ... in loop's suite, control is immediately passed to the top of the loop and the next iteration begins. If the loop runs to completion it terminates, and any else suite is executed. If the loop is broken out of (due to a break or return), control is immediately passed to the statement following the loop—and any optional else suite is skipped. Similarly, if an exception occurs, Python skips the else clause and looks for a suitable exception handler (this is covered in the next section).

enumer-
ate()
129 ☜

Here is a for ... in loop version of the list_find() function, and like the while loop version, it shows the else clause in action:

```
def list_find(lst, target):
    for index, x in enumerate(lst):
```

```
        if x == target:
            break
    else:
        index = -1
    return index
```

As this code snippet implies, the variables created in the for ... in loop's *expression* continue to exist after the loop has terminated. Like all local variables, they cease to exist at the end of their enclosing scope.

Exception Handling

Python indicates errors and exceptional conditions by raising exceptions, although some third-party Python libraries use more old-fashioned techniques, such as "error" return values.

Catching and Raising Exceptions

Exceptions are caught using try ... except blocks, whose general syntax is:

```
try:
    try_suite
except exception_group1 as variable1:
    except_suite1
...
except exception_groupN as variableN:
    except_suiteN
else:
    else_suite
finally:
    finally_suite
```

There must be at least one except block, but both the else and the finally blocks are optional. The else block's suite is executed when the try block's suite has finished normally—but it is not executed if an exception occurs. If there is a finally block, it is always executed at the end.

Each except clause's exception group can be a single exception or a parenthesized tuple of exceptions. For each group, the as *variable* part is optional; if used, the variable contains the exception that occurred, and can be accessed in the exception block's suite.

If an exception occurs in the try block's suite, each except clause is tried in turn. If the exception matches an exception group, the corresponding suite is executed. To match an exception group, the exception must be of the same type as the (or one of the) exception types listed in the group, or the same type as the (or one of the) group's exception types' subclasses.★

For example, if a KeyError exception occurs in a dictionary lookup, the first except clause that has an Exception class will match since KeyError is an (indirect) subclass of Exception. If no group lists Exception (as is normally the case), but one did have a LookupError, the KeyError will match, because KeyError is a subclass of LookupError. And if no group lists Exception or LookupError, but one does list KeyError, then that group will match. Figure 4.1 shows an extract from the exception hierarchy.

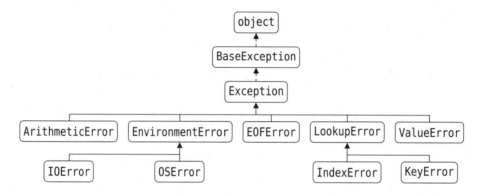

Figure 4.1 *Some of Python's exception hierarchy*

Here is an example of an *incorrect* use:

```
try:
    x = d[5]
except LookupError:    # WRONG ORDER
    print("Lookup error occurred")
except KeyError:
    print("Invalid key used")
```

If dictionary d has no item with key 5, we want the most specific exception, KeyError, to be raised, rather than the more general LookupError exception. But here, the KeyError except block will never be reached. If a KeyError is raised, the LookupError except block will match it because LookupError is a base class of KeyError, that is, LookupError appears higher than KeyError in the exception hierarchy. So when we use multiple except blocks, we must always order

★ As we will see in Chapter 6, in object-oriented programming it is common to have a class hierarchy, that is, one class—data type—inheriting from another. In Python, the start of this hierarchy is the object class; every other class inherits from this class, or from another class that inherits from it. A subclass is a class that inherits from another class, so all Python classes (except object) are subclasses since they all inherit object.

them from most specific (lowest in the hierarchy) to least specific (highest in the hierarchy).

```
try:
    x = d[k / n]
except Exception:    # BAD PRACTICE
    print("Something happened")
```

Note that it is usually bad practice to use `except Exception` since this will catch all exceptions and could easily mask logical errors in our code. In this example, we might have intended to catch `KeyErrors`, but if `n` is `0`, we will unintentionally—and silently—catch a `ZeroDivisionError` exception.

It is also possible to write `except:`, that is, to have no exception group at all. An except block like this will catch any exception, including those that inherit `BaseException` but not `Exception` (these are not shown in Figure 4.1). This has the same problems as using `except Exception`, only worse, and should never normally be done.

If none of the except blocks matches the exception, Python will work its way up the call stack looking for a suitable exception handler. If none is found the program will terminate and print the exception and a traceback on the console.

If no exceptions occur, any optional `else` block is executed. And in all cases—that is, if no exceptions occur, if an exception occurs and is handled, or if an exception occurs that is passed up the call stack—any `finally` block's suite is *always* executed. If no exception occurs, or if an exception occurs and is handled by one of the except blocks, the `finally` block's suite is executed at the end; but if an exception occurs that doesn't match, first the `finally` block's suite is executed, and then the exception is passed up the call stack. This guarantee of execution can be very useful when we want to ensure that resources are properly released. Figure 4.2 illustrates the general `try ... except ... finally` block control flows.

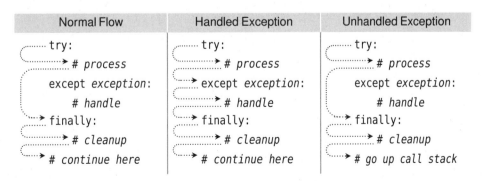

Normal Flow	Handled Exception	Unhandled Exception
`try:`	`try:`	`try:`
`# process`	`# process`	`# process`
`except exception:`	`except exception:`	`except exception:`
`# handle`	`# handle`	`# handle`
`finally:`	`finally:`	`finally:`
`# cleanup`	`# cleanup`	`# cleanup`
`# continue here`	`# continue here`	`# go up call stack`

Figure 4.2 *Try ... except ... finally control flows*

Here is a final version of the list_find() function, this time using exception-handling:

```
def list_find(lst, target):
    try:
        index = lst.index(target)
    except ValueError:
        index = -1
    return index
```

Here, we have effectively used the try ... except block to turn an exception into a return value; the same approach can also be used to catch one kind of exception and raise another instead—a technique we will see shortly.

Python also offers a simpler try ... finally block which is sometimes useful:

```
try:
    try_suite
finally:
    finally_suite
```

No matter what happens in the try block's suite (apart from the computer or program crashing!), the finally block's suite will be executed. The with statement used with a context manager (both covered in Chapter 8) can be used to achieve a similar effect to using a try ... finally block.

One common pattern of use for try ... except ... finally blocks is for handling file errors. For example, the noblanks.py program reads a list of filenames on the command line, and for each one produces another file with the same name, but with its extension changed to .nb, and with the same contents except for no blank lines. Here's the program's read_data() function:

```
def read_data(filename):
    lines = []
    fh = None
    try:
        fh = open(filename, encoding="utf8")
        for line in fh:
            if line.strip():
                lines.append(line)
    except (IOError, OSError) as err:
        print(err)
        return []
    finally:
        if fh is not None:
            fh.close()
    return lines
```

We set the file object, fh, to None because it is possible that the open() call will fail, in which case nothing will be assigned to fh (so it will stay as None), and an exception will be raised. If one of the exceptions we have specified occurs (IOError or OSError), after printing the error message we return an empty list. But note that *before* returning, the finally block's suite will be executed, so the file will be safely closed—if it had been successfully opened in the first place.

Notice also that if an encoding error occurs, even though we don't catch the relevant exception (ValueError), the file will still be safely closed. In such cases the finally block's suite is executed and then the exception is passed up the call stack—there is no return value since the function finishes as a result of the unhandled exception. And in this case, since there is no suitable except block to catch encoding error exceptions, the program will terminate and print a traceback.

We could have written the except clause slightly less verbosely:

```
except EnvironmentError as err:
    print(err)
    return []
```

This works because EnvironmentError is the base class for both IOError and OSError.

In Chapter 8 we will show a slightly more compact idiom for ensuring that files are safely closed, that does not require a finally block.

> Context managers
> ☞ 359

Raising Exceptions

Exceptions provide a useful means of changing the flow of control. We can take advantage of this either by using the built-in exceptions, or by creating our own, raising either kind when we want to. There are two syntaxes for raising exceptions:

```
raise exception(args)
raise
```

When the first syntax is used the exception that is specified should be either one of the built-in exceptions, or a custom exception that is derived from Exception. If we give the exception some text as its argument, this text will be output if the exception is printed when it is caught. When the second syntax is used, that is, when no exception is specified, raise will reraise the currently active exception—and if there isn't one it will raise a TypeError.

Custom Exceptions

Custom exceptions are custom data types (classes). Creating classes is covered in Chapter 6, but since it is easy to create simple custom exception types, we will show the syntax here:

```
class exceptionName(baseException): pass
```

The base class should be Exception or a class that inherits from Exception.

One use of custom exceptions is to break out of deeply nested loops. For example, if we have a table object that holds records (rows), which hold fields (columns), which have multiple values (items), we could search for a particular value with code like this:

```
found = False
for row, record in enumerate(table):
    for column, field in enumerate(record):
        for index, item in enumerate(field):
            if item == target:
                found = True
                break
        if found:
            break
    if found:
        break
if found:
    print("found at ({0}, {1}, {2})".format(row, column, index))
else:
    print("not found")
```

The 15 lines of code are complicated by the fact that we must break out of each loop separately. An alternative solution is to use a custom exception:

```
class FoundException(Exception): pass

try:
    for row, record in enumerate(table):
        for column, field in enumerate(record):
            for index, item in enumerate(field):
                if item == target:
                    raise FoundException()
except FoundException:
    print("found at ({0}, {1}, {2})".format(row, column, index))
else:
    print("not found")
```

This cuts the code down to ten lines, or 11 including defining the exception, and is much easier to read. If the item is found we raise our custom exception and the except block's suite is executed—and the else block is skipped. And if the item is not found, no exception is raised and so the else suite is executed at the end.

Let's look at another example to see some of the different ways that exception-handling can be done. All of the snippets are taken from the checktags.py program, a program that reads all the HTML files it is given on the command line and performs some simple tests to verify that tags begin with "<" and end with ">", and that entities are correctly formed. The program defines four custom exceptions:

```
class InvalidEntityError(Exception): pass
class InvalidNumericEntityError(InvalidEntityError): pass
class InvalidAlphaEntityError(InvalidEntityError): pass
class InvalidTagContentError(Exception): pass
```

The second and third exceptions inherit from the first; we will see why this is useful when we discuss the code that uses the exceptions. The parse() function that uses the exceptions is more than 70 lines long, so we will show only those parts that are relevant to exception-handling.

```
fh = None
try:
    fh = open(filename, encoding="utf8")
    errors = False
    for lino, line in enumerate(fh, start=1):
        for column, c in enumerate(line, start=1):
            try:
```

The code begins conventionally enough, setting the file object to None and putting all the file handling in a try block. The program reads the file line by line and reads each line character by character.

Notice that we have two try blocks; the outer one is used to handle file object exceptions, and the inner one is used to handle parsing exceptions.

```
        ...
        elif state == PARSING_ENTITY:
            if c == ";":
                if entity.startswith("#"):
                    if frozenset(entity[1:]) - HEXDIGITS:
                        raise InvalidNumericEntityError()
                elif not entity.isalpha():
                    raise InvalidAlphaEntityError()
            ...
```

The function has various states, for example, after reading an ampersand (&), it enters the PARSING_ENTITY state, and stores the characters between (but excluding) the ampersand and semicolon in the entity string.

The part of the code shown here handles the case when a semicolon has been found while reading an entity. If the entity is numeric (of the form "&#", with hexadecimal digits, and then ";", for example, "&#20AC;"), we convert the numeric part of it into a set and take away from the set all the hexadecimal digits; if anything is left at least one invalid character was present and we raise a custom exception. If the entity is alphabetic (of the form "&", with letters, and then";", for example, "©"), we raise a custom exception if any of its letters is not alphabetic.

set type
112 ✎

```
    ...
    except (InvalidEntityError,
            InvalidTagContentError) as err:
        if isinstance(err, InvalidNumericEntityError):
            error = "invalid numeric entity"
        elif isinstance(err, InvalidAlphaEntityError):
            error = "invalid alphabetic entity"


        elif isinstance(err, InvalidTagContentError):
            error = "invalid tag"
        print("ERROR {0} in {1} on line {2} column {3}"
                .format(error, filename, lino, column))
        if skip_on_first_error:
            raise
    ...
```

If a parsing exception is raised we catch it in this except block. By using the InvalidEntityError base class, we catch both InvalidNumericEntityError and InvalidAlphaEntityError exceptions. We then use isinstance() to check which type of exception occurred, and to set the error message accordingly. The built-in isinstance() function returns True if its first argument is the same type as the type (or one of that type's base types) given as its second argument.

isin-
stance()
☞ 232

We could have used a separate except block for each of the three custom parsing exceptions, but in this case combining them means that we avoided repeating the last four lines (from the print() call to raise), in each one.

The program has two modes of use. If skip_on_first_error is False, the program continues checking a file even after a parsing error has occurred; this can lead to multiple error messages being output for each file. If skip_on_first_error is True, once a parsing error has occurred, after the (one and only) error message is printed, raise is called to reraise the parsing exception and the outer (per-file) try block is left to catch it.

```
        ...
        elif state == PARSING_ENTITY:
            raise EOFError("missing ';' at end of " + filename)
        ...
```

At the end of parsing a file, we need to check to see whether we have been left in the middle of an entity. If we have, we raise an EOFError, the built-in end-of-file exception, but give it our own message text. We could just as easily have raised a custom exception.

```
    except (InvalidEntityError, InvalidTagContentError):
        pass # Already handled
    except EOFError as err:
        print("ERROR unexpected EOF:", err)
    except EnvironmentError as err:
        print(err)
    finally:
        if fh is not None:
            fh.close()
```

For the outer try block we have used separate except blocks since the behavior we want varies. If we have a parsing exception, we know that an error message has already been output and the purpose is simply to break out of reading the file and to move on to the next file, so we don't need to do anything in the exception handler. If we get an EOFError it could be caused by a genuine premature end of file or it could be the result of us raising the exception ourselves. In either case, we print an error message, and the exception's text. If an EnvironmentError occurs (i.e., if an IOError or an OSError occurs), we simply print its message. And finally, no matter what, if the file was opened, we close it.

Custom Functions

Functions are a means by which we can package up and parameterize functionality. Four kinds of functions can be created in Python: global functions, local functions, lambda functions, and methods.

Every function we have created so far has been a *global* function. Global objects (including functions) are accessible to any code in the same module (i.e., the same .py file) in which the object is created. Global objects can also be accessed from other modules, as we will see in the next chapter.

Local functions (also called nested functions) are functions that are defined inside other functions. These functions are visible only to the function where they are defined; they are especially useful for creating small helper functions that have no use elsewhere. We first show them in Chapter 7.

Online Documentation

Although this book provides solid coverage of the Python 3 language and the built-in functions and most commonly used modules in the standard library, Python's online documentation provides a considerable amount of reference documentation, both on the language, and particularly on Python's extensive standard library. The documentation is available online at docs.python.org and is also provided with Python itself.

On Windows the documentation is supplied in the Windows help file format. Click Start→All Programs→Python 3.x→Python Manuals to launch the Windows help browser. This tool has both an Index and a Search function that makes finding documentation easy. Unix users have the documentation in HTML format. In addition to the hyperlinks, there are various index pages. There is also a very convenient Quick Search function available on the left-hand side of each page.

The most frequently used online document for new users is the Library Reference, and for experienced users the Global Module Index. Both of these have links to pages covering Python's entire standard library—and in the case of the Library Reference, links to pages covering all of Python's built-in functionality as well.

It is well worth skimming through the documentation, particularly the Library Reference or the Global Module Index, to see what Python's standard library offers, and clicking through to the documentation of whichever topics are of interest. This should provide an initial impression of what is available and should also help you to establish a mental picture of where you can find the documentation you are interested in. (A brief summary of Python's standard library is provided in Chapter 5.)

Help is also available from the interpreter itself. If you call the built-in help() function with no arguments, you will enter the online help system—simply follow the instructions to get the information you want, and type "q" or "quit" to return to the interpreter. If you know what module or data type you want help on, you can call help() with the module or data type as its argument. For example, help(str) provides information on the str data type, including all of its methods, help(dict.update) provides information on the dict collection data type's update() method, and help(os) displays information about the os module (providing it has been imported).

Once familiar with Python, it is often sufficient to just be reminded about what attributes (e.g., what methods) a data type provides. This information is available using the dir() function—for example, dir(str) lists all the string methods, and dir(os) lists all the os module's constants and functions (again, providing the module has been imported).

Lambda functions are expressions, so they can be created at their point of use; however, they are much more limited than normal functions.

Methods are functions that are associated with a particular data type and can be used only in conjunction with the data type—they are introduced in Chapter 6 when we cover object-oriented programming.

Python provides many built-in functions, and the standard library and third-party libraries add hundreds more (thousands if we count all the methods), so in many cases the function we want has already been written. For this reason, it is always worth checking Python's online documentation to see what is already available. See the "Online Documentation" sidebar.

The general syntax for creating a (global or local) function is:

```
def functionName(parameters):
    suite
```

The parameters are optional, and if there is more than one they are written as a sequence of comma-separated identifiers, or as a sequence of *identifier=value* pairs as we will discuss shortly. For example, here is a function that calculates the area of a triangle using Heron's formula:

```
def heron(a, b, c):
    s = (a + b + c) / 2
    return math.sqrt(s * (s - a) * (s - b) * (s - c))
```

Inside the function, each parameter, a, b, and c, is initialized with the corresponding value that was passed as an argument. When the function is called, we must supply all of the arguments, for example, heron(3, 4, 5). If we give too few or too many arguments, a TypeError exception will be raised. When we do a call like this we are said to be using *positional arguments*, because each argument passed is set as the value of the parameter in the corresponding position. So in this case, a is set to 3, b to 4, and c to 5, when the function is called.

Every function in Python returns a value, although it is perfectly acceptable (and common) to ignore the return value. The return value is either a single value or a tuple of values, and the values returned can be collections, so there are no practical limitations on what we can return. We can leave a function at any point by using the return statement. If we use return with no arguments, or if we don't have a return statement at all, the function will return None. (In Chapter 6 we will cover the yield statement which can be used instead of return in certain kinds of functions.)

Some functions have parameters for which there can be a sensible default. For example, here is a function that counts the letters in a string, defaulting to the ASCII letters:

```
def letter_count(text, letters=string.ascii_letters):
    letters = frozenset(letters)
    count = 0
    for char in text:
        if char in letters:
            count += 1
    return count
```

We have specified a default value for the letters parameter by using the *parameter=default* syntax. This allows us to call letter_count() with just one argument, for example, letter_count("Maggie and Hopey"). Here, inside the function, letters will be the string that was given as the default value. But we can still change the default, for example, using an extra positional argument, letter_count("Maggie and Hopey", "aeiouAEIOU"), or using a keyword argument (covered next), letter_count("Maggie and Hopey", letters="aeiouAEIOU").

The parameter syntax does not permit us to follow parameters with default values with parameters that don't have defaults, so def bad(a, b=1, c): won't work. On the other hand, we are not forced to pass our arguments in the order they appear in the function's definition—instead, we can use *keyword arguments*, passing each argument in the form *name=value*.

Here is a tiny function that returns the string it is given, or if it is longer than the specified length, it returns a shortened version with an indicator added:

```
def shorten(text, length=25, indicator="..."):
    if len(text) > length:
        text = text[:length - len(indicator)] + indicator
    return text
```

Here are a few example calls:

```
shorten("The Road")                          # returns: 'The Road'
shorten(length=7, text="The Road")           # returns: 'The ...'
shorten("The Road", indicator="&", length=7) # returns: 'The Ro&'
shorten("The Road", 7, "&")                   # returns: 'The Ro&'
```

Because both length and indicator have default values, either or both can be omitted entirely, in which case the default is used—this is what happens in the first call. In the second call we use keyword arguments for both of the specified parameters, so we can order them as we like. The third call mixes both positional and keyword arguments. We used a positional first argument (positional arguments must always precede keyword arguments), and then two keyword arguments. The fourth call simply uses positional arguments.

The difference between a mandatory parameter and an optional parameter is that a parameter with a default is optional (because Python can use the default), and a parameter with no default is mandatory (because Python can-

Read-
ing and
writing
text files
sidebar

122 ☞

not guess). The careful use of default values can simplify our code and make calls much cleaner. Recall that the built-in `open()` function has one mandatory argument (filename), and six optional arguments. By using a mixture of positional and keyword arguments we are able to specify those arguments we care about, while omitting the others. This leaves us free to write things like `open(filename, encoding="utf8")`, rather than being forced to supply every argument like this: `open(filename, "r", None, "utf8", None, None, True)`. Another benefit of using keyword arguments is that they make function calls much more readable, particularly for Boolean arguments.

When default values are given they are created at the time the `def` statement is executed (i.e., when the function is created), *not* when the function is called. For immutable arguments like numbers and strings this doesn't make any difference, but for mutable arguments a subtle trap is lurking.

```
def append_if_even(x, lst=[]):  # WRONG!
    if x % 2 == 0:
        lst.append(x)
    return lst
```

When this function is created the `lst` parameter is set to refer to a new list. And whenever this function is called with just the first parameter, the default list will be the one that was created at the same time as the function itself—so no new list is created. Normally, this is not the behavior we want—we expect a new empty list to be created each time the function is called with no second argument. Here is a new version of the function, this time using the correct idiom for default mutable arguments:

```
def append_if_even(x, lst=None):
    if lst is None:
        lst = []
    if x % 2 == 0:
        lst.append(x)
    return lst
```

Here we create a new list every time the function is called without a list argument. And if a list argument is given, we use it, just the same as the previous version of the function. This idiom of having a default of `None` and creating a fresh object should be used for dictionaries, lists, sets, and any other mutable data types that we want to use as default arguments. Here is a slightly shorter version of the function which has exactly the same behavior:

```
def append_if_even(x, lst=None):
    lst = [] if lst is None else lst
    if x % 2 == 0:
        lst.append(x)
    return lst
```

Using a conditional expression we can save a line of code for each parameter that has a mutable default argument.

Names and Docstrings

Using good names for a function and its parameters goes a long way toward making the purpose and use of the function clear to other programmers—and to ourselves some time after we have created the function. Here are a few rules of thumb that you might like to consider.

- Use a naming scheme, and use it consistently. In this book we use *UP-PERCASE* for constants, *TitleCase* for classes (including exceptions), *camel-Case* for GUI (Graphical User Interface) functions and methods (covered in Chapter 13), and *lowercase* or *lowercase_with_underscores* for everything else.

- For all names, avoid abbreviations, unless they are both standardized and widely used.

- Be proportional with variable and parameter names: x is a perfectly good name for an *x*-coordinate and i is fine for a loop counter, but in general the name should be long enough to be descriptive. The name should describe the data's meaning rather than its type (e.g., *amount_due* rather than *money*), unless the use is generic to a particular type—see, for example, the text parameter in the shorten() example (page 167).

- Functions and methods should have names that say what they *do* or what they *return* (depending on their emphasis), but never how they do it—since that might change.

Here are a few naming examples:

```
def find(l, s, i=0):                            # BAD
def linear_search(l, s, i=0):                   # BAD
def first_index_of(sorted_name_list, name, start=0):  # GOOD
```

All three functions return the index position of the first occurrence of a name in a list of names, starting from the given starting index and using an algorithm that assumes the list is already sorted.

The first one is bad because the name gives no clue as to what will be found, and its parameters (presumably) indicate the required types (list, string, integer) without indicating what they mean. The second one is bad because the function name describes the algorithm originally used—it might have been changed since. This may not matter to users of the function, but it will probably confuse maintainers if the name implies a linear search, but the algorithm implemented has been changed to a binary search. The third one is good because the function name says what is returned, and the parameter names clearly indicate what is expected.

None of the functions have any way of indicating what happens if the name isn't found—do they return, say, -1, or do they raise an exception? Somehow such information needs to be documented for users of the function.

We can add documentation to any function by using a *docstring*—this is simply a string that comes immediately after the def line, and before the function's code proper begins. For example, here is the shorten() function we saw earlier, but this time reproduced in full:

```
def shorten(text, length=25, indicator="..."):
    """Returns text or a truncated copy with the indicator added

    text is any string; length is the maximum length of the returned
    string (including any indicator); indicator is the string added at
    the end to indicate that the text has been shortened

    >>> shorten("The Road")
    'The Road'
    >>> shorten("No Country for Old Men", 20)
    'No Country for Ol...'
    >>> shorten("Cities of the Plain", 15, "*")
    'Cities of the *'
    """
    if len(text) > length:
        text = text[:length - len(indicator)] + indicator
    return text
```

It is not unusual for a function's documentation to be longer than the function itself. One convention is to make the first line of the docstring a brief one-line description, then have a blank line followed by a full description, and then to reproduce some examples as they would appear if typed in interactively. In Chapter 5 we will see how examples in function documentation can be used to provide unit tests.

Argument and Parameter Unpacking

Sequence unpacking

105 ☞

We saw in the previous chapter that we can use the sequence unpacking operator (*) to supply positional arguments. For example, if we wanted to compute the area of a triangle and had the lengths of the sides in a list, we could make the call like this, heron(sides[0], sides[1], sides[2]), or simply unpack the list and do the much simpler call, heron(*sides). And if the list (or other sequence) has more items than the function has parameters, we can use slicing to extract exactly the right number of arguments.

We can also use the sequence unpacking operator in a function's parameter list. This is useful when we want to create functions that can take a variable number of positional arguments. Here is a product() function that computes the product of the arguments it is given:

```
def product(*args):
    result = 1
    for arg in args:
        result *= arg
    return result
```

This function has one parameter called args. Having the * in front means that inside the function the args parameter will be a tuple with its items set to however many positional arguments are given. Here are a few example calls:

```
product(1, 2, 3, 4)     # args == (1, 2, 3, 4); returns: 24
product(5, 3, 8)        # args == (5, 3, 8); returns: 120
product(11)             # args == (11,); returns: 11
```

We can have keyword arguments following positional arguments, as this function to calculate the sum of its arguments, each raised to the given power, shows:

```
def sum_of_powers(*args, power=1):
    result = 0
    for arg in args:
        result += arg ** power
    return result
```

The function can be called with just positional arguments, for example, sum_of_powers(1, 3, 5), or with both positional and keyword arguments, for example, sum_of_powers(1, 3, 5, power=2).

It is also possible to use * as a "parameter" in its own right. This is used to signify that there can be no positional arguments after the *, although keyword arguments are allowed. Here is a modified version of the heron() function. This time the function takes exactly three positional arguments, and has one optional keyword argument.

```
def heron2(a, b, c, *, units="meters"):
    s = (a + b + c) / 2
    area = math.sqrt(s * (s - a) * (s - b) * (s - c))
    return "{0} {1}".format(area, units)
```

Here are a few example calls:

```
heron2(25, 24, 7)                 # returns: '84.0 meters'
heron2(41, 9, 40, units="inches") # returns: '180.0 inches'
```

```
    heron2(25, 24, 7, "inches")        # WRONG! raises TypeError
```

In the third call we have attempted to pass a fourth positional argument, but the * does not allow this and causes a TypeError to be raised.

By making the * the first parameter we can prevent *any* positional arguments from being used, and force callers to use keyword arguments. Here is such a (fictitious) function's signature:

```
    def print_setup(*, paper="Letter", copies=1, color=False):
```

We can call print_setup() with no arguments, and accept the defaults. Or we can change some or all of the defaults, for example, print_setup(paper="A4", color=True). But if we attempt to use positional arguments, for example, print_setup("A4"), a TypeError will be raised.

Just as we can unpack a sequence to populate a function's positional arguments, we can also unpack a mapping using the mapping unpacking operator, asterisk asterisk (**).* We can use ** to pass a dictionary to the print_setup() function. For example:

```
    options = dict(paper="A4", color=True)
    print_setup(**options)
```

Here the options dictionary's key–value pairs are unpacked with each key's value being assigned to the parameter whose name is the same as the key. If the dictionary contains a key for which there is no corresponding parameter, a TypeError is raised. Any argument for which the dictionary has no corresponding item is set to its default value—but if there is no default, a TypeError is raised.

We can also use the mapping unpacking operator with parameters. This allows us to create functions that will accept as many keyword arguments as are given. Here is an add_person_details() function that takes Social Security number and surname positional arguments, and any number of keyword arguments:

```
    def add_person_details(ssn, surname, **kwargs):
        print("SSN =", ssn)
        print("    surname =", surname)
        for key in sorted(kwargs):
            print("    {0} = {1}".format(key, kwargs[key]))
```

This function could be called with just the two positional arguments, or with additional information, for example, add_person_details(83272171, "Luther", forename="Lexis", age=47). This provides us with a lot of flexibility. And we

---

*As we saw in Chapter 2, when used as a binary operator, ** is the pow() operator.

can of course accept both a variable number of positional arguments and a variable number of keyword arguments:

```
def print_args(*args, **kwargs):
    for i, arg in enumerate(args):
        print("positional argument {0} = {1}".format(i, arg))
    for key in kwargs:
        print("keyword argument {0} = {1}".format(key, kwargs[key]))
```

This function just prints the arguments it is given. It can be called with no arguments, or with any number of positional and keyword arguments.

Accessing Variables in the Global Scope

It is sometimes convenient to have a few global variables that are accessed by various functions in the program. This is usually okay for "constants", but is not a good practice for variables, although for short one-off programs it isn't always unreasonable.

The digit_names.py program takes an optional language ("en" or "fr") and a number on the command line and outputs the names of each of the digits it is given. So if it is invoked with "123" on the command line, it will output "one two three". The program has three global variables:

```
Language = "en"

ENGLISH = {0: "zero", 1: "one", 2: "two", 3: "three", 4: "four",
           5: "five", 6: "six", 7: "seven", 8: "eight", 9: "nine"}
FRENCH = {0: "zéro", 1: "un", 2: "deux", 3: "trois", 4: "quatre",
          5: "cinq", 6: "six", 7: "sept", 8: "huit", 9: "neuf"}
```

We have followed the convention that all uppercase variable names indicate constants, and have set the default language to English. (Python does not provide a direct way to create constants, instead relying on programmers to respect the convention.) Elsewhere in the program we access the Language variable, and use it to choose the appropriate dictionary to use:

```
def print_digits(digits):
    dictionary = ENGLISH if Language == "en" else FRENCH
    for digit in digits:
        print(dictionary[int(digit)], end=" ")
    print()
```

When Python encounters the Language variable in this function it looks in the local (function) scope and doesn't find it. So it then looks in the global (.py file) scope, and finds it there. The end keyword argument used with the first print() call is explained in "The print() Function" sidebar.

The print() Function

The print() function accepts any number of positional arguments, and has three keyword arguments, sep, end, and file. All the keyword arguments have defaults. The sep parameter's default is a space; if two or more positional arguments are given, each is printed with the sep in between, but if there is just one positional argument this parameter does nothing. The end parameter's default is \n, which is why a newline is printed at the end of calls to print(). The file parameter's default is sys.stdout, the standard output stream, which is usually the console.

Any of the keyword arguments can be given the values we want instead of using the defaults. For example, file can be set to a file object that is open for writing or appending, and both sep and end can be set to other strings, including the empty string.

If we need to print several items on the same line, one common pattern is to print the items using print() calls where end is set to a suitable separator, and then at the end to call print() with no arguments, since this just prints a newline. For an example, see the print_digits() function (page 170).

Here is the code from the program's main() function. It changes the Language variable's value if necessary, and calls print_digits() to produce the output.

```
def main():
    if len(sys.argv) == 1 or sys.argv[1] in {"-h", "--help"}:
        print("usage: {0} [en|fr] number".format(sys.argv[0]))
        sys.exit()

    args = sys.argv[1:]
    if args[0] in {"en", "fr"}:
        global Language
        Language = args.pop(0)
    print_digits(args.pop(0))
```

What stands out here is the use of the global statement. This statement is used to tell Python that a variable exists at the global (file) scope, and that assignments to the variable should be applied to the global variable, rather than cause a local variable of the same name to be created.

If we did not use the global statement the program would run, but when Python encountered the Language variable in the if statement it would look for it in the local (function) scope, and not finding it would create a new local variable called Language, leaving the global Language unchanged. This subtle bug would show up as an error only when the program was run with the "fr" argument, because then the local Language variable would be created and set to "fr", but the global Language variable used in the print_digits() function would remain unchanged as "en".

For nontrivial programs it is best not to use global variables except as constants, in which case there is no need to use the global statement.

Lambda Functions

Lambda functions are functions created using the following syntax:

```
lambda parameters: expression
```

The *parameters* are optional, and if supplied they are normally just comma-separated variable names, that is, positional arguments, although the complete argument syntax supported by def statements can be used. The *expression* cannot contain branches or loops (although conditional expressions are allowed), and cannot have a return (or yield) statement. The result of a lambda expression is an anonymous function. When a lambda function is called it returns the result of computing the *expression* as its result. If the *expression* is a tuple it should be enclosed in parentheses.

Generator functions ☞ 268

Here is a simple lambda function for adding an *s* (or not) depending on whether its argument is 1:

```
s = lambda x: "" if x == 1 else "s"
```

The lambda expression returns an anonymous function which we assign to the variable s. Any (callable) variable can be called using parentheses, so given the count of files processed in some operation we could output a message using the s() function like this: print("{0} file{1} processed".format(count, s(count))).

Lambda functions are often used as the key function for the built-in sorted() function and for the list.sort() method. Suppose we have a list of elements as 3-tuples of (group, number, name), and we wanted to sort this list in various ways. Here is an example of such a list:

```
elements = [(2, 12, "Mg"), (1, 11, "Na"), (1, 3, "Li"), (2, 4, "Be")]
```

If we sort this list, we get this result:

```
[(1, 3, 'Li'), (1, 11, 'Na'), (2, 4, 'Be'), (2, 12, 'Mg')]
```

sorted() 130, 134 ☞

We saw earlier when we covered the sorted() function that we can provide a key function to alter the sort order. For example, if we wanted to sort the list by number and name, rather than the natural ordering of group, number, and name, we could write a tiny function, def ignore0(e): return e[1], e[2], which could be provided as the key function. Creating lots of little functions like this can be inconvenient, so a frequently used alternative is a lambda function:

```
elements.sort(key=lambda e: (e[1], e[2]))
```

Here the key function is `lambda e: (e[1], e[2])` with e being each 3-tuple element in the list. The parentheses around the `lambda` expression are required when the expression is a tuple and the lambda function is created as a function's argument. We could use slicing to achieve the same effect:

```
elements.sort(key=lambda e: e[1:3])
```

A slightly more elaborate version gives us sorting in case-insensitive name, number order:

```
elements.sort(key=lambda e: (e[2].lower(), e[1]))
```

Here are two equivalent ways to create a function that calculates the area of a triangle using the conventional $\frac{1}{2} \times base \times height$ formula:

```
area = lambda b, h: 0.5 * b * h
```
```
def area(b, h):
    return 0.5 * b * h
```

We can call `area(6, 5)`, whether we created the function using a `lambda` expression or using a `def` statement, and the result will be the same.

Another neat use of lambda functions is when we want to create default dictionaries. Recall from the previous chapter that if we access a default dictionary using a nonexistent key, a suitable item is created with the given key and with a default value. Here are a few examples:

Default dictionaries

126 ☜

```
minus_one_dict = collections.defaultdict(lambda: -1)
point_zero_dict = collections.defaultdict(lambda: (0, 0))
message_dict = collections.defaultdict(lambda: "No message available")
```

If we access the `minus_one_dict` with a nonexistent key, a new item will be created with the given key and with a value of -1. Similarly for the `point_zero_dict` where the value will be the tuple `(0, 0)`, and for the `message_dict` where the value will be the "No message available" string.

Assertions

What happens if a function receives arguments with invalid data? What happens if we make a mistake in the implementation of an algorithm and perform an incorrect computation? The *worst* thing that can happen is that the program executes without any (apparent) problem and no one is any the wiser. One way to help avoid such insidious problems is to write tests—something we will briefly look at in Chapter 5. Another way is to state the preconditions and postconditions and to indicate an error if any of these are not met. Ideally, we should use tests and also state preconditions and postconditions.

Preconditions and postconditions can be specified using `assert` statements, which have the syntax:

```
assert boolean_expression, optional_expression
```

If the *boolean_expression* evaluates to `False` an `AssertionError` exception is raised. If the optional *optional_expression* is given, it is used as the argument to the `AssertionError` exception—this is useful for providing error messages. Note, though, that assertions are designed for developers, not end-users. Problems that occur in normal program use such as missing files or invalid command-line arguments should be handled by other means, such as providing an error or log message.

Here are two new versions of the `product()` function. Both versions are equivalent in that they *require* that all the arguments passed to them are nonzero, and consider a call with a 0 argument to be a coding error.

```
def product(*args): # pessimistic          def product(*args): # optimistic
    assert all(args), "0 argument"              result = 1
    result = 1                                  for arg in args:
    for arg in args:                                result *= arg
        result *= arg                           assert result, "0 argument"
    return result                               return result
```

The "pessimistic" version on the left checks all the arguments (or up to the first 0 argument) on every call. The "optimistic" version on the right just checks the result; after all, if any argument was 0, then the result will be 0.

If one of these `product()` functions is called with a 0 argument an Assertion-Error exception will be raised, and output similar to the following will be written to the error stream (`sys.stderr`, usually the console):

```
Traceback (most recent call last):
  File "program.py", line 456, in <module>
    x = product(1, 2, 0, 4, 8)
  File "program.py", line 452, in product
    assert result, "0 argument"
AssertionError: 0 argument
```

Python automatically provides a traceback that gives the filename, function, and line number, as well as the error message we specified.

Once a program is ready for public release (and of course passes all its tests and does not violate any assertions), what do we do about the `assert` statements? We can tell Python not to execute `assert` statements—in effect, to throw them away at runtime. This can be done by running the program at the command line with the `-O` option, for example, `python -O program.py`. Another approach is to set the `PYTHONOPTIMIZE` environment variable to `0`. If the docstrings are of no use to our users (and normally they wouldn't be), we can use the -OO option which in effect strips out both `assert` statements and docstrings: Note that there is no environment variable for setting this option. Some developers take a simpler approach: They produce a copy of their program with all `assert` statements commented out, and providing this passes their tests, they release the assertion-free version.

Example: make_html_skeleton.py

In this section we draw together some of the techniques covered in this chapter and show them in the context of a complete example program.

Very small Web sites are often created and maintained by hand. One way to make this slightly more convenient is to have a program that can generate skeleton HTML files that can later be fleshed out with content. The make_html_skeleton.py program is an interactive program that prompts the user for various details and then creates a skeleton HTML file. The program's main() function has a loop so that users can create skeleton after skeleton, and it retains common data (e.g., copyright information) so that users don't have to type it in more than once. Here is a transcript of a typical interaction:

```
make_html_skeleton.py

Make HTML Skeleton

Enter your name (for copyright): Harold Pinter
Enter copyright year [2008]: 2009
Enter filename: career-synopsis
Enter title: Career Synopsis
Enter description (optional): synopsis of the career of Harold Pinter
Enter a keyword (optional): playwright
Enter a keyword (optional): actor
Enter a keyword (optional): activist
Enter a keyword (optional):
Enter the stylesheet filename (optional): style
Saved skeleton career-synopsis.html

Create another (y/n)? [y]:

Make HTML Skeleton

Enter your name (for copyright) [Harold Pinter]:
Enter copyright year [2009]:
Enter filename:
Cancelled

Create another (y/n)? [y]: n
```

Notice that for the second skeleton the name and year had as their defaults the values entered previously, so they did not need to be retyped. But no default for the filename is provided, so when that was not given the skeleton was cancelled.

Now that we have seen how the program is used, we are ready to study the code. The program begins with two imports:

```
import datetime
import xml.sax.saxutils
```

The datetime module provides some simple functions for creating date-time.date and datetime.time objects. The xml.sax.saxutils module has a useful xml.sax.saxutils.escape() function that takes a string and returns an equivalent string with the special HTML characters ("&", "<", and ">") in their escaped forms ("&", "<", and ">").

Three global strings are defined; these are used as templates.

```
COPYRIGHT_TEMPLATE = "Copyright (c) {0} {1}. All rights reserved."

STYLESHEET_TEMPLATE = ('<link rel="stylesheet" type="text/css" '
                       'media="all" href="{0}" />\n')

HTML_TEMPLATE = """<?xml version="1.0"?>
<!DOCTYPE html PUBLIC "-//W3C//DTD XHTML 1.0 Strict//EN" \
"http://www.w3.org/TR/xhtml1/DTD/xhtml1-strict.dtd">
<html xmlns="http://www.w3.org/1999/xhtml" lang="en" xml:lang="en">
<head>
<title>{title}</title>
<!-- {copyright} -->
<meta name="Description" content="{description}" />
<meta name="Keywords" content="{keywords}" />
<meta equiv="content-type" content="text/html; charset=utf-8" />
{stylesheet}\
</head>
<body>

</body>
</html>
"""
```

str. format() 74 ☜☜

These strings will be used as templates in conjunction with the str.format() method. In the case of HTML_TEMPLATE we have used names rather than index positions for the field names, for example, {title}. We will see shortly that we must use keyword arguments to provide values for these.

```
class CancelledError(Exception): pass
```

One custom exception is defined; we will see it in use when we look at a couple of the program's functions.

The program's main() function is used to set up some initial information, and to provide a loop. On each iteration the user has the chance to enter some information for the HTML page they want generated, and after each one they are given the chance to finish.

```
def main():
    information = dict(name=None, year=datetime.date.today().year,
                       filename=None, title=None, description=None,
                       keywords=None, stylesheet=None)
    while True:
        try:
            print("\nMake HTML Skeleton\n")
            populate_information(information)
            make_html_skeleton(**information)
        except CancelledError:
            print("Cancelled")
        if (get_string("\nCreate another (y/n)?", default="y").lower()
            not in {"y", "yes"}):
            break
```

The datetime.date.today() function returns a datetime.date object that holds today's date. We want just the year attribute. All the other items of information are set to None since there are no sensible defaults that can be set.

Inside the while loop the program prints a title, then calls the populate_infor-mation() function with the information dictionary. This dictionary is updated inside the populate_information() function. Next, the make_html_skeleton() function is called—this function takes a number of arguments, but rather than give explicit values for each one we have simply unpacked the information dictionary.

If the user cancels, for example, by not providing mandatory information, the program prints out "Cancelled". At the end of each iteration (whether cancelled or not), the user is asked whether they want to create another skeleton—if they don't, we break out of the loop and the program terminates.

```
def populate_information(information):
    name = get_string("Enter your name (for copyright)", "name",
                       information["name"])
    if not name:
        raise CancelledError()
    year = get_integer("Enter copyright year", "year",
                       information["year"], 2000,
                       datetime.date.today().year + 1, True)
```

```
if year == 0:
    raise CancelledError()
filename = get_string("Enter filename", "filename")
if not filename:
    raise CancelledError()
if not filename.endswith((".htm", ".html")):
    filename += ".html"
...
information.update(name=name, year=year, filename=filename,
                   title=title, description=description,
                   keywords=keywords, stylesheet=stylesheet)
```

We have omitted the code for getting the title and description texts, HTML keywords, and the stylesheet file. All of them use the get_string() function that we will look at shortly. It is sufficient to note that this function takes a message prompt, the "name" of the relevant variable (for use in error messages), and an optional default value. Similarly, the get_integer() function takes a message prompt, variable name, default value, minimum and maximum values, and whether 0 is allowed.

At the end we update the information dictionary with the new values using keyword arguments. For each *key=value* pair the *key* is the name of a key in the dictionary whose value will be replaced with the given *value*—and in this case each *value* is a variable with the same name as the corresponding key in the dictionary.

This function has no explicit return value (so it returns None). It may also be terminated if a CancelledError exception is raised, in which case the exception is passed up the call stack to main() and handled there.

We will look at the make_html_skeleton() function in two parts.

```
def make_html_skeleton(year, name, title, description, keywords,
                       stylesheet, filename):
    copyright = COPYRIGHT_TEMPLATE.format(year,
                                xml.sax.saxutils.escape(name))
    title = xml.sax.saxutils.escape(title)
    description = xml.sax.saxutils.escape(description)
    keywords = ",".join([xml.sax.saxutils.escape(k)
                        for k in keywords]) if keywords else ""
    stylesheet = (STYLESHEET_TEMPLATE.format(stylesheet)
                if stylesheet else "")
    html = HTML_TEMPLATE.format(title=title, copyright=copyright,
                                description=description,
                                keywords=keywords,
                                stylesheet=stylesheet)
```

To get the copyright text we call str.format() on the COPYRIGHT_TEMPLATE, supplying the year and name (suitably HTML-escaped) as positional arguments to replace {0} and {1}. For the title and description we produce HTML-escaped copies of their texts.

For the HTML keywords we have two cases to deal with, and we distinguish them using a conditional expression. If no keywords have been entered, we set the keywords string to be the empty using. Otherwise, we use a list comprehension to iterate over all the keywords to produce a new list of strings, with each one being HTML-escaped. This list is then joined into a single string with a comma separating each item using str.join().

The stylesheet text is created in a similar way to the copyright text, but within the context of a conditional expression so that the text is the empty string if no stylesheet is specified.

| str. |
| format() |
| 74 ✍ |

The html text is created from the HTML_TEMPLATE, with keyword arguments used to provide the data for the replacement fields rather than the positional arguments used for the other template strings.

```
fh = None
try:
    fh = open(filename, "w", encoding="utf8")
    fh.write(html)
except EnvironmentError as err:
    print("ERROR", err)
else:
    print("Saved skeleton", filename)
finally:
    if fh is not None:
        fh.close()
```

Once the HTML has been prepared we write it to the file with the given filename. We inform the user that the skeleton has been saved—or of the error message if something went wrong. As usual we use a finally clause to ensure that the file is closed if it was opened.

```
def get_string(message, name="string", default=None,
               minimum_length=0, maximum_length=80):
    message += ": " if default is None else " [{0}]: ".format(default)
    while True:
        try:
            line = input(message)
            if not line:
                if default is not None:
                    return default
                if minimum_length == 0:
```

```
                    return ""
            else:
                raise ValueError("{0} may not be empty".format(
                        name))
        if not (minimum_length <= len(line) <= maximum_length):
            raise ValueError("{0} must have at least {1} and "
                    "at most {2} characters".format(
                    name, minimum_length, maximum_length))
        return line
    except ValueError as err:
        print("ERROR", err)
```

This function has one mandatory argument, message, and four optional arguments. If a default value is given we include it in the message string so that the user can see the default they would get if they just press Enter without typing any text. The rest of the function is enclosed in an infinite loop. The loop can be broken out of by the user entering a valid string—or by accepting the default (if given) by just pressing Enter.

The user could also break out of the loop, and indeed out of the entire program, by typing Ctrl+C—this would cause a KeyboardInterrupt exception to be raised, and since this is not handled by any of the program's exception handlers, would cause the program to terminate and print a traceback. Should we leave such a "loophole"? If we don't, and there is a bug in our program, we could leave the user stuck in an infinite loop with no way out except to kill the process. Unless there is a very strong reason to prevent Ctrl+C from terminating a program, it should not be caught by any exception handler.

Notice that this function is not specific to the make_html_skeleton.py program—it could be reused in many interactive programs of this type. Such reuse could be achieved by copying and pasting, but that would lead to maintenance headaches—in the next chapter we will see how to create custom modules with functionality that can be shared across any number of programs.

```
    def get_integer(message, name="integer", default=None, minimum=0,
            maximum=100, allow_zero=True):
        ...
```

This function is so similar in structure to the get_string() function that it would add nothing to reproduce it here. (It is included in the source code that accompanies the book, of course.) The allow_zero parameter can be useful when 0 is not a valid value but where we want to permit one invalid value to signify that the user has cancelled. Another approach would be to pass an invalid default value, and if that is returned, take it to mean that the user has cancelled.

The last statement in the program is simply a call to main(). Overall the program is slightly more than 150 lines and shows several features of the Python language introduced in this chapter and the previous ones.

Summary

This chapter covered the complete syntax for all of Python's control structures. It also showed how to raise and catch exceptions, and how to create custom exception types.

Most of the chapter was devoted to custom functions. We saw how to create functions and presented some rules of thumb for naming functions and their parameters. We also saw how to provide documentation for functions. Python's versatile parameter syntax and argument passing were covered in detail, including both fixed and variable numbers of positional and keyword arguments, and default values for arguments of both immutable and mutable data types. We also briefly recapped sequence unpacking with * and showed how to do mapping unpacking with **.

If we need to assign a new value to a global variable inside a function, we can do so by declaring that the variable is global, thereby preventing Python from creating a local variable and assigning to that. In general, though, it is best to use global variables only for constants.

Lambda functions are often used as key functions, or in other contexts where functions must be passed as parameters. This chapter showed how to create lambda functions, both as anonymous functions and as a means of creating small named one-line functions by assigning them to a variable.

The chapter also covered the use of the assert statement. This statement is very useful for specifying the preconditions and postconditions that we expect to be true on every use of a function, and can be a real aid to robust programming and bug hunting.

In this chapter we covered all the fundamentals of creating functions, but many other techniques are available to us. These include creating dynamic functions (creating functions at runtime, possibly with implementations that differ depending on circumstances), covered in Chapter 5; local (nested) functions, covered in Chapter 7; and recursive functions, generator functions, and so on, covered in Chapter 8.

Although Python has a considerable amount of built-in functionality, and a very extensive standard library, it is still likely that we will write some functions that would be useful in many of the programs we develop. Copying and pasting such functions would lead to maintenance nightmares, but fortunately Python provides a clean easy-to-use solution: custom modules. In the next chapter we will learn how to create our own modules with our own functions inside them. We will also see how to import functionality from the standard library and from our own modules, and will briefly review what the standard library has to offer so that we can avoid reinventing the wheel.

Exercise

Write an interactive program that maintains lists of strings in files.

When the program is run it should create a list of all the files in the current directory that have the .lst extension. Use os.listdir(".") to get all the files and filter out those that don't have the .lst extension. If there are no matching files the program should prompt the user to enter a filename—adding the .lst extension if the user doesn't enter it. If there are one or more .lst files they should be printed as a numbered list starting from 1. The user should be asked to enter the number of the file they want to load, or 0, in which case they should be asked to give a filename for a new file.

If an existing file was specified its items should be read. If the file is empty, or if a new file was specified, the program should show a message, "no items are in the list".

If there are no items, two options should be offered: "Add" and "Quit". Once the list has one or more items, the list should be shown with each item numbered from 1, and the options offered should be "Add", "Delete", "Save" (unless already saved), and "Quit". If the user chooses "Quit" and there are unsaved changes they should be given the chance to save. Here is a transcript of a session with the program (with most blank lines removed, and without the "List Keeper" title shown above the list each time):

```
Choose filename: movies

-- no items are in the list --
[A]dd  [Q]uit [a]: a
Add item: Love Actually

1: Love Actually
[A]dd  [D]elete  [S]ave  [Q]uit [a]: a
Add item: About a Boy

1: About a Boy
2: Love Actually
[A]dd  [D]elete  [S]ave  [Q]uit [a]:
Add item: Alien

1: About a Boy
2: Alien
3: Love Actually
[A]dd  [D]elete  [S]ave  [Q]uit [a]: k
```

```
ERROR: invalid choice--enter one of 'AaDdSsQq'
Press Enter to continue...
[A]dd  [D]elete  [S]ave  [Q]uit [a]: d
Delete item number (or 0 to cancel): 2

1: About a Boy
2: Love Actually
[A]dd  [D]elete  [S]ave  [Q]uit [a]: s
Saved 2 items to movies.lst
Press Enter to continue...

1: About a Boy
2: Love Actually
[A]dd  [D]elete  [Q]uit [a]:
Add item: Four Weddings and a Funeral

1: About a Boy
2: Four Weddings and a Funeral
3: Love Actually
[A]dd  [D]elete  [S]ave  [Q]uit [a]: q
Save unsaved changes (y/n) [y]:
Saved 3 items to movies.lst
```

Keep the main() function fairly small (less than 30 lines) and use it to provide the program's main loop. Write a function to get the new or existing filename (and in the latter case to load the items), and a function to present the options and get the user's choice of option. Also write functions to add an item, delete an item, print a list (of either items or filenames), load the list, and save the list. Either copy the get_string() and get_integer() functions from make_html_skeleton.py, or write your own versions.

When printing the list or the filenames, print the item numbers using a field width of 1 if there are less than ten items, of 2 if there are less than 100 items, and of 3 otherwise.

Keep the items in case-insensitive alphabetical order, and keep track of whether the list is "dirty" (has unsaved changes). Offer the "Save" option only if the list is dirty and ask the user whether they want to save unsaved changes when they quit only if the list is dirty. Adding or deleting an item will make the list dirty; saving the list will make it clean again.

A model solution is provided in listkeeper.py; it is less than 200 lines of code.

5

- Modules and Packages
- Overview of Python's Standard Library

Modules

Whereas functions allow us to parcel up pieces of code so that they can be reused throughout a program, modules provide a means of collecting sets of functions (and as we will see in the next chapter, custom data types) together so that they can be used by any number of programs. Python also has facilities for creating *packages*—these are sets of modules that are grouped together, usually because their modules provide related functionality or because they depend on each other.

This chapter's first section describes the syntaxes for importing functionality from modules and packages—whether from the standard library, or from our own custom modules and packages. The section then goes on to show how to create custom packages and custom modules. Two custom module examples are shown, the first introductory and the second illustrating how to handle many of the practical issues that arise, such as platform independence and testing.

Online documentation 162

The second section provides a brief overview of Python's standard library. It is important to be aware of what the library has to offer, since using predefined functionality makes programming much faster than creating everything from scratch. Also, many of the standard library's modules are widely used, well tested, and robust. In addition to the overview, a few small examples are used to illustrate some common use cases. And cross-references are provided for modules covered in other chapters.

Modules and Packages

A Python module, simply put, is a .py file. A module can contain any Python code we like. All the programs we have written so far have been contained in a single .py file, and so they are modules as well as programs. The key difference is that programs are designed to be run, whereas modules are designed to be imported and used by programs.

Not all modules have associated .py files—for example, the sys module is built into Python, and some modules are written in other languages (most commonly, C). However, much of Python's library is written in Python, so, for example, if we write import collections we can create named tuples by calling collections.namedtuple(), and the functionality we are accessing is in the collections.py module file. It makes no difference to our programs what language a module is written in, since all modules are imported and used in the same way.

Several syntaxes can be used when importing. For example:

```
import importable
import importable1, importable2, ..., importableN
import importable as preferred_name
```

Here *importable* is usually a module such as collections, but could be a package or a module in a package, in which case each part is separated with a dot (.), for example, os.path. The first two syntaxes are the ones we use throughout this book. They are the simplest and also the safest because they avoid the possibility of having name conflicts, since they force us to always use fully qualified names.

Packages
☞ 189

The third syntax allows us to give a name of our choice to the package or module we are importing—theoretically this could lead to name clashes, but in practice the as syntax is used to avoid them. Renaming is particularly useful when experimenting with different implementations of a module. For example, if we had two modules MyModuleA and MyModuleB that had the same API (Application Programming Interface), we could write import MyModuleA as MyModule in a program, and later on seamlessly switch to using import MyModuleB as MyModule.

Where should import statements go? It is common practice to put all the import statements at the beginning of .py files, after the shebang line, and after the module's documentation. And as we said back in Chapter 1, we recommend importing standard library modules first, then third-party library modules, and finally our own modules.

Here are some other import syntaxes:

```
from importable import object as preferred_name
from importable import object1, object2, ..., objectN
from importable import (object1, object2, object3, object4, object5,
    object6, ..., objectN)
from importable import *
```

These syntaxes can cause name conflicts since they make the imported objects (variables, functions, data types, or modules) directly accessible. If we want to use the from ... import syntax to import lots of objects, we can use multiple lines either by escaping each newline except the last, or by enclosing the object names in parentheses, as the third syntax illustrates.

In the last syntax, the * means "import everything that is not private", which in practical terms means either that every object in the module is imported except for those whose names begin with a leading underscore, or, if the module has a global __all__ variable that holds a list of names, that all the objects named in the __all__ variable are imported.

__all__
☞ 190

Here are a few import examples:

```
import os
print(os.path.basename(filename))     # safe fully qualified access

import os.path as path
print(path.basename(filename))  # risk of name collision with path

from os import path
print(path.basename(filename))  # risk of name collision with path

from os.path import basename
print(basename(filename))    # risk of name collision with basename

from os.path import *
print(basename(filename))              # risk of many name collisions
```

The from *importable* import * syntax imports all the objects from the module (or all the modules from the package)—this could be hundreds of names. In the case of from os.path import *, almost 40 names are imported, including dirname, exists, and split, any of which might be names we would prefer to use for our own variables or functions.

For example, if we write from os.path import dirname, we can conveniently call dirname() without qualification. But if further on in our code we write dirname = ".", the object reference dirname will now be bound to the string "." instead of to the dirname() function, so if we try calling dirname() we will get a TypeError exception because dirname now refers to a string and strings are not callable.

In view of the potential for name collisions the import * syntax creates, some programming teams specify in their guidelines that only the import *importable* syntax may be used. However, certain large packages, particularly GUI (Graphical User Interface) libraries, are often imported this way because they have large numbers of functions and classes (custom data types) that can be tedious to type out by hand.

A question that naturally arises is, how does Python know where to look for the modules and packages that are imported? The built-in sys module has a list called sys.path that holds a list of the directories that constitute the *Python path*. The first directory is the directory that contains the program itself, even if the program was invoked from another directory. If the PYTHONPATH environment variable is set, the paths specified in it are the next ones in the list, and the final paths are those needed to access Python's standard library—these are set when Python is installed.

When we first import a module, if it isn't built-in, Python looks for the module in each path listed in sys.path in turn. One consequence of this is that if we create a module or program with the same name as one of Python's library modules, ours will be found first, inevitably causing problems. To avoid this, never create a program or module with the same name as one of the Python library's top-level directories or modules—unless you are providing your own implementation of that module and are deliberately overriding it. (A top-level module is one whose .py file is in one of the directories in the Python path, rather than in one of those directories' subdirectories.) For example, on Windows the Python path usually includes a directory called C:\Python30\Lib, so on that platform we should not create a module called Lib.py, nor a module with the same name as any of the modules in the C:\Python30\Lib directory.

One quick way to check whether a module name is in use is to try to import the module. This can be done at the console by calling the interpreter with the -c ("execute code") command-line option followed by an import statement. For example, if we want to see whether there is a module called Music.py (or a top-level directory in the Python path called Music), we can type the following at the console:

```
python -c "import Music"
```

If we get an ImportError exception we know that no module or top-level directory of that name is in use; any other output (or none) means that the name is taken. Unfortunately, this does not guarantee that the name will always be okay, since we might later on install a third-party Python package or module that has a conflicting name, although in practice this is a very rare problem.

For example, if we created a module file called os.py, it would conflict with the library's os module. But if we create a module file called path.py, this would be okay since it would be imported as the path module whereas the library module would be imported as os.path. In this book we use an uppercase letter for the first letter of custom module filenames; this avoids name conflicts (at least on Unix) because standard library module filenames are lowercase.

A program might import some modules which in turn import modules of their own, including some that have already been imported. This does not cause any problems. Whenever a module is imported Python first checks to see whether it has already been imported. If it has not, Python executes the module's byte-code compiled code, thereby creating the variables, functions, and other objects it provides, and internally records that the module has been imported.

At every subsequent import of the module Python will detect that the module has already been imported and will do nothing.

When Python needs a module's byte-code compiled code, it generates it automatically—this differs from, say, Java, where compiling to byte code must be done explicitly. First Python looks for a file with the same name as the module's .py file but with the extension .pyo—this is an optimized byte-code compiled version of the module. If there is no .pyo file (or if it is older than the .py file, that is, if it is out of date), Python looks for a file with the extension .pyc—this is a nonoptimized byte-code compiled version of the module. If Python finds an up-to-date byte-code compiled version of the module, it loads it; otherwise, Python loads the .py file and compiles a byte-code compiled version. Either way, Python ends up with the module in memory in byte-code compiled form.

If Python had to byte-compile the .py file, it saves a .pyc version (or .pyo if –O was specified on Python's command line, or is set in the PYTHONOPTIMIZE environment variable), providing the directory is writable. Saving the byte code can be avoided by using the –B command-line option, or by setting the PYTHONDONT-WRITEBYTECODE environment variable.

Using byte-code compiled files leads to faster start-up times since the interpreter only has to load and run the code, rather than load, compile, (save if possible), and run the code; runtimes are not affected, though. When Python is installed, the standard library modules are usually byte-code compiled as part of the installation process.

Packages

A package is simply a directory that contains a set of modules and a file called __init__.py. Suppose, for example, that we had a fictitious set of module files for reading and writing various graphics file formats, such as Bmp.py, Jpeg.py, Png.py, Tiff.py, and Xpm.py, all of which provided the functions load(), save(), and so on.* We could keep the modules in the same directory as our program, but for a large program that uses scores of custom modules the graphics modules will be dispersed. By putting them in their own subdirectory, say, Graphics, they can be kept together. And if we put an empty __init__.py file in the Graphics directory along with them, the directory will become a package:

```
Graphics/
    __init__.py
    Bmp.py
    Jpeg.py
```

---

*Extensive support for handling graphics files is provided by a variety of third-party modules, most notably the Python Imaging Library (www.pythonware.com/products/pil).

```
Png.py
Tiff.py
Xpm.py
```

As long as the Graphics directory is a subdirectory inside our program's directory or is in the Python path, we can import any of these modules and make use of them. We must be careful to ensure that our top-level module name (Graphics) is not the same as any top-level name in the standard library so as to avoid name conflicts. (On Unix this is easily done by starting with an uppercase letter since all of the standard library's modules have lowercase names.) Here's how we can import and use our module:

```
import Graphics.Bmp
image = Graphics.Bmp.load("bashful.bmp")
```

For short programs some programmers prefer to use shorter names, and Python makes this possible using two slightly different approaches.

```
import Graphics.Jpeg as Jpeg
image = Jpeg.load("doc.jpeg")
```

Here we have imported the Jpeg module from the Graphics package and told Python that we want to refer to it simply as Jpeg rather than using its fully qualified name, Graphics.Jpeg.

```
from Graphics import Png
image = Png.load("dopey.png")
```

This code snippet imports the Png module directly from the Graphics package. This syntax (from ... import) makes the Png module directly accessible.

We are not obliged to use the original package names in our code. For example:

```
from Graphics import Tiff as picture
image = picture.load("grumpy.tiff")
```

Here we are using the Tiff module, but have in effect renamed it inside our program as the picture module.

In some situations it is convenient to load in all of a package's modules using a single statement. To do this we must edit the package's __init__.py file to contain a statement which specifies which modules we want loaded. This statement must assign a list of module names to the special variable __all__. For example, here is the necessary line for the Graphics/__init__.py file:

```
__all__ = ["Bmp", "Jpeg", "Png", "Tiff", "Xpm"]
```

That is all that is required, although we are free to put any other code we like in the __init__.py file. Now we can write a different kind of import statement:

```
from Graphics import *
image = Xpm.load("sleepy.xpm")
```

The from *package* import * syntax directly imports all the modules named in the __all__ list. So, after this import, not only is the Xpm module directly accessible, but so are all the others.

As noted earlier, this syntax can also be applied to a module, that is, from *module* import *, in which case all the functions, variables, and other objects defined in the module (apart from those whose names begin with a leading underscore) will be imported. If we want to control exactly what is imported when the from *module* import * syntax is used, we can define an __all__ list in the module itself, in which case doing from *module* import * will import only those objects named in the __all__ list.

So far we have shown only one level of nesting, but Python allows us to nest packages as deeply as we like. So we could have a subdirectory inside the Graphics directory, say, Vector, with module files inside that, such as Eps.py and Svg.py:

```
Graphics/
    __init__.py
    Bmp.py
    Jpeg.py
    Png.py
    Tiff.py
    Vector/
        __init__.py
        Eps.py
        Svg.py
    Xpm.py
```

For the Vector directory to be a package it must have an __init__.py file, and as noted, this can be empty or could have an __all__ list as a convenience for programmers who want to import using from Graphics.Vector import *.

To access a nested package we just build on the syntax we have already used:

```
import Graphics.Vector.Eps
image = Graphics.Vector.Eps.load("sneezy.eps")
```

The fully qualified name is rather long, so some programmers try to keep their module hierarchies fairly flat to avoid this.

```
import Graphics.Vector.Svg as Svg
image = Svg.load("snow.svg")
```

We can always use our own short name for a module, as we have done here, although this does increase the risk of having a name conflict.

Custom Modules

Since modules are just .py files they can be created without formality. In this section we will look at two custom modules. The first module, TextUtil (in file TextUtil.py), contains just three functions: is_balanced() which returns True if the string it is passed has balanced parentheses of various kinds, shorten() (shown earlier, on page 167), and simplify(), a function that can strip spurious whitespace and other characters from a string. In the coverage of this module we will also see how to execute the code in docstrings as unit tests.

The second module, CharGrid (in file CharGrid.py), holds a grid of characters and allows us to "draw" lines, rectangles, and text onto the grid and to render the grid on the console. This module shows some techniques that we have not seen before and is more typical of larger, more complex modules.

The TextUtil Module

The structure of this module (and most others) differs little from that of a program. The first line is the shebang line, and then we have some comments (typically the copyright and license information). Next it is common to have a triple quoted string that provides an overview of the module's contents, often including some usage examples—this is the module's docstring. Here is the start of the TextUtil.py file (but with the license comment lines omitted):

```
#!/usr/bin/env python3
# Copyright (c) 2008 Qtrac Ltd. All rights reserved.
"""
This module provides a few string manipulation functions.

>>> is_balanced("(Python (is (not (lisp)))))")
True
>>> shorten("The Crossing", 10)
'The Cro...'
>>> simplify(" some    text    with  spurious  whitespace  ")
'some text with spurious whitespace'
"""

import string
```

This module's docstring is available to programs (or other modules) that import the module as TextUtil.__doc__. After the module docstring come the imports, in this case just one, and then the rest of the module.

shorten()

167 ☞

We have already seen the shorten() function reproduced in full, so we will not repeat it here. And since our focus is on modules rather than on functions, although we will show the simplify() function in full, including its docstring, we will show only the code for is_balanced().

This is the simplify() function, broken into two parts:

```python
def simplify(text, whitespace=string.whitespace, delete=""):
    r"""Returns the text with multiple spaces reduced to single spaces

    The whitespace parameter is a string of characters, each of which
    is considered to be a space.
    If delete is not empty it should be a string, in which case any
    characters in the delete string are excluded from the resultant
    string.

    >>> simplify(" this     and\n that\t too")
    'this and that too'
    >>> simplify("  Washington   D.C.\n")
    'Washington D.C.'
    >>> simplify("  Washington   D.C.\n", delete=",;:.")
    'Washington DC'
    >>> simplify(" disemvoweled ", delete="aeiou")
    'dsmvwld'
    """
```

After the def line comes the function's docstring, laid out conventionally with a single line description, a blank line, further description, and then some examples written as though they were typed in interactively. Because the quoted strings are inside a docstring we must either escape the backslashes inside them, or do what we have done here and use a raw triple quoted string.

Raw
strings

62 ☞

```python
result = []
word = ""
for char in text:
    if char in delete:
        continue
    elif char in whitespace:
        if word:
            result.append(word)
            word = ""
    else:
        word += char
```

```
    if word:
        result.append(word)
return " ".join(result)
```

The result list is used to hold "words"—strings that have no whitespace or deleted characters. The given text is iterated over character by character, with deleted characters skipped. If a whitespace character is encountered and a word is in the making, the word is added to the result list and set to be an empty string; otherwise, the whitespace is skipped. Any other character is added to the word being built up. At the end a single string is returned consisting of all the words in the result list joined with a single space between each one.

The is_balanced() function follows the same pattern of having a def line, then a docstring with a single-line description, a blank line, further description, and some examples, and then the code itself. Here is the code without the docstring:

```
def is_balanced(text, brackets="()[]{}<>"):
    counts = {}
    left_for_right = {}
    for left, right in zip(brackets[::2], brackets[1::2]):
        assert left != right, "the bracket characters must differ"
        counts[left] = 0
        left_for_right[right] = left
    for c in text:
        if c in counts:
            counts[c] += 1
        elif c in left_for_right:
            left = left_for_right[c]
            if counts[left] == 0:
                return False
            counts[left] -= 1
    return not any(counts.values())
```

The function builds two dictionaries. The counts dictionary's keys are the opening characters ("(", "[", "{", and "<"), and its values are integers. The left_for_right dictionary's keys are the closing characters (")", "]", "}", and ">"), and its values are the corresponding opening characters. Once the dictionaries are set up the function iterates character by character over the text. Whenever an opening character is encountered, its corresponding count is incremented. Similarly, when a closing character is encountered, the function finds out what the corresponding opening character is. If the count for that character is 0 it means we have reached one closing character too many so can immediately return False; otherwise, the relevant count is decremented. At the end every count should be 0 if all the pairs are balanced, so if any one of them is not 0 the function returns False; otherwise, it returns True.

Up to this point everything has been much like any other .py file. If TextUtil.py was a program there would presumably be some more functions, and at the end we would have a single call to one of those functions to start off the processing. But since this is a module that is intended to be imported, defining functions is sufficient. And now, any program or module can import TextUtil and make use of it:

```
import TextUtil

text = "   a    puzzling   conundrum   "
text = TextUtil.simplify(text) # text == 'a puzzling conundrum'
```

If we want the TextUtil module to be available to a particular program, we just need to put TextUtil.py in the same directory as the program. If we want TextUtil.py to be available to all our programs, there are a few approaches that can be taken. One approach is to put the module in the Python distribution's site-packages subdirectory—this is usually C:\Python30\Lib\site-packages on Windows, but it varies on Mac OS X and other Unixes. This directory is in the Python path, so any module that is here will always be found. A second approach is to create a directory specifically for the custom modules we want to use for all our programs, and to set the PYTHONPATH environment variable to this directory. A third approach is to put the module in the *local* site-packages subdirectory—this is %APPDATA%/Python/Python30/site-packages on Windows and ~/.local/lib/python3.0/site-packages on Unix (including Mac OS X) and is in the Python path. The second and third approaches have the advantage of keeping our own code separate from the official installation.

Having the TextUtil module is all very well, but if we end up with lots of programs using it we might want to be more confident that it works as advertised. One really simple way to do this is to execute the examples in the docstrings and make sure that they produce the expected results. This can be done by adding just three lines at the end of the module's .py file:

```
if __name__ == "__main__":
    import doctest
    doctest.testmod()
```

Whenever a module is imported Python creates a variable for the module called __name__ and stores the module's name in this variable. A module's name is simply the name of its .py file but without the extension. So in this example, when the module is imported __name__ will have the value "TextUtil", and the if condition will not be met, so the last two lines will not be executed. This means that these last three lines have virtually no cost when the module is imported.

Whenever a .py file is run Python creates a variable for the program called __name__ and sets it to the string "__main__". So if we were to *run* TextUtil.py as though it were a program, Python will set __name__ to "__main__" and the if condition will evaluate to True and the last two lines will be executed.

The doctest.testmod() function uses Python's introspection features to discover all the functions in the module and their docstrings, and attempts to execute all the docstring code snippets it finds. Running a module like this produces output only if there are errors. This can be disconcerting at first since it doesn't look like anything happened at all, but if we pass a command-line flag of -v, we will get output like this:

```
Trying:
    is_balanced("(Python (is (not (lisp)))")
Expecting:
    True
ok
...
Trying:
    simplify(" disemvoweled ", delete="aeiou")
Expecting:
    'dsmvwld'
ok
4 items passed all tests:
    3 tests in __main__
    5 tests in __main__.is_balanced
    3 tests in __main__.shorten
    4 tests in __main__.simplify
15 tests in 4 items.
15 passed and 0 failed.
Test passed.
```

We have used an ellipsis to indicate a lot of lines that have been omitted. If there are functions (or classes or methods) that don't have tests, these are listed when the -v option is used. Notice that the doctest module found the tests in the module's docstring as well as those in the functions' docstrings.

Examples in docstrings that can be executed as tests are called *doctests*. Note that when we write doctests, we are able to call simplify() and the other functions unqualified (since the doctests occur inside the module itself). Outside the module, assuming we have done import TextUtil, we must use the qualified names, for example, TextUtil.is_balanced().

In the next subsection we will see how to do more thorough tests—in particular, testing cases where we expect failures, for example, invalid data causing exceptions. We will also address some other issues that arise when creating modules, including module initialization, accounting for platform differences, and ensuring that if the from *module* import * syntax is used, only the objects we want to be made public are actually imported into the importing program or module.

The CharGrid Module

The CharGrid module holds a grid of characters in memory. It provides functions for "drawing" lines, rectangles, and text on the grid, and for rendering the grid onto the console. Here are the module's docstring's doctests:

```
>>> resize(14, 50)
>>> add_rectangle(0, 0, *get_size())
>>> add_vertical_line(5, 10, 13)
>>> add_vertical_line(2, 9, 12, "!")
>>> add_horizontal_line(3, 10, 20, "+")
>>> add_rectangle(0, 0, 5, 5, "%")
>>> add_rectangle(5, 7, 12, 40, "#", True)
>>> add_rectangle(7, 9, 10, 38, " ")
>>> add_text(8, 10, "This is the CharGrid module")
>>> add_text(1, 32, "Pleasantville", "@")
>>> add_rectangle(6, 42, 11, 46, fill=True)
>>> render(False)
```

The CharGrid.add_rectangle() function takes at least four arguments, the top-left corner's row and column and the bottom-right corner's row and column. The character used to draw the outline can be given as a fifth argument, and a Boolean indicating whether the rectangle should be filled (with the same character as the outline) as a sixth argument. The first time we call it we pass the third and fourth arguments by unpacking the 2-tuple (width, height), returned by the CharGrid.get_size() function.

By default, the CharGrid.render() function clears the screen before printing the grid, but this can be prevented by passing False as we have done here. Here is the grid that results from the preceding doctests:

```
%%%%%************************************************
%   %                          @@@@@@@@@@@@@@@  *
%   %                          @Pleasantville@  *
%   %    ++++++++++            @@@@@@@@@@@@@@@  *
%%%%%                                          *
*        ###############################       *
*        ###############################  **** *
*        ##                           ##  **** *
*        ## This is the CharGrid module ##  **** *
* !      ##                           ##  **** *
* !    | ###############################  **** *
* !    | ###############################       *
*      |                                       *
****************************************************
```

The module begins in the same way as the `TextUtil` module, with a shebang line, copyright and license comments, and a module docstring that describes the module and has the doctests quoted earlier. Then the code proper begins with two imports, one of the `sys` module and the other of the `subprocess` module. The `subprocess` module is covered more fully in Chapter 9.

The module has two error-handling policies in place. Several functions have a `char` parameter whose actual argument must always be a string containing exactly one character; a violation of this requirement is considered to be a fatal coding error, so `assert` statements are used to verify the length. But passing out-of-range row or column numbers is considered erroneous but normal, so custom exceptions are raised when this happens.

We will now review some illustrative and key parts of the module's code, beginning with the custom exceptions:

```
class RangeError(Exception): pass
class RowRangeError(RangeError): pass
class ColumnRangeError(RangeError): pass
```

None of the functions in the module that raise an exception ever raise a `RangeError`; they always raise the specific exception depending on whether an out-of-range row or column was given. But by using a hierarchy, we give users of the module the choice of catching the specific exception, or to catch either of them by catching their `RangeError` base class. Note also that inside doctests the exception names are used as they appear here, but if the module is imported with `import CharGrid`, the exception names are, of course, `CharGrid.RangeError`, `CharGrid.RowRangeError`, and `CharGrid.ColumnRangeError`.

```
_CHAR_ASSERT_TEMPLATE = ("char must be a single character: '{0}' "
                         "is too long")
_max_rows = 25
_max_columns = 80
_grid = []
_background_char = " "
```

Here we define some private data for internal use by the module. We use leading underscores so that if the module is imported using `from CharGrid import *`, none of these variables will be imported. (An alternative approach would be to set an `__all__` list.) The `_CHAR_ASSERT_TEMPLATE` is a string for use with the `str.format()` function; we will see it used to give an error message in assert statements. We will discuss the other variables as we encounter them.

```
if sys.platform.startswith("win"):
    def clear_screen():
        subprocess.call(["cmd.exe", "/C", "cls"])
else:
```

```
def clear_screen():
    subprocess.call(["clear"])
clear_screen.__doc__ = """Clears the screen using the underlying \
window system's clear screen command"""
```

The means of clearing the console screen is platform-dependent. On Windows we must execute the cmd.exe program with appropriate arguments and on most Unix systems we execute the clear program. The subprocess module's subprocess.call() function lets us run an external program, so we can use it to clear the screen in the appropriate platform-specific way. The sys.platform string holds the name of the operating system the program is running on, for example, "win32" or "linux2". So one way of handling the platform differences would be to have a single clear_screen() function like this:

```
def clear_screen():
    command = (["clear"] if not sys.platform.startswith("win") else
               ["cmd.exe", "/C", "cls"])
    subprocess.call(command)
```

The disadvantage of this approach is that even though we know the platform cannot change while the program is running, we perform the check every time the function is called.

To avoid checking which platform the program is being run on every time the clear_screen() function is called, we have created a platform-specific clear_screen() function once when the module is imported, and from then on we always use it. This is possible because the def statement is a Python statement like any other; when the interpreter reaches the if it executes either the first or the second def statement, *dynamically* creating one or the other clear_screen() function. Since the function is not defined inside another function (or inside a class as we will see in the next chapter), it is still a global function, accessible like any other function in the module.

After creating the function we explicitly set its docstring; this avoids us having to write the same docstring in two places, and also illustrates that a docstring is simply one of the attributes of a function. Other attributes include the function's module and its name.

```
def resize(max_rows, max_columns, char=None):
    """Changes the size of the grid, wiping out the contents and
    changing the background if the background char is not None
    """
    assert max_rows > 0 and max_columns > 0, "too small"
    global _grid, _max_rows, _max_columns, _background_char
    if char is not None:
        assert len(char) == 1, _CHAR_ASSERT_TEMPLATE.format(char)
        _background_char = char
```

```
        _max_rows = max_rows
        _max_columns = max_columns
        _grid = [[_background_char for column in range(_max_columns)]
                    for row in range(_max_rows)]
```

This function uses an assert statement to enforce the policy that it is a coding error to attempt to resize the grid smaller than 1×1. If a background character is specified an assert is used to guarantee that it is a string of exactly one character; if it is not, the assertion error message is the _CHAR_ASSERT_TEMPLATE's text with the {0} replaced with the given char string.

Unfortunately, we must use the global statement because we need to update a number of global variables inside this function. This is something that using an object-oriented approach can help us to avoid, as we will see in Chapter 6.

List com-
prehen-
sions
110 ☞ The _grid is created using a list comprehension inside a list comprehension. Using list replication such as [[*char*] * *columns*] * *rows* will not work because the inner list will be shared (shallow-copied). We could have used nested for ... in loops instead:

```
        _grid = []
        for row in range(_max_rows):
            _grid.append([])
            for column in range(_max_columns):
                _grid[-1].append(_background_char)
```

This code is arguably trickier to understand than the list comprehension, and is much longer.

We will review just one of the drawing functions to give a flavor of how the drawing is done, since our primary concern is with the implementation of the module. Here is the add_horizontal_line() function, split into two parts:

```
        def add_horizontal_line(row, column0, column1, char="-"):
            """Adds a horizontal line to the grid using the given char

            >>> add_horizontal_line(8, 20, 25, "=")
            >>> char_at(8, 20) == char_at(8, 24) == "="
            True
            >>> add_horizontal_line(31, 11, 12)
            Traceback (most recent call last):
            ...
            RowRangeError
            """
```

The docstring has two tests, one that is expected to work and another that is expected to raise an exception. When dealing with exceptions in doctests the pattern is to specify the "Traceback" line, since that is always the same and tells the doctest module an exception is expected, then to use an ellipsis to stand for the intervening lines (which vary), and ending with the exception line we expect to get. The char_at() function is one of those provided by the module; it returns the character at the given row and column position in the grid.

```
assert len(char) == 1, _CHAR_ASSERT_TEMPLATE.format(char)
try:
    for column in range(column0, column1):
        _grid[row][column] = char
except IndexError:
    if not 0 <= row <= _max_rows:
        raise RowRangeError()
    raise ColumnRangeError()
```

The code begins with the same character length check that is used in the resize() function. Rather than explicitly checking the row and column arguments, the function works by assuming that the arguments are valid. If an IndexError exception occurs because a nonexistent row or column is accessed, we catch the exception and raise the appropriate module-specific exception in its place. This style of programming is known colloquially as "it's easier to ask forgiveness than permission", and is generally considered more *Pythonic* (good Python programming style) than "look before you leap", where checks are made in advance. Relying on exceptions to be raised rather than checking in advance is more efficient when exceptions are rare. (Assertions don't count as "look before you leap" because they should never occur—and are often commented out—in deployed code.)

Almost at the end of the module, after all the functions have been defined, there is a single call to resize():

```
resize(_max_rows, _max_columns)
```

This call initializes the grid to the default size (25×80) and ensures that code that imports the module can safely make use of it immediately. Without this call, every time the module was imported, the importing program or module would have to call resize() to initialize the grid, forcing programmers to remember that fact and also leading to multiple initializations.

```
if __name__ == "__main__":
    import doctest
    doctest.testmod()
```

The last three lines of the module are the standard ones for modules that use the doctest module to check their doctests.

The CharGrid module has an important failing: It supports only a single character grid. One solution to this would be to hold a collection of grids in the mod-

ule, but that would mean that users of the module would have to provide a key
or index with every function call to identify which grid they were referring to.
In cases where multiple instances of an object are required, a better solution is
to create a module that defines a class (a custom data type), since we can create as many class instances (objects of the data type) as we like. An additional
benefit of creating a class is that we should be able to avoid using the global
statement by storing class (static) data. We will see how to create classes in the
next chapter.

Overview of Python's Standard Library

Python's standard library is generally described as "batteries included", and
certainly a wide range of functionality is available, spread over almost 200
packages and modules. In this section we present a broad overview of what is
on offer, taking a thematic approach, but excluding those packages and modules that are of very specialized interest and those which are platform-specific.
In many cases a small example is shown to give a flavor of some of the packages
and modules; cross-references are provided for those packages and modules
that are covered elsewhere in the book.

String Handling

The string module provides some useful constants such as string.ascii_let-
ters and string.hexdigits. It also provides the string.Formatter class which we
can subclass to provide custom string formatters.* The textwrap module can be
used to wrap lines of text to a specified width, and to minimize indentation.

The struct module provides functions for packing and unpacking numbers,
Booleans, and strings to and from bytes objects using their binary representations. This can be useful when handling data to be sent to or received from low-
level libraries written in C. The struct and textwrap modules are used by the
convert-incidents.py program covered in Chapter 7.

> bytes type
> ☞ 286
> The struct module
> ☞ 287

The difflib module provides classes and methods for comparing sequences,
such as strings, and is able to produce output both in standard "diff" formats
and in HTML.

Python's most powerful string handling module is the re (regular expression)
module. This is covered in Chapter 12.

---

*The term *subclassing* (or *specializing*) is used for when we create a custom data type (a class)
based on another class. Chapter 6 gives full coverage of this topic.

The io.StringIO class can provide a string-like object that behaves like an in-memory text file. This can be convenient if we want to use the same code that writes to a file to write to a string.

Example: The io.StringIO Class

Python provides two different ways of writing text to files. One way is to use a file object's write() method, and the other is to use the print() function with the file keyword argument set to a file object that is open for writing. For example:

```
print("An error message", file=sys.stdout)
sys.stdout.write("Another error message\n")
```

Both lines of text are printed to sys.stdout, a file object that represents the "standard output stream"—this is normally the console and differs from sys.stderr, the "error output stream" only in that the latter is unbuffered. (Python automatically creates and opens sys.stdin, sys.stdout, and sys.stderr at program start-up.) The print() function adds a newline by default, although we can stop this by giving the end keyword argument set to an empty string.

In some situations it is useful to be able to capture into a string the output that is intended to go to a file. This can be achieved using the io.StringIO class which provides an object that can be used just like a file object, but which holds any data written to it in a string. If the io.StringIO object is given an initial string, it can also be read as though it were a file.

We can access io.StringIO if we do import io, and we can use it to capture output destined for a file object such as sys.stdout:

```
sys.stdout = io.StringIO()
```

If this line is put at the beginning of a program, after the imports but before any use is made of sys.stdout, any text that is sent to sys.stdout will actually be sent to the io.StringIO file-like object which this line has created and which has replaced the standard sys.stdout file object. Now, when the print() and sys.stdout.write() lines shown earlier are executed, their output will go to the io.StringIO object instead of the console. (At any time we can restore the original sys.stdout with the statement sys.stdout = sys.__stdout__.)

We can obtain all the strings that have been written to the io.StringIO object by calling the io.StringIO.getvalue() function, in this case by calling sys.stdout.getvalue()—the return value is a string containing all the lines that have been written. This string could be printed, or saved to a log or sent over a network connection like any other string. We will see another example of io.StringIO use a bit further on (page 216).

Command-Line Programming

If we need a program to be able to process text that may have been redirected in the console or that may be in files listed on the command line, we can use the fileinput module's fileinput.input() function. This function iterates over all the lines redirected from the console (if any) and over all the lines in the files listed on the command line, as one continuous sequence of lines. The module can report the current filename and line number at any time using fileinput.filename() and fileinput.lineno(), and can handle some kinds of compressed files.

Two separate modules are provided for handling command-line options, optparse and getopt. The getopt module is popular because it is simple to use and has been in the library for a long time. The optparse module is newer and more powerful.

Example: The optparse Module

csv2-
html.py
example

90 ☜

Back in Chapter 2 we described the csv2html.py program. In that chapter's exercises we proposed extending the program to accept the command-line arguments, "maxwidth" taking an integer and "format" taking a string. The model solution (csv2html2_ans.py) has a 26-line function to process the arguments. Here is the start of the main() function for csv2html2_opt.py, a version of the program that uses the optparse module to handle the command-line arguments rather than a custom function:

```
def main():
    parser = optparse.OptionParser()
    parser.add_option("-w", "--maxwidth", dest="maxwidth", type="int",
            help=("the maximum number of characters that can be "
                    "output to string fields [default: %default]"))
    parser.add_option("-f", "--format", dest="format",
            help=("the format used for outputting numbers "
                    "[default: %default]"))
    parser.set_defaults(maxwidth=100, format=".0f")
    opts, args = parser.parse_args()
```

Only nine lines of code are needed, plus the import optparse statement. Furthermore, we do not need to explicitly provide -h and --help options; these are handled by the optparse module to produce a suitable usage message using the texts from the help keyword arguments, and with any "%default" text replaced with the option's default value.

Notice also that the options now use the conventional Unix style of having both short and long option names that start with a hyphen. Short names are convenient for interactive use at the console; long names are more understandable when used in shell scripts. For example, to set the maximum width to 80 we can use any of -w80, -w 80, --width=80, or --width 80. After the command line is parsed, the options are available using the dest names, for example, opts.maxwidth and opts.format. Any command-line arguments that have not been processed (usually filenames) are in the args list.

If an error occurs when parsing the command line, the optparse parser will call sys.exit(2). This leads to a clean program termination and returns 2 to the operating system as the program's result value. Conventionally, a return value of 2 signifies a usage error, 1 signifies any other kind of error, and 0 means success. When sys.exit() is called with no arguments it returns 0 to the operating system.

Mathematics and Numbers

In addition to the built-in int, float, and complex numbers, the library provides the decimal.Decimal and fractions.Fraction numbers. Three numeric libraries are available: math for the standard mathematical functions, cmath for complex number mathematical functions, and random which provides many functions for random number generation; these modules were introduced in Chapter 2.

Python's numeric abstract base classes (classes that can be inherited from but that cannot be used directly) are in the numbers module. They are useful for checking that an object, say, *x*, is any kind of number using isinstance(*x*, numbers.Number), or is a specific kind of number, for example, isinstance(*x*, numbers.Rational) or isinstance(*x*, numbers.Integral).

Those involved in scientific and engineering programming will find the third-party NumPy package to be useful. This module provides highly efficient *n*-dimensional arrays, basic linear algebra functions and Fourier transforms, and tools for integration with C, C++, and Fortran code. The SciPy package incorporates NumPy and extends it to include modules for statistical computations, signal and image processing, genetic algorithms, and a great deal more. Both are freely available from www.scipy.org.

Times and Dates

The calendar and datetime modules provide functions and classes for date and time handling. However, they are based on an idealized Gregorian calendar, so are not suitable for dealing with pre-Gregorian dates. Time and date handling is a very complex topic—the calendars in use have varied in different places and at different times, a day is not precisely 24 hours, a year is not exactly 365 days, and daylight saving time and time zones vary. The datetime.datetime class (but not the datetime.date class) has provisions for handling time zones, but does not do so out of the box. Third-party modules are available to make good this deficiency, for example, dateutil from www.labix.org/python-dateutil, and mxDateTime from www.egenix.com/products/python/mxBase/mxDateTime.

The time module handles timestamps. These are simply numbers that hold the number of seconds since the epoch (1970-01-01T00:00:00 on Unix). This module can be used to get a timestamp of the machine's current time in UTC (Coordinated Universal Time), or as a local time that accounts for daylight saving time, and to create date, time, and date/time strings formatted in various ways. It can also parse strings that have dates and times.

Example: The calendar, datetime, and time Modules

Objects of type datetime.datetime are usually created programmatically, whereas objects that hold UTC date/times are usually received from external sources, such as file timestamps. Here are some examples:

```
import calendar, datetime, time
moon_datetime_a = datetime.datetime(1969, 7, 20, 20, 17, 40)
moon_time = calendar.timegm(moon_datetime_a.utctimetuple())
moon_datetime_b = datetime.datetime.utcfromtimestamp(moon_time)
moon_datetime_a.isoformat()     # returns: '1969-07-20T20:17:40'
moon_datetime_b.isoformat()     # returns: '1969-07-20T20:17:40'
time.strftime("%Y-%m-%dT%H:%M:%S", time.gmtime(moon_time))
```

The moon_datetime_a variable is of type datetime.datetime and holds the date and time that Apollo 11 landed on the moon. The moon_time variable is of type int and holds the number of seconds since the epoch to the moon landing—this number is provided by the calendar.timegm() function which takes a time_struct object returned by the datetime.datetime.utctimetuple() function, and returns the number of seconds that the time_struct represents. (Since the moon landing occurred before the Unix epoch, the number is negative.) The moon_datetime_b variable is of type datetime.datetime and is created from the moon_time integer to show the conversion from the number of seconds since the epoch to a datetime.datetime object.* The last three lines all return identical ISO 8601-format date/time strings.

The current UTC date/time is available as a datetime.datetime object by calling datetime.datetime.utcnow(), and as the number of seconds since the epoch by calling time.time(). For the local date/time, use datetime.datetime.now() or time.mktime(time.localtime()).

---

*Unfortunately for Windows users, the datetime.datetime.utcfromtimestamp() function can't handle negative timestamps, that is, timestamps for dates prior to January 1, 1970.

Algorithms and Collection Data Types

The bisect module provides functions for searching sorted sequences such as sorted lists, and for inserting items while preserving the sort order. This module's functions use the binary search algorithm, so they are very fast. The heapq module provides functions for turning a sequence such as a list into a heap—a collection data type where the first item (at index position 0) is always the smallest item, and for inserting and removing items while keeping the sequence as a heap.

Default dictionary

126 ☜

Named tuple

103 ☜
The collections package provides the collections.defaultdict dictionary and the collections.namedtuple collection data types that we have previously discussed. In addition, this package provides the collections.UserList and collections.UserDict types, although subclassing the built-in list and dict types is probably more common than using these types. Another type is collections.deque, which is similar to a list, but whereas a list is very fast for adding and removing items at the end, a collections.deque is very fast for adding and removing items both at the beginning and at the end.*

Python's non-numeric abstract base classes (classes that can be inherited from but that cannot be used directly) are also in the collections package. They are discussed in Chapter 8.

The array module provides the array.array sequence type that can store numbers or characters in a very space-efficient way. It has similar behavior to lists except that the type of object it can store is fixed when it is created, so unlike lists it cannot store objects of different types. The third-party NumPy package mentioned earlier also provides efficient arrays.

The weakref module provides functionality for creating weak references—these behave like normal object references, except that if the only reference to an object is a weak reference, the object can still be scheduled for garbage collection. This prevents objects from being kept in memory simply because we have a reference to them. Naturally, we can check whether the object a weak reference refers to still exists, and can access the object if it does.

Example: The heapq Module

The heapq module provides functions for converting a list into a heap and for adding and removing items from the heap while preserving the *heap property*. A heap is a binary tree that respects the heap property, which is that the first item (at index position 0) is always the smallest item.° Each of a heap's

---

*Python 3.1 is scheduled to include collections.OrderedDict, an insertion-ordered dictionary.

°Strictly speaking, the heapq module provides a *min heap*; heaps where the first item is always the largest are *max heaps*.

subtrees is also a heap, so they too respect the heap property. Here is how a heap could be created from scratch:

```
import heapq
heap = []
heapq.heappush(heap, (5, "rest"))
heapq.heappush(heap, (2, "work"))
heapq.heappush(heap, (4, "study"))
```

If we already have a list, we can turn it into a heap with heapq.heapify(*alist*); this will do any necessary reordering in-place. The smallest item can be removed from the heap using heapq.heappop(*heap*).

```
for x in heapq.merge([1, 3, 5, 8], [2, 4, 7], [0, 1, 6, 8, 9]):
    print(x, end=" ") # prints: 0 1 1 2 3 4 5 6 7 8 8 9
```

The heapq.merge() function takes any number of sorted iterables as arguments and returns an iterator that iterates over all the items from all the iterables in order.

File Formats, Encodings, and Data Persistence

The standard library has extensive support for a variety of standard file formats and encodings. The base64 module has functions for reading and writing using the Base16, Base32, and Base64 encodings specified in RFC 3548.* The quopri module has functions for reading and writing "quoted-printable" format. This format is defined in RFC 1521 and is used for MIME (Multipurpose Internet Mail Extensions) data. The uu module has functions for reading and writing uuencoded data. RFC 1832 defines the External Data Representation Standard and module xdrlib provides functions for reading and writing data in this format.

Character encodings

85 ☞

Modules are also provided for reading and writing archive files in the most popular formats. The bz2 module can handle .bz2 files, the gzip module handles .gz files, the tarfile module handles .tar, .tar.gz (also .tgz), and .tar.bz2 files, and the zipfile module handles .zip files. We will see an example of using the tarfile module in this subsection, and later on (page 216) there is a small example that uses the gzip module; we will also see the gzip module in action again in Chapter 7.

Support is also provided for handling some audio formats, with the aifc module for AIFF (Audio Interchange File Format) and the wave module for (uncompressed) .wav files. Some forms of audio data can be manipulated using the

---

* RFC (Request for Comments) documents are used to specify various Internet technologies. Each one has a unique identification number and many of them have become officially adopted standards.

audioop module, and the sndhdr module provides a couple of functions for determining what kind of sound data is stored in a file and some of its properties, such as the sampling rate.

A format for configuration files (similar to old-style Windows .ini files) is specified in RFC 822, and the configparser module provides functions for reading and writing such files.

Many applications, for example, Excel, can read and write CSV (Comma Separated Value) data, or variants such as tab-delimited data. The csv module can read and write these formats, and can account for the idiosyncracies that prevent CSV files from being straightforward to handle directly.

In addition to its support of various file formats, the standard library also has packages and modules that provide data persistence. The pickle module is used to store and retrieve arbitrary Python objects (including entire collections) to and from disk; this module is covered in Chapter 7. The library also supports DBM files of various kinds—these are like dictionaries except that their items are stored on disk rather than in memory, and both their keys and their values must be bytes objects or strings. The shelve module, covered in Chapter 11, can be used to provide DBM files with string keys and arbitrary Python objects as values—the module seamlessly converts the Python objects to and from bytes objects behind the scenes. The DBM modules, Python's database API, and using the built-in SQLite database are all covered in Chapter 11.

Example: The base64 Module

The base64 module is mostly used for handling binary data that is embedded in emails as ASCII text. It can also be used to store binary data inside .py files. The first step is to get the binary data into Base64 format. Here we assume that the base64 module has been imported and that the path and filename of a .png file are in the variable left_align_png:

```
binary = open(left_align_png, "rb").read()
ascii_text = ""
for i, c in enumerate(base64.b64encode(binary)):
    if i and i % 68 == 0:
        ascii_text += "\\\n"
    ascii_text += chr(c)
```

left_align.png

This code snippet reads the file in binary mode and converts it to a Base64 string of ASCII characters. Every sixty-eighth character a backslash-newline combination is added. This limits the width of the lines of ASCII characters to 68, but ensures that when the data is read back the newlines will be ignored

bytes
type

☞ 286

(because the backslash will escape them). The ASCII text obtained like this can
be stored as a `bytes` literal in a `.py` file, for example:

```
LEFT_ALIGN_PNG = b"""\
iVBORw0KGgoAAAANSUhEUgAAACAAAAAgCAYAAABzenr0AAAABGdBTUEAALGPC/xhBQAA\
...
bmquu8PAmVT2+CwVV6rCyA9UfFMCkI+bN6p18tCWqcUzrDOwBh2zVCR+JZVeAAAAAElF\
TkSuQmCC"""
```

We've omitted most of the lines as indicated by the ellipsis.

The data can be converted back to its original binary form like this:

```
binary = base64.b64decode(LEFT_ALIGN_PNG)
```

The binary data could be written to a file using `open(filename, "wb").write(
binary)`. Keeping binary data in `.py` files is much less compact than keeping
it in its original form, but can be useful if we want to provide a program that
requires some binary data as a single `.py` file.

Example: The tarfile Module

Most versions of Windows don't come with support for the `.tar` format that
is so widely used on Unix systems. This inconvenient omission can easily be
rectified using Python's `tarfile` module, which can create and unpack `.tar` and
`.tar.gz` archives (known as *tarballs*), and with the right libraries installed,
`.tar.bz2` archives. The `untar.py` program can unpack tarballs using the `tarfile`
module; here we will just show some key extracts, starting with the first import
statement:

```
BZ2_AVAILABLE = True
try:
    import bz2
except ImportError:
    BZ2_AVAILABLE = False
```

The `bz2` module is used to handle the bzip2 compression format, but importing
it will fail if Python was built without access to the bzip2 library. (The Python
binary for Windows is always built with bzip2 compression built-in; it is only
on some Unix builds that it might be absent.) We account for the possibility
that the module is not available using a `try` … `except` block, and keep a Boolean
variable that we can refer to later (although we don't quote the code that
uses it).

```
UNTRUSTED_PREFIXES = tuple(["/", "\\"] +
        [c + ":" for c in string.ascii_letters])
```

This statement creates the tuple ('/', '\', 'A:', 'B:', ..., 'Z:', 'a:', 'b:', ..., 'z:'). Any filename in the tarball being unpacked that begins with one of these is suspect—tarballs should not use absolute paths since then they risk overwriting system files, so as a precaution we will not unpack any file whose name starts with one of these prefixes.

```python
def untar(archive):
    tar = None
    try:
        tar = tarfile.open(archive)
        for member in tar.getmembers():
            if member.name.startswith(UNTRUSTED_PREFIXES):
                print("untrusted prefix, ignoring", member.name)
            elif ".." in member.name:
                print("suspect path, ignoring", member.name)
            else:
                tar.extract(member)
                print("unpacked", member.name)
    except (tarfile.TarError, EnvironmentError) as err:
        error(err)
    finally:
        if tar is not None:
            tar.close()
```

Each file in a tarball is called a *member*. The tarfile.getmembers() function returns a list of tarfile.TarInfo objects, one for each member. The member's filename, including its path, is in the tarfile.TarInfo.name attribute. If the name begins with an untrusted prefix, or contains .. in its path, we output an error message; otherwise, we call tarfile.extract() to save the member to disk. The tarfile module has its own set of custom exceptions, but we have taken the simplistic approach that if any exception occurs we output the error message and finish.

```python
def error(message, exit_status=1):
    print(message)
    sys.exit(exit_status)
```

We have just quoted the error() function for completeness. The (unquoted) main() function prints a usage message if -h or --help is given; otherwise, it performs some basic checks before calling untar() with the tarball's filename.

File, Directory, and Process Handling

The shutil module provides high-level functions for file and directory handling, including shutil.copy() and shutil.copytree() for copying files and entire directory trees, shutil.move() for moving directory trees, and shutil.rmtree() for removing entire directory trees, including nonempty ones.

Temporary files and directories should be created using the tempfile module which provides the necessary functions, for example, tempfile.mkstemp(), and creates the temporaries in the most secure manner possible.

The filecmp module can be used to compare files with the filecmp.cmp() function and to compare entire directories with the filecmp.cmpfiles() function.

One very powerful and effective use of Python programs is to orchestrate the running of other programs. This can be done using the subprocess module which can start other processes, communicate with them using pipes, and retrieve their results. This module is covered in Chapter 9. An even more powerful alternative is to use the multiprocessing module which provides extensive facilities for offloading work to multiple processes and for accumulating results, and can often be used as an alternative to multithreading.

The os module provides platform-independent access to operating system functionality. The os.environ variable holds a mapping object whose items are environment variable names and their values. The program's working directory is provided by os.getcwd() and can be changed using os.chdir(). The module also provides functions for low-level file-descriptor-based file handling. The os.access() function can be used to determine whether a file exists or whether it is readable or writable, and the os.listdir() function returns a list of the entries (e.g., the files and directories, but excluding the . and .. entries), in the directory it is given. The os.stat() function returns various items of information about a file or directory, such as its mode, access time, and size.

Directories can be created using os.mkdir(), or if intermediate directories need to be created, using os.makedirs(). Empty directories can be removed using os.rmdir(), and directory trees that contain only empty directories can be removed using os.removedirs(). Files or directories can be removed using os.remove(), and can be renamed using os.rename().

The os.walk() function iterates over an entire directory tree, retrieving the name of every file and directory in turn.

The os module also provides many low-level platform-specific functions, for example, to work with file descriptors, and to fork (only on Unix systems), spawn, and exec.

Whereas the os module provides functions for interacting with the operating system, especially in the context of the file system, the os.path module provides a mixture of string manipulation (of paths), and some file system convenience functions. The os.path.abspath() function returns the absolute path of its argument, with redundant path separators and .. elements removed. The os.path.split() function returns a 2-tuple with the first element containing the path and the second the filename (which will be empty if a path with no filename was given). These two parts are also available directly using os.path.basename() and os.path.dirname(). A filename can also be split into two parts, name and extension, using os.path.splitext(). The os.path.join() function takes any number of path strings and returns a single path using the platform-specific path separator.

If we need several pieces of information about a file or directory we can use os.stat(), but if we need just one piece, we can use the relevant os.path function, for example, os.path.exists(), os.path.getsize(), os.path.isfile(), or os.path.isdir().

The mimetypes module has the mimetypes.guess_type() function that tries to guess the given file's MIME type.

Example: The os and os.path Modules

Here is how we can use the os and os.path modules to create a dictionary where each key is a filename (including its path) and where each value is the timestamp (seconds since the epoch) when the file was last modified, for those files in the given path:

```
date_from_name = {}
for name in os.listdir(path):
    fullname = os.path.join(path, name)
    if os.path.isfile(fullname):
        date_from_name[fullname] = os.path.getmtime(fullname)
```

This code is pretty straightforward, but can be used only for the files in a single directory. If we need to traverse an entire directory tree we can use the os.walk() function.

Here is a code snippet taken from the finddup.py program.* The code creates a dictionary where each key is a 2-tuple (file size, filename) where the filename excludes the path, and where each value is a list of the full filenames that match their key's filename and have the same file size:

```
data = collections.defaultdict(list)

for root, dirs, files in os.walk(path):
    for filename in files:
        fullname = os.path.join(root, filename)
        key = (os.path.getsize(fullname), filename)
        data[key].append(fullname)
```

---

*A much more sophisticated find duplicates program, findduplicates-t.py, which uses multiple threads and MD5 checksums, is covered in Chapter 9.

For each directory, os.walk() returns the root and two lists, one of the subdirectories in the directory and the other of the files in the directory. To get the full path for a filename we need to combine just the root and the filename. Notice that we do not have to recurse into the subdirectories ourselves—os.walk() does that for us. Once the data has been gathered, we can iterate over it to produce a report of possible duplicate files:

```
for size, filename in sorted(data):
    names = data[(size, filename)]
    if len(names) > 1:
        print("{0} ({1} bytes) may be duplicated "
                "({2} files):".format(filename, size, len(names)))
        for name in names:
            print("\t{0}".format(name))
```

Because the dictionary keys are (size, filename) tuples, we don't need to use a key function to get the data sorted in size order. If any (size, filename) tuple has more than one filename in its list, these might be duplicates.

```
...
shell32.dll (8460288 bytes) may be duplicated (2 files):
        \windows\system32\shell32.dll
        \windows\system32\dllcache\shell32.dll
```

This is the last item taken from the 3 282 lines of output produced by running finddup.py \windows on a Windows XP system.

Networking and Internet Programming

Packages and modules for networking and Internet programming are a major part of Python's standard library. At the lowest level, the socket module provides the most fundamental network functionality, with functions for creating sockets, doing DNS (Domain Name System) lookups, and handling IP (Internet Protocol) addresses. Encrypted and authenticated sockets can be set up using the ssl module. The socketserver module provides TCP (Transmission Control Protocol) and UDP (User Datagram Protocol) servers. These servers can handle requests directly, or can create a separate process (by forking) or a separate thread to handle each request. Asynchronous client and server socket handling can be achieved using the asyncore module and the higher-level asynchat module that is built on top of it.

Python has defined the WSGI (Web Server Gateway Interface) to provide a standard interface between web servers and web applications written in Python. In support of the standard the wsgiref package provides a reference implementation of WSGI that has modules for providing WSGI-compliant HTTP servers, and for handling response header and CGI (Common Gateway

Interface) scripts. In addition, the http.server module provides an HTTP server which can be given a request handler (a standard one is provided), to run CGI scripts. The http.cookies and http.cookiejar modules provide functions for managing cookies, and CGI script support is provided by the cgi and cgitb modules.

Client access to HTTP requests is provided by the http.client module, although the higher-level urllib package's modules, urllib.parse, urllib.request, urllib.response, urllib.error, and urllib.robotparser, provide easier and more convenient access to URLs. Grabbing a file from the Internet is as simple as:

```
fh = urllib.request.urlopen("http://www.python.org/index.html")
html = fh.read().decode("utf8")
```

The urllib.request.urlopen() function returns an object that behaves much like a file object opened in read binary mode. Here we retrieve the Python Web site's index.html file (as a bytes object), and store it as a string in the html variable. It is also possible to grab files and store them in local files with the urllib.request.urlretrieve() function.

HTML and XHTML documents can be parsed using the html.parser module, URLs can be parsed and created using the urllib.parse module, and robots.txt files can be parsed with the urllib.robotparser module. Data that is represented using JSON (JavaScript Object Notation) can be read and written using the json module.

In addition to HTTP server and client support, the library provides XML-RPC (Remote Procedure Call) support with the xmlrpc.client and xmlrpc.server modules. Additional client functionality is provided for FTP (File Transport Protocol) by the ftplib module, for NNTP (Network News Transport Protocol) by the nntplib module, and for TELNET with the telnetlib module.

The smtpd module provides an SMTP (Simple Mail Transport Protocol) server, and the email client modules are smtplib for SMTP, imaplib for IMAP4 (Internet Message Access Protocol), and poplib for POP3 (Post Office Protocol). Mailboxes in various formats can be accessed using the mailbox module. Individual messages (including multipart messages) can be created and manipulated using the email module.

If the standard library's packages and modules are insufficient in this area, Twisted (www.twistedmatrix.com) provides a comprehensive third-party networking library. Many third-party web programming libraries are also available, including Django (www.djangoproject.com) and Turbogears (www.turbogears.org) for creating web applications, and Plone (www.plone.org) and Zope (www.zope.org) which provide complete web frameworks and content management systems. All of these libraries are written in Python.

XML

There are two widely used approaches to parsing XML documents. One is the DOM (Document Object Model) and the other is SAX (Simple API for XML). Two DOM parsers are provided, one by the `xml.dom` module and the other by the `xml.dom.minidom` module. A SAX parser is provided by the `xml.sax` module. We have already used the `xml.sax.saxutils` module for its `xml.sax.saxutils.escape()` function (to XML-escape "&", "<", and ">"). There is also an `xml.sax.saxutils.quoteattr()` function that does the same thing but additionally escapes quotes (to make the text suitable for a tag's attribute), and `xml.sax.saxutils.unescape()` to do the opposite conversion.

Two other parsers are available. The `xml.parsers.expat` module can be used to parse XML documents with expat, providing the expat library is available, and the `xml.etree.ElementTree` can be used to parse XML documents using a kind of dictionary/list interface. (By default, the DOM and element tree parsers themselves use the expat parser under the hood.)

Writing XML manually and writing XML using DOM and element trees, and parsing XML using the DOM, SAX, and element tree parsers, is covered in Chapter 7.

Example: The xml.etree.ElementTree Module

Python's DOM and SAX parsers provide the APIs that experienced XML programmers are used to, and the `xml.etree.ElementTree` module offers a more Pythonic approach to parsing and writing XML. The element tree module is a fairly recent addition to the standard library,[*] and so may not be familiar to some readers. In view of this, we will present a very short example here to give a flavor of it—Chapter 7 provides a more substantial example and provides comparative code using DOM and SAX.

The U.S. government's NOAA (National Oceanic and Atmospheric Administration) Web site provides a wide variety of data, including an XML file that lists the U.S. weather stations. The file is more than 20 000 lines long and contains details of around two thousand stations. Here is a typical entry:

```
<station>
    <station_id>KBOS</station_id>
    <state>MA</state>
    <station_name>Boston, Logan International Airport</station_name>
    ...
    <xml_url>http://weather.gov/data/current_obs/KBOS.xml</xml_url>
</station>
```

---

[*]The `xml.etree.ElementTree` module first appeared in Python 2.5.

We have cut out a few lines and reduced the indentation that is present in the file. The file is about 840K in size, so we have compressed it using gzip to a more manageable 72K. Unfortunately, the element tree parser requires either a filename or a file object to read, but we cannot give it the compressed file since that will just appear to be random binary data. We can solve this problem with two initial steps:

```
binary = gzip.open(filename).read()
fh = io.StringIO(binary.decode("utf8"))
```

io.
StringIO
203 ☜
The gzip module's gzip.open() function is similar to the built-in open() except that it reads gzip-compressed files (those with extension .gz) as raw binary data. We need the data available as a file that the element tree parser can work with, so we use the bytes.decode() method to convert the binary data to a string using UTF-8 encoding (which is what the XML file uses), and we create a file-like io.StringIO object with the string containing the entire XML file as its data.
bytes
type

☞ 286

```
tree = xml.etree.ElementTree.ElementTree()
root = tree.parse(fh)
stations = []
for element in tree.getiterator("station_name"):
    stations.append(element.text)
```

Here we create a new xml.etree.ElementTree.ElementTree object and give it a file object from which to read the XML we want it to parse. As far as the element tree parser is concerned it has been passed a file object open for reading, although in fact it is reading a string inside an io.StringIO object. We want to extract the names of all the weather stations, and this is easily achieved using the xml.etree.ElementTree.ElementTree.getiterator() method which returns an iterator that returns all the xml.etree.ElementTree.Element objects that have the given tag name. We just use the element's text attribute to retrieve the text. Like os.walk(), we don't have to do any recursion ourselves; the iterator method does that for us. Nor do we have to specify a tag—in which case the iterator will return every element in the entire XML document.

Other Modules

We don't have the space to cover the nearly 200 packages and modules that are available in the standard library. Nonetheless, this general overview should be sufficient to get a flavor of what the library provides and some of the key packages in the major areas it serves. In this section's final subsection we discuss just a few more areas of interest.

In the previous section we saw how easy it is to create tests in docstrings and to run them using the doctest module. The library also has a unit-testing framework provided by the unittest module—this is a Python version of the Java JUnit test framework. The doctest module also provides some basic integration with the unittest module. Several third-party testing frameworks are also available, for example, py.test from codespeak.net/py/dist/ and nose from www.somethingaboutorange.com/mrl/projects/nose/.

Noninteractive applications such as servers often report problems by writing to log files. The logging module provides a uniform interface for logging, and in addition to being able to log to files, it can log using HTTP GET or POST requests, or using email or sockets.

The library provides many modules for introspection and code manipulation, and although most of them are beyond the scope of this book, one that is worth mentioning is pprint which has functions for "pretty printing" Python objects, including collection data types, which is sometimes useful for debugging. We will see a simple use of the inspect module that introspects live objects in Chapter 8.

The threading module provides support for creating threaded applications, and the queue module provides three different kinds of thread-safe queues. Threading is covered in Chapter 9.

Python has no native support for GUI programming, but several GUI libraries can be used by Python programs. The Tk library is available using the tkinter module, and is usually installed as standard. GUI programming is introduced in Chapter 13.

The abc (Abstract Base Class) module provides the functions necessary for creating abstract base classes. This module is covered in Chapter 8.

Shallow and deep copying

136 ☞

The copy module provides the copy.copy() and copy.deepcopy() functions that were discussed in Chapter 3.

Access to *foreign functions*, that is, to functions in shared libraries (.dll files on Windows, .dylib files on Mac OS X, and .so files on Linux), is available using the ctypes module. Python also provides a C API, so it is possible to create custom data types and functions in C and make these available to Python. Both the ctypes module and Python's C API are beyond the scope of this book.

If none of the packages and modules mentioned in this section provides the functionality you need, before writing anything from scratch it is worth checking the Python documentation's Global Module Index to see whether a suitable module is available, since we have not been able to mention every one here. And failing that, try looking at the Python Package Index (pypi.python.org/pypi) which contains several thousand Python add-ons ranging from small one-file modules all the way up to large library and framework packages containing anything from scores to hundreds of modules.

Summary

The chapter began by introducing the various syntaxes that can be used for importing packages, modules, and objects inside modules. We noted that many programmers only use the import *importable* syntax so as to avoid name clashes, and that we must be careful not to give a program or module the same name as a top-level Python module or directory.

Also discussed were Python packages. These are simply directories with an __init__.py file and one or more .py modules inside them. The __init__.py file can be empty, but to support the from *importable* import * syntax, we can create an __all__ special variable in the __init__.py file set to a list of module names. We can also put any common initialization code in the __init__.py file. It was noted that packages can be nested simply by creating subdirectories and having each of these contain its own __init__.py file.

Two custom modules were described. The first just provided a few functions and had very simple doctests. The second was more elaborate with its own exceptions, the use of dynamic function creation to create a function with a platform-specific implementation, private global data, a call to an initialization function, and more elaborate doctests.

About half the chapter was devoted to a high-level overview of Python's standard library. Several string handling modules were mentioned and a couple of io.StringIO examples were presented. One example showed how to write text to a file using either the built-in print() function or a file object's write() method, and how to use an io.StringIO object in place of a real file. In previous chapters we handled command-line options by reading sys.argv ourselves, but in the coverage of the library's support for command-line programming we introduced the optparse module which greatly simplifies command-line argument handling—we will use this module extensively from now on.

Mention was made of Python's excellent support for numbers, and the library's numeric types and its three modules of mathematical functions, as well as the support for scientific and engineering mathematics provided by the SciPy project. Both library and third-party date/time handling classes were briefly described and examples of how to obtain the current date/time and how to convert between datetime.datetime and the number of seconds since the epoch were shown. Also discussed were the additional collection data types and the algorithms for working with ordered sequences that the standard library provides, along with some examples of using the heapq module's functions.

The modules that support various file encodings (besides character encodings) were discussed, as well as the modules for packing and unpacking the most popular archive formats, and those that have support for audio data. An example showing how to use the Base64 encoding to store binary data in .py files was given, and also a program to unpack tarballs. Considerable support is provided for handling directories and files—and all of this is abstracted into platform-independent functions. Examples were shown for creating a dictionary with filename keys and last modified timestamp values, and for doing a recursive search of a directory to identify possible duplicate files based on their name and size.

A large part of the library is devoted to networking and Internet programming. We very briefly surveyed what is available, from raw sockets (including encrypted sockets), to TCP and UDP servers, to HTTP servers and support for the WSGI. Also mentioned were the modules for handling cookies, CGI scripts, and HTTP data, and for parsing HTML, XHTML, and URLs. Other modules that were mentioned included those for handling XML-RPC and for handling higher-level protocols such as FTP and NNTP, as well as the email client and server support using SMTP and client support for IMAP4 and POP3.

The library's comprehensive support for XML writing and parsing was also mentioned, including the DOM, SAX, and element tree parsers, and the expat module. And an example was given using the element tree module. Mention was also made of some of the many other packages and modules that the library provides.

Python's standard library represents an extremely useful resource that can save enormous amounts of time and effort, and in many cases allows us to write much smaller programs by relying on the functionality that the library provides. In addition, literally thousands of third-party packages are available to fill any gaps the standard library may have. All of this predefined functionality allows us to focus much more on what we want our programs to do, while leaving the library modules to take care of most of the details.

This chapter brings us to the end of the fundamentals of procedural programming. Later chapters, and particularly Chapter 8, will look at more advanced and specialized procedural techniques, and the following chapter introduces object-oriented programming. Using Python as a purely procedural language is both possible and practical—especially for small programs—but for medium to large programs, for custom packages and modules, and for long-term maintainability, the object-oriented approach usually wins out. Fortunately, all that we have covered up to now is both useful and relevant in object-oriented programming, so the subsequent chapters will continue to build up our Python knowledge and skills based on the foundations that have now been laid.

Exercise

Write a program to show directory listings, rather like the dir command in Windows or ls in Unix. The benefit of creating our own listing program is that we can build in the defaults we prefer and can use the same program on all platforms without having to remember the differences between dir and ls. Create a program that supports the following interface:

```
Usage: ls.py [options] [path1 [path2 [... pathN]]]

The paths are optional; if not given . is used.

Options:
  -h, --help      show this help message and exit
  -H, --hidden    show hidden files [default: off]
  -m, --modified  show last modified date/time [default: off]
  -o ORDER, --order=ORDER
                  order by ('name', 'n', 'modified', 'm', 'size', 's')
                  [default: name]
  -r, --recursive recurse into subdirectories [default: off]
  -s, --sizes     show sizes [default: off]
```

(The output has been modified slightly to fit the book's page width.)

Here is an example of output on a small directory using the command line ls.py -ms -os misc/:

```
2007-04-10 15:49:01            322 misc/chars.pyw
2007-08-01 11:24:57          1,039 misc/pfa-bug.pyw
2007-10-12 09:00:27          2,445 misc/test.lout
2007-04-10 15:50:31          2,848 misc/chars.png
2008-02-11 14:17:03         12,184 misc/abstract.pdf
2008-02-05 14:22:38        109,788 misc/klmqtintro.lyx
2007-12-13 12:01:14      1,359,950 misc/tracking.pdf
                                   misc/phonelog/

7 files, 1 directory
```

We used option grouping in the command line (optparse handles this automatically for us), but the same could have been achieved using separate options, for example, ls.py -m -s -os misc/, or by even more grouping, ls.py -msos misc/, or by using long options, ls.py --modified --sizes --order=size misc/, or any combination of these. Note that we define a "hidden" file or directory as one whose name begins with a dot (.).

The exercise is quite challenging. You will need to read the optparse documentation to see how to provide options that set a True value, and how to offer a fixed list of choices. If the user sets the recursive option you will need to process the files (but not the directories) using os.walk(); otherwise, you will have to use os.listdir() and process both files and directories yourself.

One rather tricky aspect is avoiding hidden directories when recursing. They can be cut out of os.walk()'s dirs list—and therefore skipped by os.walk()—by modifying that list. But be careful not to assign to the dirs variable itself, since that won't change the list it refers to but will simply (and uselessly) replace it; the approach used in the model solution is to assign to a slice of the whole list, that is, `dirs[:] = [dir for dir in dirs if not dir.startswith(".")]`.

`locale. set- locale()`

`81 ☞`

The best way to get grouping characters in the file sizes is to import the `locale` module, call `locale.setlocale()` to get the user's default locale, and use the `n` format character. Overall, `ls.py` is about 130 lines split over four functions.

- The Object-Oriented Approach
- Custom Classes
- Custom Collection Classes

Object-Oriented Programming

In all the previous chapters we used objects extensively, but our style of programming has been strictly procedural. Python is a multiparadigm language—it allows us to program in procedural, object-oriented, and functional style, or in any mixture of styles, since it does not force us to program in any one particular way.

It is perfectly possible to write any program in procedural style, and for very small programs (up to, say, 500 lines), doing so is rarely a problem. But for most programs, and especially for medium-size and large programs, object-oriented programming offers many advantages.

This chapter covers all the fundamental concepts and techniques for doing object-oriented programming in Python. The first section is especially for those who are less experienced and for those coming from a procedural programming background (such as C or Fortran). The section starts by looking at some of the problems that can arise with procedural programming that object-oriented programming can solve. Then it briefly describes Python's approach to object-oriented programming and explains the relevant terminology. After that, the chapter's two main sections begin.

The second section covers the creation of custom data types that hold single items (although the items themselves may have many attributes), and the third section covers the creation of custom collection data types that can hold any number of objects of any types. These sections cover most aspects of object-oriented programming in Python, although we defer some more advanced material to Chapter 8.

The Object-Oriented Approach

In this section we will look at some of the problems of a purely procedural approach by considering a situation where we need to represent circles, potentially lots of them. The minimum data required to represent a circle is its (x, y) position and its radius. One simple approach is to use a 3-tuple for each circle. For example:

```
circle = (11, 60, 8)
```

One drawback of this approach is that it isn't obvious what each element of the tuple represents. We could mean (x, y, radius) or, just as easily, (radius, x, y). Another drawback is that we can access the elements by index position only. If we have two functions, distance_from_origin(x, y) and edge_distance_from_origin(x, y, *radius*), we would need to use tuple unpacking to call them with a circle tuple:

```
distance = distance_from_origin(*circle[:2])
distance = edge_distance_from_origin(*circle)
```

Both of these assume that the circle tuples are of the form (x, y, radius). We can solve the problem of knowing the element order and of using tuple unpacking by using a named tuple:

```
import collections
Circle = collections.namedtuple("Circle", "x y radius")
circle = Circle(13, 84, 9)
distance = distance_from_origin(circle.x, circle.y)
```

This allows us to create Circle 3-tuples with named attributes which makes function calls much easier to understand, since to access elements we can use their names. Unfortunately, problems remain. For example, there is nothing to stop an invalid circle from being created:

```
circle = Circle(33, 56, -5)
```

It doesn't make sense to have a circle with a negative radius, but the circle named tuple is created here without raising an exception—just as it would be if the radius was given as a variable that held a negative number. The error will be noticed only if we call the edge_distance_from_origin() function—and then only if that function actually checks for a negative radius. This inability to validate when creating an object is probably the worst aspect of taking a purely procedural approach.

If we want circles to be mutable so that we can move them by changing their coordinates or resize them by changing their radius, we can do so by using the collections.namedtuple._replace() method:

```
circle = circle._replace(radius=12)
```

Just as when we create a Circle, there is nothing to stop us from (or warn us about) setting invalid data.

If the circles were going to need lots of changes, we might opt to use a mutable data type such as a list, for the sake of convenience:

```
circle = [36, 77, 8]
```

This doesn't give us any protection from putting in invalid data, and the best we can do about accessing elements by name is to create some constants so that we can write things like circle[RADIUS] = 5. But using a list brings additional problems—for example, we can legitimately call circle.sort()! Using a dictionary might be an alternative, for example, circle = dict(x=36, y=77, radius=8), but again there is no way to ensure a valid radius and no way to prevent inappropriate methods from being called.

Object-Oriented Concepts and Terminology

What we need is some way to package up the data that is needed to represent a circle, and some way to restrict the methods that can be applied to the data so that only valid operations are possible. Both of these things can be achieved by creating a custom Circle data type. We will see how to create a Circle data type in later in this section, but first we need to cover some preliminaries and explain some terminology. Don't worry if the terminology is unfamiliar at first; it will become much clearer once we reach the examples.

We use the terms *class*, *type*, and *data type* interchangeably. In Python we can create custom classes that are fully integrated and that can be used just like the built-in data types. We have already encountered many classes, for example, dict, int, and str. We use the term *object*, and occasionally the term *instance*, to refer to an instance of a particular class. For example, 5 is an int object and "oblong" is a str object.

Most classes encapsulate both data and the methods that can be applied to that data. For example, the str class holds a string of Unicode characters as its data and supports methods such as str.upper(). Many classes also support additional features; for example, we can concatenate two strings (or any two sequences) using the + operator and find a sequence's length using the built-in len() function. Such features are provided by *special methods*—these are like normal methods except that their names always begin and end with two underscores, and are predefined. For example, if we want to create a class that supports concatenation using the + operator and also the len() function, we can do so by implementing the __add__() and __len__() special methods in our class. Conversely, we should never define any method with a name that begins and ends with two underscores unless it is one of the predefined special methods and is appropriate to our class. This will ensure that we never get conflicts with later versions of Python even if they introduce new predefined special methods.

Objects usually have attributes—methods are callable attributes, and other attributes are data. For example, a `complex` object has `imag` and `real` attributes and lots of methods, including special methods like `__add__()` and `__sub__` (to support the binary + and – operators), and normal methods like `conjugate()`. Data attributes (often referred to simply as "attributes") are normally implemented as *instance variables*, that is, variables that are unique to a particular object. We will see examples of this, and also examples of how to provide data attributes as *properties*. A property is an item of object data that is accessed like an instance variable but where the accesses are handled by methods behind the scenes. As we will see, using properties makes it easy to do data validation.

Inside a method (which is just a function whose first argument is the instance on which it is called to operate), several kinds of variables are potentially accessible. The object's instance variables can be accessed by qualifying their name with the instance itself. Local variables can be created inside the method; these are accessed without qualification. Class variables (sometimes called static variables) can be accessed by qualifying their name with the class name, and global variables, that is, module variables, are accessed without qualification.

Some of the Python literature uses the concept of a *namespace*, a mapping from names to objects. Modules are namespaces—for example, after the statement `import math` we can access objects in the `math` module by qualifying them with their namespace name (e.g., `math.pi` and `math.sin()`). Similarly, classes and objects are also namespaces; for example, if we have `z = complex(1, 2)`, the `z` object's namespace has two attributes which we can access (`z.real` and `z.imag`).

One of the advantages of object orientation is that if we have a class, we can *specialize* it. This means that we make a new class that inherits all the attributes (data and methods) from the original class, usually so that we can add or replace methods or add more instance variables. We can *subclass* (another term for *specialize*), any Python class, whether built-in or from the standard library, or one of* our own custom classes. The ability to subclass is one of the great advantages offered by object-oriented programming since it makes it straightforward to use an existing class that has tried and tested functionality as the basis for a new class that extends the original, adding new data attributes or new functionality in a very clean and direct way. Furthermore, we can pass objects of our new class to functions and methods that were written for the original class and they will work correctly.

We use the term *base class* to refer to a class that is inherited; a base class may be the immediate ancestor, or may be further up the inheritance tree. Another term for base class is *super class*. We use the term *subclass, derived*

---

*Some library classes that are implemented in C cannot be subclassed; such classes specify this in their documentation.

class, or *derived* to describe a class that inherits from (i.e., specializes) another class. In Python every built-in and library class and every class we create is derived directly or indirectly from the ultimate base class—object. Figure 6.1 illustrates some of the inheritance terminology.

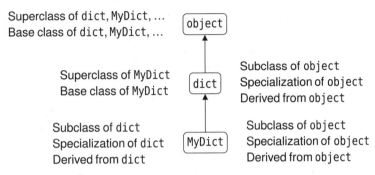

Superclass of dict, MyDict, ...
Base class of dict, MyDict, ...

object

Superclass of MyDict
Base class of MyDict

dict

Subclass of object
Specialization of object
Derived from object

Subclass of dict
Specialization of dict
Derived from dict

MyDict

Subclass of object
Specialization of object
Derived from object

Figure 6.1 *Some object-oriented inheritance terminology*

Any method can be overridden, that is, reimplemented, in a subclass; this is the same as Java (apart from Java's "final" methods).* If we have an object of class MyDict (a class that inherits dict) and we call a method that is defined by both dict and MyDict, Python will correctly call the MyDict version—this is known as *dynamic method binding*, also called *polymorphism*. If we need to call the base class version of a method inside a reimplemented method we can do so by using the built-in super() function.

Python also supports *duck typing*—"if it walks like a duck and quacks like a duck, it is a duck". In other words, if we want to call certain methods on an object, it doesn't matter what class the object is, only that it has the methods we want to call. In the preceding chapter we saw that when we needed a file object we could provide one by calling the built-in open() function—or by creating an io.StringIO object and providing that instead, since io.StringIO objects have the same API (Application Programming Interface), that is, the same methods, as the file objects returned by open() in text mode.

Inheritance is used to model is-a relationships, that is, where a class's objects are essentially the same as some other class's objects, but with some variations, such as extra data attributes and extra methods. Another approach is to use *aggregation* (also called *composition*)—this is where a class includes one or more instance variables that are of other classes. Aggregation is used to model has-a relationships. In Python, every class uses inheritance—because all custom classes have object as their ultimate base class, and most classes also use aggregation since most classes have instance variables of various types.

---

*In C++ terminology, all Python methods are virtual.

Some object-oriented languages have two features that Python does not provide. The first is overloading, that is, having methods with the same name but with different parameter lists in the same class. Thanks to Python's versatile argument-handling capabilities this is never a limitation in practice. The second is access control—there are no bulletproof mechanisms for enforcing data privacy. However, if we create attributes (instance variables or methods) that begin with two leading underscores, Python will prevent unintentional accesses so that they can be considered to be private. (This is done by name mangling; we will see an example in Chapter 8.)

Just as we use an uppercase letter as the first letter of custom modules, we will do the same thing for custom classes. We can define as many classes as we like, either directly in a program or in modules—class names don't have to match module names, and modules may contain as many class definitions as we like.

Now that we have seen some of the problems that classes can solve, introduced the necessary terminology, and covered some background matters, we can begin to create some custom classes.

Custom Classes

In earlier chapters we created custom classes: custom exceptions. Here are two new syntaxes for creating custom classes:

```
class className:
    suite
```

```
class className(base_classes):
    suite
```

Since the exception subclasses we created did not add any new attributes (no instance data or methods) we used a suite of pass (i.e., nothing added), and since the suite was just one statement we put it on the same line as the class statement itself. Note that just like def statements, class is a statement, so we can create classes dynamically if we want to. A class's methods are created using def statements in the class's suite. Class instances are created by calling the class with any necessary arguments; for example, x = complex(4, 8) creates a complex number and sets x to be an object reference to it.

Attributes and Methods

Let's start with a very simple class, Point, that holds an (x, y) coordinate. The class is in file Shape.py, and its complete implementation (excluding docstrings) is show here:

```
class Point:
```

```
    def __init__(self, x=0, y=0):
        self.x = x
        self.y = y

    def distance_from_origin(self):
        return math.hypot(self.x, self.y)

    def __eq__(self, other):
        return self.x == other.x and self.y == other.y

    def __repr__(self):
        return "Point({0.x!r}, {0.y!r})".format(self)

    def __str__(self):
        return "({0.x!r}, {0.y!r})".format(self)
```

Since no base classes are specified, Point is a direct subclass of object, just as though we had written class Point(object). Before we discuss each of the methods, let's see some examples of their use:

```
import Shape
a = Shape.Point()
repr(a)                      # returns: 'Point(0, 0)'
b = Shape.Point(3, 4)
str(b)                       # returns: '(3, 4)'
b.distance_from_origin()     # returns: 5.0
b.x = -19
str(b)                       # returns: '(-19, 4)'
a == b, a != b               # returns: (False, True)
```

The Point class has two data attributes, self.x and self.y, and five methods (not counting inherited methods), four of which are special methods; they are illustrated in Figure 6.2. Once the Shape module is imported, the Point class can be used like any other. The data attributes can be accessed directly (e.g., y = a.y), and the class integrates nicely with all of Python's other classes by providing support for the equality operator (==) and for producing strings in representational and string forms. And Python is smart enough to supply the inequality operator (!=) based on the equality operator. (It is also possible to specify each operator individually if we want total control, for example, if they are not exact opposites of each other.)

Python automatically supplies the first argument in method calls—it is an object reference to the object itself (called *this* in C++ and Java). We must include this argument in the parameter list, and by convention the parameter is called self. All object attributes (data and method attributes) must be qualified by self. This requires a little bit more typing compared with some other languages, but has the advantage of providing absolute clarity: we always know that we are accessing an object attribute if we qualify with self.

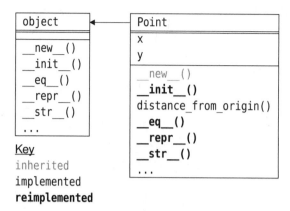

Figure 6.2 *The Point class's inheritance hierarchy*

To create an object, two steps are necessary. First a raw or uninitialized object must be created, and then the object must be initialized, ready for use. Some object-oriented languages (such as C++ and Java) combine these two steps into one, but Python keeps them separate. When an object is created (e.g., p = Shape.Point()), first the special method __new__() is called to create the object, and then the special method __init__() is called to initialize it.

In practice almost every Python class we create will require us to reimplement only the __init__() method, since the object.__new__() method is almost always sufficient and is automatically called if we don't provide our own __new__() method. (Later in this chapter we will show a rare example where we do need to reimplement __new__().) Not having to reimplement methods in a subclass is another benefit of object-oriented programming—if the base class method is sufficient we don't have to reimplement it in our subclass. This works because if we call a method on an object and the object's class does not have an implementation of that method, Python will automatically go through the object's base classes, and their base classes, and so on, until it finds the method—and if the method is not found an AttributeError exception is raised.

Alternative Fuzzy-Bool
☞ 246

For example, if we execute p = Shape.Point(), Python begins by looking for the method Point.__new__(). Since we have not reimplemented this method, Python looks for the method in Point's base classes. In this case there is only one base class, object, and this has the required method, so Python calls object.__new__() and creates a raw uninitialized object. Then Python looks for the initializer, __init__(), and since we have reimplemented it, Python doesn't need to look further and calls Point.__init__(). Finally, Python sets p to be an object reference to the newly created and initialized object of type Point.

Because they are so short and a few pages away, for convenience we will show each method again before discussing it.

```
    def __init__(self, x=0, y=0):
        self.x = x
        self.y = y
```

The two instance variables, self.x and self.y, are created in the initializer, and assigned the values of the x and y parameters. Since Python will find this initializer when we create a new Point object, the object.__init__() method will not be called. This is because as soon as Python has found the required method it calls it and doesn't look further.

Object-oriented purists might start the method off with a call to the base class __init__() method by calling super().__init__(). The effect of calling the super() function like this is to call the base class's __init__() method. For classes that directly inherit object there is no need to do this, and in this book we call base class methods only when necessary—for example, when creating classes that are designed to be subclassed, or when creating classes that don't directly inherit object. This is to some extent a matter of coding style—it is perfectly reasonable to always call super().__init__() at the start of a custom class's __init__() method.

```
    def distance_from_origin(self):
        return math.hypot(self.x, self.y)
```

This is a conventional method that performs a computation based on the object's instance variables. It is quite common for methods to be fairly short and to have only the object they are called on as an argument, since often all the data the method needs is available inside the object.

```
    def __eq__(self, other):
        return self.x == other.x and self.y == other.y
```

Methods should not have names that begin and end with two underscores—unless they are one of the predefined special methods. Python provides special methods for all the comparison operators as shown in Table 6.1.

All instances of custom classes support == by default, and the comparison always returns False. We can override this behavior by reimplementing the __eq__() special method as we have done here. Python will supply the __ne__() (not equal) inequality operator (!=) automatically if we implement __eq__() but don't implement __ne__().

By default, all instances of custom classes are hashable, so hash() can be called on them and they can be used as dictionary keys and stored in sets. But if we reimplement __eq__(), instances are no longer hashable. We will see how to fix this when we discuss the FuzzyBool class later on.

Fuzzy-
Bool

☞ 244

By implementing this special method we can compare Point objects, but if we were to try to compare a Point with an object of a different type—say, int—we

Table 6.1 *Comparison Special Methods*

Special Method	Usage	Description
`__lt__(self, other)`	`x < y`	Returns True if x is less than y
`__le__(self, other)`	`x <= y`	Returns True if x is less than or equal to y
`__eq__(self, other)`	`x == y`	Returns True if x is equal to y
`__ne__(self, other)`	`x != y`	Returns True if x is not equal to y
`__ge__(self, other)`	`x >= y`	Returns True if x is greater than or equal to y
`__gt__(self, other)`	`x > y`	Returns True if x is greater than y

would get an `AttributeError` exception (since `int`s don't have an x attribute). On the other hand, we *can* compare `Point` objects with other objects that coincidentally just happen to have an x attribute (thanks to Python's duck typing), but this may lead to surprising results.

If we want to avoid inappropriate comparisons there are a few approaches we can take. One is to use an assertion, for example, `assert isinstance(other, Point)`. Another is to raise a `TypeError` to indicate that comparisons between the two types are not supported, for example, `if not isinstance(other, Point): raise TypeError()`. The third way (which is also the most Pythonically correct) is to do this: `if not isinstance(other, Point): return NotImplemented`. In this third case, if `NotImplemented` is returned, Python will then try calling `other.__eq__(self)` to see whether the `other` type supports the comparison with the `Point` type, and if there is no such method or if that method also returns `NotImplemented`, Python will give up and raise a `TypeError` exception. (Note that only reimplementations of the comparison special methods listed in Table 6.1 may return `NotImplemented`.)

The built-in `isinstance()` function takes an object and a class (or a tuple of classes), and returns True if the object is of the given class (or of one of the tuple of classes), or of one of the class's (or one of the tuple of classes') base classes.

```
def __repr__(self):
    return "Point({0.x!r}, {0.y!r})".format(self)
```

`str.`
`format()`
`74 ☞`

The built-in `repr()` function calls the `__repr__()` special method for the object it is given and returns the result. The string returned is one of two kinds. One kind is where the string returned can be evaluated using the built-in `eval()` function to produce an object equivalent to the one `repr()` was called on. The other kind is used where this is not possible; we will see an example later on. Here is how we can go from a `Point` object to a string and back to a `Point` object:

```
p = Shape.Point(3, 9)
repr(p)                                # returns: 'Point(3, 9)'
q = eval(p.__module__ + "." + repr(p))
repr(q)                                # returns: 'Point(3, 9)'
```

import
185 ☞

We must give the module name when eval()-ing if we used import Shape. (This would not be necessary if we had done the import differently, for example, from Shape import Point.) Python provides every object with a few private attributes, one of which is __module__, a string that holds the object's module name, which in this example is "Shape".

At the end of this snippet we have two Point objects, p and q, both with the same attribute values, so they compare as equal. The eval() function returns the result of executing the string it is given—which must contain a valid Python statement.

Dynamic code execution

☞ 334

```
def __str__(self):
    return "({0.x!r}, {0.y!r})".format(self)
```

The built-in str() function works like the repr() function, except that it calls the object's __str__() special method. The result is intended to be understandable to human readers and is not expected to be suitable for passing to the eval() function. Continuing the previous example, str(p) (or str(q)) would return the string '(3, 9)'.

We have now covered the simple Point class—and also covered a lot of behind-the-scenes details that are important to know but which can mostly be left in the background. The Point class holds an (x, y) coordinate—a fundamental part of what we need to represent a circle, as we discussed at the beginning of the chapter. In the next subsection we will see how to create a custom Circle class, inheriting from Point so that we don't have to duplicate the code for the x and y attributes or for the distance_from_origin() method.

Inheritance and Polymorphism

The Circle class builds on the Point class using inheritance. The Circle class adds one additional data attribute (radius), and three new methods. It also reimplements a few of Point's methods. Here is the complete class definition:

```
class Circle(Point):

    def __init__(self, radius, x=0, y=0):
        super().__init__(x, y)
        self.radius = radius

    def edge_distance_from_origin(self):
        return abs(self.distance_from_origin() - self.radius)
```

```
    def area(self):
        return math.pi * (self.radius ** 2)

    def circumference(self):
        return 2 * math.pi * self.radius

    def __eq__(self, other):
        return self.radius == other.radius and super().__eq__(other)

    def __repr__(self):
        return "Circle({0.radius!r}, {0.x!r}, {0.y!r})".format(self)

    def __str__(self):
        return repr(self)
```

Inheritance is achieved simply by listing the class (or classes) that we want our class to inherit in the class line.* Here we have inherited the Point class—the inheritance hierarchy for Circle is shown in Figure 6.3.

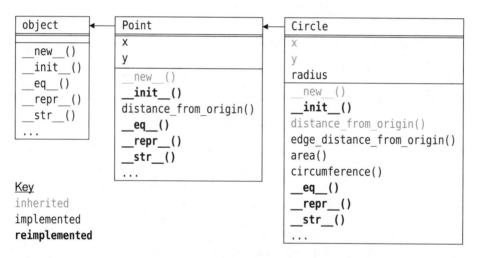

Figure 6.3 *The Circle class's inheritance hierarchy*

Inside the __init__() method we use super() to call the base class's __init__() method—this creates and initializes the self.x and self.y attributes. Users of the class could supply an invalid radius, such as -2; in the next subsection we will see how to prevent such problems by making attributes more robust using properties.

The area() and circumference() methods are straightforward. The edge_distance_from_origin() method calls the distance_from_origin() method as part

---

* Multiple inheritance, abstract base types, and other advanced object-oriented techniques are covered in Chapter 8.

of its computation. Since the `Circle` class does not provide an implementation of the `distance_from_origin()` method, the one provided by the `Point` base class will be found and used. Contrast this with the reimplementation of the `__eq__()` method. This method compares this circle's radius with the other circle's radius, and if they are equal it then explicitly calls the base class's `__eq__()` method using `super()`. If we did not use `super()` we would have infinite recursion, since `Circle.__eq__()` would then just keep calling itself. Notice also that we don't have to pass the `self` argument in the `super()` calls since Python automatically passes it for us.

Here are a couple of usage examples:

```
p = Shape.Point(28, 45)
c = Shape.Circle(5, 28, 45)
p.distance_from_origin()        # returns: 53.0
c.distance_from_origin()        # returns: 53.0
```

We can call the `distance_from_origin()` method on a `Point` or on a `Circle`, since `Circle`s can stand in for `Point`s.

Polymorphism means that any object of a given class can be used as though it were an object of any of its class's base classes. This is why when we create a subclass we need to implement only the additional methods we require and have to reimplement only those existing methods we want to replace. And when reimplementing methods, we can use the base class's implementation if necessary by using `super()` inside the reimplementation.

In the `Circle`'s case we have implemented additional methods, such as `area()` and `circumference()`, and reimplemented methods we needed to change. The reimplementations of `__repr__()` and `__str__()` are necessary because without them the base class methods will be used and the strings returned will be of `Point`s instead of `Circle`s. The reimplementations of `__init__()` and `__eq__()` are necessary because we must account for the fact that `Circle`s have an additional attribute, and in both cases we make use of the base class implementations of the methods to minimize the work we must do.

The `Point` and `Circle` classes are as complete as we need them to be. We could provide additional methods, such as other comparison special methods if we wanted to be able to order `Point`s or `Circle`s. Another thing that we might want to do for which no method is provided is to copy a `Point` or `Circle`. Most Python classes don't provide a `copy()` method (exceptions being `dict.copy()` and `set.copy()`). If we want to copy a `Point` or `Circle` we can easily do so by importing the copy module and using the `copy.copy()` function. (There is no need to use `copy.deepcopy()` for `Point` and `Circle` objects since they contain only immutable instance variables.)

Shallow
and
deep
copying

136 ☜

Using Properties to Control Attribute Access

In the previous subsection the Point class included a distance_from_origin()
method, and the Circle class had the area(), circumference(), and edge_dis-
tance_from_origin() methods. All these methods return a single float value, so
from the point of view of a user of these classes they could just as well be data
attributes, but read-only, of course. In the ShapeAlt.py file alternative implementations of Point and Circle are provided, and all the methods mentioned
here are provided as properties. This allows us to write code like this:

```
circle = Shape.Circle(5, 28, 45)   # assumes: import ShapeAlt as Shape
circle.radius                      # returns: 5
circle.edge_distance_from_origin   # returns: 48.0
```

Here are the implementations of the getter methods for the ShapeAlt.Circle
class's area and edge_ distance_from_origin properties:

```
@property
def area(self):
    return math.pi * (self.radius ** 2)

@property
def edge_distance_from_origin(self):
    return abs(self.distance_from_origin - self.radius)
```

If we provide only getters as we have done here, the properties are read-only.
The code for the area property is the same as for the previous area() method.
The edge_distance_from_origin's code is slightly different from before because it
now accesses the base class's distance_from_origin property instead of calling
a distance_from_origin() method. The most notable difference to both is the
property *decorator*. A decorator is a function that takes a function or method
as its argument and returns a "decorated" version, that is, a version of the
function or method that is modified in some way. A decorator is indicated by
preceding its name with an at symbol (@). For now, just treat decorators as
syntax—in Chapter 8 we will see how to create custom decorators.

The property() decorator function is built-in and takes up to four arguments: a
getter function, a setter function, a deleter function, and a docstring. The
effect of using @property is the same as calling the property() function with just
one argument, the getter function. We could have created the area property
like this:

```
def area(self):
    return math.pi * (self.radius ** 2)
area = property(area)
```

We rarely use this syntax, since using a decorator is shorter and clearer.

In the previous subsection we noted that no validation is performed on the Circle's radius attribute. We can provide validation by making radius into a property. This does not require any changes to the Circle.__init__() method, and any code that accesses the Circle.radius attribute will continue to work unchanged—only now the radius will be validated whenever it is set.

Python programmers normally use properties rather than the explicit getters and setters (e.g., getRadius() and setRadius()) that are so commonly used in other object-oriented languages. This is because it is so easy to change a data attribute into a property without affecting the use of the class.

To turn an attribute into a readable/writable property we must create a private attribute where the data is actually held and supply getter and setter methods. Here is the radius's getter, setter, and docstring in full:

```
@property
def radius(self):
    """The circle's radius

    >>> circle = Circle(-2)
    Traceback (most recent call last):
    ...
    AssertionError: radius must be nonzero and non-negative
    >>> circle = Circle(4)
    >>> circle.radius = -1
    Traceback (most recent call last):
    ...
    AssertionError: radius must be nonzero and non-negative
    >>> circle.radius = 6
    """
    return self.__radius

@radius.setter
def radius(self, radius):
    assert radius > 0, "radius must be nonzero and non-negative"
    self.__radius = radius
```

We use an assert to ensure a nonzero and non-negative radius and store the radius's value in the private attribute self.__radius. Notice that the getter and setter (and deleter if we needed one) all have the same name—it is the decorators that distinguish them, and the decorators rename them appropriately so that no name conflicts occur.

The decorator for the setter may look strange at first sight. Every property that is created has a getter, setter, and deleter attribute, so once the radius property is created using @property, the radius.getter, radius.setter, and radius.deleter attributes become available. The radius.getter is set to the getter method by the @property decorator. The other two are set up by Python so that they do nothing (so the attribute cannot be written to or deleted), unless they are used as decorators, in which case they in effect replace themselves with the method they are used to decorate.

The Circle's initializer, Circle.__init__(), includes the statement self.radius = radius; this will call the radius property's setter, so if an invalid radius is given when a Circle is created an AssertionError exception will be raised. Similarly, if an attempt is made to set an existing Circle's radius to an invalid value, again the setter will be called and an exception raised. The docstring includes doctests to test that the exception is correctly raised in these cases.

Both the Point and Circle types are custom data types that have sufficient functionality to be useful. Most of the data types that we are likely to create are like this, but occasionally it is necessary to create a custom data type that is complete in every respect. We will see examples of this in the next subsection.

Creating Complete and Fully Integrated Data Types

When creating a complete data type two possibilities are open to us. One is to create the data type from scratch. Although the data type will inherit object (as all Python classes do), every data attribute and method that the data type requires (apart from __new__()) must be provided. The other possibility is to inherit from an existing data type that is similar to the one we want to create. In this case the work usually involves reimplementing those methods we want to behave differently and "unimplementing" those methods we don't want at all.

In the following subsubsection we will implement a FuzzyBool data type from scratch, and in the subsubsection after that we will implement the same type but will use inheritance to reduce the work we must do. The built-in bool type is two-valued (True and False), but in some areas of AI (Artificial Intelligence), fuzzy Booleans are used, which have values corresponding to "true" and "false", and also to intermediates between them. In our implementations we will use floating-point values with 0.0 denoting False and 1.0 denoting True. In this system, 0.5 means 50 percent true, and 0.25 means 25 percent true, and so on. Here are some usage examples (they work the same with either implementation):

```
a = FuzzyBool.FuzzyBool(.875)
b = FuzzyBool.FuzzyBool(.25)
a >= b                             # returns: True
bool(a), bool(b)                   # returns: (True, False)
~a                                 # returns: FuzzyBool(0.125)
```

```
a & b                                  # returns: FuzzyBool(0.25)
b |= FuzzyBool.FuzzyBool(.5)           # b is now: FuzzyBool(0.5)
"a={0:.1%} b={1:.0%}".format(a, b)     # returns: 'a=87.5% b=50%'
```

We want the FuzzyBool type to support the complete set of comparison operators (<, <=, ==, !=, >=, >), and the three basic logical operations, not (~), and (&), and or (|). In addition to the logical operations we want to provide a couple of other logical methods, conjunction() and disjunction(), that take as many FuzzyBools as we like and return the appropriate resultant FuzzyBool. And to complete the data type we want to provide conversions to types bool, int, float, and str, and have an eval()-able representational form. The final requirements are that FuzzyBool supports str.format() format specifications, that FuzzyBools can be used as dictionary keys or as members of sets, and that FuzzyBools are immutable—but with the provision of augmented assignment operators (&= and |=) to ensure that they are convenient to use.

Table 6.1 (page 232) lists the comparison special methods, Table 6.2 (page 240) lists the fundamental special methods, and Table 6.3 (page 243) lists the numeric special methods—these include the bitwise operators (~, &, and |) which FuzzyBools use for their logical operators, and also arithmetic operators such as + and – which FuzzyBool does not implement because they are inappropriate.

Creating Data Types from Scratch

To create the FuzzyBool type from scratch means that we must provide an attribute to hold the FuzzyBool's value and all the methods that we require. Here are the class line and the initializer, taken from FuzzyBool.py:

```
class FuzzyBool:

    def __init__(self, value=0.0):
        self.__value = value if 0.0 <= value <= 1.0 else 0.0
```

Shape-
Alt.
Circle.
radius
proper-
ty
237 ☜

We have made the value attribute private because we want FuzzyBool to behave like immutables, so allowing access to the attribute would be wrong. Also, if an out-of-range value is given we force it to take a fail-safe value of 0.0 (false). In the previous subsection's ShapeAlt.Circle class we used a stricter policy, raising an exception if an invalid radius value was used when creating a new Circle object. The FuzzyBool's inheritance tree is shown in Figure 6.4.

The simplest logical operator is logical NOT, for which we have coopted the bitwise inversion operator (~):

```
    def __invert__(self):
        return FuzzyBool(1.0 - self.__value)
```

Table 6.2 *Fundamental Special Methods*

Special Method	Usage	Description
`__bool__(self)`	`bool(x)`	If provided, returns a truth value for x; useful for `if x: ...`
`__format__(self, format_spec)`	`"{0}".format(x)`	Provides `str.format()` support for custom classes
`__hash__(self)`	`hash(x)`	If provided, x can be used as a dictionary key or held in a set
`__init__(self, args)`	`x = X(args)`	Called when an object is initialized
`__new__(cls, args)`	`x = X(args)`	Called when an object is created
`__repr__(self)`	`repr(x)`	Returns a string representation of x; where possible `eval(repr(x)) == x`
`__repr__(self)`	`ascii(x)`	Returns a string representation of x using only ASCII characters
`__str__(self)`	`str(x)`	Returns a human-comprehensible string representation of x

Reimplementing __new__() ☞ 246

str. format() 77 ☜❚

The __del__() Special Method

The `__del__(self)` special method is called when an object is destroyed—at least in theory. In practice, `__del__()` may never be called, even at program termination. Furthermore, when we write del *x*, all that happens is that the object reference *x* is deleted and the count of how many object references refer to the object that was referred to by *x* is decreased by 1. Only when this count reaches 0 is `__del__()` likely to be called, but Python offers no guarantee that it will ever be called. In view of this, `__del__()` is very rarely reimplemented—none of the examples in this book reimplements it—and it should not be used to free up resources, so it is not suitable to be used for closing files, disconnecting network connections, or disconnecting database connections.

Python provides two separate mechanisms for ensuring that resources are properly released. One is to use a `try ... finally` block as we have seen before and will see again in Chapter 7, and the other is to use a context object in conjunction with a `with` statement—this is covered in Chapter 8.

The bitwise logical AND operator (&) is provided by the `__and__()` special method, and the in-place version (&=) is provided by `__iand__()`:

```python
def __and__(self, other):
    return FuzzyBool(min(self.__value, other.__value))
```

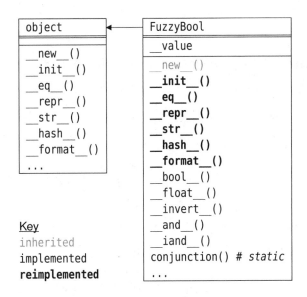

Figure 6.4 *The FuzzyBool class's inheritance hierarchy*

```
def __iand__(self, other):
    self.__value = min(self.__value, other.__value)
    return self
```

The bitwise AND operator returns a new FuzzyBool based on this one and the other one, whereas the augmented assignment (in-place) version updates the private value. Strictly speaking, this is not immutable behavior, but it does match the behavior of some other Python immutables, such as int, where, for example, using += looks like the left-hand operand is being changed but in fact it is re-bound to refer to a new int object that holds the result of the addition, although in this case no rebinding is needed because we really do change the FuzzyBool itself. The reason that we return self is to support the chaining of operations.

We could also implement __rand__(). This method is called when self and other are of different types and the __and__() method is not implemented for that particular pair of types. This isn't needed for the FuzzyBool class. Most of the special methods for binary operators have both "i" (in-place) and "r" (reflect, that is, swap operands) versions.

We have not shown the implementation for __or__() which provides the bitwise | operator, or for __ior__() which provides the in-place |= operator, since both are the same as the equivalent AND methods except that we take the maximum value instead of the minimum value of self and other.

```
def __repr__(self):
    return ("{0}({1})".format(self.__class__.__name__,
```

```
                                self.__value))
```

We have created an eval()-able representational form. For example, given f =
FuzzyBool.FuzzyBool(.75); repr(f) will produce the string 'FuzzyBool(0.75)'.

All objects have some special attributes automatically supplied by Python,
one of which is called __class__, a reference to the object's class. All classes
have a private __name__ attribute, again provided automatically. We have used
these attributes to provide the class name used for the representation form.
This means that if the FuzzyBool class is subclassed just to add extra methods,
the inherited __repr__() method will work correctly without needing to be
reimplemented, since it will pick up the subclass's class name.

```
          def __str__(self):
              return str(self.__value)
```

For the string form we just return the floating-point value formatted as a
string. We don't have to use super() to avoid infinite recursion because we call
str() on the self.__value attribute, not on the instance itself.

```
          def __bool__(self):
              return self.__value > 0.5

          def __int__(self):
              return round(self.__value)

          def __float__(self):
              return self.__value
```

The __bool__() special method converts the instance to a Boolean, so it must always return either True or False. The __int__() special method provides integer
conversion. We have used the built-in round() function because int() simply
truncates (so would return 0 for any FuzzyBool value except 1.0). Floating-point
conversion is easy because the value is already a floating-point number.

```
          def __lt__(self, other):
              return self.__value < other.__value

          def __eq__(self, other):
              return self.__value == other.__value
```

To provide the complete set of comparisons (<, <=, ==, !=, >=, >) it is necessary to
implement at least three of them, <, <=, and ==, since Python can infer > from
<, != from ==, and >= from <=. We have shown only two representative methods
here since all of them are very similar.[*]

Com-
plete
compar-
isons

☞ 369

---

[*] In fact, we implemented only the __lt__() and __eq__() methods quoted here—the other
comparison methods were automatically generated; we will see how in Chapter 8.

Table 6.3 *Numeric and Bitwise Special Methods*

Special Method	Usage	Special Method	Usage
__abs__(self)	abs(x)	__complex__(self)	complex(x)
__float__(self)	float(x)	__int__(self)	int(x)
__index__(self)	bin(x) oct(x) hex(x)	__round__(self, *digits*)	round(x, *digits*)
__pos__(self)	+x	__neg__(self)	-x
__add__(self, other)	x + y	__sub__(self, other)	x - y
__iadd__(self, other)	x += y	__isub__(self, other)	x -= y
__radd__(self, other)	y + x	__rsub__(self, other)	y - x
__mul__(self, other)	x * y	__mod__(self, other)	x % y
__imul__(self, other)	x *= y	__imod__(self, other)	x %= y
__rmul__(self, other)	y * x	__rmod__(self, other)	y % x
__floordiv__(self, other)	x // y	__truediv__(self, other)	x / y
__ifloordiv__(self, other)	x //= y	__itruediv__(self, other)	x /= y
__rfloordiv__(self, other)	y // x	__rtruediv__(self, other)	y / x
__divmod__(self, other)	divmod(x, y)	__rdivmod__(self, other)	divmod(y, x)
__pow__(self, other)	x ** y	__and__(self, other)	x & y
__ipow__(self, other)	x **= y	__iand__(self, other)	x &= y
__rpow__(self, other)	y ** x	__rand__(self, other)	y & x
__xor__(self, other)	x ^ y	__or__(self, other)	x | y
__ixor__(self, other)	x ^= y	__ior__(self, other)	x |= y
__rxor__(self, other)	y ^ x	__ror__(self, other)	y | x
__lshift__(self, other)	x << y	__rshift__(self, other)	x >> y
__ilshift__(self, other)	x <<= y	__irshift__(self, other)	x >>= y
__rlshift__(self, other)	y << x	__rrshift__(self, other)	y >> x
		__invert__(self)	~x

```
def __hash__(self):
    return hash(id(self))
```

By default, instances of custom classes support operator == (which always returns False), and are hashable (so can be dictionary keys and can be added
to sets). But if we reimplement the __eq__() special method to provide proper
equality testing, instances are no longer hashable. This can be fixed by providing a __hash__() special method as we have done here.

Python provides hash functions for strings, numbers, frozen sets, and other
classes. Here we have simply used the built-in hash() function (which can
operate on any type which has a __hash__() special method), and given it the
object's unique ID from which to calculate the hash. (We can't use the private
self.__value since that can change as a result of augmented assignment,
whereas an object's hash value must never change.)

The built-in id() function returns a unique integer for the object it is given
as its argument. This integer is usually the object's address in memory, but
all that we can assume is that no two objects have the same ID. Behind the
scenes the is operator uses the id() function to determine whether two object
references refer to the same object.

```
def __format__(self, format_spec):
    return format(self.__value, format_spec)
```

The built-in format() function is only really needed in class definitions. It takes
a single object and an optional format specification and returns a string with
the object suitably formatted.

When an object is used in a format string the object's __format__() method is
called with the object and the format specification as arguments. The method
returns the instance suitably formatted as we saw earlier.

All the built-in classes already have suitable __format__() methods; here we
make use of the float.__format__() method by passing the floating-point value
and the format string we have been given. We could have achieved exactly the
same thing like this:

```
def __format__(self, format_spec):
    return self.__value.__format__(format_spec)
```

Using the format() function requires a tiny bit less typing and is clearer to read.
Nothing forces us to use the format() function at all, so we could invent our own
format specification language and interpret it inside the __format__() method,
as long as we return a string.

```
@staticmethod
def conjunction(*fuzzies):
    return FuzzyBool(min([float(x) for x in fuzzies]))
```

Fuzzy-
Bool
usage
exam-
ples
238 ☞

The built-in staticmethod() function is designed to be used as a decorator as we have done here. Static methods are simply methods that do *not* get self or any other first argument specially passed by Python.

The & operator can be chained, so given FuzzyBool's f, g, and h, we can get the conjunction of all of them by writing f & g & h. This works fine for small numbers of FuzzyBools, but if we have a dozen or more it starts to become rather inefficient since each & represents a function call. With the method given here we can achieve the same thing using a single function call of Fuzzy-Bool.FuzzyBool.conjunction(f, g, h). This can be written more concisely using a FuzzyBool instance, but since static methods don't get self, if we call one using an instance and we want to process that instance we must pass it ourselves—for example, f.conjunction(f, g, h).

We have not shown the corresponding disjunction() method since it differs only in its name and that it uses max() rather than min().

Some Python programmers consider the use of static methods to be un-Python-ic, and use them only if they are converting code from another language (such as C++ or Java), or if they have a method that does not use self. In Python, rather than using static methods it is usually better to create a module function instead, as we will see in the next subsubsection, or a class method, as we will see in the last section.

In a similar vein, creating a variable inside a class definition but outside any method creates a static (class) variable. For constants it is usually more convenient to use private module globals, but class variables can often be useful for sharing data among all of a class's instances.

We have now completed the implementation of the FuzzyBool class "from scratch". We have had to reimplement 15 methods (17 if we had done the minimum of all four comparison operators), and have implemented two static methods. In the following subsubsection we will show an alternative implementation, this time based on the inheritance of float. It involves the reimplementations of just eight methods and the implementation of two module functions—and the "unimplementation" of 32 methods.

In most object-oriented languages inheritance is used to create new classes that have all the methods and attributes of the classes they inherit, as well as the additional methods and attributes that we want the new class to have. Python fully supports this, allowing us to add new methods, or to reimplement inherited methods so as to modify their behavior. But in addition, Python allows us to effectively unimplement methods, that is, to make the new class behave as though it does not have some of the methods that it inherits. Doing this might not appeal to object-oriented purists since it breaks polymorphism, but in Python at least, it can occasionally be a useful technique.

Creating Data Types from Other Data Types

The FuzzyBool implementation in this subsubsection is in the file Fuzzy-BoolAlt.py. One immediate difference from the previous version is that instead of providing static methods for conjunction() and disjunction(), we have provided them as module functions. For example:

```
def conjunction(*fuzzies):
    return FuzzyBool(min(fuzzies))
```

The code for this is much simpler than before because FuzzyBoolAlt.FuzzyBool objects are float subclasses, and so can be used directly in place of a float without needing any conversion. (The inheritance tree is shown in Figure 6.5.) Accessing the function is also cleaner than before. Instead of having to specify both the module and the class (or using an instance), having done import FuzzyBoolAlt we can just write FuzzyBoolAlt.conjunction().

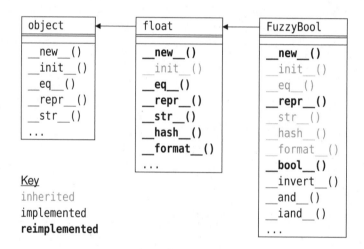

Figure 6.5 *The alternative FuzzyBool class's inheritance hierarchy*

Here is the FuzzyBool's class line and its __new__() method:

```
class FuzzyBool(float):

    def __new__(cls, value=0.0):
        return super().__new__(cls,
                value if 0.0 <= value <= 1.0 else 0.0)
```

When we create a new class it is usually mutable and relies on object.__new__() to create the raw uninitialized object. But in the case of immutable classes we need to do the creation and initialization in one step since once an immutable object has been created it cannot be changed.

The __new__() method is called before any object has been created (since object creation is what __new__() does), so it cannot have a self object passed to it since one doesn't yet exist. In fact, __new__() is a *class method*—these are similar to normal methods except that they are called on the class rather than on an instance and Python supplies as their first argument the class they are called on. The variable name cls for class is just a convention, in the same way that self is the conventional name for the object itself.

So when we write f = FuzzyBool(0.7), under the hood Python calls Fuzzy-Bool.__new__(FuzzyBool, 0.7) to create a new object—say, *fuzzy*—and then calls *fuzzy*.__init__() to do any further initialization, and finally returns an object reference to the *fuzzy* object—it is this object reference that f is set to. Most of __new__()'s work is passed on to the base class implementation, object.__new__(); all we do is make sure that the value is in range.

Class methods are set up by using the built-in classmethod() function used as a decorator. But as a convenience we don't have to bother writing @classmethod before def __new__() because Python already knows that this method is always a class method. We do need to use the decorator if we want to create other class methods, though, as we will see in the chapter's final section.

Now that we have seen a class method we can clarify the different kinds of methods that Python provides. Class methods have their first argument added by Python and it is the method's class; normal methods have their first argument added by Python and it is the instance the method was called on; and static methods have no first argument added. And all the kinds of methods get any arguments we pass to them (as their second and subsequent arguments in the case of class and normal methods, and as their first and subsequent arguments for static methods).

```
def __invert__(self):
    return FuzzyBool(1.0 - float(self))
```

This method is used to provide support for the bitwise NOT operator (~) just the same as before. Notice that instead of accessing a private attribute that holds the FuzzyBool's value we use self directly. This is thanks to inheriting float which means that a FuzzyBool can be used wherever a float is expected—providing none of the FuzzyBool's "unimplemented" methods are used, of course.

```
def __and__(self, other):
    return FuzzyBool(min(self, other))

def __iand__(self, other):
    return FuzzyBool(min(self, other))
```

The logic for these is also the same as before (although the code is subtly different), and just like the __invert__() method we can use both self and other

directly as though they were floats. We have omitted the OR versions since
they differ only in their names (__or__() and __ior__()) and that they use max()
rather than min().

```
def __repr__(self):
    return ("{0}({1})".format(self.__class__.__name__,
                             super().__repr__()))
```

We must reimplement the __repr__() method since the base class version
float.__repr__() just returns the number as a string, whereas we need the class
name to make the representation eval()-able. For the str.format()'s second argument we cannot just pass self since that will result in an infinite recursion
of calls to this __repr__() method, so instead we call the base class implementation.

We don't have to reimplement the __str__() method because the base class
version, float.__str__(), is sufficient and will be used in the absence of a
FuzzyBool.__str__() reimplementation.

```
def __bool__(self):
    return self > 0.5

def __int__(self):
    return round(self)
```

When a float is used in a Boolean context it is False if its value is 0.0 and True
otherwise. This is not the appropriate behavior for FuzzyBools, so we have had
to reimplement this method. Similarly, using int(self) would simply truncate,
turning everything but 1.0 into 0, so here we use round() to produce 0 for values
up to 0.5 and 1 for values up to and including the maximum of 1.0.

We have not reimplemented the __hash__() method, the __format__() method,
or any of the methods that are used to provide the comparison operators, since
all those provided by the float base class work correctly for FuzzyBools.

The methods we have reimplemented provide a complete implementation of
the FuzzyBool class—and have required far less code than the implementation
presented in the previous subsection. However, this new FuzzyBool class
has inherited more than 30 methods which don't make sense for FuzzyBools.
For example, none of the basic numeric and bitwise shift operators (+, -, *, /, <<,
>>, etc.) can sensibly be applied to FuzzyBools. Here is how we could begin to
"unimplement" addition:

```
def __add__(self, other):
    raise NotImplementedError()
```

We would also have to write the same code for the __iadd__() and __radd__()
methods to completely prevent addition. (Note that NotImplementedError is a
standard exception and is different from the built-in NotImplemented object.) An

alternative to raising a `NotImplementedError` exception, especially if we want
to more closely mimic the behavior of Python's built-in classes, is to raise
a `TypeError`. Here is how we can make `FuzzyBool.__add__()` behave just like
built-in classes that are faced with an invalid operation:

```
def __add__(self, other):
    raise TypeError("unsupported operand type(s) for +: "
                    "'{0}' and '{1}'".format(
            self.__class__.__name__, other.__class__.__name__))
```

For unary operations, we want to unimplement in a way that mimics the
behavior of built-in types, the code is slightly easier:

```
def __neg__(self):
    raise TypeError("bad operand type for unary -: '{0}'".format(
            self.__class__.__name__))
```

For comparison operators, there is a much simpler idiom. For example, to
unimplement ==, we would write:

```
def __eq__(self, other):
    return NotImplemented
```

If a method implementing a comparison operator (<, <=, ==, !=, >=, >), returns
the built-in `NotImplemented` object and an attempt is made to use the method,
Python will first try the reverse comparison by swapping the operands (in
case the `other` object has a suitable comparison method since the `self` object
does not), and if that doesn't work Python raises a `TypeError` exception with a
message that explains that the operation is not supported for operands of the
types used. But for all noncomparison methods that we don't want, we must
raise either a `NotImplementedError` or a `TypeError` exception as we did for the
`__add__()` and `__neg__()` methods shown earlier.

It would be tedious to unimplement every method we don't want as we have
done here, although it does work and has the virtue of being easy to understand. Here we will look at a more advanced technique for unimplementing
methods—it is used in the `FuzzyBoolAlt` module—but it is probably best to skip
to the next section (starting on page 251) and return here only if the need arises
in practice.

Here is the code for unimplementing the two unary operations we don't want:

```
for name, operator in (("__neg__", "-"),
                       ("__index__", "index()")):
    message = ("bad operand type for unary {0}: '{{self}}'"
               .format(operator))
    exec("def {0}(self): raise TypeError(\"{1}\".format("
         "self=self.__class__.__name__))".format(name, message))
```

The built-in exec() function dynamically executes the code passed to it from the object it is given. In this case we have given it a string, but it is also possible to pass some other kinds of objects. By default, the code is executed in the context of the enclosing scope, in this case within the definition of the FuzzyBool class, so the def statements that are executed create FuzzyBool methods which is what we want. The code is executed just once, when the FuzzyBoolAlt module is imported. Here is the code that is generated for the first tuple ("__neg__", "-"):

Dynamic programming ☞ 339

```
def __neg__(self):
    raise TypeError("bad operand type for unary -: '{self}'"
                    .format(self=self.__class__.__name__))
```

We have made the exception and error message match those that Python uses for its own types. The code for handling binary methods and *n*-ary functions (such as pow()) follows a similar pattern but with a different error message. For completeness, here is the code we have used:

```
for name, operator in (("__xor__", "^"), ("__ixor__", "^="),
        ("__add__", "+"), ("__iadd__", "+="), ("__radd__", "+"),
        ("__sub__", "-"), ("__isub__", "-="), ("__rsub__", "-"),
        ("__mul__", "*"), ("__imul__", "*="), ("__rmul__", "*"),
        ("__pow__", "**"), ("__ipow__", "**="),
        ("__rpow__", "**"), ("__floordiv__", "//"),
        ("__ifloordiv__", "//="), ("__rfloordiv__", "//"),
        ("__truediv__", "/"), ("__itruediv__", "/="),
        ("__rtruediv__", "/"), ("__divmod__", "divmod()"),
        ("__rdivmod__", "divmod()"), ("__mod__", "%"),
        ("__imod__", "%="), ("__rmod__", "%"),
        ("__lshift__", "<<"), ("__ilshift__", "<<="),
        ("__rlshift__", "<<"), ("__rshift__", ">>"),
        ("__irshift__", ">>="), ("__rrshift__", ">>")):
    message = ("unsupported operand type(s) for {0}: "
               "'{{self}}'{{join}} {{args}}".format(operator))
    exec("def {0}(self, *args):\n"
    "    types = [\"'\" + arg.__class__.__name__ + \"'\" "
    "for arg in args]\n"
    "    raise TypeError(\"{1}\".format("
    "self=self.__class__.__name__, "
    "join=(\" and\" if len(args) == 1 else \",\"),"
    "args=\", \".join(types)))".format(name, message))
```

This code is slightly more complicated than before because for binary operators we must output messages where the two types are listed as *type1 and type2*, but for three or more types we must list them as *type1, type2, type3* to mimic

the built-in behavior. Here is the code that is generated for the first tuple
("__xor__", "^"):

```
def __xor__(self, *args):
    types = ["'" + arg.__class__.__name__ + "'" for arg in args]
    raise TypeError("unsupported operand type(s) for ^: "
                    "'{self}'{join} {args}".format(
                    self=self.__class__.__name__,
                    join=(" and" if len(args) == 1 else ","),
                    args=", ".join(types)))
```

The two for ... in loop blocks we have used here can be simply cut and pasted,
and then we can add or remove unary operators and methods from the first
one and binary or *n*-ary operators and methods from the second one to unimplement whatever methods are not required.

With this last piece of code in place, if we had two FuzzyBools, f and g, and tried
to add them using f + g, we would get a TypeError exception with the message
"unsupported operand type(s) for +: 'FuzzyBool' and 'FuzzyBool'", which is
exactly the behavior we want.

Creating classes the way we did for the first FuzzyBool implementation is
much more common and is sufficient for almost every purpose. However, if
we need to create an immutable class, the way to do it is to reimplement object.__new__() having inherited one of Python's immutable types such as
float, int, str, or tuple, and then implement all the other methods we need.
The disadvantage of doing this is that we may need to unimplement some
methods—this breaks polymorphism, so in most cases using aggregation as we
did in the first FuzzyBool implementation is a much better approach.

Custom Collection Classes

In this section's subsections we will look at custom classes that are responsible
for large amounts of data. The first class we will review, Image, is one that holds
image data. This class is typical of many data-holding custom classes in that it
not only provides in-memory access to its data, but also has methods for saving
and loading the data to and from disk. The second and third classes we will
study, SortedList and SortedDict, are designed to fill a rare and surprising gap
in Python's standard library for intrinsically sorted collection data types.

Creating Classes That Aggregate Collections

A simple way of representing a 2D color image is as a two-dimensional array
with each array element being a color. So to represent a 100 × 100 image we
must store 10 000 colors. For the Image class (in file Image.py), we will take a

potentially more efficient approach. An Image stores a single background color, plus the colors of those points in the image that differ from the background color. This is done by using a dictionary as a kind of sparse array, with each key being an (x, y) coordinate and the corresponding value being the color of that point. If we had a 100×100 image and half its points are the background color, we would need to store only $5\,000 + 1$ colors, a considerable saving in memory.

The Image.py module follows what should now be a familiar pattern: It starts with a shebang line, then copyright information in comments, then a module docstring with some doctests, and then the imports, in this case of the os and pickle modules. We will briefly cover the use of the pickle module when we cover saving and loading images. After the imports we create some custom exception classes:

Pickles
☞ 282

```
class ImageError(Exception): pass
class CoordinateError(ImageError): pass
```

We have shown only the first two exception classes; the others (LoadError, SaveError, ExportError, and NoFilenameError) are all created the same way and all inherit from ImageError. Users of the Image class can choose to test for any of the specific exceptions, or just for the base class ImageError exception.

The rest of the module consists of the Image class and at the end the standard three lines for running the module's doctests. Before looking at the class and its methods, let's look at how it can be used:

```
border_color = "#FF0000"    # red
square_color = "#0000FF"    # blue
width, height = 240, 60
midx, midy = width // 2, height // 2
image = Image.Image(width, height, "square_eye.img")
for x in range(width):
    for y in range(height):
        if x < 5 or x >= width - 5 or y < 5 or y >= height - 5:
            image[x, y] = border_color
        elif midx - 20 < x < midx + 20 and midy - 20 < y < midy + 20:
            image[x, y] = square_color
image.save()
image.export("square_eye.xpm")
```

Notice that we can use the item access operator ([]) for setting colors in the image. Brackets can also be used for getting or deleting (effectively setting to the background color) the color at a particular (x, y) coordinate. The coordinates are passed as a single tuple object (thanks to the comma operator), the same as if we wrote image[(x, y)]. Achieving this kind of seamless syntax integration is easy in Python—we just have to implement the appropriate special methods, which in the case of the item access operator are __getitem__(), __setitem__(), and __delitem__().

The Image class uses HTML-style hexadecimal strings to represent colors. The background color must be set when the image is created; otherwise, it defaults to white. The Image class saves and loads images in its own custom format, but it can also export in the .xpm format which is understood by many image processing applications. The .xpm image produced by the code snippet is shown in Figure 6.6.

Figure 6.6 *The square_eye.xpm image*

We will now review the Image class's methods, starting with the class line and the initializer:

```
class Image:

    def __init__(self, width, height, filename="",
                 background="#FFFFFF"):
        self.filename = filename
        self.__background = background
        self.__data = {}
        self.__width = width
        self.__height = height
        self.__colors = {self.__background}
```

When an Image is created, the user (i.e., the class's user) must provide a width and height, but the filename and background color are optional since defaults are provided. The self.__data dictionary's keys are (*x,y*) coordinates and its values are color strings. The self.__colors set is initialized with the background color; it is used to keep track of the unique colors used by the image.

All the data attributes are private except for the filename, so we must provide a means by which users of the class can access them. This is easily done using properties.[*]

```
    @property
    def background(self):
        return self.__background

    @property
```

---

[*] In Chapter 8 we will see a completely different approach to providing attribute access, using special methods such as __getattr__() and __setattr__(), that is useful in some circumstances.

```
    def width(self):
        return self.__width

    @property
    def height(self):
        return self.__height

    @property
    def colors(self):
        return set(self.__colors)
```

When returning a data attribute from an object we need to be aware of whether the attribute is of an immutable or mutable type. It is always safe to return immutable attributes since they can't be changed, but for mutable attributes we must consider some trade-offs. Returning a reference to a mutable attribute is very fast and efficient because no copying takes place—but it also means that the caller now has access to the object's internal state and might change it in a way that invalidates the object. One policy to consider is to always return a copy of mutable data attributes, unless profiling shows a significant negative effect on performance. (In this case, an alternative to keeping the set of unique colors would be to return set(self.__data.values()) | {self.__background} whenever the set of colors was needed.)

Copying collections

136 ☞

```
    def __getitem__(self, coordinate):
        assert len(coordinate) == 2, "coordinate should be a 2-tuple"
        if (not (0 <= coordinate[0] < self.width) or
                not (0 <= coordinate[1] < self.height)):
            raise CoordinateError(str(coordinate))
        return self.__data.get(tuple(coordinate), self.__background)
```

This method returns the color for a given coordinate using the item access operator ([ ]). The special methods for the item access operators and some other collection-relevant special methods are listed in Table 6.4.

We have chosen to apply two policies for item access. The first policy is that a precondition for using an item access method is that the coordinate it is passed is a sequence of length 2 (usually a 2-tuple), and we use an assertion to ensure this. The second policy is that any coordinate values are accepted, but if either is out of range, we raise a custom exception.

We have used the dict.get() method with a default value of the background color to retrieve the color for the given coordinate. This ensures that if the color has never been set for the coordinate the background color is correctly returned instead of a KeyError exception being raised.

```
    def __setitem__(self, coordinate, color):
        assert len(coordinate) == 2, "coordinate should be a 2-tuple"
```

Table 6.4 *Collection Special Methods*

Special Method	Usage	Description
`__contains__(self, x)`	`x in y`	Returns True if x is in sequence y or if x is a key in mapping y
`__delitem__(self, k)`	`del y[k]`	Deletes the k-th item of sequence y or the item with key k in mapping y
`__getitem__(self, k)`	`y[k]`	Returns the k-th item of sequence y or the value for key k in mapping y
`__iter__(self)`	`for x in y: pass`	Returns an iterator for sequence y's items or mapping y's keys
`__len__(self)`	`len(y)`	Returns the number of items in y
`__reversed__(self)`	`reversed(y)`	Returns a backward iterator for sequence y's items or mapping y's keys
`__setitem__(self, k, v)`	`y[k] = v`	Sets the k-th item of sequence y or the value for key k in mapping y, to v

```
    if (not (0 <= coordinate[0] < self.width) or
        not (0 <= coordinate[1] < self.height)):
        raise CoordinateError(str(coordinate))
    if color == self.__background:
        self.__data.pop(tuple(coordinate), None)
    else:
        self.__data[tuple(coordinate)] = color
        self.__colors.add(color)
```

If the user sets a coordinate's value to the background color we can simply delete the corresponding dictionary item since any coordinate not in the dictionary is assumed to have the background color. We must use dict.pop() and give a dummy second argument rather than use del because doing so avoids a KeyError being raised if the key (coordinate) is not in the dictionary.

If the color is different from the background color, we set it for the given coordinate and add it to the set of the unique colors used by the image.

```
    def __delitem__(self, coordinate):
        assert len(coordinate) == 2, "coordinate should be a 2-tuple"
        if (not (0 <= coordinate[0] < self.width) or
            not (0 <= coordinate[1] < self.height)):
            raise CoordinateError(str(coordinate))
        self.__data.pop(tuple(coordinate), None)
```

If a coordinate's color is deleted the effect is to make that coordinate's color the background color. Again we use dict.pop() to remove the item since it will work correctly whether or not an item with the given coordinate is in the dictionary.

We have not provided a __len__() implementation since it does not make sense for a two-dimensional object. Also, we cannot provide a representational form since an Image cannot be created fully formed just by calling Image(), so we do not provide __repr__() (or __str__()) implementations either. If a user calls repr() or str() on an Image object, the object.__repr__() base class implementation will return a suitable string, for example, '<Image.Image object at 0x9c794ac>'. This is a standard format used for non-eval()-able objects. The hexadecimal number is the object's ID—this is unique (normally it is the object's address in memory), but transient.

We want users of the Image class to be able to save and load their image data, so we have provided two methods, save() and load(), to carry out these tasks.

We have chosen to save the data by *pickling* it. In Python-speak pickling is a way of serializing (converting into a sequence of bytes, or into a string) a Python object. What is so powerful about pickling is that the pickled object can be a collection data type, such as a list or a dictionary, and even if the pickled object has other objects inside it (including other collections, which may include other collections, etc.), the whole lot will be pickled—and without duplicating objects that occur more than once.

A pickle can be read back directly into a Python variable—we don't have to do any parsing or other interpretation ourselves. So using pickles is ideal for saving and loading ad hoc collections of data, especially for small programs and for programs created for personal use. However, pickles have no security mechanisms (no encryption, no digital signature), so loading a pickle that comes from an untrusted source could be dangerous. In view of this, for programs that are not purely for personal use, it is best to create a custom file format that is specific to the program. In Chapter 7 we show how to read and write custom binary, text, and XML file formats.

```python
def save(self, filename=None):
    if filename is not None:
        self.filename = filename
    if not self.filename:
        raise NoFilenameError()

    fh = None
    try:
        data = [self.width, self.height, self.__background,
                self.__data]
        fh = open(self.filename, "wb")
        pickle.dump(data, fh, pickle.HIGHEST_PROTOCOL)
    except (EnvironmentError, pickle.PicklingError) as err:
        raise SaveError(str(err))
```

```
finally:
    if fh is not None:
        fh.close()
```

The first part of the function is concerned purely with the filename. If the
Image object was created with no filename and no filename has been set since,
then the save() method must be given an explicit filename (in which case it
behaves as "save as" and sets the internally used filename). If no filename is
specified the current filename is used, and if there is no current filename and
none is given an exception is raised.

We create a list (data) to hold the objects we want to save, including the
self.__data dictionary of coordinate–color items, but excluding the set of
unique colors since that data can be reconstructed. Then we open the file to
write in binary mode and call the pickle.dump() function to write the data object
to the file. And that's it!

The pickle module can serialize data using various formats (called *protocols*
in the documentation), with the one to use specified by the third argument to
pickle.dump(). Protocol 0 is ASCII and is useful for debugging. We have used
protocol 3 (pickle.HIGHEST_PROTOCOL), a compact binary format which is why
we had to open the file in binary mode. When reading pickles no protocol is
specified—the pickle.load() function is smart enough to work out the protocol
for itself.

```
def load(self, filename=None):
    if filename is not None:
        self.filename = filename
    if not self.filename:
        raise NoFilenameError()

    fh = None
    try:
        fh = open(self.filename, "rb")
        data = pickle.load(fh)
        (self.__width, self.__height, self.__background,
         self.__data) = data
        self.__colors = (set(self.__data.values()) |
                         {self.__background})
    except (EnvironmentError, pickle.UnpicklingError) as err:
        raise LoadError(str(err))
    finally:
        if fh is not None:
            fh.close()
```

This function starts off the same as the save() function to get the filename of
the file to load. The file must be opened in read binary mode, and the data is
read using the single statement, data = pickle.load(fh). The data object is an

exact reconstruction of the one we saved, so in this case it is a list with the width and height integers, the background color string, and the dictionary of coordinate–color items. We use tuple unpacking to assign each of the data list's items to the appropriate variable, so any previously held image data is (correctly) lost.

The set of unique colors is reconstructed by making a set of all the colors in the coordinate–color dictionary and then adding the background color.

```
def export(self, filename):
    if filename.lower().endswith(".xpm"):
        self.__export_xpm(filename)
    else:
        raise ExportError("unsupported export format: " +
                          os.path.splitext(filename)[1])
```

We have provided one generic export method that uses the file extension to determine which private method to call—or raises an exception for file formats that cannot be exported. In this case we only support saving to .xpm files (and then only for images with fewer than 8 930 colors). We haven't quoted the __export_xpm() method because it isn't really relevant to this chapter's theme, but it is in the book's source code, of course.

We have now completed our coverage of the custom Image class. This class is typical of those used to hold program-specific data, providing access to the data items it contains, the ability to save and load all its data to and from disk, and with only the essential methods it needs provided. In the next two subsections we will see how to create two generic custom collection types that offer complete APIs.

Creating Collection Classes Using Aggregation

In this subsection we will develop a complete custom collection data type, SortedList, that holds a list of items in sorted order. The items are sorted using their less than operator (<), provided by the __lt__() special method, or by using a key function if one is given. The class tries to match the API of the built-in list class to make it as easy to learn and use as possible, but some methods cannot sensibly be provided—for example, using the concatenation operator (+) could result in items being out of order, so we do not implement it.

As always when creating custom classes we have the choice of inheriting a class that is similar to the one we want to make or creating a class from scratch and aggregating instances of any other classes we need inside it. For this subsection's SortedList we use aggregation for the data, and for the following subsection's SortedDict we will use both aggregation and inheritance.

In Chapter 8 we will see that classes can make promises about the API they offer. For example, a `list` provides the `MutableSequence` API which means that it supports the `in` operator, the `iter()` and `len()` built-in functions, and the item access operator (`[]`) for getting, setting, and deleting items, and an `insert()` method. The `SortedList` class implemented here does not support item setting and does not have an `insert()` method, so it does not provide a `MutableSequence` API. If we were to create `SortedList` by inheriting `list`, the resultant class would claim to be a mutable sequence but would not have the complete API. In view of this the `SortedList` does not inherit `list` and so makes no promises about its API. On the other hand, the next subsection's `SortedDict` class supports the complete `MutableMapping` API that the `dict` class provides, so we can make it a `dict` subclass.

Here are some basic examples of using a `SortedList`:

```
letters = SortedList.SortedList(("H", "c", "B", "G", "e"), str.lower)
# str(letters) == "['B', 'c', 'e', 'G', 'H']"
letters.add("G")
letters.add("f")
letters.add("A")
# str(letters) == "['A', 'B', 'c', 'e', 'f', 'G', 'G', 'H']"
letters[2] # returns: 'c'
```

A `SortedList` object *aggregates* (is composed of) two private attributes; a function, `self.__key()` (held as object reference `self.__key`), and a list, `self.__list`.

Lambda functions

172 ☞

The key function is passed as the second argument (or using the key keyword argument if no initial sequence is given). If no key function is specified the following private module function is used:

```
_identity = lambda x: x
```

This is the identity function: It simply returns its argument unchanged, so when it is used as a `SortedList`'s key function it means that the sort key for each object in the list is the object itself.

The `SortedList` type does not allow the item access operator (`[]`) to change an item (so it does not implement the `__setitem__()` special method), nor does it provide the `append()` or `extend()` method since these might invalidate the ordering. The only way to add items is to pass a sequence when the `SortedList` is created or to add them later using the `SortedList.add()` method. On the other hand, we can safely use the item access operator for getting or deleting the item at a given index position since neither operation affects the ordering, so both the `__getitem__()` and `__delitem__()` special methods are implemented.

We will now review the class method by method, starting as usual with the `class` line and the initializer:

```
class SortedList:

    def __init__(self, sequence=None, key=None):
        self.__key = key or _identity
        assert hasattr(self.__key, "__call__")
        if sequence is None:
            self.__list = []
        elif (isinstance(sequence, SortedList) and
                sequence.key == self.__key):
            self.__list = sequence.__list[:]
        else:
            self.__list = sorted(list(sequence), key=self.__key)
```

Since a function's name is an object reference (to its function), we can hold functions in variables just like any other object reference. Here the private self.__key variable holds a reference to the key function that was passed in, or to the identity function. The method's first statement relies on the fact that the or operator returns its first operand if it is True in a Boolean context (which a not-None key function is), or its second operand otherwise. A slightly longer but more obvious alternative would have been self.__key = key if key is not None else _identity.

Once we have the key function, we use an assert to ensure that it is callable. The built-in hasattr() function returns True if the object passed as its first argument has the attribute whose name is passed as its second argument. There are corresponding setattr() and delattr() functions—these functions are covered in Chapter 8. All callable objects, for example, functions and methods, have a __call__ attribute.

To make the creation of SortedLists as similar as possible to the creation of lists we have an optional sequence argument that corresponds to the single optional argument that list() accepts. The SortedList class aggregates a list collection in the private variable self.__list and keeps the items in the aggregated list in sorted order using the given key function.

The elif clause uses type testing to see whether the given sequence is a SortedList and if that is the case whether it has the same key function as this sorted list. If these conditions are met we simply shallow-copy the sequence's list without needing to sort it. If most key functions are created on the fly using lambda, even though two may have the same code they will not compare as equal, so the efficiency gain may not be realized in practice.

```
    @property
    def key(self):
        return self.__key
```

Once a sorted list is created its key function is fixed, so we keep it as a private variable to prevent users from changing it. But some users may want to get a reference to the key function (as we will see in the next subsection), and so we have made it accessible by providing the read-only key property.

```
def add(self, value):
    index = self.__bisect_left(value)
    if index == len(self.__list):
        self.__list.append(value)
    else:
        self.__list.insert(index, value)
```

When this method is called the given value must be inserted into the private self.__list in the correct position to preserve the list's order. The private SortedList.__bisect_left() method returns the required index position as we will see in a moment. If the new value is larger than any other value in the list it must go at the end, so the index position will be equal to the list's length (list index positions go from 0 to len(L) – 1)—if this is the case we append the new value. Otherwise, we insert the new value at the given index position—which will be at index position 0 if the new value is smaller than any other value in the list.

```
def __bisect_left(self, value):
    key = self.__key(value)
    left, right = 0, len(self.__list)
    while left < right:
        middle = (left + right) // 2
        if self.__key(self.__list[middle]) < key:
            left = middle + 1
        else:
            right = middle
    return left
```

This private method calculates the index position where the given value belongs in the list. It computes the comparison key for the given value using the sorted list's key function, and compares the comparison key with the computed comparison keys of the items that the method examines. The algorithm used is *binary search* (also called *binary chop*), which has excellent performance even on very large lists—for example, at most, 21 comparisons are required to find a value's position in a list of 1 000 000 items.[*] Compare this with a plain unsorted list which uses linear search and needs an average of 500 000 comparisons, and at worst 1 000 000 comparisons, to find a value in a list of 1 000 000 items.

```
def remove(self, value):
    index = self.__bisect_left(value)
```

---

[*] Python's bisect module provides the bisect.bisect_left() function and some others, but at the time of this writing none of the bisect module's functions can work with a key function.

```
        if index < len(self.__list) and self.__list[index] == value:
            del self.__list[index]
        else:
            raise ValueError("{0}.remove(x): x not in list".format(
                              self.__class__.__name__))
```

This method is used to remove the first occurrence of the given value. It uses the SortedList.__bisect_left() method to find the index position where the value belongs and then tests to see whether that index position is within the list and that the item at that position is the same as the given value. If the conditions are met the item is removed; otherwise, a ValueError exception is raised (which is what list.remove() does in the same circumstances).

```
    def remove_every(self, value):
        count = 0
        index = self.__bisect_left(value)
        while (index < len(self.__list) and
               self.__list[index] == value):
            del self.__list[index]
            count += 1
        return count
```

This method is similar to the SortedList.remove() method, and is an extension of the list API. It starts off by finding the index position where the first occurrence of the value belongs in the list, and then loops as long as the index position is within the list and the item at the index position is the same as the given value. The code is slightly subtle since at each iteration the matching item is deleted, and as a consequence, after each deletion the item at the index position is the item that followed the deleted item.

```
    def count(self, value):
        count = 0
        index = self.__bisect_left(value)
        while (index < len(self.__list) and
               self.__list[index] == value):
            index += 1
            count += 1
        return count
```

This method returns the number of times the given value occurs in the list (which could be 0). It uses a very similar algorithm to SortedList.remove_every(), only here we must increment the index position in each iteration.

```
    def index(self, value):
        index = self.__bisect_left(value)
        if index < len(self.__list) and self.__list[index] == value:
            return index
```

```
            raise ValueError("{0}.index(x): x not in list".format(
                       self.__class__.__name__))
```

Since a SortedList is ordered we can use a fast binary search to find (or not find) the value in the list.

```
        def __delitem__(self, index):
            del self.__list[index]
```

The __delitem__() special method provides support for the del L[n] syntax, where L is a sorted list and n is an integer index position. We don't test for an out-of-range index since if one is given the self.__list[index] call will raise an IndexError exception, which is the behavior we want.

```
        def __getitem__(self, index):
            return self.__list[index]
```

This method provides support for the x = L[n] syntax, where L is a sorted list and n is an integer index position.

```
        def __setitem__(self, index, value):
            raise TypeError("use add() to insert a value and rely on "
                            "the list to put it in the right place")
```

We don't want the user to change an item at a given index position (so L[n] = x is disallowed); otherwise, the sorted list's order might be invalidated. The TypeError exception is the one used to signify that an operation is not supported by a particular data type.

```
        def __iter__(self):
            return iter(self.__list)
```

This method is easy to implement since we can just return an iterator to the private list using the built-in iter() function. This method is used to support the for *value* in *iterable* syntax.

Note that if a sequence is required it is this method that is used. So to convert a SortedList, L, to a plain list we can call list(L), and behind the scenes Python will call SortedList.__iter__(L) to provide the sequence that the list() function requires.

```
        def __reversed__(self):
            return reversed(self.__list)
```

This provides support for the built-in reversed() function so that we can write, for example, for *value* in reversed(*iterable*).

```
        def __contains__(self, value):
            index = self.__bisect_left(value)
```

```
return (index < len(self.__list) and
        self.__list[index] == value)
```

The __contains__() method provides support for the in operator. Once again we are able to use a fast binary search rather than the slow linear search used by a plain list.

```
def clear(self):
    self.__list = []

def pop(self, index=-1):
    return self.__list.pop(index)

def __len__(self):
    return len(self.__list)

def __str__(self):
    return str(self.__list)
```

The SortedList.clear() method discards the existing list and replaces it with a new empty list. The SortedList.pop() method removes and returns the item at the given index position, or raises an IndexError exception if the index is out of range. For the pop(), __len__(), and __str__() methods, we simply pass on the work to the aggregated self.__list object.

We do not reimplement the __repr__() special method, so the base class object.__repr__() will be called when the user writes repr(L) and L is a SortedList. This will produce a string such as '<SortedList.SortedList object at 0x97e7cec>', although the hexadecimal ID will vary, of course. We cannot provide a sensible __repr__() implementation because we would need to give the key function and we cannot represent a function object reference as an eval()-able string.

We have not implemented the insert(), reverse(), or sort() method because none of them is appropriate. If any of them are called an AttributeError exception will be raised.

If we copy a sorted list using the L[:] idiom we will get a plain list object, rather than a SortedList. The easiest way to get a copy is to import the copy module and use the copy.copy() function—this is smart enough to copy a sorted list (and instances of most other custom classes) without any help. However, we have decided to provide an explicit copy() method:

```
def copy(self):
    return SortedList(self, self.__key)
```

By passing self as the first argument we ensure that self.__list is simply shallow-copied rather than being copied and re-sorted. (This is thanks to the __init__() method's type-testing elif clause.) The theoretical performance advantage of copying this way is not available to the `copy.copy()` function, but we can easily make it available by adding this line:

```
__copy__ = copy
```

When `copy.copy()` is called it tries to use the object's `__copy__()` special method, falling back to its own code if one isn't provided. With this line in place `copy.copy()` will now use the `SortedList.copy()` method for sorted lists. (It is also possible to provide a `__deepcopy__()` special method, but this is slightly more involved—the `copy` module's online documentation has the details.)

We have now completed the implementation of the `SortedList` class. In the next subsection we will make use of a `SortedList` to provide a sorted list of keys for the `SortedDict` class.

Creating Collection Classes Using Inheritance

The `SortedDict` class shown in this subsection attempts to mimic a `dict` as closely as possible. The major difference is that a `SortedDict`'s keys are always ordered based on a specified key function or on the identity function. Sorted-Dict provides the same API as `dict` (except for having a non-`eval()`-able `repr()`), plus two extra methods that make sense only for an ordered collection.[*]

Here are a few examples of use to give a flavor of how `SortedDict` works:

```
d = SortedDict.SortedDict(dict(s=1, A=2, y=6), str.lower)
d["z"] = 4
d["T"] = 5
del d["y"]
d["n"] = 3
d["A"] = 17
str(d) # returns: "{'A': 17, 'n': 3, 's': 1, 'T': 5, 'z': 4}"
```

The `SortedDict` implementation uses both aggregation and inheritance. The sorted list of keys is aggregated as an instance variable, whereas the `SortedDict` class itself inherits the `dict` class. We will start our code review by looking at the `class` line and the initializer, and then we will look at all of the other methods in turn.

```
class SortedDict(dict):

    def __init__(self, dictionary=None, key=None, **kwargs):
        dictionary = dictionary or {}
        super().__init__(dictionary)
        if kwargs:
```

---

[*]The `SortedDict` class presented here is different from the one in *Rapid GUI Programming with Python and Qt* by this author, ISBN 0132354187, and from the one in the Python Package Index.

```
        super().update(kwargs)
        self.__keys = SortedList.SortedList(super().keys(), key)
```

The `dict` base class is specified in the `class` line. The initializer tries to mimic the `dict()` function, but adds a second argument for the key function. The `super().__init__()` call is used to initialize the `SortedDict` using the base class `dict.__init__()` method. Similarly, if keyword arguments have been used, we use the base class `dict.update()` method to add them to the dictionary. (Note that only one occurrence of any keyword argument is accepted, so none of the keys in the `kwargs` keyword arguments can be "dictionary" or "key".)

We keep a copy of all the dictionary's keys in a sorted list stored in the `self.__keys` variable. We pass the dictionary's keys to initialize the sorted list using the base class's `dict.keys()` method—we must not use `SortedDict.keys()` because that relies on the `self.__keys` variable which will exist only *after* the `SortedList` of keys has been created.

```
        def update(self, dictionary=None, **kwargs):
            if dictionary is None:
                pass
            elif isinstance(dictionary, dict):
                super().update(dictionary)
            else:
                for key, value in dictionary.items():
                    super().__setitem__(key, value)
            if kwargs:
                super().update(kwargs)
            self.__keys = SortedList.SortedList(super().keys(),
                                                self.__keys.key)
```

This method is used to update one dictionary's items with another dictionary's items, or with keyword arguments, or both. Items which exist only in the other dictionary are added to this one, and for items whose keys appear in both dictionaries, the other dictionary's value replaces the original value. We have had to extend the behavior slightly in that we keep the original dictionary's key function, even if the other dictionary is a `SortedDict`.

The updating is done in two phases. First we update the dictionary's items. If the given dictionary is a `dict` subclass (which includes `SortedDict`, of course), we use the base class `dict.update()` to perform the update—using the base class version is essential to avoid calling `SortedDict.update()` recursively and going into an infinite loop. If the dictionary is not a `dict` we iterate over the dictionary's items and set each key–value pair individually. (If the dictionary object is not a `dict` and does not have an `items()` method an `AttributeError` exception will quite rightly be raised.) If keyword arguments have been used we again call the base class `update()` method to incorporate them.

A consequence of the updating is that the self.__keys list becomes out of date, so we replace it with a new SortedList with the dictionary's keys (again obtained from the base class, since the SortedDict.keys() method relies on the self.__keys list which we are in the process of updating), and with the original sorted list's key function.

```
@classmethod
def fromkeys(cls, iterable, value=None, key=None):
    return cls({k: value for k in iterable}, key)
```

The dict API includes the dict.fromkeys() class method. This method is used to create a new dictionary based on an iterable. Each element in the iterable becomes a key, and each key's value is either None or the specified value.

Because this is a class method the first argument is provided automatically by Python and is the class. For a dict the class will be dict, and for a SortedDict it is SortedDict. The return value is a dictionary of the given class. For example:

```
class MyDict(SortedDict.SortedDict): pass
d = MyDict.fromkeys("VEINS", 3)
str(d)    # returns: "{'E': 3, 'I': 3, 'N': 3, 'S': 3, 'V': 3}"
d.__class__.__name__    # returns: 'MyDict'
```

So when inherited class methods are called, their cls variable is set to the correct class, just like when normal methods are called and their self variable is set to the current object. This is different from and better than using a static method because a static method is tied to a particular class and does not know whether it is being executed in the context of its original class or that of a subclass.

```
def __setitem__(self, key, value):
    if key not in self:
        self.__keys.add(key)
    return super().__setitem__(key, value)
```

This method implements the d[key] = value syntax. If the key isn't in the dictionary we add it to the list of keys, relying on the SortedList to put it in the right place. Then we call the base class method, and return its result to the caller to support chaining, for example, x = d[key] = value.

Notice that in the if statement we check to see whether the key already exists in the SortedDict by using not in self. Because SortedDict inherits dict, a SortedDict can be used wherever a dict is expected, and in this case self is a SortedDict. When we reimplement dict methods in SortedDict, if we need to call the base class implementation to get it to do some of the work for us, we must be careful to call the method using super(), as we do in this method's last statement; doing so prevents the reimplementation of the method from calling itself and going into infinite recursion.

Generator Functions

A *generator function* or *generator method* is one which contains a yield expression. When a generator function is called it returns an iterator. Values are extracted from the iterator one at a time by calling its __next__() method. At each call to __next__() the generator function's yield expression's value (None if none is specified) is returned. If the generator function finishes or executes a return a StopIteration exception is raised.

In practice we rarely call __next__() or catch a StopIteration. Instead, we just use a generator like any other iterable. Here are two almost equivalent functions. The one on the left returns a list and the one on the right returns a generator.

```
# Build and return a list
def letter_range(a, z):
    result = []                         # Return each value on demand
    while ord(a) < ord(z):      def letter_range(a, z):
        result.append(a)                while ord(a) < ord(z):
        a = chr(ord(a) + 1)                 yield a
    return result                           a = chr(ord(a) + 1)
```

We can iterate over the result produced by either function using a for loop, for example, for letter in letter_range("m", "v"):. But if we want a list of the resultant letters, although calling letter_range("m", "v") is sufficient for the left-hand function, for the right-hand generator function we must use list(letter_range("m", "v")).

Generator functions and methods (and generator expressions) are covered more fully in Chapter 8.

We do not reimplement the __getitem__() method since the base class version works fine and has no effect on the ordering of the keys.

```
def __delitem__(self, key):
    try:
        self.__keys.remove(key)
    except ValueError:
        raise KeyError(key)
    return super().__delitem__(key)
```

This method provides the del d[key] syntax. If the key is not present the SortedList.remove() call will raise a ValueError exception. If this occurs we catch the exception and raise a KeyError exception instead so as to match the dict class's API. Otherwise, we return the result of calling the base class implementation to delete the item with the given key from the dictionary itself.

```
def setdefault(self, key, value=None):
    if key not in self:
        self.__keys.add(key)
    return super().setdefault(key, value)
```

This method returns the value for the given key if the key is in the dictionary; otherwise, it creates a new item with the given key and value and returns the value. For the SortedDict we must make sure that the key is added to the keys list if the key is not already in the dictionary.

```
def pop(self, key, *args):
    if key not in self:
        if len(args) == 0:
            raise KeyError(key)
        return args[0]
    self.__keys.remove(key)
    return super().pop(key, args)
```

If the given key is in the dictionary this method returns the corresponding value and removes the key–value item from the dictionary. The key must also be removed from the keys list.

The implementation is quite subtle because the pop() method must support two different behaviors to match dict.pop(). The first is d.pop(k); here the value for key k is returned, or if there is no key k, a KeyError is raised. The second is d.pop(k, value); here the value for key k is returned, or if there is no key k, value (which could be None) is returned. In all cases, if key k exists, the corresponding item is removed.

```
def popitem(self):
    item = super().popitem()
    self.__keys.remove(item[0])
    return item
```

The dict.popitem() method removes and returns a random key–value item from the dictionary. We must call the base class version first since we don't know in advance which item will be removed. We remove the item's key from the keys list, and then return the item.

```
def clear(self):
    super().clear()
    self.__keys.clear()
```

Here we clear all the dictionary's items and all the keys list's items.

```
def values(self):
    for key in self.__keys:
        yield self[key]
```

```
def items(self):
    for key in self.__keys:
        yield (key, self[key])

def __iter__(self):
    return iter(self.__keys)

keys = __iter__
```

Dictionaries have four methods that return iterators: `dict.values()` for the dictionary's values, `dict.items()` for the dictionary's key–value items, `dict.keys()` for the keys, and the `__iter__()` special method that provides support for the `iter(d)` syntax, and operates on the keys. (Actually, the base class versions of these methods return dictionary views, but for most purposes the behavior of the iterators implemented here is the same.)

Since the `__iter__()` method and the `keys()` method have identical behavior, instead of implementing `keys()`, we simply create an object reference called keys and set it to refer to the `__iter__()` method. With this in place, users of `SortedDict` can call `d.keys()` or `iter(d)` to get an iterator over a dictionary's keys, just the same as they can call `d.values()` to get an iterator over the dictionary's values.

The `values()` and `items()` methods are generator methods—see the "Generator Functions" sidebar (page 268) for a brief explanation of generator methods. In both cases they iterate over the sorted keys list, so they always return iterators that iterate in key order (with the key order depending on the key function given to the initializer). For the `items()` and `values()` methods, the values are looked up using the `d[k]` syntax (which uses `dict.__getitem__()` under the hood), since we can treat self as a dict.

Generators
☞ 331

```
def __repr__(self):
    return object.__repr__(self)

def __str__(self):
    return ("{" + ", ".join(["{0!r}: {1!r}".format(k, v)
                            for k, v in self.items()]) + "}")
```

We cannot provide an `eval()`-able representation of a `SortedDict` because we can't produce an `eval()`-able representation of the key function. So for the `__repr__()` reimplementation we bypass `dict.__repr__()`, and instead call the ultimate base class version, `object.__repr__()`. This produces a string of the kind used for non-`eval()`-able representations, for example, `'<Sorted­Dict.SortedDict object at 0xb71fff5c>'`.

We have implemented the `SortedDict.__str__()` method ourselves because we want the output to show the items in key sorted order. The method could have been written like this instead:

```
            items = []
            for key, value in self.items():
                items.append("{0!r}: {1!r}".format(key, value))
            return "{" + ", ".join(items) + "}"
```

Using a list comprehension is shorter and avoids the need for the temporary items variable.

The base class methods dict.get(), dict.__getitem__() (for the v = d[k] syntax), dict.__len__() (for len(d)), and dict.__contains__() (for x in d) all work fine as they are and don't affect the key ordering, so we have not needed to reimplement them.

The last dict method that we must reimplement is copy().

```
        def copy(self):
            d = SortedDict()
            super(SortedDict, d).update(self)
            d.__keys = self.__keys.copy()
            return d
```

The easiest reimplementation is simply def copy(self): return SortedDict(self). We've chosen a slightly more complicated solution that avoids re-sorting the already sorted keys. We create an empty sorted dictionary, then update it with the items in the original sorted dictionary using the base class dict.update() to avoid the SortedDict.update() reimplementation, and replace the dictionary's self.__keys SortedList with a shallow copy of the original one.

When super() is called with no arguments it works on the base class and the self object. But we can make it work on any class and any object by passing in a class and an object explicitly. Using this syntax, the super() call works on the immediate *base* class of the class it is given, so in this case the code has the same effect as (and could be written as) dict.update(d, self).

In view of the fact that Python's sort algorithm is very fast, and is particularly well optimized for partially sorted lists, the efficiency gain is likely to be little or nothing except for huge dictionaries. However, the implementation shows that at least in principle, a custom copy() method can be more efficient than using the copy_of_x = ClassOfX(x) idiom that Python's built-in types support. And just as we did for SortedList, we have set __copy__ = copy so that the copy.copy() function uses our custom copy method rather than its own code.

```
        def value_at(self, index):
            return self[self.__keys[index]]

        def set_value_at(self, index, value):
            self[self.__keys[index]] = value
```

These two methods represent an extension to the dict API. Since, unlike a plain dict, a SortedDict is ordered, it follows that the concept of key index positions is applicable. For example, the first item in the dictionary is at index position 0, and the last at position len(d) – 1. Both of these methods operate on the dictionary item whose key is at the index-th position in the sorted keys list. Thanks to inheritance, we can look up values in the SortedDict using the item access operator ([]) applied directly to self, since self is a dict. If an out-of-range index is given the methods raise an IndexError exception.

We have now completed the implementation of the SortedDict class. It is not often that we need to create complete generic collection classes like this, but when we do, Python's special methods allow us to fully integrate our class so that its users can treat it like any of the built-in or standard library classes.

Summary

This chapter covered all the fundamentals of Python's support for object-oriented programming. We began by showing some of the disadvantages of a purely procedural approach and how these could be avoided by using object orientation. We then described some of the most common terminology used in object-oriented programming, including many "duplicate" terms such as *base class* and *super class*.

We saw how to create simple classes with data attributes and custom methods. We also saw how to inherit classes and how to add additional data attributes and additional methods, and how methods can be "unimplemented". Unimplementing is needed when we inherit a class but want to restrict the methods that our subclass provides, but it should be used with care since it breaks the expectation that a subclass can be used wherever one of its base classes can be used, that is, it breaks polymorphism.

Custom classes can be seamlessly integrated so that they support the same syntaxes as Python's built-in and library classes. This is achieved by implementing special methods. We saw how to implement special methods to support comparisons, how to provide representational and string forms, and how to provide conversions to other types such as int and float when it makes sense to do so. We also saw how to implement the __hash__() method to make a custom class's instances usable as dictionary keys or as members of a set.

Data attributes by themselves provide no mechanism for ensuring that they are set to valid values. We saw how easy it is to replace data attributes with properties—this allows us to create read-only properties, and for writable properties makes it easy to provide validation.

Most of the classes we create are "incomplete" since we tend to provide only the methods that we actually need. This works fine in Python, but in addition it is possible to create complete custom classes that provide every relevant method. We saw how to do this for single valued classes, both by using aggregation and more compactly by using inheritance. We also saw how to do this for multivalued (collection) classes. Custom collection classes can provide the same facilities as the built-in collection classes, including support for in, len(), iter(), reversed(), and the item access operator ([]).

We learned that object creation and initialization are separate operations and that Python allows us to control both, although in almost every case we only need to customize initialization. We also learned that although it is always safe to return an object's immutable data attributes, we should normally only ever return copies of an object's mutable data attributes to avoid the object's internal state leaking out and being accidentally invalidated.

Python provides normal methods, static methods, class methods, and module functions. We saw that most methods are normal methods, with class methods being occasionally useful. Static methods are rarely used, since class methods or module functions are almost always better alternatives.

The built-in repr() method calls an object's __repr__() special method. Where possible, eval(repr(x)) == x, and we saw how to support this. When an eval()-able representation string cannot be produced we use the base class object.__repr__() method to produce a non-eval()-able representation in a standard format.

Type testing using the built-in isinstance() function can provide some efficiency benefits, although object-oriented purists would almost certainly avoid its use. Accessing base class methods is achieved by calling the built-in super() function, and is essential to avoid infinite recursion when we need to call a base class method inside a subclass's reimplementation of that method.

Generator functions and methods do lazy evaluation, returning (via the yield expression) each value one at a time on request and raising a StopIteration when (and if) they run out of values. Generators can be used wherever an iterator is expected, and for finite generators, all their values can be extracted into a tuple or list by passing the iterator returned by the generator to tuple() or list().

The object-oriented approach almost invariably simplifies code compared with a purely procedural approach. With custom classes we can guarantee that only valid operations are available (since we implement only appropriate methods), and that no operation can put an object into an invalid state (e.g., by using properties to apply validation). Once we start using object orientation our style of programming is likely to change from being about global data structures and the global functions that are applied to the data, to creating classes and implementing the methods that are applicable to them. Object orientation makes it possible to package up data and those methods that make sense for the data. This helps us avoid mixing up all our data and functions together, and makes it easier to produce maintainable programs since functionality is kept separated out into individual classes.

Exercises   ⦀

The first two exercises involve modifying classes we covered in this chapter, and the last two exercises involve creating new classes from scratch.

1. Modify the `Point` class (from `Shape.py` or `ShapeAlt.py`), to support the following operations, where p, q, and r are `Points` and n is a number:

   ```
   p = q + r    # Point.__add__()
   p += q       # Point.__iadd__()
   p = q - r    # Point.__sub__()
   p -= q       # Point.__isub__()
   p = q * n    # Point.__mul__()
   p *= n       # Point.__imul__()
   p = q / n    # Point.__truediv__()
   p /= n       # Point.__itruediv__()
   p = q // n   # Point.__floordiv__()
   p //= n      # Point.__ifloordiv__()
   ```

   The in-place methods are all four lines long, including the def line, and the other methods are each just two lines long, including the def line, and of course they are all very similar and quite simple. With a minimal description and a doctest for each it adds up to around one hundred thirty new lines. A model solution is provided in `Shape_ans.py`; the same code is also in `ShapeAlt_ans.py`.

2. Modify the `Image.py` class to provide a `resize(width, height)` method. If the new width or height is smaller than the current value, any colors outside the new boundaries must be deleted. If either width or height is None then use the existing width or height. At the end, make sure you regenerate the `self.__colors` set. Return a Boolean to indicate whether a change was made or not. The method can be implemented in fewer than 20 lines (fewer than 35 including a docstring with a simple doctest). A solution is provided in `Image_ans.py`.

3. Implement a `Transaction` class that takes an amount, a date, a currency (default "USD"—U.S. dollars), a USD conversion rate (default 1), and a description (default None). All of the data attributes must be private. Provide the following read-only properties: amount, date, currency, usd_conversion_rate, description, and usd (calculated from amount * usd_conversion_rate). This class can be implemented in about sixty lines including some simple doctests. A model solution for this exercise (and the next one) is in file `Account.py`.

4. Implement an Account class that holds an account number, an account name, and a list of Transactions. The number should be a read-only property; the name should be a read-write property with an assertion to ensure that the name is at least four characters long. The class should support the built-in len() function (returning the number of transactions), and should provide two calculated read-only properties: balance which should return the account's balance in USD and all_usd which should return True if all the transactions are in USD and False otherwise. Three other methods should be provided: apply() to apply (add) a transaction, save(), and load(). The save() and load() methods should use a binary pickle with the filename being the account number with extension .acc; they should save and load the account number, the name, and all the transactions. This class can be implemented in about ninety lines with some simple doctests that include saving and loading—use code such as name = os.path.join(tempfile.gettempdir(), account_name) to provide a suitable temporary filename, and make sure you delete the temporary file after the tests have finished. A model solution is in file Account.py.

- Writing and Reading Binary Data
- Writing and Parsing Text Files
- Writing and Parsing XML Files
- Random Access Binary Files

File Handling

Most programs need to save and load information, such as data or state information, to and from files. Python provides many different ways of doing this. We already briefly discussed handling text files in Chapter 3 and pickles in the preceding chapter. In this chapter we will cover file handling in much more depth.

All the techniques presented in this chapter are platform-independent. This means that a file saved using one of the example programs on one operating system/processor architecture combination can be loaded by the same program on a machine with a different operating system/processor architecture combination. And this can be true of your programs too if you use the same techniques as the example programs.

The chapter's first three sections cover the common case of saving and loading an entire data collection to and from disk. The first section shows how to do this using binary file formats, with one subsection using (optionally compressed) pickles, and the other subsection showing how to do the work manually. The second section shows how to handle text files. Writing text is easy, but reading it back can be tricky if we need to handle nontextual data such as numbers and dates. We show two approaches to parsing text, doing it manually and using regular expressions. The third section shows how to read and write XML files. This section covers writing and parsing using element trees, writing and parsing using the DOM (Document Object Model), and writing manually and parsing using SAX (Simple API for XML).

The fourth section shows how to handle random access binary files. This is useful when each data item is the same size and where we have more items than we want in (or can fit into) memory.

Which is the best file format to use for holding entire collections—binary, text, or XML? Which is the best way to handle each format? These questions are too context-dependent to have a single definitive answer, especially since there are

Name	Data Type	Notes
report_id	str	Minimum length 8 and no whitespace
date	datetime.date	
airport	str	Nonempty and no newlines
aircraft_id	str	Nonempty and no newlines
aircraft_type	str	Nonempty and no newlines
pilot_percent_hours_on_type	float	Range 0.0 to 100.0
pilot_total_hours	int	Positive and nonzero
midair	bool	
narrative	str	Multiline

Figure 7.1 *Aircraft incident record*

pros and cons for each format and for each way of handling them. We show all of them to help you make an informed decision on a case-by-case basis.

Binary formats are usually very fast to save and load and they can be very compact. Binary data doesn't need parsing since each data type is stored using its natural representation. Binary data is not human readable or editable, and without knowing the format in detail it is not possible to create separate tools to work with binary data.

Text formats are human readable and editable, and this can make text files easier to process with separate tools or to change using a text editor. Text formats can be tricky to parse and it is not always easy to give good error messages if a text file's format is broken (e.g., by careless editing).

XML formats are human readable and editable, although they tend to be verbose and create large files. Like text formats, XML formats can be processed using separate tools. Parsing XML is straightforward (providing we use an XML parser rather than do it manually), and some parsers have good error reporting. XML parsers can be slow, so reading very large XML files can take a lot more time than reading an equivalent binary or text file. XML includes metadata such as the character encoding (either implicitly or explicitly) that is not often provided in text files, and this can make XML more portable than text files.

Text formats are usually the most convenient for end-users, but sometimes performance issues are such that a binary format is the only reasonable choice. However, it is always useful to provide import/export for XML since this makes it possible to process the file format with third-party tools without preventing the most optimal text or binary format being used by the program for normal processing.

Format	Reader/Writer	Reader + Writer Lines of Code	Total Lines of Code	Output File Size (~KB)
Binary	Pickle (gzip compressed)	20 + 16 =	36	160
Binary	Pickle	20 + 16 =	36	416
Binary	Manual (gzip compressed)	60 + 34 =	94	132
Binary	Manual	60 + 34 =	94	356
Plain text	Regex reader/manual writer	39 + 28 =	67	436
Plain text	Manual	53 + 28 =	81	436
XML	Element tree	37 + 27 =	64	460
XML	DOM	44 + 36 =	80	460
XML	SAX reader/manual writer	55 + 37 =	92	464

Figure 7.2 *Aircraft incident file format reader/writer comparison*

This chapter's first three sections all use the same data collection: a set of aircraft incident records. Figure 7.1 shows the names, data types, and validation constraints that apply to aircraft incident records. It doesn't really matter what data we are processing. The important thing is that we learn to process the fundamental data types including strings, integers, floating-point numbers, Booleans, and dates, since if we can handle these we can handle any other kind of data.

By using the same set of aircraft incident data for binary, text, and XML formats, it makes it possible to compare and contrast the different formats and the code necessary for handling them. Figure 7.2 shows the number of lines of code for reading and writing each format, and the totals.

The file sizes are approximate and based on a particular sample of 596 aircraft incident records.* Compressed binary file sizes for the same data saved under different filenames may vary by a few bytes since the filename is included in the compressed data and filename lengths vary. Similarly, the XML file sizes vary slightly since some XML writers use entities (" for " and ' for ') for quotes inside text data, and others don't.

The first three sections all quote code from the same program: convert-incidents.py. This program is used to read aircraft incident data in one format and to write it in another format. Here is the program's console help text. (We have reformatted the output slightly to fit the book's page width.)

```
Usage: convert-incidents.py [options] infile outfile
```

---

*The data we used is based on real aircraft incident data available from the FAA (U.S. government's Federal Aviation Administration, www.faa.gov).

Reads aircraft incident data from infile and writes the data to
outfile. The data formats used depend on the file extensions:
.aix is XML, .ait is text (UTF-8 encoding), .aib is binary,
.aip is pickle, and .html is HTML (only allowed for the outfile).
All formats are platform-independent.

```
Options:
  -h, --help      show this help message and exit
  -f, --force     write the outfile even if it exists [default: off]
  -v, --verbose   report results [default: off]
  -r READER, --reader=READER
                  reader (XML): 'dom', 'd', 'etree', 'e', 'sax', 's'
                  reader (text): 'manual', 'm', 'regex', 'r'
                  [default: etree for XML, manual for text]
  -w WRITER, --writer=WRITER
                  writer (XML): 'dom', 'd', 'etree', 'e',
                  'manual', 'm' [default: manual]
  -z, --compress  compress .aib/.aip outfile [default: off]
  -t, --test      execute doctests and exit (use with -v for verbose)
```

The options are more complex than would normally be required since an
end-user will not care which reader or writer we use for any particular format.
In a more realistic version of the program the reader and writer options would
not exist and we would implement just one reader and one writer for each
format. Similarly, the test option exists to help us test the code and would not
be present in a production version.

The program defines one custom exception:

```
class IncidentError(Exception): pass
```

Aircraft incidents are held as Incident objects. Here is the class line and
the initializer:

```
class Incident:

    def __init__(self, report_id, date, airport, aircraft_id,
                 aircraft_type, pilot_percent_hours_on_type,
                 pilot_total_hours, midair, narrative=""):
        assert len(report_id) >= 8 and len(report_id.split()) == 1, \
               "invalid report ID"
        self.__report_id = report_id
        self.date = date
        self.airport = airport
        self.aircraft_id = aircraft_id
        self.aircraft_type = aircraft_type
        self.pilot_percent_hours_on_type = pilot_percent_hours_on_type
```

```
self.pilot_total_hours = pilot_total_hours
self.midair = midair
self.narrative = narrative
```

The report ID is validated when the Incident is created and is available as the read-only report_id property. All the other data attributes are read/write properties. For example, here is the date property's code:

```
@property
def date(self):
    return self.__date

@date.setter
def date(self, date):
    assert isinstance(date, datetime.date), "invalid date"
    self.__date = date
```

All the other properties follow the same pattern, differing only in the details of their assertions, so we won't reproduce them here. Since we have used assertions, the program will fail if an attempt is made to create an Incident with invalid data, or to set one of an existing incident's read/write properties to an invalid value. We have chosen this uncompromising approach because we want to be sure that the data we save and load is always valid, and if it isn't we want the program to terminate and complain rather than silently continue.

The collection of incidents is held as an IncidentCollection. This class is a dict subclass, so we get a lot of functionality, such as support for the item access operator ([]) to get, set, and delete incidents, by inheritance. Here is the class line and a few of the class's methods:

```
class IncidentCollection(dict):

    def values(self):
        for report_id in self.keys():
            yield self[report_id]

    def items(self):
        for report_id in self.keys():
            yield (report_id, self[report_id])

    def __iter__(self):
        for report_id in sorted(super().keys()):
            yield report_id

    keys = __iter__
```

We have not needed to reimplement the initializer since dict.__init__() is sufficient. The keys are report IDs and the values are Incidents. We have reimplemented the values(), items(), and keys() methods so that their iterators work in report ID order. This works because the values() and items() methods iterate over the keys returned by IncidentCollection.keys()—and this method (which is just another name for IncidentCollection.__iter__()), iterates in sorted order over the keys provided by the base class dict.keys() method.

In addition, the IncidentCollection class has export() and import_() methods. (We use the trailing underscore to distinguish the method from the built-in import statement.) The export() method is passed a filename, and optionally a writer and a compress flag, and based on the filename and writer, it hands off the work to a more specific method such as export_xml_dom() or export_xml_etree(). The import_() method takes a filename and an optional reader and works similarly. The import methods that read binary formats are not told whether the file is compressed—they are expected to work this out for themselves and behave appropriately.

Writing and Reading Binary Data

Binary formats, even without compression, usually take up the least amount of disk space and are usually the fastest to save and load. Easiest of all is to use pickles, although handling binary data manually should produce the smallest file sizes.

Pickles with Optional Compression

Pickles offer the simplest approach to saving and loading data from Python programs, but as we noted in the preceding chapter, pickles have no security mechanisms (no encryption, no digital signature), so loading a pickle that comes from an untrusted source could be dangerous. The security concern arises because pickles can import arbitrary modules and call arbitrary functions, so we could be given a pickle where the data has been manipulated in such a way as to, for example, make the interpreter execute something harmful when the pickle is loaded. Nonetheless, pickles are often ideal for handling ad hoc data, especially for programs for personal use.

It is usually easier when creating file formats to write the saving code before the loading code, so we will begin by seeing how to save the incidents into a pickle.

```
def export_pickle(self, filename, compress=False):
    fh = None
    try:
        if compress:
            fh = gzip.open(filename, "wb")
        else:
            fh = open(filename, "wb")
```

```
                    pickle.dump(self, fh, pickle.HIGHEST_PROTOCOL)
                    return True
             except (EnvironmentError, pickle.PicklingError) as err:
                 print("{0}: export error: {1}".format(
                        os.path.basename(sys.argv[0]), err))
                 return False
             finally:
                 if fh is not None:
                    fh.close()
```

If compression has been requested, we use the gzip module's gzip.open() function to open the file; otherwise, we use the built-in open() function. We must use "write binary" mode ("wb") when pickling data in binary format. (In Python 3.0, pickle.HIGHEST_PROTOCOL is protocol 3, a compact binary pickle format.*)

For error handling we have chosen to report errors to the user as soon as they occur, and to return a Boolean to the caller indicating success or failure. And we have used a finally block to ensure that the file is closed at the end, whether there was an error or not. In Chapter 8 we will use a more compact idiom to ensure that files are closed that avoids the need for a finally block.

> Context managers
> ☞ 359

This code is very similar to what we saw in the preceding chapter, but there is one subtle point to note. The pickled data is self, a dict. But the dictionary's values are Incident objects, that is, objects of a custom class. The pickle module is smart enough to be able to save objects of most custom classes without us needing to intervene.

In general, Booleans, numbers, and strings can be pickled, as can instances of classes including custom classes, providing their private __dict__ is picklable. In addition, any built-in collection types (tuples, lists, sets, dictionaries) can be pickled, providing they contain only picklable objects (including collection types, so recursive structures are supported). It is also possible to pickle other kinds of objects or instances of custom classes that can't normally be pickled (e.g., because they have a nonpicklable attribute), either by giving some help to the pickle module or by implementing custom pickle and unpickle functions. All the relevant details are provided in the pickle module's online documentation.

> __dict__
> ☞ 353

To read back the pickled data we need to distinguish between a compressed and an uncompressed pickle. Any file that is compressed using gzip compression begins with a particular *magic number*. A magic number is a sequence of one or more bytes at the beginning of a file that is used to indicate the file's type. For gzip files the magic number is the two bytes 0x1F 0x8B, which we store in a bytes variable:

---

*Protocol 3 is Python 3-specific. If we want pickles that are readable and writable by both Python 2 and Python 3 programs, we must use protocol 2 instead.

```
GZIP_MAGIC = b"\x1F\x8B"
```

For more about the bytes data type, see "The Bytes and Bytearray Data Types"
sidebar (page 286), and Tables 7.1, 7.2, and 7.3 (pages 288–290), which list
their methods.

Here is the code for reading an incidents pickle file:

```
def import_pickle(self, filename):
    fh = None
    try:
        fh = open(filename, "rb")
        magic = fh.read(len(GZIP_MAGIC))
        if magic == GZIP_MAGIC:
            fh.close()
            fh = gzip.open(filename, "rb")
        else:
            fh.seek(0)
        self.clear()
        self.update(pickle.load(fh))
        return True
    except (EnvironmentError, pickle.UnpicklingError) as err:
        print("{0}: import error: {1}".format(
            os.path.basename(sys.argv[0]), err))
        return False
    finally:
        if fh is not None:
            fh.close()
```

We don't know whether the given file is compressed. In either case we begin
by opening the file in "read binary" mode, and then we read the first two bytes.
If these bytes are the same as the gzip magic number we close the file and
create a new file object using the gzip.open() function. And if the file is not
compressed we use the file object returned by open(), calling its seek() method
to restore the file pointer to the beginning so that the next read (made inside
the pickle.load() function) will be from the start.

We can't assign to self since that would wipe out the IncidentCollection object
that is in use, so instead we clear all the incidents to make the dictionary empty
and then use dict.update() to populate the dictionary with all the incidents
from the IncidentCollection dictionary loaded from the pickle.

Note that it does not matter whether the processor's byte ordering is big- or
little-endian, because for the magic number we read individual bytes, and for
the data the pickle module handles endianness for us.

Raw Binary Data with Optional Compression ‖

Writing our own code to handle raw binary data gives us complete control over our file format. It should also be safer than using pickles, since maliciously invalid data will be handled by our code rather than executed by the interpreter.

When creating custom binary file formats it is wise to create a magic number to identify your file type, and a version number to identify the version of the file format in use. Here are the definitions used in the convert-incidents.py program:

```
MAGIC = b"AIB\x00"
FORMAT_VERSION = b"\x00\x01"
```

We have used four bytes for the magic number and two for the version. Endianness is not an issue because these will be written as individual bytes, not as the byte representations of integers, so they will always be the same on any processor architecture.

To write and read raw binary data we must have some means of converting Python objects to and from suitable binary representations. Most of the functionality we need is provided by the struct module, briefly described in "The Struct Module" sidebar (page 287), and by the bytes and bytearray data types, briefly described in The "Bytes and Bytearray Data Types" sidebar (page 286).

Unfortunately, the struct module can handle strings only of a specified length, and we need variable length strings for the report and aircraft IDs, as well as for the airport, the aircraft type, and the narrative texts. To meet this need we have created a function, pack_string(), which takes a string and returns a bytes object which contains two components: The first is an integer length count, and the second is a sequence of length count UTF-8 encoded bytes representing the string's text.

Since the only place the pack_string() function is needed is inside the export_binary() function, we have put the definition of pack_string() inside the export_binary() function. This means that pack_string() is not visible outside the export_binary() function, and makes clear that it is just a local helper function. Here is the start of the export_binary() function, and the complete nested pack_string() function:

Local functions

☞ 341

```
    def export_binary(self, filename, compress=False):

        def pack_string(string):
            data = string.encode("utf8")
            format = "<H{0}s".format(len(data))
            return struct.pack(format, len(data), data)
```

str.
trans-
late()

73 ☞

The Bytes and Bytearray Data Types

Python provides two data types for handling raw bytes: bytes which is immutable, and bytearray which is mutable. Both types hold a sequence of zero or more 8-bit unsigned integers (bytes) with each byte in the range 0...255.

Both types are very similar to strings and provide many of the same methods, including support for slicing. In addition, bytearrays also provide some mutating list-like methods. All their methods are listed in Tables 7.1 (page 288) and 7.2 (page 289).

Whereas a slice of a bytes or bytearray returns an object of the same type, accessing a single byte using the item access operator ([]) returns an int—the value of the specified byte. For example:

```
word = b"Animal"
x = b"A"
word[0] == x       # returns: False  # word[0] == 65;   x == b"A"
word[:1] == x      # returns: True   # word[:1] == b"A"; x == b"A"
word[0] == x[0]    # returns: True   # word[0] == 65;    x[0] == 65
```

Here are some other bytes and bytearray examples:

```
data = b"5 Hills \x35\x20\x48\x69\x6C\x6C\x73"
data.upper()                            # returns: b'5 HILLS 5 HILLS'
data.replace(b"ill", b"at")             # returns: b'5 Hats 5 Hats'
bytes.fromhex("35 20 48 69 6C 6C 73")   # returns: b'5 Hills'
bytes.fromhex("352048696C6C73")         # returns: b'5 Hills'
data = bytearray(data)                  # data is now a bytearray
data.pop(10)                            # returns: 72 (ord("H"))
data.insert(10, ord("B"))               # data == b'5 Hills 5 Bills'
```

Methods that make sense only for strings, such as bytes.upper(), assume that the bytes are encoded using ASCII. The bytes.fromhex() class method ignores whitespace and interprets each two-digit substring as a hexadecimal number, so "35" is taken to be a byte of value 0x35, and so on.

Charac-
ter
encod-
ings

85 ☞

The str.encode() method returns a bytes object with the string encoded according to the specified encoding. UTF-8 is a very convenient encoding because it can represent any Unicode character and is especially compact when representing ASCII characters (just one byte each). The format variable is set to hold a struct format based on the string's length. For example, given the string "en.wikipedia.org", the format will be "<H16s" (little-endian byte order, 2-byte unsigned integer, 16-byte byte string), and the bytes object that is returned will be b'\x10\x00en.wikipedia.org'. Conveniently, Python shows bytes objects in a compact form using printable ASCII characters where possible, and hexadecimal escapes (and some special escapes like \t and \n) otherwise.

The Struct Module

The struct module provides struct.pack(), struct.unpack(), and some other functions, and the struct.Struct() class. The struct.pack() function takes a struct format string and one or more values and returns a bytes object that holds all the values represented in accordance with the format. The struct.unpack() function takes a format and a bytes or bytearray object and returns a tuple of the values that were originally packed using the format. For example:

```
data = struct.pack("<2h", 11, -9)    # data == b'\x0b\x00\xf7\xff'
items = struct.unpack("<2h", data)  # items == (11, -9)
```

Format strings consist of one or more characters. Most characters represent a value of a particular type. If we need more than one value of a type we can either write the character as many times as there are values of the type ("hh"), or precede the character with a count as we have done here ("2h").

Many format characters are described in the struct module's online documentation, including "b" (8-bit signed integer), "B" (8-bit unsigned integer), "h" (16-bit signed integer—used in the examples here), "H" (16-bit unsigned integer), "i" (32-bit signed integer), "I" (32-bit unsigned integer), "q" (64-bit signed integer), "Q" (64-bit unsigned integer), "f" (32-bit float), "d" (64-bit float—this corresponds to Python's float type), "?" (Boolean), "s" (bytes or bytearray object—byte strings), and many others.

For some data types such as multibyte integers, the processor's endianness makes a difference to the byte order. We can force a particular byte order to be used regardless of the processor architecture by starting the format string with an endianness character. In this book we always use "<", which means little-endian since that's the native endianness for the widely used Intel and AMD processors. Big-endian (also called network byte order) is signified by ">" (or by "!"). If no endianness is specified the machine's endianness is used. We recommend always specifying the endianness even if it is the same as the machine being used since doing so keeps the data portable.

The struct.calcsize() function takes a format and returns how many bytes a struct using the format will occupy. A format can also be stored by creating a struct.Struct() object giving it the format as its argument, with the size of the struct.Struct() object given by its size attribute. For example:

```
TWO_SHORTS = struct.Struct("<2h")
data = TWO_SHORTS.pack(11, -9)      # data == b'\x0b\x00\xf7\xff'
items = TWO_SHORTS.unpack(data)    # items == (11, -9)
```

In both examples, 11 is 0x000b, but this is transformed into the bytes 0x0b 0x00 because we have used little-endian byte ordering.

Table 7.1 *Bytes and Bytearray Methods #1*

Charac-
ter
encod-
ings

85 ☞

Syntax	Description
ba.append(i)	Appends int i (in range 0...255) to bytearray ba
b.capitalize()	Returns a copy of bytes/bytearray b with the first character capitalized (if it is an ASCII letter)
b.center(width, byte)	Returns a copy of b centered in length width padded with spaces or optionally with the given *byte*
b.count(x, start, end)	Returns the number of occurrences of bytes/bytearray x in bytes/bytearray b (or in the *start:end* slice of b)
b.decode(encoding, error)	Returns a str object that represents the bytes using the UTF-8 encoding or using the specified *encoding* and handling errors according to the optional *error* argument
b.endswith(x, start, end)	Returns True if b (or the *start:end* slice of b) ends with bytes/bytearray x or with any of the bytes/bytearrays in tuple x; otherwise, returns False
b.expandtabs(size)	Returns a copy of bytes/bytearray b with tabs replaced with spaces in multiples of 8 or of *size* if specified
ba.extend(seq)	Extends bytearray ba with all the ints in sequence seq; all the ints must be in the range 0...255
b.find(x, start, end)	Returns the leftmost position of bytes/bytearray x in b (or in the *start:end* slice of b) or -1 if not found. Use the rfind() method to find the rightmost position.
b.fromhex(h)	Returns a bytes object with bytes corresponding to the hexadecimal integers in str h
b.index(x, start, end)	Returns the leftmost position of x in b (or in the *start:end* slice of b) or raises ValueError if not found. Use the rindex() method to find the rightmost position.
ba.insert(p, i)	Inserts integer i (in range 0...255) at position p in ba
b.isalnum()	Returns True if bytes/bytearray b is nonempty and every character in b is an ASCII alphanumeric character
b.isalpha()	Returns True if bytes/bytearray b is nonempty and every character in b is an ASCII alphabetic character
b.isdigit()	Returns True if bytes/bytearray b is nonempty and every character in b is an ASCII digit
b.islower()	Returns True if bytes/bytearray b has at least one lowercaseable ASCII character and all its lowercaseable characters are lowercase
b.isspace()	Returns True if bytes/bytearray b is nonempty and every character in b is an ASCII whitespace character

Table 7.2 *Bytes and Bytearray Methods #2*

Syntax	Description
b.istitle()	Returns True if b is nonempty and title-cased
b.isupper()	Returns True if b has at least one uppercaseable ASCII character and all its uppercaseable characters are uppercase
b.join(seq)	Returns the concatenation of every bytes/bytearray in sequence seq, with b (which may be empty) between each one
b.ljust(width, *byte*)	Returns a copy of bytes/bytearray b left-aligned in length width padded with spaces or optionally with the given *byte*. Use the rjust() method to right-align.
b.lower()	Returns an ASCII-lowercased copy of bytes/bytearray b
b.partition(sep)	Returns a tuple of three bytes objects—the part of b before the leftmost bytes/bytearray sep, sep itself, and the part of b after sep; or if sep isn't in b returns b and two empty bytes objects. Use the rpartition() method to partition on the rightmost occurrence of sep.
ba.pop(p)	Removes and returns the int at index position p in ba
ba.remove(i)	Removes the first occurrence of int i from bytearray ba
b.replace(x, y, *n*)	Returns a copy of b with every (or a maximum of *n* if given) occurrence of bytes/bytearray x replaced with y
ba.reverse()	Reverses bytearray ba's bytes in-place
b.split(*x*, *n*)	Returns a list of bytes splitting at most *n* times on *x*. If *n* isn't given, splits everywhere possible; if *x* isn't given, splits on whitespace. Use rsplit() to split from the right.
b.splitlines(*f*)	Returns the list of lines produced by splitting b on line terminators, stripping the terminators unless *f* is True
b.startswith(x, *start*, *end*)	Returns True if bytes/bytearray b (or the *start*:*end* slice of b) starts with bytes/bytearray x or with any of the bytes/bytearrays in tuple x; otherwise, returns False
b.strip(*x*)	Returns a copy of b with leading and trailing whitespace (or the bytes in bytes/bytearray *x*) removed; lstrip() strips only at the start, and rstrip() strips only at the end
b.swapcase()	Returns a copy of b with uppercase ASCII characters lowercased and lowercase ASCII characters uppercased
b.title()	Returns a copy of b where the first ASCII letter of each word is uppercased and all other ASCII letters are lowercased
b.translate(bt, *d*)	Returns a copy of b that has no bytes from *d*, and where each other byte is replaced by the byte-th byte from bytes bt

Table 7.3 *Bytes and Bytearray Methods #3*

Syntax	Description
b.upper()	Returns an ASCII-uppercased copy of bytes/bytearray b
b.zfill(w)	Returns a copy of b, which if shorter than w is padded with leading zeros (0x30 characters) to make it w bytes long

The pack_string() function can handle strings of up to 65 535 UTF-8 characters. We could easily switch to using a different kind of integer for the byte count; for example, a 4-byte signed integer (format "i") would allow for strings of up to 2^{31}-1 (more than 2 billion) characters.

The struct module does provide a similar built-in format, "p", that stores a single byte as a character count followed by up to 255 characters. For packing, the code using "p" format is slightly simpler than doing all the work ourselves. But "p" format restricts us to a maximum of 255 UTF-8 characters and provides almost no benefit when unpacking. (For the sake of comparison, versions of pack_string() and unpack_string() that use "p" format are included in the convert-incidents.py source file.)

We can now turn our attention to the rest of the code in the export_binary() method.

```
fh = None
try:
    if compress:
        fh = gzip.open(filename, "wb")
    else:
        fh = open(filename, "wb")
    fh.write(MAGIC)
    fh.write(FORMAT_VERSION)
    for incident in self.values():
        data = bytearray()
        data.extend(pack_string(incident.report_id))
        data.extend(pack_string(incident.airport))
        data.extend(pack_string(incident.aircraft_id))
        data.extend(pack_string(incident.aircraft_type))
        data.extend(pack_string(incident.narrative.strip()))
        data.extend(NumbersStruct.pack(
                    incident.date.toordinal(),
                    incident.pilot_percent_hours_on_type,
                    incident.pilot_total_hours,
                    incident.midair))
        fh.write(data)
    return True
```

We have omitted the except and finally blocks since they are the same as the ones shown in the preceding subsection, apart from the particular exceptions that the except block catches.

We begin by opening the file in "write binary" mode, either a normal file or a gzip compressed file depending on the compress flag. We then write the 4-byte magic number that is (hopefully) unique to our program, and the 2-byte version number.[*] Using a version number makes it easier to change the format in the future—when we read the version number we can use it to determine which code to use for reading.

Next we iterate over all the incidents, and for each one we create a bytearray. We add each item of data to the byte array, starting with the variable length strings. The date.toordinal() method returns a single integer representing the stored date; the date can be restored by passing this integer to the date-time.date.fromordinal() method. The NumbersStruct is defined earlier in the program with this statement:

```
NumbersStruct = struct.Struct("<Idi?")
```

This format specifies little-endian byte order, an unsigned 32-bit integer (for the date ordinal), a 64-bit float (for the percentage hours on type), a 32-bit integer (for the total hours flown), and a Boolean (for whether the incident was midair). The structure of an entire aircraft incident record is shown schematically in Figure 7.3.

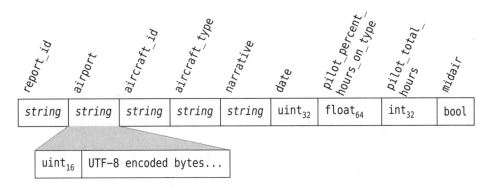

Figure 7.3 *The structure of a binary aircraft incident record*

Once the bytearray has all the data for one incident, we write it to disk. And once all the incidents have been written we return True (assuming no error occurred). The finally block ensures that the file is closed just before we return.

---

[*]There is no central repository for magic numbers like there is for domain names, so we can never guarantee uniqueness.

Reading back the data is not as straightforward as writing it—for one thing we have more error checking to do. Also, reading back variable length strings is slightly tricky. Here is the start of the import_binary() method and the complete nested unpack_string() function that we use to read back the variable length strings:

```
def import_binary(self, filename):

    def unpack_string(fh, eof_is_error=True):
        uint16 = struct.Struct("<H")
        length_data = fh.read(uint16.size)
        if not length_data:
            if eof_is_error:
                raise ValueError("missing or corrupt string size")
            return None
        length = uint16.unpack(length_data)[0]
        if length == 0:
            return ""
        data = fh.read(length)
        if not data or len(data) != length:
            raise ValueError("missing or corrupt string")
        format = "<{0}s".format(length)
        return struct.unpack(format, data)[0].decode("utf8")
```

Since each incident record begins with its report ID string, when we attempt to read this string and we succeed, we are at the start of a new record. But if we fail, we've reached the end of the file and can finish. We set the eof_is_error flag to False when attempting to read a report ID since if there is no data, it just means we have finished. For all other strings we accept the default of True because if any other string has no data, it is an error. (Even an empty string will be preceded by a 16-bit unsigned integer length.)

We begin by attempting to read the string's length. If this fails we return None to signify end of file (if we are attempting to read a new incident), or we raise a ValueError exception to indicate corrupt or missing data. The struct.unpack() function and the struct.Struct.unpack() method always return a tuple, even if it contains only a single value. We unpack the length data and store the number it represents in the length variable. Now we know how many bytes we must read to get the string. If the length is zero we simply return an empty string. Otherwise, we attempt to read the specified number of bytes. If we don't get any data or if the data is not the size we expected (i.e., it is too little), we raise a ValueError exception.

If we have the right number of bytes we create a suitable format string for the struct.unpack() function, and we return the string that results from unpacking the data and decoding the bytes as UTF-8. (In theory, we could replace the last two lines with return data.decode("utf8"), but we prefer to go through the unpacking process since it is possible—though unlikely—that the "s" format performs some transformation on our data which must be reversed when reading back.)

We will now look at the rest of the import_binary() method, breaking it into two parts for ease of explanation.

```
fh = None
try:
    fh = open(filename, "rb")
    magic = fh.read(len(GZIP_MAGIC))
    if magic == GZIP_MAGIC:
        fh.close()
        fh = gzip.open(filename, "rb")
    else:
        fh.seek(0)
    magic = fh.read(len(MAGIC))
    if magic != MAGIC:
        raise ValueError("invalid .aib file format")
    version = fh.read(len(FORMAT_VERSION))
    if version > FORMAT_VERSION:
        raise ValueError("unrecognized .aib file version")
    self.clear()
```

The file may or may not be compressed, so we use the same technique that we used for reading pickles to open the file using gzip.open() or the built-in open() function.

Once the file is open and we are at the beginning, we read the first four bytes (len(MAGIC)). If these don't match our magic number we know that it isn't a binary aircraft incident data file and so we raise a ValueError exception. Next we read in the 2-byte version number. It is at this point that we would use different reading code depending on the version. Here we just check that the version isn't a later one than this program is able to read.

If the magic number is correct and the version is one we can handle, we are ready to read in the data, so we begin by clearing out all the existing incidents so that the dictionary is empty.

```
while True:
    report_id = unpack_string(fh, False)
    if report_id is None:
        break
    data = {}
    data["report_id"] = report_id
    for name in ("airport", "aircraft_id",
                "aircraft_type", "narrative"):
```

```
        data[name] = unpack_string(fh)
        other_data = fh.read(NumbersStruct.size)
        numbers = NumbersStruct.unpack(other_data)
        data["date"] = datetime.date.fromordinal(numbers[0])
        data["pilot_percent_hours_on_type"] = numbers[1]
        data["pilot_total_hours"] = numbers[2]
        data["midair"] = numbers[3]
        incident = Incident(**data)
        self[incident.report_id] = incident
    return True
```

The while block loops until we run out of data. We start by trying to get a report ID. If we get None we've reached the end of the file and can break out of the loop. Otherwise, we create a dictionary called data to hold the data for one incident and attempt to get the rest of the incident's data. For the strings we use the unpack_string() method, and for the other data we read it all in one go using the NumbersStruct struct. Since we stored the date as an ordinal we must do the reverse conversion to get a date back. But for the other items, we can just use the unpacked data—no validation or conversion is required since we wrote the correct data types in the first place and have read back the same data types using the format held in the NumbersStruct struct.

If any error occurs, for example, if we fail to unpack all the numbers, an exception will be raised and will be handled in the except block. (We haven't shown the except and finally blocks because they are structurally the same as those shown in the preceding subsection for the import_pickle() method.)

Toward the end we make use of the convenient mapping unpacking syntax to create an Incident object which we then store in the incidents dictionary.

Apart from the handling of variable length strings, the struct module makes it very easy to save and load data in binary format. And for variable length strings the pack_string() and unpack_string() methods shown here should serve most purposes perfectly well.

Map-
ping
unpack-
ing

169 ☞

Writing and Parsing Text Files

Writing text is easy, but reading it back can be problematic, so we need to choose the structure carefully so that it is not too difficult to parse. Figure 7.4 shows an example aircraft incident record in the text format we are going to use. When we write the incident records to a file we will follow each one with a blank line, but when we parse the file we will accept zero or more blank lines between incident records.

Writing Text

Each incident record begins with the report ID enclosed in brackets ([ ]). This is followed by all the one-line data items written in *key=value* form. For the multi-line narrative text we precede the text with a start marker (.NARRATIVE_START.) and follow it with an end marker (.NARRATIVE_END.), and we indent all the text in between to ensure that no line of text could be confused with a start or end marker.

```
[20070927022009C]
date=2007-09-27
aircraft_id=1675B
aircraft_type=DHC-2-MK1
airport=MERLE K (MUDHOLE) SMITH
pilot_percent_hours_on_type=46.1538461538
pilot_total_hours=13000
midair=0
.NARRATIVE_START.
    ACCORDING TO THE PILOT, THE DRAG LINK FAILED DUE TO AN OVERSIZED
    TAIL WHEEL TIRE LANDING ON HARD SURFACE.
.NARRATIVE_END.
```

Figure 7.4 *An example text format aircraft incident record*

Here is the code for the export_text() function, but excluding the except and finally blocks since they are the same as ones we have seen before, except for the exceptions handled:

```
def export_text(self, filename):
    wrapper = textwrap.TextWrapper(initial_indent="    ",
                                   subsequent_indent="    ")
    fh = None
    try:
        fh = open(filename, "w", encoding="utf8")
        for incident in self.values():
            narrative = "\n".join(wrapper.wrap(
                    incident.narrative.strip()))
            fh.write("[{0.report_id}]\n"
                    "date={0.date!s}\n"
                    "aircraft_id={0.aircraft_id}\n"
                    "aircraft_type={0.aircraft_type}\n"
                    "airport={airport}\n"
                    "pilot_percent_hours_on_type="
                    "{0.pilot_percent_hours_on_type}\n"
```

```
            "pilot_total_hours={0.pilot_total_hours}\n"
            "midair={0.midair:d}\n"
            ".NARRATIVE_START.\n{narrative}\n"
            ".NARRATIVE_END.\n\n".format(incident,
        airport=incident.airport.strip(),
        narrative=narrative))
    return True
```

The line breaks in the narrative text are not significant, so we can wrap the text as we like. Normally we would use the textwrap module's textwrap.wrap() function, but here we need to both indent and wrap, so we begin by creating a textwrap.TextWrap object, initialized with the indentation we want to use (four spaces for the first and subsequent lines). By default, the object will wrap lines to a width of 70 characters, although we can change this by passing another keyword argument.

We could have written this using a triple quoted string, but we prefer to put in the newlines manually. The textwrap.TextWrap object provides a wrap() method that takes a string as input, in this case the narrative text, and returns a list of strings with suitable indentation and each no longer than the wrap width. We then join this list of lines into a single string using newline as the separator. The incident date is held as a datetime.date object; we have forced str.format() to use the string representation when writing the date—this very conveniently produces the date in ISO 8601, YYYY-MM-DD format. We have told str.format() to write the midair bool as an integer—this produces 1 for True and 0 for False. In general, using str.format() makes writing text very easy because it handles all of Python's data types (and custom types if we implement the __str__() or __format__() special method) automatically.

datetime
module

205 ☞

str.
format()

74 ☞

__for-
mat__()

244 ☞

Parsing Text

The method for reading and parsing text format aircraft incident records is longer and more involved than the one used for writing. When reading the file we could be in one of several states. We could be in the middle of reading narrative lines; we could be at a *key=value* line; or we could be at a report ID line at the start of a new incident. We will look at the import_text_manual() method in five parts.

```
def import_text_manual(self, filename):
    fh = None
    try:
        fh = open(filename, encoding="utf8")
        self.clear()
        data = {}
        narrative = None
```

The method begins by opening the file in "read text" mode. Then we clear the dictionary of incidents and create the `data` dictionary to hold the data for a single incident in the same way as we did when reading binary incident records. The `narrative` variable is used for two purposes: as a state indicator and to store the current incident's narrative text. If `narrative` is `None` it means that we are not currently reading a narrative; but if it is a string (even an empty one) it means we are in the process of reading narrative lines.

```python
for lino, line in enumerate(fh, start=1):
    line = line.rstrip()
    if not line and narrative is None:
        continue
    if narrative is not None:
        if line == ".NARRATIVE_END.":
            data["narrative"] = textwrap.dedent(
                                    narrative).strip()
            if len(data) != 9:
                raise IncidentError("missing data on "
                            "line {0}".format(lino))
            incident = Incident(**data)
            self[incident.report_id] = incident
            data = {}
            narrative = None
        else:
            narrative += line + "\n"
```

Since we are reading line by line we can keep track of the current line number and use this to provide more informative error messages than is possible when reading binary files. We begin by stripping off any trailing whitespace from the line, and if this leaves us with an empty line (and providing we are not in the middle of a narrative), we simply skip to the next line. This means that the number of blank lines between incidents doesn't matter, but that we preserve any blank lines that are in narrative texts.

If the `narrative` is not `None` we know that we are in a narrative. If the line is the narrative end marker we know that we have not only finished reading the narrative, but also finished reading all the data for the current incident. In this case we put the narrative text into the `data` dictionary (having removed the indentation with the `textwrap.dedent()` function), and providing we have the nine pieces of data we need, we create a new incident and store it in the dictionary. Then we clear the `data` dictionary and reset the `narrative` variable ready for the next record. On the other hand, if the line isn't the narrative end marker, we append it to the narrative—including the newline that was stripped off at the beginning.

```
elif (not data and line[0] == "["
                and line[-1] == "]"):
    data["report_id"] = line[1:-1]
```

If the narrative is None then we are at either a new report ID or are reading some other data. We could be at a new report ID only if the data dictionary is empty (because it starts that way and because we clear it after reading each incident), and if the line begins with [and ends with]. If this is the case we put the report ID into the data dictionary. This means that this elif condition will not be True again until the data dictionary is next cleared.

```
elif "=" in line:
    key, value = line.split("=", 1)
    if key == "date":
        data[key] = datetime.datetime.strptime(value,
                                    "%Y-%m-%d").date()
    elif key == "pilot_percent_hours_on_type":
        data[key] = float(value)
    elif key == "pilot_total_hours":
        data[key] = int(value)
    elif key == "midair":
        data[key] = bool(int(value))
    else:
        data[key] = value
elif line == ".NARRATIVE_START.":
    narrative = ""
else:
    raise KeyError("parsing error on line {0}".format(
                    lino))
```

If we are not in a narrative and are not reading a new report ID there are only three more possibilities: We are reading *key=value* items, we are at a narrative start marker, or something has gone wrong.

In the case of reading a line of *key=value* data, we split the line on the first = character, specifying a maximum of one split—this means that the value can safely include = characters. All the data read is in the form of Unicode strings, so for date, numeric, and Boolean data types we must convert the value string accordingly.

For dates we use the datetime.datetime.strptime() function ("string parse time") which takes a format string and returns a datetime.datetime object. We have used a format string that matches the ISO 8601 date format, and we use datetime.datetime.date() to retrieve a datetime.date object from the resultant datetime.datetime object, since we want only a date and not a date/time. We rely on Python's built-in type functions, float() and int(), for the numeric conversions. Note, though that, for example, int("4.0") will raise a ValueError; if we want to be more liberal in accepting integers, we could use int(float("4.0")), or if we wanted to round rather than truncate, round(float("4.0")). To get a bool is slightly subtler—for example, bool("0") returns True (a nonempty string is True), so we must first convert the string to an int.

Invalid, missing, or out-of-range values will always cause an exception to be raised. If any of the conversions fail they raise a ValueError exception. And if any values are out of range an IncidentError exception will be raised when the data is used to create a corresponding Incident object.

If the line doesn't contain an = character, we check to see whether we've read the narrative start marker. If we have, we set the narrative variable to be an empty string. This means that the first if condition will be True for subsequent lines, at least until the narrative end marker is read.

If none of the if or elif conditions is True then an error has occurred, so in the final else clause we raise a KeyError exception to signify this.

```
            return True
    except (EnvironmentError, ValueError, KeyError,
            IncidentError) as err:
        print("{0}: import error: {1}".format(
            os.path.basename(sys.argv[0]), err))
        return False
    finally:
        if fh is not None:
            fh.close()
```

After reading all the lines, we return True to the caller—unless an exception occurred, in which case the except block catches the exception, prints an error message for the user, and returns False. And no matter what, if the file was opened, it is closed at the end.

Parsing Text Using Regular Expressions

Readers unfamiliar with regular expressions ("regexes") are recommended to read Chapter 12 before reading this section—or to skip ahead to the following section (page 302), and return here later if desired.

Using regular expressions to parse text files can often produce shorter code than doing everything by hand as we did in the previous subsection, but it can be more difficult to provide good error reporting. We will look at the import_text_regex() method in two parts, first looking at the regular expressions and then at the parsing—but omitting the except and finally blocks since they have nothing new to teach us.

```
def import_text_regex(self, filename):
    incident_re = re.compile(
                    r"\[(?P<id>[^]]+)\](?P<keyvalues>.+?)"
                    r"^\.NARRATIVE_START\.$(?P<narrative>.*?)"
                    r"^\.NARRATIVE_END\.$",
                    re.DOTALL|re.MULTILINE)
    key_value_re = re.compile(r"^\s*(?P<key>[^=]+)\s*=\s*"
                              r"(?P<value>.+)\s*$", re.MULTILINE)
```

raw strings

62 ☜

The regular expressions are written as raw strings. This saves us from having to double each backslash (writing each \ as \\)—for example, without using raw strings the second regular expression would have to be written as "^\\s*(?P<key>[^=]+)\\s*=\\s*(?P<value>.+)\\s*$". In this book we always use raw strings for regular expressions.

The first regular expression, incident_re, is used to capture an entire incident record. One effect of this is that any spurious text *between* records will not be noticed. This regular expression really has two parts. The first is \[(?P<id>[^]]+)\](?P<keyvalues>.+?) which matches a [, then matches and captures into the id match group as many non-] characters as it can, then matches a] (so this gives us the report ID), and then matches as few—but at least one—of any characters (including newlines because of the re.DOTALL flag), into the keyvalues match group. The characters matched for the keyvalues match group are the minimum necessary to take us to the second part of the regular expression.

The second part of the first regular expression is ^\.NARRATIVE_START\.$ (?P<narrative>.*?)^\.NARRATIVE_END\.$ and this matches the literal text .NARRATIVE_START., then as few characters as possible which are captured into the narrative match group, and then the literal text .NARRATIVE_END., at the end of the incident record. The re.MULTILINE flag means that in this regular expression ^ matches at the start of every line (rather than just at the start of the string), and $ matches at the end of every line (rather than just at the end of the string), so the narrative start and end markers are matched only at the start of lines.

The second regular expression, key_value_re, is used to capture *key=value* lines, and it matches at the start of every line in the text it is given to match against, where the line begins with any amount of whitespace (including none), followed by non-= characters which are captured into the key match group, followed by an = character, followed by all the remaining characters in the line (excluding any leading or trailing whitespace), and captures them into the value match group.

The fundamental logic used to parse the file is the same as we used for the manual text parser that we covered in the previous subsection, only this time we extract incident records and incident data within those records using regular expressions rather than reading line by line.

```
fh = None
try:
    fh = open(filename, encoding="utf8")
    self.clear()
    for incident_match in incident_re.finditer(fh.read()):
        data = {}
        data["report_id"] = incident_match.group("id")
        data["narrative"] = textwrap.dedent(
                    incident_match.group("narrative")).strip()
        keyvalues = incident_match.group("keyvalues")
        for match in key_value_re.finditer(keyvalues):
            data[match.group("key")] = match.group("value")
        data["date"] = datetime.datetime.strptime(
                        data["date"], "%Y-%m-%d").date()
        data["pilot_percent_hours_on_type"] = (
                float(data["pilot_percent_hours_on_type"]))
        data["pilot_total_hours"] = int(
                data["pilot_total_hours"])
        data["midair"] = bool(int(data["midair"]))
        if len(data) != 9:
            raise IncidentError("missing data")
        incident = Incident(**data)
        self[incident.report_id] = incident
    return True
```

The re.finditer() method returns an iterator which produces each nonoverlapping match in turn. We create a data dictionary to hold one incident's data as we have done before, but this time we get the report ID and narrative text from each match of the incident_re regular expression. We then extract all the *key=value* strings in one go using the keyvalues match group, and apply the key_value_re regular expression's re.finditer() method to iterate over each individual *key=value* line. For each (key, value) pair found, we put them in the data dictionary—so all the values go in as strings. Then, for those values which should not be strings, we replace them with a value of the appropriate type using the same string conversions that we used when parsing the text manually.

We have added a check to ensure that the data dictionary has nine items because if an incident record is corrupt, the key_value.finditer() iterator might match too many or too few *key=value* lines. The end is the same as before—we create a new Incident object and put it in the incidents dictionary, then return True. If anything went wrong, the except suite will issue a suitable error message and return False, and the finally suite will close the file.

One of the things that makes both the manual and the regular expression text parsers as short and straightforward as they are is Python's exception-handling. The parsers don't have to check any of the conversions of strings to dates, numbers, or Booleans, and they don't have to do any range checking (the Incident class does that). If any of these things fail, an exception will be raised, and we handle all the exceptions neatly in one place at the end. Another benefit of using exception-handling rather than explicit checking is that the code scales well—even if the record format changes to include more data items, the error handling code doesn't need to grow any larger.

Writing and Parsing XML Files

Some programs use an XML file format for all the data they handle, whereas others use XML as a convenient import/export format. The ability to import and export XML is useful and is always worth considering even if a program's main format is a text or binary format.

Python offers three ways of writing XML files: manually writing the XML, creating an element tree and using its write() method, and creating a DOM and using its write() method. For reading and parsing XML files there are four approaches that can be used: manually reading and parsing the XML (not recommended and not covered here—it can be quite difficult to handle some of the more obscure and advanced details correctly), or using an element tree, DOM, or SAX parser.

The aircraft incident XML format is shown in Figure 7.5. In this section we will show how to write this format manually and how to write it using an element tree and a DOM, as well as how to read and parse this format using the element tree, DOM, and SAX parsers. If you don't care which approach is used to read or write the XML, you could just read the Element Trees subsection that follows, and then skip to the chapter's final section (Random Access Binary Files; page 313).

Element Trees

Writing the data using an element tree is done in two phases: First an element tree representing the data must be created, and second the tree must be written to a file. Some programs might use the element tree as their data structure, in which case they already have the tree and can simply write out the data. We will look at the export_xml_etree() method in two parts:

```
def export_xml_etree(self, filename):
    root = xml.etree.ElementTree.Element("incidents")
    for incident in self.values():
```

```
<?xml version="1.0" encoding="UTF-8"?>
<incidents>
<incident report_id="20070222008099G" date="2007-02-22"
    aircraft_id="80342" aircraft_type="CE-172-M"
    pilot_percent_hours_on_type="9.09090909091"
    pilot_total_hours="440" midair="0">
<airport>BOWERMAN</airport>
<narrative>
ON A GO-AROUND FROM A NIGHT CROSSWIND LANDING ATTEMPT THE AIRCRAFT HIT
A RUNWAY EDGE LIGHT DAMAGING ONE PROPELLER.
</narrative>
</incident>
<incident>

    ...
</incident>
    :
</incidents>
```

Figure 7.5 *An example XML format aircraft incident record in context*

```
element = xml.etree.ElementTree.Element("incident",
        report_id=incident.report_id,
        date=incident.date.isoformat(),
        aircraft_id=incident.aircraft_id,
        aircraft_type=incident.aircraft_type,
        pilot_percent_hours_on_type=str(
                incident.pilot_percent_hours_on_type),
        pilot_total_hours=str(incident.pilot_total_hours),
        midair=str(int(incident.midair)))
airport = xml.etree.ElementTree.SubElement(element,
                                            "airport")
airport.text = incident.airport.strip()
narrative = xml.etree.ElementTree.SubElement(element,
                                            "narrative")
narrative.text = incident.narrative.strip()
root.append(element)
tree = xml.etree.ElementTree.ElementTree(root)
```

We begin by creating the root element (<incidents>). Then we iterate over all the incident records. For each one we create an element (<incident>) to hold the data for the incident, and use keyword arguments to provide the attributes. All the attributes must be text, so we convert the date, numeric, and Boolean data items accordingly. We don't have to worry about escaping "&", "<", and ">" (or about quotes in attribute values), since the element tree module (and the DOM and SAX modules) automatically take care of these details.

Each <incident> has two subelements, one holding the airport name and the other the narrative text. When subelements are created we must provide the parent element and the tag name. An element's read/write text attribute is used to hold its text.

Once the <incident> has been created with all its attributes and its <airport> and <narrative> subelements, we add the incident to the hierarchy's root (<incidents>) element. At the end we have a hierarchy of elements that contains all the incident record data, which we then trivially convert into an element tree.

```
try:
    tree.write(filename, "UTF-8")
except EnvironmentError as err:
    print("{0}: import error: {1}".format(
            os.path.basename(sys.argv[0]), err))
    return False
return True
```

Writing the XML to represent an entire element tree is simply a matter of telling the tree to write itself to the given file using the given encoding.

Up to now when we have specified an encoding we have almost always used the string "utf8". This works fine for Python's built-in open() function which can accept a wide range of encodings and a variety of names for them, such as "UTF-8", "UTF8", "utf-8", and "utf8". But for XML files the encoding name can be only one of the official names, so "utf8" is not acceptable, which is why we have used "UTF-8".★

Reading an XML file using an element tree is not much harder than writing one. Again there are two phases: First we read and parse the XML file, and then we traverse the resultant element tree to read off the data to populate the incidents dictionary. Again this second phase is not necessary if the element tree itself is being used as the in-memory data store. Here is the import_xml_etree() method, split into two parts.

```
def import_xml_etree(self, filename):
    try:
        tree = xml.etree.ElementTree.parse(filename)
    except (EnvironmentError,
            xml.parsers.expat.ExpatError) as err:
        print("{0}: import error: {1}".format(
                os.path.basename(sys.argv[0]), err))
```

★ See www.w3.org/TR/2006/REC-xml11-20060816/#NT-EncodingDecl and www.iana.org/assignments/character-sets for information about XML encodings.

```
                      return False
```

By default, the element tree parser uses the expat XML parser under the hood which is why we must be ready to catch expat exceptions.

```
            self.clear()
            for element in tree.findall("incident"):
                try:
                    data = {}
                    for attribute in ("report_id", "date", "aircraft_id",
                            "aircraft_type",
                            "pilot_percent_hours_on_type",
                            "pilot_total_hours", "midair"):
                        data[attribute] = element.get(attribute)
                    data["date"] = datetime.datetime.strptime(
                                    data["date"], "%Y-%m-%d").date()
                    data["pilot_percent_hours_on_type"] = (
                            float(data["pilot_percent_hours_on_type"]))
                    data["pilot_total_hours"] = int(
                            data["pilot_total_hours"])
                    data["midair"] = bool(int(data["midair"]))
                    data["airport"] = element.find("airport").text.strip()
                    narrative = element.find("narrative").text
                    data["narrative"] = (narrative.strip()
                                    if narrative is not None else "")
                    incident = Incident(**data)
                    self[incident.report_id] = incident
                except (ValueError, LookupError, IncidentError) as err:
                    print("{0}: import error: {1}".format(
                        os.path.basename(sys.argv[0]), err))
                    return False
            return True
```

Once we have the element tree we can iterate over every <incident> using the xml.etree.ElementTree.findall() method. Each incident is returned as an xml.etree.Element object. We use the same technique for handling the element attributes as we did in the previous section's import_text_regex() method—first we store all the values in the data dictionary, and then we convert those values which are dates, numbers, or Booleans to the correct type. For the airport and narrative subelements we use the xml.etree.Element.find() method to find them and read their text attributes. If a text element has no text its text attribute will be None, so we must account for this when reading the narrative text element since it might be empty. In all cases, the attribute values and text returned to us do not contain XML escapes since they are automatically unescaped.

As with all the XML parsers used to process aircraft incident data, an exception will occur if the aircraft or narrative element is missing, or if one of the attributes is missing, or if one of the conversions fails, or if any of the numeric data is out of range—this ensures that invalid data will cause parsing to stop and for an error message to be output. The code at the end for creating and storing incidents and for handling exceptions is the same as we have seen before.

DOM (Document Object Model)

The DOM is a standard API for representing and manipulating an XML document in memory. The code for creating a DOM and writing it to a file, and for parsing an XML file using a DOM, is structurally very similar to the element tree code, only slightly longer.

We will begin by reviewing the export_xml_dom() method in two parts. This method works in two phases: First a DOM is created to reflect the incident data, and then the DOM is written out to a file. Just as with an element tree, some programs might use the DOM as their data structure, in which case they can simply write out the data.

```
def export_xml_dom(self, filename):
    dom = xml.dom.minidom.getDOMImplementation()
    tree = dom.createDocument(None, "incidents", None)
    root = tree.documentElement
    for incident in self.values():
        element = tree.createElement("incident")
        for attribute, value in (
                ("report_id", incident.report_id),
                ("date", incident.date.isoformat()),
                ("aircraft_id", incident.aircraft_id),
                ("aircraft_type", incident.aircraft_type),
                ("pilot_percent_hours_on_type",
                 str(incident.pilot_percent_hours_on_type)),
                ("pilot_total_hours",
                 str(incident.pilot_total_hours)),
                ("midair", str(int(incident.midair)))):
            element.setAttribute(attribute, value)
        for name, text in (("airport", incident.airport),
                           ("narrative", incident.narrative)):
            text_element = tree.createTextNode(text)
            name_element = tree.createElement(name)
            name_element.appendChild(text_element)
            element.appendChild(name_element)
        root.appendChild(element)
```

The method begins by getting a DOM implementation. By default, the implementation is provided by the expat XML parser. The `xml.dom.minidom` module provides a simpler and smaller DOM implementation than that provided by the `xml.dom` module, although the objects it uses are from the `xml.dom` module. Once we have a DOM implementation we can create a document. The first argument to `xml.dom.DOMImplementation.createDocument()` is the namespace URI which we don't need, so we pass `None`; the second argument is a qualified name (the tag name for the root element), and the third argument is the document type, and again we pass `None` since we don't have a document type. Having gotten the tree that represents the document, we retrieve the root element and then proceed to iterate over all the incidents.

For each incident we create an `<incident>` element, and for each attribute we want the incident to have we call `setAttribute()` with the attribute's name and value. Just as with the element tree, we don't have to worry about escaping "&", "<", and ">" (or about quotes in attribute values). For the airport and narrative text elements we must create a text element to hold the text and a normal element (with the appropriate tag name) as the text element's parent—we then add the normal element (and the text element it contains) to the current incident element. With the incident element complete, we add it to the root.

```
fh = None
try:
    fh = open(filename, "w", encoding="utf8")
    tree.writexml(fh, encoding="UTF-8")
    return True
```

XML encoding 304 ☞

We have omitted the except and `finally` blocks since they are the same as ones we have already seen. What this piece of code makes clear is the difference between the encoding string used for the built-in `open()` function and the encoding string used for XML files, as we discussed earlier.

Importing an XML document into a DOM is similar to importing into an element tree, but like exporting, it requires more code. We will look at the import_xml_dom() function in three parts, starting with the `def` line and the nested get_text() function.

```
def import_xml_dom(self, filename):

    def get_text(node_list):
        text = []
        for node in node_list:
            if node.nodeType == node.TEXT_NODE:
                text.append(node.data)
        return "".join(text).strip()
```

The get_text() function iterates over a list of nodes (e.g., a node's child nodes), and for each one that is a text node, it extracts the node's text and appends it

to a list of texts. At the end the function returns all the text it has gathered as
a single string, with whitespace stripped from both ends.

```
try:
    dom = xml.dom.minidom.parse(filename)
except (EnvironmentError,
        xml.parsers.expat.ExpatError) as err:
    print("{0}: import error: {1}".format(
            os.path.basename(sys.argv[0]), err))
    return False
```

Parsing an XML file into a DOM is easy since the module does all the hard work
for us, but we must be ready to handle expat errors since just like an element
tree, the expat XML parser is the default parser used by the DOM classes
under the hood.

```
self.clear()
for element in dom.getElementsByTagName("incident"):
    try:
        data = {}
        for attribute in ("report_id", "date", "aircraft_id",
                "aircraft_type",
                "pilot_percent_hours_on_type",
                "pilot_total_hours", "midair"):
            data[attribute] = element.getAttribute(attribute)
        data["date"] = datetime.datetime.strptime(
                            data["date"], "%Y-%m-%d").date()
        data["pilot_percent_hours_on_type"] = (
                float(data["pilot_percent_hours_on_type"]))
        data["pilot_total_hours"] = int(
                data["pilot_total_hours"])
        data["midair"] = bool(int(data["midair"]))
        airport = element.getElementsByTagName("airport")[0]
        data["airport"] = get_text(airport.childNodes)
        narrative = element.getElementsByTagName(
                                            "narrative")[0]
        data["narrative"] = get_text(narrative.childNodes)
        incident = Incident(**data)
        self[incident.report_id] = incident
    except (ValueError, LookupError, IncidentError) as err:
        print("{0}: import error: {1}".format(
                os.path.basename(sys.argv[0]), err))
        return False
return True
```

Once the DOM exists we clear the current incidents data and iterate over all Local func- tions ☞ 341 the incident tags. For each one we extract the attributes, and for date, numeric, and Booleans we convert them to the correct types in exactly the same way as we did when using an element tree. The only really significant difference between using a DOM and an element tree is in the handling of text nodes. We use the xml.dom.Element.getElementsByTagName() method to get the child elements with the given tag name—in the cases of <airport> and <narrative> we know there is always one of each, so we take the first (and only) child element of each type. Then we use the nested get_text() function to iterate over these tags' child nodes to extract their texts.

As usual, if any error occurs we catch the relevant exception, print an error message for the user, and return False.

The differences in approach between DOM and element tree are not great, and since they both use the same expat parser under the hood, they're both reasonably fast.

Manually Writing XML

Writing a preexisting element tree or DOM as an XML document can be done with a single method call. But if our data is not already in one of these forms we must create an element tree or DOM first, in which case it may be more convenient to simply write out our data directly.

When writing XML files we must make sure that we properly escape text and attribute values, and that we write a well-formed XML document. Here is the export_xml_manual() method for writing out the incidents in XML:

```python
def export_xml_manual(self, filename):
    fh = None
    try:
        fh = open(filename, "w", encoding="utf8")
        fh.write('<?xml version="1.0" encoding="UTF-8"?>\n')
        fh.write("<incidents>\n")
        for incident in self.values():
            fh.write('<incident report_id={report_id} '
                    'date="{0.date!s}" '
                    'aircraft_id={aircraft_id} '
                    'aircraft_type={aircraft_type} '
                    'pilot_percent_hours_on_type='
                    '"{0.pilot_percent_hours_on_type}" '
                    'pilot_total_hours="{0.pilot_total_hours}" '
                    'midair="{0.midair:d}">\n'
                    '<airport>{airport}</airport>\n'
                    '<narrative>\n{narrative}\n</narrative>\n'
```

```
                         '</incident>\n'.format(incident,
                report_id=xml.sax.saxutils.quoteattr(
                                  incident.report_id),
                aircraft_id=xml.sax.saxutils.quoteattr(
                                  incident.aircraft_id),
                aircraft_type=xml.sax.saxutils.quoteattr(
                                  incident.aircraft_type),
                airport=xml.sax.saxutils.escape(incident.airport),
                narrative="\n".join(textwrap.wrap(
                        xml.sax.saxutils.escape(
                            incident.narrative.strip()), 70))))
        fh.write("</incidents>\n")
        return True
```

As we have often done in this chapter, we have omitted the except and finally blocks.

We write the file using the UTF-8 encoding and must specify this to the built-in open() function. Strictly speaking, we don't have to specify the encoding in the <?xml?> declaration since UTF-8 is the default encoding, but we prefer to be explicit. We have chosen to quote all the attribute values using double quotes ("), and so for convenience have used single quotes to quote the string we put the incidents in to avoid the need to escape the quotes.

The sax.saxutils.quoteattr() function is similar to the sax.saxutils.escape() function we use for XML text in that it properly escapes "&", "<", and ">" characters. In addition, it escapes quotes (if necessary), and returns a string that has quotes around it ready for use. This is why we have not needed to put quotes around the report ID and other string attribute values.

The newlines we have inserted and the text wrapping for the narrative are purely cosmetic. They are designed to make the file easier for humans to read and edit, but they could just as easily be omitted.

Writing the data in HTML format is not much different from writing XML. The convert-incidents.py program includes the export_html() function as a simple example of this, although we won't review it here because it doesn't really show anything new.

Parsing XML with SAX (Simple API for XML)

Unlike the element tree and DOM, which represent an entire XML document in memory, SAX parsers work incrementally, which can potentially be both faster and less memory-hungry. A performance advantage cannot be assumed, however, especially since both the element tree and DOM use the fast expat parser.

SAX parsers work by announcing "parsing events" when they encounter start tags, end tags, and other XML elements. To be able to handle those events that we are interested in we must create a suitable handler class, and provide certain predefined methods which are called when matching parsing events take place. The most commonly implemented handler is a content handler, although it is possible to provide error handlers and other handlers if we want finer control.

Here is the complete `import_xml_sax()` method. It is very short because most of the work is done by the custom `IncidentSaxHandler` class:

```
def import_xml_sax(self, filename):
    fh = None
    try:
        handler = IncidentSaxHandler(self)
        parser = xml.sax.make_parser()
        parser.setContentHandler(handler)
        parser.parse(filename)
        return True
    except (EnvironmentError, ValueError, IncidentError,
            xml.sax.SAXParseException) as err:
        print("{0}: import error: {1}".format(
                os.path.basename(sys.argv[0]), err))
        return False
```

We create the one handler we want to use and then we create a SAX parser and set its content handler to be the one we have created. Then we give the filename to the parser's `parse()` method and return `True` if no parsing errors occured.

We pass `self` (i.e., this `IncidentCollection` dict subclass) to the custom `IncidentSaxHandler` class's initializer. The handler clears the old incidents away and then builds up a dictionary of incidents as the file is parsed. Once the parse is complete the dictionary contains all the incidents that have been read.

```
class IncidentSaxHandler(xml.sax.handler.ContentHandler):

    def __init__(self, incidents):
        super().__init__()
        self.__data = {}
        self.__text = ""
        self.__incidents = incidents
        self.__incidents.clear()
```

Custom SAX handler classes must inherit the appropriate base class. This ensures that for any methods we don't reimplement (because we are not interested in the parsing events they handle), the base class version will be called—and will safely do nothing.

We start by calling the base class's initializer. This is generally good practice for all subclasses, although it is not necessary (though harmless) for direct object subclasses. The self.__data dictionary is used to keep one incident's data, the self.__text string is used to keep the text of an airport name or of a narrative depending on which we are reading, and the self.__incidents dictionary is an object reference to the IncidentCollection dictionary which the handler updates directly. (An alternative design would be to have an independent dictionary inside the handler and to copy it to the IncidentCollection at the end using dict.clear() and then dict.update().)

```
def startElement(self, name, attributes):
    if name == "incident":
        self.__data = {}
        for key, value in attributes.items():
            if key == "date":
                self.__data[key] = datetime.datetime.strptime(
                                   value, "%Y-%m-%d").date()
            elif key == "pilot_percent_hours_on_type":
                self.__data[key] = float(value)
            elif key == "pilot_total_hours":
                self.__data[key] = int(value)
            elif key == "midair":
                self.__data[key] = bool(int(value))
            else:
                self.__data[key] = value
    self.__text = ""
```

Whenever a start tag and its attributes are read the xml.sax.handler.Content-Handler.startElement() method is called with the tag name and the tag's attributes. In the case of an aircraft incidents XML file, the start tags are <incidents>, which we ignore; <incident>, whose attributes we use to populate some of the self.__data dictionary; and <airport> and <narrative>, both of which we ignore. We always clear the self.__text string when we get a start tag because no text tags are nested in the aircraft incident XML file format.

We don't do any exception-handling in the IncidentSaxHandler class. If an exception occurs it will be passed up to the caller, in this case the import_xml_sax() method, which will catch it and output a suitable error message.

```
def endElement(self, name):
    if name == "incident":
        if len(self.__data) != 9:
            raise IncidentError("missing data")
        incident = Incident(**self.__data)
        self.__incidents[incident.report_id] = incident
    elif name in frozenset({"airport", "narrative"}):
```

```
        self.__data[name] = self.__text.strip()
    self.__text = ""
```

When an end tag is read the `xml.sax.handler.ContentHandler.endElement()` method is called. If we have reached the end of an incident we should have all the necessary data, so we create a new `Incident` object and add it to the incidents dictionary. If we have reached the end of a text element, we add an item to the `self.__data` dictionary with the text that has been accumulated so far. At the end we clear the `self.__text` string ready for its next use. (Strictly speaking, we don't have to clear it, since we clear it when we get a start tag, but clearing it could make a difference in some XML formats, for example, where tags can be nested.)

```
        def characters(self, text):
            self.__text += text
```

When the SAX parser reads text it calls the `xml.sax.handler.ContentHandler.characters()` method. There is no guarantee that this method will be called just once with all the text; the text might come in chunks. This is why we simply use the method to accumulate text, and actually put the text into the dictionary only when the relevant end tag is reached. (A more efficient implementation would have `self.__text` be a list with the body of this method being `self.__text.append(text)`, and with the other methods adapted accordingly.)

Using the SAX API is very different from using element tree or DOM, but it is just as effective. We can provide other handlers, and can reimplement additional methods in the content handler to get as much control as we like. The SAX parser itself does not maintain any representation of the XML document—this makes SAX ideal for reading XML into our own custom data collections, and also means that there is no SAX "document" to write out as XML, so for writing XML we must use one of the approaches described earlier in this section.

Random Access Binary Files

In the earlier sections we worked on the basis that all of a program's data was read into memory in one go, processed, and then all written out in one go. Modern computers have so much RAM that this is a perfectly viable approach, even for large data sets. However, in some situations holding the data on disk and just reading the bits we need and writing back changes might be a better solution. The disk-based random access approach is most easily done using a key–value database (a "DBM"), or a full SQL database—both are covered in Chapter 11—but in this section we will show how to handle random access files by hand.

We will first present the `BinaryRecordFile.BinaryRecordFile` class. Instances of this class represent a generic readable/writable binary file, structured as a sequence of fixed length records. We will then look at the `BikeStock.BikeStock` class which holds a collection of `BikeStock.Bike` objects as records in a `BinaryRecordFile.BinaryRecordFile` to see how to make use of binary random access files.

A Generic BinaryRecordFile Class

The `BinaryRecordFile.BinaryRecordFile` class's API is similar to a list in that we can get/set/delete a record at a given index position. When a record is deleted, it is simply marked "deleted"; this saves having to move all the records that follow it up to fill the gap, and also means that after a deletion all the original index positions remain valid. Another benefit is that a record can be undeleted simply by unmarking it. The price we pay for this is that deleting records doesn't save any disk space. We will solve this by providing methods to "compact" the file, eliminating deleted records (and invalidating index positions).

Before reviewing the implementation, let's look at some basic usage:

```
Contact = struct.Struct("<15si")
contacts = BinaryRecordFile.BinaryRecordFile(filename, Contact.size)
```

Here we create a struct (little-endian byte order, a 15-byte byte string, and a 4-byte signed integer) that we will use to represent each record. Then we create a `BinaryRecordFile.BinaryRecordFile` instance with a filename and with a record size to match the struct we are using. If the file exists it will be opened with its contents left intact; otherwise, it will be created—in either case it will be opened in binary read/write mode.

```
contacts[4] = Contact.pack("Abe Baker".encode("utf8"), 762)
contacts[5] = Contact.pack("Cindy Dove".encode("utf8"), 987)
```

We can treat the file like a list using the item access operator ([]); here we assign two byte strings (bytes objects, each containing an encoded string and an integer) at two record index positions in the file. These assignments will overwrite any existing content; and if the file doesn't already have six records, the earlier records will be created with every byte set to 0x00.

```
contact_data = Contact.unpack(contacts[5])
contact_data[0].decode("utf8").rstrip(chr(0)) # returns: 'Cindy Dove'
```

Since the string "Cindy Dove" is shorter than the 15 UTF-8 characters in the struct, when it is packed it is padded with 0x00 bytes at the end. So when we retrieve the record, the `contact_data` will hold the 2-tuple (b'Cindy

Dove\x00\x00\x00\x00\x00', 987). To get the name, we must decode the UTF-8 to produce a Unicode string, and strip off the 0x00 padding bytes.

Now that we've had a glimpse of the class in action, we are ready to review the code. The `BinaryRecordFile.BinaryRecordFile` class is in file `BinaryRecord-File.py`. After the usual preliminaries the file begins with the definitions of a couple of private byte values:

```
_DELETED = b"\x01"
_OKAY = b"\x02"
```

Each record starts with a "state" byte which is either `_DELETED` or `_OKAY` (or `b"\x00"` in the case of blank records).

Here is the `class` line and the initializer:

```
class BinaryRecordFile:

    def __init__(self, filename, record_size, auto_flush=True):
        self.__record_size = record_size + 1
        mode = "w+b" if not os.path.exists(filename) else "r+b"
        self.__fh = open(filename, mode)
        self.auto_flush = auto_flush
```

There are two different record sizes. The `BinaryRecordFile.record_size` is the one set by the user and is the record size from the user's point of view. The private `BinaryRecordFile.__record_size` is the real record size and includes the state byte.

We are careful not to truncate the file when we open it if it already exists (by using a mode of `"r+b"`), and to create it if it does not exist (by using a mode of `"w+b"`)—the `"+"` part of the mode string is what signifies reading *and* writing. If the `BinaryRecordFile.auto_flush` Boolean is `True`, the file is flushed before every read and after every write.

```
    @property
    def record_size(self):
        return self.__record_size - 1

    @property
    def name(self):
        return self.__fh.name

    def flush(self):
        self.__fh.flush()

    def close(self):
        self.__fh.close()
```

Table 7.4 *File Object Attributes and Methods #1*

Syntax	Description
f.close()	Closes file object f and sets attribute f.closed to True
f.closed	Returns True if the file is closed
f.encoding	The encoding used for bytes ↔ str conversions
f.fileno()	Returns the underlying file's file descriptor. (Available only for file objects that have file descriptors.)
f.flush()	Flushes the file object f
f.isatty()	Returns True if the file object is associated with a console. (Available only for file objects that refer to actual files.)
f.mode	The mode file object f was opened with
f.name	File object f's filename (if it has one)
f.newlines	The kinds of newline strings encountered in text file f
f.__next__()	Returns the next line from file object f. In most cases, this method is used implicitly, for example, for *line* in f.
f.peek(*n*)	Returns *n* bytes without moving the file pointer position
f.read(*count*)	Reads at most *count* bytes from file object f. If *count* is not specified then every byte is read from the current file position to the end. Returns a bytes object when reading in binary mode and a str when reading in text mode. If there is no more to read (end of file), an empty bytes or str is returned.
f.readable()	Returns True if f was opened for reading
f.readinto(*ba*)	Reads at most len(ba) bytes into bytearray ba and returns the number of bytes read—this is 0 at end of file. (Available only in binary mode.)
f.readline(*count*)	Reads the next line (or up to *count* bytes if *count* is specified and reached before the \n character), including the \n
f.readlines(*sizehint*)	Reads all the lines to the end of the file and returns them as a list. If *sizehint* is given, then reads approximately up to *sizehint* bytes if the underlying file object supports this.
f.seek(offset, whence)	Moves the file pointer position (where the next read or write will take place) to the given offset if *whence* is not given or is os.SEEK_SET. Moves the file pointer to the given offset (which may be negative) relative to the current position if *whence* is os.SEEK_CUR or relative to the end if *whence* is os.SEEK_END. Writes are always done at the end in append "a" mode no matter where the file pointer is. In text mode only the return value of tell() method calls should be used as offsets.

Table 7.5 *File Object Attributes and Methods #2*

Syntax	Description
f.seekable()	Returns True if f supports random access
f.tell()	Returns the current file pointer position relative to the start of the file
f.truncate(*size*)	Truncates the file to the current file pointer position, or to the given *size* if *size* is specified
f.writable()	Returns True if f was opened for writing
f.write(s)	Writes bytes/bytearray object s to the file if opened in binary mode or a str object s to the file if opened in text mode
f.writelines(*seq*)	Writes the sequence of objects (strings for text files, byte strings for binary files) to the file

We have made the record size and filename into read-only properties. The record size we report to the user is the one they requested and matches their records. The flush and close methods simply delegate to the file object.

```
def __setitem__(self, index, record):
    assert isinstance(record, (bytes, bytearray)), \
            "binary data required"
    assert len(record) == self.record_size, (
        "record must be exactly {0} bytes".format(
        self.record_size))
    self.__fh.seek(index * self.__record_size)
    self.__fh.write(_OKAY)
    self.__fh.write(record)
    if self.auto_flush:
        self.__fh.flush()
```

This method supports the *brf[i]* = *data* syntax where *brf* is a binary record file, *i* a record index position, and *data* a byte string. Notice that the record must be the same size as the size is specified when the binary record file was created. If the arguments are okay, we move the file position pointer to the first byte of the record—notice that here we use the real record size, that is, we account for the state byte. The seek() method moves the file pointer to an absolute byte position by default. A second argument can be given to make the movement relative to the current position or to the end. (The attributes and methods provided by file objects are listed in Tables 7.4 and 7.5.)

Since the item is being set it obviously hasn't been deleted, so we write the _OKAY state byte, and then we write the user's binary record data. The binary record file does not know or care about the record structure that is being used—only that records are of the right size.

We do not check whether the index is in range. If the index is beyond the end of the file the record will be written in the correct position and every byte between the previous end of the file and the new record will automatically be set to b"\x00". Such blank records are neither _OKAY nor _DELETED, so we can distinguish them when we need to.

```
def __getitem__(self, index):
    self.__seek_to_index(index)
    state = self.__fh.read(1)
    if state != _OKAY:
        return None
    return self.__fh.read(self.record_size)
```

When retrieving a record there are four cases that we must account for: The record doesn't exist, that is, the given index is beyond the end; the record is blank; the record has been deleted; and the record is okay. If the record doesn't exist the private __seek_to_index() method will raise an IndexError exception. Otherwise, it will seek to the byte where the record begins and we can read the state byte. If the state is not _OKAY the record must either be blank or be deleted, in which case we return None; otherwise, we read and return the record. (Another strategy would be to raise a custom exception for blank or deleted records, say, BlankRecordError or DeletedRecordError, instead of returning None.)

```
def __seek_to_index(self, index):
    if self.auto_flush:
        self.__fh.flush()
    self.__fh.seek(0, os.SEEK_END)
    end = self.__fh.tell()
    offset = index * self.__record_size
    if offset >= end:
        raise IndexError("no record at index position {0}".format(
                         index))
    self.__fh.seek(offset)
```

This is a private supporting method used by some of the other methods to move the file position pointer to the first byte of the record at the given index position. We begin by checking to see whether the given index is in range. We do this by seeking to the end of the file (byte offset of 0 from the end), and using the tell() method to retrieve the byte position we have seeked to. If the record's offset (index position × real record size) is at or after the end then the index is out of range and we raise a suitable exception. Otherwise, we seek to the offset position ready for the next read or write.

```
def __delitem__(self, index):
    self.__seek_to_index(index)
    state = self.__fh.read(1)
```

```
    if state != _OKAY:
        return
    self.__fh.seek(index * self.__record_size)
    self.__fh.write(_DELETED)
    if self.auto_flush:
        self.__fh.flush()
```

First we move the file position pointer to the right place. If the index is in
range (i.e., if no IndexError exception has occurred), and providing the record
isn't blank or already deleted, we delete the record by overwriting its state byte
with _DELETED.

```
def undelete(self, index):
    self.__seek_to_index(index)
    state = self.__fh.read(1)
    if state == _DELETED:
        self.__fh.seek(index * self.__record_size)
        self.__fh.write(_OKAY)
        if self.auto_flush:
            self.__fh.flush()
        return True
    return False
```

This method begins by finding the record and reading its state byte. If the
record is deleted we overwrite the state byte with _OKAY and return True to
the caller to indicate success; otherwise (for blank or nondeleted records), we
return False.

```
def __len__(self):
    if self.auto_flush:
        self.__fh.flush()
    self.__fh.seek(0, os.SEEK_END)
    end = self.__fh.tell()
    return end // self.__record_size
```

This method reports how many records are in the binary record file. It does
this by dividing the end byte position (i.e., how many bytes are in the file) by
the size of a record.

We have now covered all the basic functionality offered by the BinaryRecord-
File.BinaryRecordFile class. There is one last matter to consider: compacting
the file to eliminate blank and deleted records. There are essentially two approaches we can take to this. One approach is to overwrite blank or deleted
records with records that have higher record index positions so that there are
no gaps, and truncating the file if there are any blank or deleted records at the
end. The inplace_compact() method does this. The other approach is to copy
the nonblank nondeleted records to a temporary file and then to rename the

temporary to the original. Using a temporary file is particularly convenient if
we also want to make a backup. The compact() method does this.

We will start by looking at the inplace_compact() method, in two parts.

```
def inplace_compact(self):
    index = 0
    length = len(self)
    while index < length:
        self.__seek_to_index(index)
        state = self.__fh.read(1)
        if state != _OKAY:
            for next in range(index + 1, length):
                self.__seek_to_index(next)
                state = self.__fh.read(1)
                if state == _OKAY:
                    self[index] = self[next]
                    del self[next]
                    break
            else:
                break
        index += 1
```

We iterate over every record, reading the state of each one in turn. If we find a
blank or deleted record we look for the next nonblank nondeleted record in the
file. If we find one we replace the blank or deleted record with the nonblank
nondeleted one and delete the original nonblank nondeleted one; otherwise,
we break out of the while loop entirely since we have run out of nonblank
nondeleted records.

```
        self.__seek_to_index(0)
        state = self.__fh.read(1)
        if state != _OKAY:
            self.__fh.truncate(0)
        else:
            limit = None
            for index in range(len(self) - 1, 0, -1):
                self.__seek_to_index(index)
                state = self.__fh.read(1)
                if state != _OKAY:
                    limit = index
                else:
                    break
            if limit is not None:
                self.__fh.truncate(limit * self.__record_size)
        self.__fh.flush()
```

If the first record is blank or deleted, then they must all be blank or deleted since the previous code moved all nonblank nondeleted records to the beginning of the file and blank and deleted ones to the end. In this case we can simply truncate the file to 0 bytes.

If there is at least one nonblank nondeleted record we iterate from the last record backward toward the first since we know that blank and deleted records have been moved to the end. The limit variable is set to the earliest blank or deleted record (or left as None if there are no blank or deleted records), and the file is truncated accordingly.

An alternative to doing the compacting in-place is to do it by copying to another file—this is useful if we want to make a backup, as the compact() method that we will review next shows.

```python
def compact(self, keep_backup=False):
    compactfile = self.__fh.name + ".$$$"
    backupfile = self.__fh.name + ".bak"
    self.__fh.flush()
    self.__fh.seek(0)
    fh = open(compactfile, "wb")
    while True:
        data = self.__fh.read(self.__record_size)
        if not data:
            break
        if data[:1] == _OKAY:
            fh.write(data)
    fh.close()
    self.__fh.close()

    os.rename(self.__fh.name, backupfile)
    os.rename(compactfile, self.__fh.name)
    if not keep_backup:
        os.remove(backupfile)
    self.__fh = open(self.__fh.name, "r+b")
```

This method creates two files, a compacted file and a backup copy of the original file. The compacted file starts out with the same name as the original but with .$$$ tacked on to the end of the filename, and similarly the backup file has the original filename with .bak tacked on to the end. We read the existing file record by record, and for those records that are nonblank and nondeleted we write them to the compacted file. (Notice that we write the real record, that is, the state byte plus the user record, each time.)

Bytes and bytear-ray sidebar

286 ☜

The line if data[:1] == _OKAY: is quite subtle. Both the data object and the _OKAY object are of type bytes. We want to compare the first byte of the data object to the (1 byte) _OKAY object. If we take a slice of a bytes object, we get a bytes object, but if we take a single byte, say, data[0], we get an int—the byte's value.

So here we compare the 1 byte slice of data (its first byte, the state byte) with the 1 byte _OKAY object. (Another way of doing it would be to write if data[0] == _OKAY[0]: which would compare the two int values.)

At the end we rename the original file as the backup and rename the compacted file as the original. We then remove the backup if keep_backup is False (the default). Finally, we open the compacted file (which now has the original filename), ready to be read or written.

The BinaryRecordFile.BinaryRecordFile class is quite low-level, but it can serve as the basis of higher-level classes that need random access to files of fixed-size records, as we will see in the next subsection.

Example: The BikeStock Module's Classes

The BikeStock module uses a BinaryRecordFile.BinaryRecordFile to provide a simple stock control class. The stock items are bicycles, each represented by a BikeStock.Bike instance, and the entire stock of bikes is held in a Bike-Stock.BikeStock instance. The BikeStock.BikeStock class aggregates a dictionary whose keys are bike IDs and whose values are record index positions, into a BinaryRecordFile.BinaryRecordFile. Here is a brief example of use to get a feel for how these classes work:

```
bicycles = BikeStock.BikeStock(bike_file)
value = 0.0
for bike in bicycles:
    value += bike.value
bicycles.increase_stock("GEKKO", 2)
for bike in bicycles:
    if bike.identity.startswith("B4U"):
        if not bicycles.increase_stock(bike.identity, 1):
            print("stock movement failed for", bike.identity)
```

This snippet opens a bike stock file and iterates over all the bicycle records it contains to find the total value (sum of price × quantity) of the bikes held. It then increases the number of "GEKKO" bikes in stock by two and increments the stock held for all bikes whose bike ID begins with "B4U" by one. All of these actions take place on disk, so any other process that reads the bike stock file will always get the most current data.

Although the BinaryRecordFile.BinaryRecordFile works in terms of indexes, the BikeStock.BikeStock class works in terms of bike IDs. This is managed by the BikeStock.BikeStock instance holding a dictionary that relates bike IDs to indexes.

We will begin by looking at the BikeStock.Bike class's class line and initializer, then we will look at a few selected BikeStock.BikeStock methods, and finally we will look at the code that provides the bridge between BikeStock.Bike objects and the binary records used to represent them in a BinaryRecord-File.BinaryRecordFile. (All the code is in the BikeStock.py file.)

```
class Bike:

    def __init__(self, identity, name, quantity, price):
        assert len(identity) > 3, ("invalid bike identity '{0}'"
                                    .format(identity))
        self.__identity = identity
        self.name = name
        self.quantity = quantity
        self.price = price
```

All of a bike's attributes are available as properties—the bike ID (self.__identity) as the read-only Bike.identity property and the others as read/write properties with some assertions for validation. In addition, the Bike.value read-only property returns the quantity multiplied by the price. (We have not shown the implementation of the properties since we have seen similar code before.)

The BikeStock.BikeStock class provides its own methods for manipulating bike objects, and they in turn use the writable bike properties.

```
class BikeStock:

    def __init__(self, filename):
        self.__file = BinaryRecordFile.BinaryRecordFile(filename,
                                            _BIKE_STRUCT.size)
        self.__index_from_identity = {}
        for index in range(len(self.__file)):
            record = self.__file[index]
            if record is not None:
                bike = _bike_from_record(record)
                self.__index_from_identity[bike.identity] = index
```

The BikeStock.BikeStock class is a custom collection class that aggregates a binary record file (self.__file) and a dictionary (self.__index_from_identity) whose keys are bike IDs and whose values are record index positions.

Once the file has been opened (and created if it didn't already exist), we iterate over its contents (if any). Each bike is retrieved and converted from a bytes object to a BikeStock.Bike using the private _bike_from_record() function, and the bike's identity and index are added to the self.__index_from_identity dictionary.

```
    def append(self, bike):
        index = len(self.__file)
        self.__file[index] = _record_from_bike(bike)
```

```
                  self.__index_from_identity[bike.identity] = index
```

Appending a new bike is a matter of finding a suitable index position and setting the record at that position to the bike's binary representation. We also take care to update the self.__index_from_identity dictionary.

```
        def __delitem__(self, identity):
            del self.__file[self.__index_from_identity[identity]]
```

Deleting a bike record is easy; we just find its record index position from its identity and delete the record at that index position. In the case of the Bike-Stock.BikeStock class we have not made use of the BinaryRecordFile.Binary-RecordFile's undeletion capability.

```
        def __getitem__(self, identity):
            record = self.__file[self.__index_from_identity[identity]]
            return None if record is None else _bike_from_record(record)
```

Bike records are retrieved by bike ID. If there is no such ID the lookup in the self.__index_from_identity dictionary will raise a KeyError exception, and if the record is blank or deleted the BinaryRecordFile.BinaryRecordFile will return None. But if a record is retrieved we return it as a BikeStock.Bike object.

```
        def __change_stock(self, identity, amount):
            index = self.__index_from_identity[identity]
            record = self.__file[index]
            if record is None:
                return False
            bike = _bike_from_record(record)
            bike.quantity += amount
            self.__file[index] = _record_from_bike(bike)
            return True

    increase_stock = (lambda self, identity, amount:
                                    self.__change_stock(identity, amount))
    decrease_stock = (lambda self, identity, amount:
                                    self.__change_stock(identity, -amount))
```

The private __change_stock() method provides an implementation for the increase_stock() and decrease_stock() methods. The bike's index position is found and the raw binary record is retrieved. Then the data is converted to a BikeStock.Bike object, the change is applied to the bike, and then the record in the file is overwritten with the binary representation of the updated bike object. (There is also a __change_bike() method that provides an implementation for the change_name() and change_price() methods, but none of these are shown because they are very similar to what's shown here.)

```
    def __iter__(self):
        for index in range(len(self.__file)):
            record = self.__file[index]
            if record is not None:
                yield _bike_from_record(record)
```

This method ensures that `BikeStock.BikeStock` objects can be iterated over, just like a list, with a `BikeStock.Bike` object returned at each iteration, and skipping blank and deleted records.

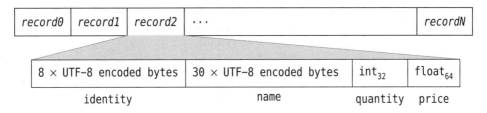

Figure 7.6 *The logical structure of a bike record file*

The private `_bike_from_record()` and `_record_from_bike()` functions isolate the binary representation of the `BikeStock.Bike` class from the `BikeStock.BikeStock` class that holds a collection of bikes. The logical structure of a bike record file is shown in Figure 7.6. The physical structure is slightly different because each record is preceded by a state byte.

```
    _BIKE_STRUCT = struct.Struct("<8s30sid")

    def _bike_from_record(record):
        ID, NAME, QUANTITY, PRICE = range(4)
        parts = list(_BIKE_STRUCT.unpack(record))
        parts[ID] = parts[ID].decode("utf8").rstrip("\x00")
        parts[NAME] = parts[NAME].decode("utf8").rstrip("\x00")
        return Bike(*parts)


    def _record_from_bike(bike):
        return _BIKE_STRUCT.pack(bike.identity.encode("utf8"),
                                 bike.name.encode("utf8"),
                                 bike.quantity, bike.price)
```

When we convert a binary record into a `BikeStock.Bike` we first convert the tuple returned by `unpack()` into a list. This allows us to modify elements, in this case to convert UTF-8 encoded bytes into strings with padding 0x00 bytes stripped off. We then use the sequence unpacking operator (*) to feed the parts to the `BikeStock.Bike` initializer. Packing the data is much simpler; we just have to make sure that we encode the strings as UTF-8 bytes.

For modern desktop systems the need for application programs to use random access binary data decreases as RAM sizes and disk speeds increase. And when such functionality is needed, it is often easiest to use a DBM file or an SQL database. Nonetheless, there are systems where the functionality shown here may be useful, for example, on embedded and other resource limited systems.

Summary

This chapter showed the most widely used techniques for saving and loading collections of data to and from files. We have seen how easy pickles are to use, and how we can handle both compressed and uncompressed files without knowing in advance whether compression has been used.

We saw how writing and reading binary data requires care, and saw that the code can be quite long if we need to handle variable length strings. But we also learned that using binary files usually results in the smallest possible file sizes and the fastest writing and reading times. We learned too that it is important to use a magic number to identify our file type and to use a version number to make it practical to change the format later on.

In this chapter we saw that plain text is the easiest format for users to read and that if the data is structured well it can be straightforward for additional tools to be created to manipulate the data. However, parsing text data can be tricky. We saw how to read text data both manually and using regular expressions.

XML is a very popular data interchange format and it is generally useful to be able to at least import and export XML even when the normal format is a binary or text one. We saw how to write XML manually—including how to correctly escape attribute values and textual data—and how to write it using an element tree and a DOM. We also learned how to parse XML using the element tree, DOM, and SAX parsers that Python's standard library provides.

In the chapter's final section we saw how to create a generic class to handle random access binary files that hold records of a fixed size, and then how to use the generic class in a specific context.

This chapter brings us to the end of all the fundamentals of Python programming. It is possible to stop reading right here and to write perfectly good Python programs based on everything you have learned so far. But it would be a shame to stop now—Python has so much more to offer, from neat techniques that can shorten and simplify code, to some mind-bending advanced facilities that are at least nice to know about, even if they are not often needed. In the next chapter we will go further with procedural and object-oriented programming, and we will also get a taste of functional programming. Then, in the following chapters we will focus more on broader programming techniques including threading, networking, database programming, regular expressions, and GUI (Graphical User Interface) programming.

Exercises

The first exercise is to create a simpler binary record file module than the one presented in this chapter—one whose record size is exactly the same as what the user specifies. The second exercise is to modify the BikeStock module to use your new binary record file module. The third exercise asks you to create a program from scratch—the file handling is quite straightforward, but some of the output formatting is rather challenging.

1. Make a new, simpler version of the BinaryRecordFile module—one that does not use a state byte. For this version the record size specified by the user is the record size actually used. New records must be added using a new append() method that simply moves the file pointer to the end and writes the given record. The _setitem_() method should only allow existing records to be replaced; one easy way of doing this is to use the _seek_to_index() method. With no state byte, _getitem_() is reduced to a mere three lines. The _delitem_() method will need to be completely rewritten since it must move all the records up to fill the gap; this can be done in just over half a dozen lines, but does require some thought. The undelete() method must be removed since it is not supported, and the compact() and inplace_compact() methods must be removed because they are no longer needed.

   All told, the changes amount to fewer than 20 new or changed lines and at least 60 deleted lines compared with the original, and not counting doctests. A solution is provided in BinaryRecordFile_ans.py.

2. Once you are confident that your simpler BinaryRecordFile class works, copy the BikeStock.py file and modify it to work with your BinaryRecordFile class. This involves changing only a handful of lines. A solution is provided in BikeStock_ans.py.

3. Debugging binary formats can be difficult, but a tool that can help is one that can do a hex dump of a binary file's contents. Create a program that has the following console help text:

   ```
   Usage: xdump.py [options] file1 [file2 [... fileN]]

   Options:
     -h, --help            show this help message and exit
     -b BLOCKSIZE, --blocksize=BLOCKSIZE
                           block size (8..80) [default: 16]
     -d, --decimal         decimal block numbers [default: hexadecimal]
   ```

```
-e ENCODING, --encoding=ENCODING
                    encoding (ASCII..UTF-32) [default: UTF-8]
```

Using this program, if we have a BinaryRecordFile that is storing records
with the structure "<i10s" (little-endian, 4-byte signed integer, 10-byte
byte string), by setting the block size to match one record (15 bytes including the state byte), we can get a clear picture of what's in the file. For example:

```
xdump.py -b15 test.dat
Block       Bytes                                   UTF-8 characters
--------    ------------------------------------    ----------------
00000000    02000000 00416C70 68610000 000000       .....Alpha.....
00000001    01140000 00427261 766F0000 000000       .....Bravo.....
00000002    02280000 00436861 726C6965 000000       .(...Charlie...
00000003    023C0000 0044656C 74610000 000000       .<...Delta.....
00000004    02500000 00456368 6F000000 000000       .P...Echo......
```

Each byte is represented by a two-digit hexadecimal number; the spacing
between each set of four bytes (i.e., between each group of eight hexadecimal digits) is purely to improve readability. Here we can see that the second record ("Bravo") has been deleted since its state byte is 0x01 rather
than the 0x02 used to indicate nonblank nondeleted records.

Use the optparse module to handle the command-line options. (By specifying an option's "type" you can get optparse to handle the string-to-integer
conversion for the block size.) It can be quite tricky to get the headings
to line up correctly for any given block size and to line up the characters
correctly for the last block, so make sure you test with various block sizes
(e.g., 8, 9, 10, ..., 40). Also, don't forget that in variable length files, the last
block may be short. As the example illustrates, use periods to stand for
nonprintable characters.

The program can be written in fewer than 70 lines spread over two
functions. A solution is given in xdump.py.

- Further Procedural Programming
- Further Object-Oriented Programming
- Functional-Style Programming

Advanced Programming Techniques

In this chapter we will look at a wide variety of different programming techniques and introduce many additional, often more advanced, Python syntaxes. Some of the material in this chapter is quite challenging, but keep in mind that the most advanced techniques are rarely needed and you can always skim the first time to get an idea of what can be done and read more carefully when the need arises.

The chapter's first section digs more deeply into Python's procedural features. It starts by showing how to use what we already covered in a novel way, and then returns to the theme of generators that we only touched on in Chapter 6. The section then introduces dynamic programming—loading modules by name at runtime and executing arbitrary code at runtime. The section returns to the theme of local (nested) functions, but in addition covers the use of the `nonlocal` keyword and recursive functions. Earlier we saw how to use Python's predefined decorators—in this section we learn how to create our own decorators. The section concludes with coverage of function annotations.

The second section covers all new material relating to object-oriented programming. It begins by introducing `__slots__`, a mechanism for minimizing the memory used by each object. It then shows how to access attributes without using properties. The section also introduces functors (objects that can be called like functions), and context managers—these are used in conjunction with the `with` keyword, and in many cases (e.g., file handling) they can be used to replace `try ... except ... finally` constructs with simpler `try ... except` constructs. The section also shows how to create custom context managers, and introduces additional advanced object-oriented features, including class decorators, abstract base classes, multiple inheritance, and metaclasses.

The third section introduces some fundamental concepts of functional programming, and introduces some useful functions from the `functools`, `itertools`, and `operator` modules. This section also shows how to use partial function application to simplify code.

All the previous chapters put together have provided us with the "standard Python toolbox". This chapter takes everything that we have already covered and turns it into the "deluxe Python toolbox", with all the original tools (techniques and syntaxes), plus many new ones that can make our programming easier, shorter, and more effective. Some of the tools can have interchangeable uses, for example, some jobs can be done using either a class decorator or a metaclass, whereas others, such as descriptors, can be used in multiple ways to achieve different effects. Some of the tools covered here, for example, context managers, we will use all the time, and others will remain ready at hand for those particular situations for which they are the perfect solution.

Further Procedural Programming

Most of this section deals with additional facilities relating to procedural programming and functions, but the very first subsection is different in that it presents a useful programming technique based on what we already covered without introducing any new syntax.

Branching Using Dictionaries

As we noted earlier, functions are objects like everything else in Python, and a function's name is an object reference that refers to the function. If we write a function's name without parentheses, Python knows we mean the object reference, and we can pass such object references around just like any others. We can use this fact to replace `if` statements that have lots of `elif` clauses with a single function call.

In Chapter 11 we will review an interactive console program called `dvds-dbm.py`, that has the following menu:

```
(A)dd  (E)dit  (L)ist  (R)emove  (I)mport  e(X)port  (Q)uit
```

The program has a function that gets the user's choice and which will return only a valid choice, in this case one of "a", "e", "l", "r", "i", "x", and "q". Here are two equivalent code snippets for calling the relevant function based on the user's choice:

```
if action == "a":
    add_dvd(db)
elif action == "e":
    edit_dvd(db)
```

```
elif action == "l":                      │
    list_dvds(db)                        │
elif action == "r":                      │
    remove_dvd(db)                       │
elif action == "i":                      │
    import_(db)                          │
elif action == "x":                      │ functions = dict(a=add_dvd, e=edit_dvd,
    export(db)                           │                  l=list_dvds, r=remove_dvd,
elif action == "q":                      │                  i=import_, x=export, q=quit)
    quit(db)                             │ functions[action](db)
```

The choice is held as a one-character string in the action variable, and the database to be used is held in the db variable. The import_() function has a trailing underscore to keep it distinct from the built-in import statement.

In the right-hand code snippet we create a dictionary whose keys are the valid menu choices, and whose values are function references. In the second statement we retrieve the function reference corresponding to the given action and call the function referred to using the call operator, (), and in this example, passing the db argument. Not only is the code on the right-hand side much shorter than the code on the left, but also it can scale (have far more dictionary items) without affecting its performance, unlike the left-hand code whose speed depends on how many elifs must be tested to find the appropriate function to call.

The convert-incidents.py program from the preceding chapter uses this technique in its import_() method, as this extract from the method shows:

```
call = {(".aix", "dom"): self.import_xml_dom,
        (".aix", "etree"): self.import_xml_etree,
        (".aix", "sax"): self.import_xml_sax,
        (".ait", "manual"): self.import_text_manual,
        (".ait", "regex"): self.import_text_regex,
        (".aib", None): self.import_binary,
        (".aip", None): self.import_pickle}
result = call[extension, reader](filename)
```

The complete method is 13 lines long; the extension parameter is computed in the method, and the reader is passed in. The dictionary keys are 2-tuples, and the values are methods. If we had used if statements, the code would be 22 lines long, and would not scale as well.

Generator Expressions and Functions

Generator functions

Back in Chapter 6 we introduced generator functions and methods. It is also possible to create generator expressions. These are syntactically almost identical to list comprehensions, the difference being that they are enclosed in parentheses rather than brackets. Here are their syntaxes:

```
(expression for item in iterable)
(expression for item in iterable if condition)
```

In the preceding chapter we created some iterator methods using `yield` expressions. Here are two equivalent code snippets that show how a simple `for … in` loop containing a `yield` expression can be coded as a generator:

```
def items_in_key_order(d):          def items_in_key_order(d):
    for key in sorted(d):               return ((key, d[key])
        yield key, d[key]                       for key in sorted(d))
```

Both functions return a generator that produces a list of key–value items for the given dictionary. If we need all the items in one go we can pass the generator returned by the functions to `list()` or `tuple()`; otherwise, we can iterate over the generator to retrieve items as we need them.

Generators provide a means of performing lazy evaluation, which means that they compute only the values that are actually needed. This can be more efficient than, say, computing a very large list in one go. Some generators produce as many values as we ask for—without any upper limit. For example:

```
def quarters(next_quarter=0.0):
    while True:
        yield next_quarter
        next_quarter += 0.25
```

This function will return 0.0, 0.25, 0.5, and so on, forever. Here is how we could use the generator:

```
result = []
for x in quarters():
    result.append(x)
    if x >= 1.0:
        break
```

The `break` statement is essential—without it the `for … in` loop will never finish. At the end the result list is `[0.0, 0.25, 0.5, 0.75, 1.0]`.

Every time we call `quarters()` we get back a generator that starts at 0.0 and increments by 0.25; but what if we want to reset the generator's current value? It is possible to pass a value into a generator, as this new version of the generator function shows:

```
def quarters(next_quarter=0.0):
    while True:
```

```
        received = (yield next_quarter)
        if received is None:
            next_quarter += 0.25
        else:
            next_quarter = received
```

The yield expression returns each value to the caller in turn. In addition, if the caller calls the generator's send() method, the value sent is received in the generator function as the result of the yield expression. Here is how we can use the new generator function:

```
result = []
generator = quarters()
while len(result) < 5:
    x = next(generator)
    if abs(x - 0.5) < sys.float_info.epsilon:
        x = generator.send(1.0)
    result.append(x)
```

We create a variable to refer to the generator and call the built-in next() function which retrieves the next item from the generator it is given. (The same effect can be achieved by calling the generator's __next__() special method, in this case, x = generator.__next__().) If the value is equal to 0.5 we send the value 1.0 into the generator (which immediately yields this value back). This time the result list is [0.0, 0.25, 1.0, 1.25, 1.5].

In the next subsection we will review the magic-numbers.py program which processes files given on the command line. Unfortunately, the Windows shell program (cmd.exe) does not provide wildcard expansion (also called *file globbing*), so if a program is run on Windows with the argument *.*, the literal text "*.*" will go into the sys.argv list instead of all the files in the current directory. We solve this problem by creating two different get_files() functions, one for Windows and the other for Unix, both of which use generators. Here's the code:

```
if sys.platform.startswith("win"):
    def get_files(names):
        for name in names:
            if os.path.isfile(name):
                yield name
            else:
                for file in glob.iglob(name):
                    if not os.path.isfile(file):
                        continue
                    yield file
else:
    def get_files(names):
        return (file for file in names if os.path.isfile(file))
```

In either case the function is expected to be called with a list of filenames, for example, sys.argv[1:], as its argument.

On Windows the function iterates over all the names listed. For each filename, the function yields the name, but for nonfiles (usually directories), the glob module's glob.iglob() function is used to return an iterator to the names of the files that the name represents after wildcard expansion. For an ordinary name like autoexec.bat an iterator that produces one item (the name) is returned, and for a name that uses wildcards like *.txt an iterator that produces all the matching files (in this case those with extension .txt) is returned. (There is also a glob.glob() function that returns a list rather than an iterator.)

On Unix the shell does wildcard expansion for us, so we just need to return a generator for all the files whose names we have been given.*

Generator functions can be used to create *coroutines*—functions that have multiple entry and exit points (the yield expressions) and that can be suspended and resumed at certain points (again at yield expressions). Coroutines are often used to provide simpler and lower-overhead alternatives to threading. Several coroutine modules are available from the Python Package Index, pypi.python.org/pypi.

Dynamic Code Execution and Dynamic Imports

There are some occasions when it is easier to write a piece of code that generates the code we need than to write the needed code directly. And in some contexts it is useful to let users enter code (e.g., functions in a spreadsheet), and to let Python execute the entered code for us rather than to write a parser and handle it ourselves—although executing arbitrary code like this is a potential security risk, of course. Another use case for dynamic code execution is to provide plug-ins to extend a program's functionality. Using plug-ins has the disadvantage that all the necessary functionality is not built into the program (which can make the program more difficult to deploy and runs the risk of plug-ins getting lost), but has the advantages that plug-ins can be upgraded individually and can be provided separately, perhaps to provide enhancements that were not originally envisaged.

Dynamic Code Execution

The easiest way to execute an expression is to use the built-in eval() function we first saw in Chapter 6. For example:

```
x = eval("(2 ** 31) - 1")    # x == 2147483647
```

---

*The glob.glob() functions are not as powerful as, say, the Unix bash shell, since although they support the *, ?, and [] syntaxes, they don't support the {} syntax.

This is fine for user-entered expressions, but what if we need to create a function dynamically? For that we can use the built-in exec() function. For example, the user might give us a formula such as $4\pi r^2$ and the name "area of sphere", which they want turned into a function. Assuming that we replace π with math.pi, the function they want can be created like this:

```
import math
code = '''
def area_of_sphere(r):
    return 4 * math.pi * r ** 2
'''
context = {}
context["math"] = math
exec(code, context)
```

We must use proper indentation—after all, the quoted code is standard Python. (Although in this case we could have written it all on a single line because the suite is just one line.)

If exec() is called with some code as its only argument there is no way to access any functions or variables that are created as a result of the code being executed. Furthermore, exec() cannot access any imported modules or any of the variables, functions, or other objects that are in scope at the point of the call. Both of these problems can be solved by passing a dictionary as the second argument. The dictionary provides a place where object references can be kept for accessing after the exec() call has finished. For example, the use of the context dictionary means that after the exec() call, the dictionary has an object reference to the area_of_sphere() function that was created by exec(). In this example we needed exec() to be able to access the math module, so we inserted an item into the context dictionary whose key is the module's name and whose value is an object reference to the corresponding module object. This ensures that inside the exec() call, math.pi is accessible.

In some cases it is convenient to provide the entire global context to exec(). This can be done by passing the dictionary returned by the globals() function. One disadvantage of this approach is that any objects created in the exec() call would be added to the global dictionary. A solution is to copy the global context into a dictionary, for example, context = globals().copy(). This still gives exec() access to imported modules and the variables and other objects that are in scope, and because we have copied, any changes to the context made inside the exec() call are kept in the context dictionary and are not propagated to the global environment. (It would appear to be more secure to use copy.deepcopy(), but if security is a concern it is best to avoid exec() altogether.) We can also pass the local context, for example, by passing locals() as a third argument—this makes objects in the local scope accessible to the code executed by exec().

After the exec() call the context dictionary contains a key called "area_of_sphere" whose value is the area_of_sphere() function. Here is how we can access and call the function:

```
area_of_sphere = context["area_of_sphere"]
area = area_of_sphere(5)        # area == 314.15926535897933
```

The area_of_sphere object is an object reference to the function we have dynamically created and can be used just like any other function. And although we created only a single function in the exec() call, unlike eval(), which can operate on only a single expression, exec() can handle as many Python statements as we like, including entire modules, as we will see in the next subsubsection.

Dynamically Importing Modules

Python provides three straightforward mechanisms that can be used to create plug-ins, all of which involve importing modules by name at runtime. And once we have dynamically imported additional modules, we can use Python's introspection functions to check the availability of the functionality we want, and to access it as required.

In this subsubsection we will review the magic-numbers.py program. This program reads the first 1 000 bytes of each file given on the command line and for each one outputs the file's type (or the text "Unknown"), and the filename. Here is an example command line and an extract from its output:

```
C:\Python30\python.exe magic-numbers.py c:\windows\*.*
...
XML................c:\windows\WindowsShell.Manifest
Unknown............c:\windows\WindowsUpdate.log
Windows Executable..c:\windows\winhelp.exe
Windows Executable..c:\windows\winhlp32.exe
Windows BMP Image...c:\windows\winnt.bmp
...
```

The program tries to load in any module that is in the same directory as the program and whose name contains the text "magic". Such modules are expected to provide a single public function, get_file_type(). Two very simple example modules, StandardMagicNumbers.py and WindowsMagicNumbers.py, that each have a get_file_type() function are provided with the book's examples.

We will review the program's main() function in two parts.

```
def main():
    modules = load_modules()
    get_file_type_functions = []
    for module in modules:
```

```
    get_file_type = get_function(module, "get_file_type")
    if get_file_type is not None:
        get_file_type_functions.append(get_file_type)
```

In a moment, we will look at three different implementations of the load_modules() function which returns a (possibly empty) list of module objects, and we will look at the get_function() function further on. For each module found we try to retrieve a get_file_type() function, and add any we get to a list of such functions.

```
for file in get_files(sys.argv[1:]):
    fh = None
    try:
        fh = open(file, "rb")
        magic = fh.read(1000)
        for get_file_type in get_file_type_functions:
            filetype = get_file_type(magic,
                                     os.path.splitext(file)[1])
            if filetype is not None:
                print("{0:.<20}{1}".format(filetype, file))
                break
        else:
            print("{0:.<20}{1}".format("Unknown", file))
    except EnvironmentError as err:
        print(err)
    finally:
        if fh is not None:
            fh.close()
```

This loop iterates over every file listed on the command line and for each one reads its first 1 000 bytes. It then tries each get_file_type() function in turn to see whether it can determine the current file's type. If the file type is determined, the details are printed and the inner loop is broken out of, with processing continuing with the next file. If no function can determine the file type—or if no get_file_type() functions were found—an "Unknown" line is printed.

We will now review three different (but equivalent) ways of dynamically importing modules, starting with the longest and most difficult approach, since it shows every step explicitly:

```
def load_modules():
    modules = []
    for name in os.listdir(os.path.dirname(__file__) or "."):
        if name.endswith(".py") and "magic" in name.lower():
            filename = name
            name = os.path.splitext(name)[0]
            if name.isidentifier() and name not in sys.modules:
```

```
                    fh = None
                    try:
                        fh = open(filename, "r", encoding="utf8")
                        code = fh.read()
                        module = type(sys)(name)
                        sys.modules[name] = module
                        exec(code, module.__dict__)
                        modules.append(module)
                    except (EnvironmentError, SyntaxError) as err:
                        sys.modules.pop(name, None)
                        print(err)
                    finally:
                        if fh is not None:
                            fh.close()
            return modules
```

We begin by iterating over all the files in the program's directory. If this is the current directory, os.path.dirname(__file__) will return an empty string which would cause os.listdir() to raise an exception, so we pass "." if necessary. For each candidate file (ends with .py and contains the text "magic"), we get the module name by chopping off the file extension. If the name is a valid identifier it is a viable module name, and if it isn't already in the global list of modules maintained in the sys.modules dictionary we can try to import it.

We read the text of the file into the code string. The next line, module = type(sys)(name), is quite subtle. When we call type() it returns the type object of the object it is given. So if we called type(1) we would get int back. If we print the type object we just get something human readable like "int", but if we call the type object as a function, we get an object of that type back. For example, we can get the integer 5 in variable x by writing x = 5, or x = int(5), or x = type(0)(5), or int_type = type(0); x = int_type(5). In this case we've used type(sys) and sys is a module, so we get back the module type object (essentially the same as a class object), and can use it to create a new module with the given name. Just as with the int example where it didn't matter what integer we used to get the int type object, it doesn't matter what module we use (as long as it is one that exists, that is, has been imported) to get the module type object.

Once we have a new (empty) module, we add it to the global list of modules to prevent the module from being accidentally reimported. This is done before calling exec() to more closely mimic the behavior of the import statement. Then we call exec() to execute the code we have read—and we use the module's dictionary as the code's context. At the end we add the module to the list of modules we will pass back. And if a problem arises, we delete the module from the global modules dictionary if it has been added—it will not have been added to the list of modules if an error occurred. Notice that exec() can handle any

Table 8.1 *Dynamic Programming and Introspection Functions*

Syntax	Description
`__import__(...)`	Imports a module by name; see text
`compile(source, file, mode)`	Returns the code object that results from compiling the source text; `file` should be the filename, or `"<string>"`; mode must be "single", "eval", or "exec"
`delattr(obj, name)`	Deletes the attribute called `name` from object `obj`
`dir(`*obj*`)`	Returns the list of names in the local scope, or if *obj* is given then *obj*'s names (e.g., its attributes and methods)
`eval(source, globals, locals)`	Returns the result of evaluating the single expression in source; if supplied, *globals* is the global context and *locals* is the local context (as dictionaries)
`exec(obj, globals, locals)`	Evaluates object `obj`, which can be a string or a code object from `compile()`, and returns `None`; if supplied, *globals* is the global context and *locals* is the local context
`getattr(obj, name,` *val*`)`	Returns the value of the attribute called `name` from object `obj`, or *val* if given and there is no such attribute
`globals()`	Returns a dictionary of the current global context
`hasattr(obj, name)`	Returns `True` if object `obj` has an attribute called `name`
`locals()`	Returns a dictionary of the current local context
`setattr(obj, name, val)`	Sets the attribute called `name` to the value `val` for the object `obj`, creating the attribute if necessary
`type(obj)`	Returns object `obj`'s type object
`vars(`*obj*`)`	Returns object *obj*'s context as a dictionary; or the local context if *obj* is not given

amount of code (whereas `eval()` evaluates a single expression—see Table 8.1), and raises a `SyntaxError` exception if there's a syntax error.

Here's the second way to dynamically load a module at runtime—the code shown here replaces the first approach's try ... except block:

```
try:
    exec("import " + name)
    modules.append(sys.modules[name])
except SyntaxError as err:
    print(err)
```

One theoretical problem with this approach is that it is potentially insecure. The name variable could begin with sys; and be followed by some destructive code.

And here is the third approach, again just showing the replacement for the first approach's try ... except block:

```
try:
    module = __import__(name)
    modules.append(module)
except (ImportError, SyntaxError) as err:
    print(err)
```

This is the easiest way to dynamically import modules and is slightly safer than using exec(), although like any dynamic import, it is by no means secure because we don't know what is being executed when the module is imported.

None of the techniques shown here handles packages or modules in different paths, but it is not difficult to extend the code to accommodate these—although it is worth reading the online documentation, especially for __import__(), if more sophistication is required.

Having imported the module we need to be able to access the functionality it provides. This can be achieved using Python's built-in introspection functions, getattr() and hasattr(). Here's how we have used them to implement the get_function() function:

```
def get_function(module, function_name):
    function = get_function.cache.get((module, function_name), None)
    if function is None:
        try:
            function = getattr(module, function_name)
            if not hasattr(function, "__call__"):
                raise AttributeError()
            get_function.cache[module, function_name] = function
        except AttributeError:
            function = None
    return function
get_function.cache = {}
```

Ignoring the cache-related code for a moment, what the function does is call getattr() on the module object with the name of the function we want. If there is no such attribute an AttributeError exception is raised, but if there is such an attribute we use hasattr() to check that the attribute itself has the __call__ attribute—something that all callables (functions and methods) have. (Further on we will see a nicer way of checking whether an attribute is

collec-
tions.
Callable
☞ 381

callable.) If the attribute exists and is callable we can return it to the caller; otherwise, we return None to signify that the function isn't available.

If hundreds of files were being processed (e.g., due to using *.* in the C:\windows directory), we don't want to go through the lookup process for every module for every file. So immediately after defining the get_function() function, we add an attribute to the function, a dictionary called cache. (In general, Python allows us to add arbitrary attributes to arbitrary objects.) The first time that get_function() is called the cache dictionary is empty, so the dict.get() call will return None. But each time a suitable function is found it is put in the dictionary with a 2-tuple of the module and function name used as the key and the function itself as the value. So the second and all subsequent times a particular function is requested the function is immediately returned from the cache and no attribute lookup takes place at all.★

The technique used for caching the get_function()'s return value for a given set of arguments is called *memoizing*. It can be used for any function that has no side effects (does not change any global variables), and that always returns the same result for the same (immutable) arguments. Since the code required to create and manage a cache for each memoized function is the same, it is an ideal candidate for a function decorator, and several @memoize decorator recipes are given in the Python Cookbook, in code.activestate.com/recipes/langs/python/. However, module objects are mutable, so some off-the-shelf memoizer decorators wouldn't work with our get_function() function as it stands. An easy solution would be to use each module's __name__ string rather than the module itself as the first part of the key tuple.

Doing dynamic module imports is easy, and so is executing arbitrary Python code using the exec() function. This can be very convenient, for example, allowing us to store code in a database. However, we have no control over what imported or exec()uted code will do. Recall that in addition to variables, functions, and classes, modules can also contain code that is executed when it is imported—if the code came from an untrusted source it might do something unpleasant. How to address this depends on circumstances, although it may not be an issue at all in some environments, or for personal projects.

Local and Recursive Functions

It is often useful to have one or more small helper functions inside another function. Python allows this without formality—we simply define the functions we need inside the definition of an existing function. Such functions are often called *nested functions* or *local functions*. We already saw examples of these in Chapter 7.

★A slightly more sophisticated get_function() that has better handling of modules without the required functionality is in the magic-numbers.py program alongside the version shown here.

One common use case for local functions is when we want to use recursion. In these cases, the enclosing function is called, sets things up, and then makes the first call to a local recursive function. Recursive functions (or methods) are ones that call themselves. Structurally, all directly recursive functions can be seen as having two cases: the *base case* and the *recursive case*. The base case is used to stop the recursion.

Recursive functions can be computationally expensive because for every recursive call another stack frame is used; however, some algorithms are most naturally expressed using recursion. Most Python implementations have a fixed limit to how many recursive calls can be made. The limit is returned by sys.getrecursionlimit() and can be changed by sys.setrecursionlimit(), although increasing the limit is most often a sign that the algorithm being used is inappropriate or that the implementation has a bug.

The classic example of a recursive function is one that is used to calculate factorials.* For example, factorial(5) will calculate 5! and return 120, that is, $1 \times 2 \times 3 \times 4 \times 5$:

```
def factorial(x):
    if x <= 1:
        return 1
    return x * factorial(x - 1)
```

This is not an efficient solution, but it does show the two fundamental features of recursive functions. If the given number, x, is 1 or less, 1 is returned and no recursion occurs—this is the base case. But if x is greater than 1 the value returned is x * factorial(x - 1), and this is the recursive case because here the factorial function calls itself. The function is guaranteed to terminate because if the initial x is less than or equal to 1 the base case will be used and the function will finish immediately, and if x is greater than 1, each recursive call will be on a number one less than before and so will eventually be 1.

To see both local functions and recursive functions in a meaningful context we will study the indented_list_sort() function from module file IndentedList.py. This function takes a list of strings that use indentation to create a hierarchy, and a string that holds one level of indent, and returns a list with the same strings but where all the strings are sorted in case-insensitive alphabetical order, with indented items sorted under their parent item, recursively, as the before and after lists shown in Figure 8.1 illustrate.

Given the before list, the after list is produced by this call: after = IndentedList.indented_list_sort(before). The default indent value is four spaces, the same as the indent used in the before list, so we did not need to set it explicitly.

---

*Python's math module provides a much more efficient math.factorial() function.

```
before = ["Nonmetals",          after = ["Alkali Metals",
    "       Hydrogen",               "       Lithium",
    "       Carbon",                 "       Potassium",
    "       Nitrogen",               "       Sodium",
    "       Oxygen",             "Inner Transitionals",
    "Inner Transitionals",           "       Actinides",
    "       Lanthanides",            "           Curium",
    "           Cerium",             "           Plutonium",
    "           Europium",           "           Uranium",
    "       Actinides",              "       Lanthanides",
    "           Uranium",            "           Cerium",
    "           Curium",             "           Europium",
    "           Plutonium",      "Nonmetals",
    "Alkali Metals",                 "       Carbon",
    "       Lithium",                "       Hydrogen",
    "       Sodium",                 "       Nitrogen",
    "       Potassium"]              "       Oxygen"]
```

Figure 8.1 *Before and after sorting an indented list*

We will begin by looking at the indented_list_sort() function as a whole, and then we will look at its two local functions.

```
def indented_list_sort(indented_list, indent="    "):
    KEY, ITEM, CHILDREN = range(3)

    def add_entry(level, key, item, children):
        ...

    def update_indented_list(entry):
        ...

    entries = []
    for item in indented_list:
        level = 0
        i = 0
        while item.startswith(indent, i):
            i += len(indent)
            level += 1
        key = item.strip().lower()
        add_entry(level, key, item, entries)

    indented_list = []
    for entry in sorted(entries):
        update_indented_list(entry)
    return indented_list
```

The code begins by creating three constants that are used to provide names for index positions used by the local functions. Then we define the two local functions which we will review in a moment. The sorting algorithm works in two stages. In the first stage we create a list of entries, each a 3-tuple consisting of a "key" that will be used for sorting, the original string, and a list of the string's child entries. The key is just a lowercased copy of the string with whitespace stripped from both ends. The level is the indentation level, 0 for top-level items, 1 for children of top-level items, and so on. In the second stage we create a new indented list and add each string from the sorted entries list, and each string's child strings, and so on, to produce a sorted indented list.

```
def add_entry(level, key, item, children):
    if level == 0:
        children.append((key, item, []))
    else:
        add_entry(level - 1, key, item, children[-1][CHILDREN])
```

This function is called for each string in the list. The children argument is the list to which new entries must be added. When called from the outer function (indented_list_sort()), this is the entries list. This has the effect of turning a list of strings into a list of entries, each of which has a top-level (unindented) string and a (possibly empty) list of child entries.

If the level is 0 (top-level), we add a new 3-tuple to the entries list. This holds the key (for sorting), the original item (which will go into the resultant sorted list), and an empty children list. This is the base case since no recursion takes place. If the level is greater than 0, the item is a child (or descendant) of the last item in the children list. In this case we recursively call add_entry() again, reducing the level by 1 and passing the children list's last item's children list as the list to add to. If the level is 2 or more, more recursive calls will take place, until eventually the level is 0 and the children list is the right one for the entry to be added to.

For example, when the "Inner Transitionals" string is reached, the outer function calls add_entry() with a level of 0, a key of "inner transitionals", an item of "Inner Transitionals", and the entries list as the children list. Since the level is 0, a new item will be appended to the children list (entries), with the key, item, and an empty children list. The next string is " Lanthanides"—this is indented, so it is a child of the "Inner Transitionals" string. The add_entry() call this time has a level of 1, a key of "lanthanides", an item of " Lanthanides", and the entries list as the children list. Since the level is 1, the add_entry() function calls itself recursively, this time with level 0 (1 - 1), the same key and item, but with the children list being the children list of the last item, that is, the "Inner Transitionals" item's children list.

Here is what the entries list looks like once all the strings have been added, but before the sorting has been done:

```
[('nonmetals',
  'Nonmetals',
  [('hydrogen', '     Hydrogen', []),
   ('carbon', '      Carbon', []),
   ('nitrogen', '     Nitrogen', []),
   ('oxygen', '      Oxygen', [])]),
 ('inner transitionals',
  'Inner Transitionals',
  [('lanthanides',
    '     Lanthanides',
    [('cerium', '        Cerium', []),
     ('europium', '        Europium', [])]),
   ('actinides',
    '     Actinides',
    [('uranium', '        Uranium', []),
     ('curium', '        Curium', []),
     ('plutonium', '        Plutonium', [])])]),
 ('alkali metals',
  'Alkali Metals',
  [('lithium', '     Lithium', []),
   ('sodium', '     Sodium', []),
   ('potassium', '     Potassium', [])])]
```

The output was produced using the pprint ("pretty print") module's pprint. pprint() function. Notice that the entries list has only three items (all of which are 3-tuples), and that each 3-tuple's last element is a list of child 3-tuples (or is an empty list).

The add_entry() function is both a local function and a recursive function. Like all recursive functions, it has a *base case* (in this function, when the level is 0) that ends the recursion, and a recursive case.

The function could be written in a slightly different way:

```
def add_entry(key, item, children):
    nonlocal level
    if level == 0:
        children.append((key, item, []))
    else:
        level -= 1
        add_entry(key, item, children[-1][CHILDREN])
```

Here, instead of passing level as a parameter, we use a nonlocal statement to access a variable in an outer enclosing scope. If we did not change level inside the function we would not need the nonlocal statement—in such a situation, Python would not find it in the local (inner function) scope, and would look at the enclosing scope and find it there. But in this version of add_entry() we need to change level's value, and just as we need to tell Python that we want to change global variables using the global statement (to prevent a new local variable from being created rather than the global variable updated), the same applies to variables that we want to change but which belong to an outer scope. Although it is often best to avoid using global altogether, it is also best to use nonlocal with care.

```
def update_indented_list(entry):
    indented_list.append(entry[ITEM])
    for subentry in sorted(entry[CHILDREN]):
        update_indented_list(subentry)
```

In the algorithm's first stage we build up a list of entries, each a (key, item, children) 3-tuple, in the same order as they are in the original list. In the algorithm's second stage we begin with a new empty indented list and iterate over the sorted entries, calling update_indented_list() for each one to build up the new indented list. The update_indented_list() function is recursive. For each top-level entry it adds an item to the indented_list, and then calls itself for each of the item's child entries. Each child is added to the indented_list, and then the function calls itself for each child's children—and so on. The base case (when the recursion stops) is when an item, or child, or child of a child, and so on has no children of its own.

Python looks for indented_list in the local (inner function) scope and doesn't find it, so it then looks in the enclosing scope and finds it there. But notice that inside the function we append items to the indented_list even though we have not used nonlocal. This works because nonlocal (and global) are concerned with object references, not with the objects they refer to. In the second version of add_entry() we had to use nonlocal for level because the += operator applied to a number rebinds the object reference to a new object—what really happens is level = level + 1, so level is set to refer to a new integer object. But when we call list.append() on the indented_list, it modifies the list itself and no rebinding takes place, and therefore nonlocal is not necessary. (For the same reason, if we have a dictionary, list, or other global collection, we can add or remove items from it without using a global statement.)

Function and Method Decorators

A decorator is a function that takes a function or method as its sole argument and returns a new function or method that incorporates the decorated function or method with some additional functionality added. We have already made use of some predefined decorators, for example, @property and @classmethod. In this subsection we will learn how to create our own function decorators, and later in this chapter we will see how to create class decorators.

Class decorators
☞ 367

For our first decorator example, let us suppose that we have many functions that perform calculations, and that some of these must always produce a positive result. We could add an assertion to each of these, but using a decorator is easier and clearer. Here's a function decorated with the @positive_result decorator that we will create in a moment:

```
@positive_result
def discriminant(a, b, c):
    return (b ** 2) - (4 * a * c)
```

Thanks to the decorator, if the result is ever less than 0, an AssertionError exception will be raised and the program will terminate. And of course, we can use the decorator on as many functions as we like. Here's the decorator's implementation:

```
def positive_result(function):
    def wrapper(*args, **kwargs):
        result = function(*args, **kwargs)
        assert result >= 0, function.__name__ + "() result isn't >= 0"
        return result
    wrapper.__name__ = function.__name__
    wrapper.__doc__ = function.__doc__
    return wrapper
```

Decorators define a new local function that calls the original function. Here, the local function is wrapper(); it calls the original function and stores the result, and it uses an assertion to guarantee that the result is positive (or that the program will terminate). The wrapper finishes by returning the result computed by the wrapped function. After creating the wrapper, we set its name and docstring to those of the original function. This helps with introspection, since we want error messages to mention the name of the original function, not the wrapper. Finally, we return the wrapper function—it is this function that will be used in place of the original.

```
def positive_result(function):
    @functools.wraps(function)
    def wrapper(*args, **kwargs):
        result = function(*args, **kwargs)
        assert result >= 0, function.__name__ + "() result isn't >= 0"
        return result
    return wrapper
```

Here is a slightly cleaner version of the @positive_result decorator. The wrapper itself is wrapped using the functools module's @functools.wraps decorator, which ensures that the wrapper() function has the name and docstring of the original function.

In some cases it would be useful to be able to parameterize a decorator, but at
first sight this does not seem possible since a decorator takes just one argument, a function or method. But there is a neat solution to this. We can call a
function with the parameters we want and that returns a decorator which can
then decorate the function that follows it. For example:

```
@bounded(0, 100)
def percent(amount, total):
    return (amount / total) * 100
```

Here, the bounded() function is called with two arguments, and returns a decorator that is used to decorate the percent() function. The purpose of the decorator in this case is to guarantee that the number returned is always in the range
0 to 100 inclusive. Here's the implementation of the bounded() function:

```
def bounded(minimum, maximum):
    def decorator(function):
        @functools.wraps(function)
        def wrapper(*args, **kwargs):
            result = function(*args, **kwargs)
            if result < minimum:
                return minimum
            elif result > maximum:
                return maximum
            return result
        return wrapper
    return decorator
```

The function creates a decorator function, that itself creates a wrapper function. The wrapper performs the calculation and returns a result that is within
the bounded range. The decorator() function returns the wrapper() function,
and the bounded() function returns the decorator.

One further point to note is that each time a wrapper is created inside the
bounded() function, the particular wrapper uses the minimum and maximum
values that were passed to bounded().

The last decorator we will create in this subsection is a bit more complex. It is a
logging function that records the name, arguments, and result of any function
it is used to decorate. For example:

```
@logged
def discounted_price(price, percentage, make_integer=False):
    result = price * ((100 - percentage) / 100)
    if not (0 < result <= price):
        raise ValueError("invalid price")
    return result if not make_integer else int(round(result))
```

If Python is run in debug mode (the normal mode), every time the discounted_price() function is called a log message will be added to the file logged.log in the machine's local temporary directory, as this log file extract illustrates:

```
called: discounted_price(100, 10) -> 90.0
called: discounted_price(210, 5) -> 199.5
called: discounted_price(210, 5, make_integer=True) -> 200
called: discounted_price(210, 14, True) -> 181
called: discounted_price(210, -8) <type 'ValueError'>: invalid price
```

If Python is run in optimized mode (using the -O command-line option or if the PYTHONOPTIMIZE environment variable is set to -O), then no logging will take place. Here's the code for setting up logging and for the decorator:

```
if __debug__:
    logger = logging.getLogger("Logger")
    logger.setLevel(logging.DEBUG)
    handler = logging.FileHandler(os.path.join(
                            tempfile.gettempdir(), "logged.log"))
    logger.addHandler(handler)

    def logged(function):
        @functools.wraps(function)
        def wrapper(*args, **kwargs):
            log = "called: " + function.__name__ + "("
            log += ", ".join(["{0!r}".format(a) for a in args] +
                            ["{0!s}={1!r}".format(k, v)
                             for k, v in kwargs.items()])
            result = exception = None
            try:
                result = function(*args, **kwargs)
                return result
            except Exception as err:
                exception = err
            finally:
                log += ((") -> " + str(result)) if exception is None
                        else ") {0}: {1}".format(type(exception),
                                                 exception))
                logger.debug(log)
                if exception is not None:
                    raise exception
        return wrapper
else:
    def logged(function):
        return function
```

In debug mode the global variable __debug__ is True. If this is the case we set up logging using the logging module, and then create the @logged decorator. The logging module is very powerful and flexible—it can log to files, rotated files, emails, network connections, HTTP servers, and more. Here we've used only the most basic facilities by creating a logging object, setting its logging level (several levels are supported), and choosing to use a file for the output.

The wrapper's code begins by setting up the log string with the function's name and arguments. We then try calling the function and storing its result. If any exception occurs we store it. In all cases the finally block is executed, and there we add the return value (or exception) to the log string and write to the log. If no exception occurred, the result is returned; otherwise, we reraise the exception to correctly mimic the original function's behavior.

If Python is running in optimized mode, __debug__ is False; in this case we define the logged() function to simply return the function it is given, so apart from the tiny overhead of this indirection when the function is first created, there is no runtime overhead at all.

Note that the standard library's trace and profile modules can run and analyse programs and modules to produce various tracing and profiling reports. Both use introspection, so unlike the @logged decorator we have used here, neither trace nor profile requires any source code changes.

Function Annotations

Functions and methods can be defined with annotations—expressions that can be used in a function's signature. Here's the general syntax:

```
def functionName(par1 : exp1, par2 : exp2, ..., parN : expN) -> rexp:
    suite
```

Every colon expression part (: expX) is an optional annotation, and so is the arrow return expression part (-> rexp). The last (or only) positional parameter (if present) can be of the form *args, with or without an annotation; similarly, the last (or only) keyword parameter (if present) can be of the form **kwargs, again with or without an annotation.

If annotations are present they are added to the function's __annotations__ dictionary; if they are not present this dictionary is empty. The dictionary's keys are the parameter names, and the values are the corresponding expressions. The syntax allows us to annotate all, some, or none of the parameters and to annotate the return value or not. Annotations have no special significance to Python. The only thing that Python does in the face of annotations is to put them in the __annotations__ dictionary; any other action is up to us. Here is an example of an annotated function that is in the Util module:

```
def is_unicode_punctuation(s : str) -> bool:
    for c in s:
        if unicodedata.category(c)[0] != "P":
            return False
    return True
```

Every Unicode character belongs to a particular category and each category is identified by a two-character identifier. All the categories that begin with *P* are punctuation characters.

Here we have used Python data types as the annotation expressions. But they have no particular meaning for Python, as these calls should make clear:

```
Util.is_unicode_punctuation("zebr\a")     # returns: False
Util.is_unicode_punctuation(s="!@#?")     # returns: True
Util.is_unicode_punctuation(("!", "@"))   # returns: True
```

The first call uses a positional argument and the second call a keyword argument, just to show that both kinds work as expected. The last call passes a tuple rather than a string, and this is accepted since Python does nothing more than record the annotations in the __annotations__ dictionary.

If we want to give meaning to annotations, for example, to provide type checking, one approach is to decorate the functions we want the meaning to apply to with a suitable decorator. Here is a very basic type-checking decorator:

```
def strictly_typed(function):
    annotations = function.__annotations__
    arg_spec = inspect.getfullargspec(function)

    assert "return" in annotations, "missing type for return value"
    for arg in arg_spec.args + arg_spec.kwonlyargs:
        assert arg in annotations, ("missing type for parameter '" +
                                    arg + "'")
    @functools.wraps(function)
    def wrapper(*args, **kwargs):
        for name, arg in (list(zip(arg_spec.args, args)) +
                          list(kwargs.items())):
            assert isinstance(arg, annotations[name]), (
                    "expected argument '{0}' of {1} got {2}".format(
                    name, annotations[name], type(arg)))
        result = function(*args, **kwargs)
        assert isinstance(result, annotations["return"]), (
                    "expected return of {0} got {1}".format(
                    annotations["return"], type(result)))
        return result
    return wrapper
```

This decorator requires that every argument and the return value must be annotated with the expected type. It checks that the function's arguments and return type are all annotated with their types when the function it is passed is created, and at runtime it checks that the types of the actual arguments match those expected.

The inspect module provides powerful introspection services for objects. Here, we have made use of only a small part of the argument specification object it returns, to get the names of each positional and keyword argument—in the correct order in the case of the positional arguments. These names are then used in conjunction with the annotations dictionary to ensure that every parameter and the return value are annotated.

The wrapper function created inside the decorator begins by iterating over every name–argument pair of the given positional and keyword arguments. Since zip() returns an iterator and dictionary.items() returns a dictionary view we cannot concatenate them directly, so first we convert them both to lists. If any actual argument has a different type from its corresponding annotation the assertion will fail; otherwise, the actual function is called and the type of the value returned is checked, and if it is of the right type, it is returned. At the end of the strictly_typed() function, we return the wrapped function as usual. Notice that the checking is done only in debug mode (which is Python's default mode—controlled by the -O command-line option and the PYTHONOPTIMIZE environment variable).

If we decorate the is_unicode_punctuation() function with the @strictly_typed decorator, and try the same examples as before using the decorated version, the annotations are acted upon:

```
is_unicode_punctuation("zebr\a")        # returns: False
is_unicode_punctuation(s="!@#?")        # returns: True
is_unicode_punctuation(("!", "@"))      # raises AssertionError
```

Now the argument types are checked, so in the last case an AssertionError is raised because a tuple is not a string or a subclass of str.

Now we will look at a completely different use of annotations. Here's a small function that has the same functionality as the built-in range() function, except that it always returns floats:

```
def range_of_floats(*args) -> "author=Reginald Perrin":
    return (float(x) for x in range(*args))
```

No use is made of the annotation by the function itself, but it is easy to envisage a tool that imported all of a project's modules and produced a list of function names and author names, extracting each function's name from its __name__ attribute, and the author names from the value of the __annotations__ dictionary's "return" item.

Annotations are a very new feature of Python, and because Python does not impose any predefined meaning on them, the uses they can be put to are limited only by our imagination. Further ideas for possible uses, and some useful links, are available from PEP 3107 "Function Annotations", www.python.org/dev/peps/pep-3107.

Further Object-Oriented Programming

In this section we will look more deeply into Python's support for object orientation, learning many techniques that can reduce the amount of code we must write, and that expand the power and capabilities of the programming features that are available to us. But we will begin with one very small and simple new feature. Here is the start of the definition of a Point class that has exactly the same behavior as the versions we created in Chapter 6:

```
class Point:

    __slots__ = ("x", "y")

    def __init__(self, x=0, y=0):
        self.x = x
        self.y = y
```

When a class is created without the use of __slots__, behind the scenes Python creates a private dictionary called __dict__ for each instance, and this dictionary holds the instance's data attributes. This is why we can add or remove attributes from objects. (For example, we added a cache attribute to the get_function() function earlier in this chapter.)

Attribute access functions

339 ✒

If we only need objects where we access the original attributes and don't need to add or remove attributes, we can create classes that don't have a __dict__. This is achieved simply by defining a class attribute called __slots__ whose value is a tuple of attribute names. Each object of such a class will have attributes of the specified names and no __dict__; no attributes can be added or removed from such classes. These objects consume less memory than conventional objects, although this is unlikely to make much difference unless large numbers of objects are created.

Controlling Attribute Access

It is sometimes convenient to have a class where attribute values are computed on the fly rather than stored. Here's the complete implementation of such a class:

```
class Ord:

    def __getattr__(self, char):
        return ord(char)
```

With the Ord class available, we can create an instance, ord = Ord(), and then have an alternative to the built-in ord() function that works for any character that is a valid identifier. For example, ord.a returns 97, ord.Z returns 90, and ord.å returns 229. (But ord.! and similar are syntax errors.)

Note that if we typed the Ord class into IDLE it would not work if we then typed ord = Ord(). This is because the instance has the same name as the built-in ord() function that the Ord class uses, so the ord() call would actually become a call to the ord instance and result in a TypeError exception. The problem would not arise if we imported a module containing the Ord class because the interactively created ord object and the built-in ord() function used by the Ord class would be in two separate modules, so one would not displace the other. If we really need to create a class interactively and to reuse the name of a built-in we can do so by ensuring that the class calls the built-in—in this case by importing the builtins module which provides unambiguous access to all the built-in functions, and calling builtins.ord() rather than plain ord().

Here's another tiny yet complete class. This one allows us to create "constants". It isn't difficult to change the values behind the class's back, but it can at least prevent simple mistakes.

```
class Const:

    def __setattr__(self, name, value):
        if name in self.__dict__:
            raise ValueError("cannot change a const attribute")
        self.__dict__[name] = value

    def __delattr__(self, name):
        if name in self.__dict__:
            raise ValueError("cannot delete a const attribute")
        raise AttributeError("'{0}' object has no attribute '{1}'"
                             .format(self.__class__.__name__, name))
```

With this class we can create a constant object, say, const = Const(), and set any attributes we like on it, for example, const.limit = 591. But once an attribute's value has been set, although it can be read as often as we like, any attempt to change or delete it will result in a ValueError exception being raised. We have not reimplemented __getattr__() because the base class object.__getattr__() method does what we want—returns the given attribute's value or raises an AttributeError exception if there is no such attribute. In the __delattr__() method we mimic the __getattr__() method's error message for nonexistent attributes, and to do this we must get the name of the class we are in as well as

Table 8.2 *Attribute Access Special Methods*

Special Method	Usage	Description
__delattr__(self, name)	del x.n	Deletes object x's n attribute
__dir__(self)	dir(x)	Returns a list of x's attribute names
__getattr__(self, name)	v = x.n	Returns the value of object x's n attribute if it isn't found directly
__getattribute__(self, name)	v = x.n	Returns the value of object x's n attribute; see text
__setattr__(self, name, value)	x.n = v	Sets object x's n attribute's value to v

the name of the nonexistent attribute. The class works because we are using the object's __dict__ which is what the base class __getattr__(), __setattr__(), and __delattr__() methods use, although here we have used only the base class's __getattr__() method. All the special methods used for attribute access are listed in Table 8.2.

There is another way of getting constants: We can use named tuples. Here are a couple of examples:

```
Const = collections.namedtuple("_", "min max")(191, 591)
Const.min, Const.max                    # returns: (191, 591)
Offset = collections.namedtuple("_", "id name description")(*range(3))
Offset.id, Offset.name, Offset.description  # returns: (0, 1, 2)
```

In both cases we have just used a throwaway name for the named tuple because we want just one named tuple instance each time, not a tuple subclass for creating instances of a named tuple. Although Python does not support an enum data type, we can use named tuples as we have done here to get a similar effect.

Image.py
251 ✎

For our last look at attribute access special methods we will return to an example we first saw in Chapter 6. In that chapter we created an Image class whose width, height, and background color are fixed when an Image is created (although they are changed if an image is loaded). We provided access to them using read-only properties. For example, we had:

```
@property
def width(self):
    return self.__width
```

This is easy to code but could become tedious if there are a lot of read-only properties. Here is a different solution that handles all the Image class's read-only properties in a single method:

```
        def __getattr__(self, name):
            if name == "colors":
                return set(self.__colors)
            classname = self.__class__.__name__
            if name in frozenset({"background", "width", "height"}):
                return self.__dict__["_{0}__{1}".format(classname, name)]
            raise AttributeError("'{0}' object has no attribute '{1}'"
                                 .format(classname, name))
```

If we attempt to access an object's attribute and the attribute is not found, Python will call the __getattr__() method (providing it is implemented, and that we have not reimplemented __getattribute__()), with the name of the attribute as a parameter. Implementations of __getattr__() must raise an AttributeError exception if they do not handle the given attribute.

For example, if we have the statement image.colors, Python will look for a colors attribute and having failed to find it, will then call Image.__getattr__(image, "colors"). In this case the __getattr__() method handles a "colors" attribute name and returns a copy of the set of colors that the image is using.

The other attributes are immutable, so they are safe to return directly to the caller. We could have written separate elif statements for each one like this:

```
    elif name == "background":
        return self.__background
```

But instead we have chosen a more compact approach. Since we know that under the hood all of an object's nonspecial attributes are held in self.__dict__, we have chosen to access them directly. For private attributes (those whose name begins with two leading underscores), the name is mangled to have the form _className__attributeName, so we must account for this when retrieving the attribute's value from the object's private dictionary.

For the name mangling needed to look up private attributes and to provide the standard AttributeError error text, we need to know the name of the class we are in. (It may not be Image because the object might be an instance of an Image subclass.) Every object has a __class__ special attribute, so self.__class__ is always available inside methods and can safely be accessed by __getattr__() without risking unwanted recursion.

Note that there is a subtle difference in that using __getattr__() and self.__class__ provides access to the attribute in the instance's class (which may be a subclass), but accessing the attribute directly uses the class the attribute is defined in.

One special method that we have not covered is __getattribute__(). Whereas the __getattr__() method is called last when looking for (nonspecial) attributes, the __getattribute__() method is called first for every attribute

access. Although it can be useful or even essential in some cases to call
__getattribute__(), reimplementing the __getattribute__() method can be
tricky. Reimplementations must be very careful not to call themselves
recursively—using super().__getattribute__() or object.__getattribute__()
is often done in such cases. Also, since __getattribute__() is called for every
attribute access, reimplementing it can easily end up degrading performance
compared with direct attribute access or properties. None of the classes presented in this book reimplements __getattribute__().

Functors

In Python a *function object* is an object reference to any callable, such as a
function, a lambda function, or a method. The definition also includes classes,
since an object reference to a class is a callable that, when called, returns an
object of the given class—for example, x = int(5). In computer science a *functor*
is an object that can be called as though it were a function, so in Python terms a
functor is just another kind of function object. Any class that has a __call__()
special method is a functor. The key benefit that functors offer is that they can
maintain some state information. For example, we could create a functor that
always strips basic punctuation from the ends of a string. We would create and
use it like this:

```
strip_punctuation = Strip(",;:.!?")
strip_punctuation("Land ahoy!")          # returns: 'Land ahoy'
```

Here we create an instance of the Strip functor initializing it with the value
",;:.!?". Whenever the instance is called it returns the string it is passed with
any punctuation characters stripped off. Here's the complete implementation
of the Strip class:

```
class Strip:

    def __init__(self, characters):
        self.characters = characters

    def __call__(self, string):
        return string.strip(self.characters)
```

We could achieve the same thing using a plain function or lambda, but if we
need to store a bit more state or perform more complex processing, a functor is
often the right solution.

A functor's ability to capture state by using a class is very versatile and powerful, but sometimes it is more than we really need. Another way to capture state
is to use a *closure*. A closure is a function or method that captures some external
state. For example:

```
def make_strip_function(characters):
    def strip_function(string):
        return string.strip(characters)
    return strip_function

strip_punctuation = make_strip_function(",;:.!?")
strip_punctuation("Land ahoy!")        # returns: 'Land ahoy'
```

The make_strip_function() function takes the characters to be stripped as its
sole argument and returns a function, strip_function(), that takes a string
argument and which strips the characters that were given at the time the
closure was created. So just as we can create as many instances of the Strip
class as we want, each with its own characters to strip, we can create as many
strip functions with their own characters as we like.

The classic use case for functors is to provide key functions for sort routines.
Here is a generic SortKey functor class (from file SortKey.py):

```
class SortKey:

    def __init__(self, *attribute_names):
        self.attribute_names = attribute_names

    def __call__(self, instance):
        values = []
        for attribute_name in self.attribute_names:
            values.append(getattr(instance, attribute_name))
        return values
```

When a SortKey object is created it keeps a tuple of the attribute names it
was initialized with. When the object is called it creates a list of the attribute
values for the instance it is passed—in the order they were specified when the
SortKey was initialized. For example, imagine we have a Person class:

```
class Person:

    def __init__(self, forename, surname, email):
        self.forename = forename
        self.surname = surname
        self.email = email
```

Suppose we have a list of Person objects in the people list. We can sort the
list by surnames like this: people.sort(key=SortKey("surname")). If there
are a lot of people there are bound to be some surname clashes, so we can
sort by surname, and then by forename within surname, like this: peo-
ple.sort(key=SortKey("surname", "forename")). And if we had people with the
same surname and forename we could add the email attribute too. And of

course, we could sort by forename and then surname by changing the order of the attribute names we give to the SortKey functor.

Another way of achieving the same thing, but without needing to create a functor at all, is to use the operator module's operator.attrgetter() function. For example, to sort by surname we could write: people.sort(key=operator.attr-getter("surname")). And similarly, to sort by surname and forename: people.sort(key=operator.attrgetter("surname", "forename")). The operator.attrgetter() function returns a function (a closure) that, when called on an object, returns those attributes of the object that were specified when the closure was created.

Functors are probably used rather less frequently in Python than in other languages that support them because Python has other means of doing the same things—for example, using closures or item and attribute getters.

Context Managers

Context managers allow us to simplify code by ensuring that certain operations are performed before and after a particular block of code is executed. The behavior is achieved because context managers define two special methods, __enter__() and __exit__(), that Python treats specially in the scope of a with statement. When a context manager is created in a with statement its __enter__() method is automatically called, and when the context manager goes out of scope after its with statement its __exit__() method is automatically called.

We can create our own custom context managers or use predefined ones—as we will see later in this subsection, the file objects returned by the built-in open() function are context managers. The syntax for using context managers is this:

```
with expression as variable:
    suite
```

The *expression* must be or must produce a context manager object; if the optional as *variable* part is specified, the variable is set to refer to the object returned by the context manager's __enter__() method (and this is often the context manager itself). Because a context manager is guaranteed to execute its "exit" code (even in the face of exceptions), context managers can be used to eliminate the need for finally blocks in many situations.

Some of Python's types are context managers—for example, all the file objects that open() can return—so we can eliminate finally blocks when doing file handling as these equivalent code snippets illustrate (assuming that process() is a function defined elsewhere):

```
fh = None                          |
try:                               |
    fh = open(filename)            |
    for line in fh:                |
        process(line)              |    try:
except EnvironmentError as err:    |        with open(filename) as fh:
    print(err)                     |            for line in fh:
finally:                           |                process(line)
    if fh is not None:             |    except EnvironmentError as err:
        fh.close()                 |        print(err)
```

A file object is a context manager whose exit code always closes the file if it was opened. The exit code is executed whether or not an exception occurs, but in the latter case, the exception is propagated. This ensures that the file gets closed and we still get the chance to handle any errors, in this case by printing a message for the user.

In fact, context managers don't have to propagate exceptions, but not doing so effectively hides any exceptions, and this would almost certainly be a coding error. All the built-in and standard library context managers propagate exceptions.

Sometimes we need to use more than one context manager at the same time. For example:

```
try:
    with open(source) as fin:
        with open(target, "w") as fout:
            for line in fin:
                fout.write(process(line))
except EnvironmentError as err:
    print(err)
```

Here we read lines from the source file and write processed versions of them to the target file.

Using nested with statements can quickly lead to a lot of indentation. Fortunately, the standard library's contextlib module provides some additional support for context managers, including the contextlib.nested() function which allows two or more context managers to be handled in the same with statement rather than having to nest with statements. Here is a replacement for the code just shown, but omitting most of the lines that are identical to before:

```
try:
    with contextlib.nested(open(source), open(target, "w")) as (
            fin, fout):
        for line in fin:
```

It isn't only file objects that are context managers. For example, several threading-related classes used for locking are context managers. Context managers can also be used with decimal.Decimal numbers; this is useful if we want to perform some calculations with certain settings (such as a particular precision) in effect.

Thread-
ing
☞ 395

If we want to create a custom context manager we must create a class that provides two methods: __enter__() and __exit__(). Whenever a with statement is used on an instance of such a class, the __enter__() method is called and the return value is used for the as *variable* (or thrown away if there isn't one). When control leaves the scope of the with statement the __exit__() method is called (with details of an exception if one has occurred passed as arguments).

Suppose we want to perform several operations on a list in an atomic manner—that is, we either want all the operations to be done or none of them so that the resultant list is always in a known state. For example, if we have a list of integers and want to append an integer, delete an integer, and change a couple of integers, all as a single operation, we could write code like this:

```
try:
    with AtomicList(items) as atomic:
        atomic.append(58289)
        del atomic[3]
        atomic[8] = 81738
        atomic[index] = 38172
except (AttributeError, IndexError, ValueError) as err:
    print("no changes applied:", err)
```

If no exception occurs, all the operations are applied to the original list (items), but if an exception occurs, no changes are made at all. Here is the code for the AtomicList context manager:

```
class AtomicList:

    def __init__(self, alist, shallow_copy=True):
        self.original = alist
        self.shallow_copy = shallow_copy


    def __enter__(self):
        self.modified = (self.original[:] if self.shallow_copy
                         else copy.deepcopy(self.original))
        return self.modified


    def __exit__(self, exc_type, exc_val, exc_tb):
        if exc_type is None:
            self.original[:] = self.modified
```

Shallow
and
deep
copying

136 ✍

When the AtomicList object is created we keep a reference to the original list and note whether shallow copying is to be used. (Shallow copying is fine for lists of numbers or strings; but for lists that contain lists or other collections, shallow copying is not sufficient.)

Then, when the AtomicList context manager object is used in the with statement its __enter__() method is called. At this point we copy the original list and return the copy so that all the changes can be made on the copy.

Once we reach the end of the with statement's scope the __exit__() method is called. If no exception occurred the exc_type ("exception type") will be None and we know that we can safely replace the original list's items with the items from the modified list. (We cannot do self.original = self.modified because that would just replace one object reference with another and would not affect the original list at all.) But if an exception occurred, we do nothing to the original list and the modified list is discarded.

The return value of __exit__() is used to indicate whether any exception that occurred should be propagated. A True value means that we have handled any exception and so no propagation should occur. Normally we always return False or something that evaluates to False in a Boolean context to allow any exception that occurred to propagate. By not giving an explicit return value, our __exit__() returns None which evaluates to False and correctly causes any exception to propagate.

Custom context managers are used in Chapter 10 to ensure that socket connections and gzipped files are closed, and some of the threading modules context managers are used in Chapter 9 to ensure that mutual exclusion locks are unlocked. You'll also get the chance to create a more generic atomic contex manager in this chapter's exercises.

Descriptors

Descriptors are classes which provide access control for the attributes of other classes. Any class that implements one or more of the descriptor special methods, __get__(), __set__(), and __delete__(), is called (and can be used as) a descriptor.

The built-in property() and classmethod() functions are implemented using descriptors. The key to understanding descriptors is that although we create an instance of a descriptor in a class as a class attribute, Python accesses the descriptor through the class's instances.

To make things clear, let's imagine that we have a class whose instances hold some strings. We want to access the strings in the normal way, for example, as a property, but we also want to get an XML-escaped version of the strings whenever we want. One simple solution would be that whenever a string is set we immediately create an XML-escaped copy. But if we had thousands of strings and only ever read the XML version of a few of them, we would be wasting a lot of processing and memory for nothing. So we will create a descriptor that will provide XML-escaped strings on demand without storing them. We will start with the beginning of the client (owner) class, that is, the class that uses the descriptor:

```
class Product:

    __slots__ = ("__name", "__description", "__price")

    name_as_xml = XmlShadow("name")
    description_as_xml = XmlShadow("description")

    def __init__(self, name, description, price):
        self.__name = name
        self.description = description
        self.price = price
```

The only code we have not shown are the properties; the name is a read-only property and the description and price are readable/writable properties, all set up in the usual way. (All the code is in the XmlShadow.py file.) We have used the __slots__ variable to ensure that the class has no __dict__ and can store only the three specified private attributes; this is not related to or necessary for our use of descriptors. The name_as_xml and description_as_xml class attributes are set to be instances of the XmlShadow descriptor. Although no Product object has a name_as_xml attribute or a description_as_xml attribute, thanks to the descriptor we can write code like this (here quoting from the module's doctests):

```
>>> product = Product("Chisel <3cm>", "Chisel & cap", 45.25)
>>> product.name, product.name_as_xml, product.description_as_xml
('Chisel <3cm>', 'Chisel &lt;3cm&gt;', 'Chisel &amp; cap')
```

This works because when we try to access, for example, the name_as_xml attribute, Python finds that the Product class has a descriptor with that name, and so uses the descriptor to get the attribute's value. Here's the complete code for the XmlShadow descriptor class:

```
class XmlShadow:

    def __init__(self, attribute_name):
        self.attribute_name = attribute_name

    def __get__(self, instance, owner=None):
        return xml.sax.saxutils.escape(
                        getattr(instance, self.attribute_name))
```

When the name_as_xml and description_as_xml objects are created we pass the name of the Product class's corresponding attribute to the XmlShadow initializer so that the descriptor knows which attribute to work on. Then, when the name_as_xml or description_as_xml attribute is looked up, Python calls the descriptor's __get__() method. The self argument is the instance of the descriptor, the instance argument is the Product instance (i.e., the product's self), and the owner argument is the owning class (Product in this case). We use the getattr() function to retrieve the relevant attribute from the product (in this case the relevant property), and return an XML-escaped version of it.

If the use case was that only a small proportion of the products were accessed for their XML strings, but the strings were often long and the same ones were frequently accessed, we could use a cache. For example:

```
class CachedXmlShadow:

    def __init__(self, attribute_name):
        self.attribute_name = attribute_name
        self.cache = {}

    def __get__(self, instance, owner=None):
        xml_text = self.cache.get(id(instance))
        if xml_text is not None:
            return xml_text
        return self.cache.setdefault(id(instance),
                xml.sax.saxutils.escape(
                        getattr(instance, self.attribute_name)))
```

We store the unique identity of the instance as the key rather than the instance itself because dictionary keys must be hashable (which IDs are), but we don't want to impose that as a requirement on classes that use the CachedXmlShadow descriptor. The key is necessary because descriptors are created per class rather than per instance. (The dict.setdefault() method conveniently returns the value for the given key, or if no item with that key is present, creates a new item with the given key and value and returns the value.)

Having seen descriptors used to generate data without necessarily storing it, we will now look at a descriptor that can be used to store all of an object's attribute data, with the object not needing to store anything itself. In the example, we will just use a dictionary, but in a more realistic context, the data might be stored in a file or a database. Here's the start of a modified version of the Point class that makes use of the descriptor (from the ExternalStorage.py file):

```
class Point:

    __slots__ = ()
    x = ExternalStorage("x")
    y = ExternalStorage("y")
```

```
def __init__(self, x=0, y=0):
    self.x = x
    self.y = y
```

By setting __slots__ to an empty tuple we ensure that the class cannot store any data attributes at all. When self.x is assigned to, Python finds that there is a descriptor with the name "x", and so uses the descriptor's __set__() method. The rest of the class isn't shown, but is the same as the original Point class shown in Chapter 6. Here is the complete ExternalStorage descriptor class:

```
class ExternalStorage:

    __slots__ = ("attribute_name",)
    __storage = {}

    def __init__(self, attribute_name):
        self.attribute_name = attribute_name

    def __set__(self, instance, value):
        self.__storage[id(instance), self.attribute_name] = value

    def __get__(self, instance, owner=None):
        if instance is None:
            return self
        return self.__storage[id(instance), self.attribute_name]
```

Each ExternalStorage object has a single data attribute, attribute_name, which holds the name of the owner class's data attribute. Whenever an attribute is set we store its value in the private class dictionary, __storage. Similarly, whenever an attribute is retrieved we get it from the __storage dictionary.

As with all descriptor methods, self is the instance of the descriptor object and instance is the self of the object that contains the descriptor, so here self is an ExternalStorage object and instance is a Point object.

Although __storage is a class attribute, we can access it as self.__storage (just as we can call methods using self.*method()*), because Python will look for it as an instance attribute, and not finding it will then look for it as a class attribute. The one (theoretical) disadvantage of this approach is that if we have a class attribute and an instance attribute with the same name, one would hide the other. (If this were really a problem we could always refer to the class attribute using the class, that is, ExternalStorage.__storage. Although hard-coding the class does not play well with subclassing in general, it doesn't really matter for private attributes since Python name-mangles the class name into them anyway.)

The implementation of the __get__() special method is slightly more sophisticated than before because we provide a means by which the ExternalStorage instance itself can be accessed. For example, if we have p = Point(3, 4), we can access the *x*-coordinate with p.x, and we can access the ExternalStorage object that holds all the xs with Point.x.

To complete our coverage of descriptors we will create the Property descriptor that mimics the behavior of the built-in property() function, at least for setters and getters. The code is in Property.py. Here is the complete NameAndExtension class that makes use of it:

```
class NameAndExtension:

    def __init__(self, name, extension):
        self.__name = name
        self.extension = extension

    @Property                   # Uses the custom Property descriptor
    def name(self):
        return self.__name

    @Property                   # Uses the custom Property descriptor
    def extension(self):
        return self.__extension

    @extension.setter           # Uses the custom Property descriptor
    def extension(self, extension):
        self.__extension = extension
```

The usage is just the same as for the built-in @property decorator and for the *@propertyName*.setter decorator. Here is the start of the Property descriptor's implementation:

```
class Property:

    def __init__(self, getter, setter=None):
        self.__getter = getter
        self.__setter = setter
        self.__name__ = getter.__name__
```

The class's initializer takes one or two functions as arguments. If it is used as a decorator, it will get just the decorated function and this becomes the getter, while the setter is set to None. We use the getter's name as the property's name. So for each property, we have a getter, possibly a setter, and a name.

```
    def __get__(self, instance, owner=None):
        if instance is None:
            return self
        return self.__getter(instance)
```

When a property is accessed we return the result of calling the getter function where we have passed the instance as its first parameter. At first sight, self.__getter() looks like a method call, but it is not. In fact, self.__getter is an attribute, one that happens to hold an object reference to a method that was passed in. So what happens is that first we retrieve the attribute (self.__getter), and then we call it as a function (). And because it is called as a function rather than as a method we must pass in the relevant self object explicitly ourselves. And in the case of a descriptor the self object (from the class that is using the descriptor) is called instance (since self is the descriptor object). The same applies to the __set__() method.

```
def __set__(self, instance, value):
    if self.__setter is None:
        raise AttributeError("'{0}' is read-only".format(
                            self.__name__))
    return self.__setter(instance, value)
```

If no setter has been specified, we raise an AttributeError; otherwise, we call the setter with the instance and the new value.

```
def setter(self, setter):
    self.__setter = setter
    return self.__setter
```

This method is called when the interpreter reaches, for example, @extension.setter, with the function it decorates as its setter argument. It stores the setter method it has been given (which can now be used in the __set__() method), and returns the setter, since decorators should return the function or method they decorate.

We have now looked at three quite different uses of descriptors. Descriptors are a very powerful and flexible feature that can be used to do lots of under-the-hood work while appearing to be simple attributes in their client (owner) class.

Class Decorators

Just as we can create decorators for functions and methods, we can also create decorators for entire classes. Class decorators take a class object (the result of the class statement), and should return a class—normally a modified version of the class they decorate. In this subsection we will study two class decorators to see how they can be implemented.

Sorted-List

258 ☜

In Chapter 6 we created the SortedList custom collection class that aggregated a plain list as the private attribute self.__list. Eight of the SortedList methods simply passed on their work to the private attribute. For example, here are how the SortedList.clear() and SortedList.pop() methods were implemented:

```
    def clear(self):
        self.__list = []

    def pop(self, index=-1):
        return self.__list.pop(index)
```

There is nothing we can do about the clear() method since there is no corresponding method for the list type, but for pop(), and the other six methods that SortedList delegates, we can simply call the list class's corresponding method. This can be done by using the @delegate class decorator from the book's Util module. Here is the start of a new version of the SortedList class:

```
    @Util.delegate("__list", ("pop", "__delitem__", "__getitem__",
                    "__iter__", "__reversed__", "__len__", "__str__"))
    class SortedList:
```

The first argument is the name of the attribute to delegate to, and the second argument is a sequence of one or more methods that we want the delegate() decorator to implement for us so that we don't have to do the work ourselves. The SortedList class in the SortedListDelegate.py file uses this approach and therefore does not have any code for the methods listed, even though it fully supports them. Here is the class decorator that implements the methods for us:

```
    def delegate(attribute_name, method_names):
        def decorator(cls):
            nonlocal attribute_name
            if attribute_name.startswith("__"):
                attribute_name = "_" + cls.__name__ + attribute_name
            for name in method_names:
                setattr(cls, name, eval("lambda self, *a, **kw: "
                                        "self.{0}.{1}(*a, **kw)".format(
                                        attribute_name, name)))
            return cls
        return decorator
```

We could not use a plain decorator because we want to pass arguments to the decorator, so we have instead created a function that takes our arguments and that returns a class decorator. The decorator itself takes a single argument, a class (just as a function decorator takes a single function or method as its argument).

We must use nonlocal so that the nested function uses the attribute_name from the outer scope rather than attempting to use one from its own scope. And we must be able to correct the attribute name if necessary to take account of the name mangling of private attributes. The decorator's behavior is quite simple: It iterates over all the method names that the delegate() function has been given, and for each one creates a new method which it sets as an attribute on the class with the given method name.

We have used eval() to create each of the delegated methods since it can be used to execute a single statement, and a lambda statement produces a method or function. For example, the code executed to produce the pop() method is:

```
lambda self, *a, **kw: self._SortedList__list.pop(*a, **kw)
```

We use the * and ** argument forms to allow for any arguments even though the methods being delegated to have specific argument lists. For example, list.pop() accepts a single index position (or nothing, in which case it defaults to the last item). This is okay because if the wrong number or kinds of arguments are passed, the list method that is called to do the work will raise an appropriate exception.

Fuzzy-
Bool
238 ☜

The second class decorator we will review was also used in Chapter 6. When we implemented the FuzzyBool class we mentioned that we had supplied only the __lt__() and __eq__() special methods (for < and ==), and had generated all the other comparison methods automatically. What we didn't show was the complete start of the class definition:

```
@Util.complete_comparisons
class FuzzyBool:
```

The other four comparison operators were provided by the complete_comparisons() class decorator. Given a class that defines only < (or < and ==), the decorator produces the missing comparison operators by using the following logical equivalences:

$$x = y \quad \Leftrightarrow \quad \neg\,(x < y \vee y < x)$$
$$x \neq y \quad \Leftrightarrow \quad \neg\,(x = y)$$
$$x > y \quad \Leftrightarrow \quad y < x$$
$$x \leq y \quad \Leftrightarrow \quad \neg\,(y < x)$$
$$x \geq y \quad \Leftrightarrow \quad \neg\,(x < y)$$

If the class to be decorated has < and ==, the decorator will use them both, falling back to doing everything in terms of < if that is the only operator supplied. (In fact, Python automatically produces > if < is supplied, != if == is supplied, and >= if <= is supplied, so it is sufficient to just implement the three operators <, <=, and == and to leave Python to infer the others. However, using the class decorator reduces the minimum that we must implement to just <. This is convenient, and also ensures that all the comparison operators use the same consistent logic.)

```
def complete_comparisons(cls):
    assert cls.__lt__ is not object.__lt__, (
            "{0} must define < and ideally ==".format(cls.__name__))
```

```
    if cls.__eq__ is object.__eq__:
        cls.__eq__ = lambda self, other: (not
                    (cls.__lt__(self, other) or cls.__lt__(other, self)))
    cls.__ne__ = lambda self, other: not cls.__eq__(self, other)
    cls.__gt__ = lambda self, other: cls.__lt__(other, self)
    cls.__le__ = lambda self, other: not cls.__lt__(other, self)
    cls.__ge__ = lambda self, other: not cls.__lt__(self, other)
    return cls
```

One problem that the decorator faces is that class object from which every
other class is ultimately derived defines all six comparison operators, all of
which raise a TypeError exception if used. So we need to know whether < and
== have been reimplemented (and are therefore usable). This can easily be done
by comparing the relevant special methods in the class being decorated with
those in object.

If the decorated class does not have a custom < the assertion fails because that
is the decorator's minimum requirement. And if there is a custom == we use
it; otherwise, we create one. Then all the other methods are created and the
decorated class, now with all six comparison methods, is returned.

Using class decorators is probably the simplest and most direct way of
changing classes. Another approach is to use metaclasses, a topic we will cover
later in this chapter.

Meta-
classes
☞ 380

Abstract Base Classes

An abstract base class (ABC) is a class that cannot be used to create objects.
Instead, the purpose of such classes is to define interfaces, that is, to in effect
list the methods and properties that classes that inherit the abstract base class
must provide. This is useful because we can use an abstract base class as a
kind of promise—a promise that any derived class will provide the methods
and properties that the abstract base class specifies.*

Abstract base classes are classes that have at least one abstract method or
property. Abstract methods can be defined with no implementation (i.e., their
suite is pass, or if we want to force reimplementation in a subclass, raise
NotImplementedError()), or with an actual (concrete) implementation that can
be invoked from subclasses, for example, when there is a common case. They
can also have other concrete (i.e., nonabstract) methods and properties.

Classes that derive from an ABC can be used to create instances only if they
reimplement all the abstract methods and abstract properties they have inherited. For those abstract methods that have concrete implementations (even if

---

* Python's abstract base classes are described in PEP 3119 (www.python.org/dev/peps/pep-3119),
which also includes a very useful rationale and is well worth reading.

Table 8.3 *The Numbers Module's Abstract Base Classes*

ABC	Inherits	API	Examples
Number	object		complex, decimal.Decimal, float, fractions.Fraction, int
Complex	Number	==, !=, +, −, *, /, abs(), bool(), complex(), conjugate(); also real and imag properties	complex, decimal.Decimal, float, fractions.Fraction, int
Real	Complex	<, <=, ==, !=, >=, >, +, −, *, /, //, %, abs(), bool(), complex(), conjugate(), divmod(), float(), math.ceil(), math.floor(), round(), trunc(); also real and imag properties	decimal.Decimal, float, fractions.Fraction, int
Rational	Real	<, <=, ==, !=, >=, >, +, −, *, /, //, %, abs(), bool(), complex(), conjugate(), divmod(), float(), math.ceil(), math.floor(), round(), trunc(); also real, imag, numerator, and denominator properties	fractions.Fraction, int
Integral	Rational	<, <=, ==, !=, >=, >, +, −, *, /, //, %, <<, >>, ~, &, ^, |, abs(), bool(), complex(), conjugate(), divmod(), float(), math.ceil(), math.floor(), pow(), round(), trunc(); also real, imag, numerator, and denominator properties	int

it is only pass), the derived class could simply use super() to use the ABC's version. Any concrete methods or properties are available through inheritance as usual. All ABCs must have a metaclass of abc.ABCMeta (from the abc module), or from one of its subclasses. We cover metaclasses a bit further on.

Meta-classes ☞ 380

Python provides two groups of abstract base classes, one in the collections module and the other in the numbers module. They allow us to ask questions about an object; for example, given a variable *x*, we can see whether it is a sequence using isinstance(*x*, collections.MutableSequence) or whether it is a whole number using isinstance(*x*, numbers.Integral). This is particularly useful in view of Python's dynamic typing where we don't necessarily know (or care) what an object's type is, but want to know whether it supports the operations we want to apply to it. The numeric and collection ABCs are listed in Tables 8.3 and 8.4. The other major ABC is io.IOBase from which all the file and stream-handling classes derive.

To fully integrate our own custom numeric and collection classes we ought to make them fit in with the standard ABCs. For example, the SortedList class is a sequence, but as it stands, isinstance(L, collections.Sequence) returns False if L is a SortedList. One easy way to fix this is to inherit the relevant ABC:

```
class SortedList(collections.Sequence):
```

By making collections.Sequence the base class, the isinstance() test will now return True. Furthermore, we will be required to implement __init__() (or __new__()), __getitem__(), and __len__() (which we do). The collections.Sequence ABC also provides concrete (i.e., nonabstract) implementations for __contains__(), __iter__(), __reversed__(), count(), and index(). In the case of SortedList, we reimplement them all, but we could have used the ABC versions if we wanted to, simply by not reimplementing them. We cannot make SortedList a subclass of collections.MutableSequence even though the list is mutable because SortedList does not have all the methods that a collections.MutableSequence must provide, such as __setitem__() and append(). (The code for this SortedList is in SortedListAbc.py. We will see an alternative approach to making a SortedList into a collections.Sequence in the Metaclasses subsection.)

Meta-
classes
☞ 380

Now that we have seen how to make a custom class fit in with the standard ABCs, we will turn to another use of ABCs: to provide an interface promise for our own custom classes. We will look at three rather different examples to cover different aspects of creating and using ABCs.

We will start with a very simple example that shows how to handle readable/writable properties. The class is used to represent domestic appliances. Every appliance that is created must have a read-only model string and a readable/writable price. We also want to ensure that the ABC's __init__() is reimplemented. Here's the ABC (from Appliance.py); we have not shown the import abc statement which is needed for the abstractmethod() and abstractproperty() functions, both of which can be used as decorators:

```
class Appliance(metaclass=abc.ABCMeta):

    @abc.abstractmethod
    def __init__(self, model, price):
        self.__model = model
        self.price = price

    def get_price(self):
        return self.__price
```

Table 8.4 *The Collections Module's Main Abstract Base Classes*

ABC	Inherits	API	Examples
Callable	object	()	All functions, methods, and lambdas
Container	object	in	bytearray, bytes, dict, frozenset, list, set, str, tuple
Hashable	object	hash()	bytes, frozenset, str, tuple
Iterable	object	iter()	bytearray, bytes, collections.deque, dict, frozenset, list, set, str, tuple
Iterator	Iterable	iter(), next()	
Sized	object	len()	bytearray, bytes, collections.deque, dict, frozenset, list, set, str, tuple
Mapping	Container, Iterable, Sized	==, !=, [], len(), iter(), in, get(), items(), keys(), values()	dict
Mutable-Mapping	Mapping	==, !=, [], del, len(), iter(), in, clear(), get(), items(), keys(), pop(), popitem(), setdefault(), update(), values()	dict
Sequence	Container, Iterable, Sized	[], len(), iter(), reversed(), in, count(), index()	bytearray, bytes, list, str, tuple
Mutable-Sequence	Container, Iterable, Sized	[], +=, del, len(), iter(), reversed(), in, append(), count(), extend(), index(), insert(), pop(), remove(), reverse()	bytearray, list
Set	Container, Iterable, Sized	<, <=, ==, !=, =>, >, &, |, ^, len(), iter(), in, isdisjoint()	frozenset, set
MutableSet	Set	<, <=, ==, !=, =>, >, &, |, ^, &=, |=, ^=, -=, len(), iter(), in, add(), clear(), discard(), isdisjoint(), pop(), remove()	set

```
    def set_price(self, price):
        self.__price = price

    price = abc.abstractproperty(get_price, set_price)


    @property
    def model(self):
        return self.__model
```

We have set the class's metaclass to be abc.ABCMeta since this is a requirement for ABCs; any abc.ABCMeta subclass can be used instead, of course. We have made __init__() an abstract method to ensure that it is reimplemented, and we have also provided an implementation which we expect (but can't force) inheritors to call. To make an abstract readable/writable property we cannot use decorator syntax; also we have not used private names for the getter and setter since doing so would be inconvenient for subclasses. The model property is not abstract, so subclasses don't need to reimplement it. No Appliance objects can be created because the class contains abstract attributes. Here is an example subclass:

```
    class Cooker(Appliance):

        def __init__(self, model, price, fuel):
            super().__init__(model, price)
            self.fuel = fuel

        price = property(lambda self: super().price,
                         lambda self, price: super().set_price(price))
```

The Cooker class must reimplement the __init__() method and the price property. For the property we have just passed on all the work to the base class. The model read-only property is inherited. We could create many more classes based on Appliance, such as Fridge, Toaster, and so on.

The next ABC we will look at is even shorter; it is an ABC for text-filtering functors (in file TextFilter.py):

```
    class TextFilter(metaclass=abc.ABCMeta):

        @abc.abstractproperty
        def is_transformer(self):
            raise NotImplementedError()


        @abc.abstractmethod
        def __call__(self):
            raise NotImplementedError()
```

The TextFilter ABC provides no functionality at all; it exists purely to define an interface, in this case an is_transformer read-only property and a __call__()

method, that all its subclasses must provide. Since the abstract property and method have no implementations we don't want subclasses to call them, so instead of using an innocuous pass statement we raise an exception if they are used (e.g., via a super() call).

Here is one simple subclass:

```
class CharCounter(TextFilter):

    @property
    def is_transformer(self):
        return False


    def __call__(self, text, chars):
        count = 0
        for c in text:
            if c in chars:
                count += 1
        return count
```

This text filter is not a transformer because rather than transforming the text it is given, it simply returns a count of the specified characters that occur in the text. Here is an example of use:

```
vowel_counter = CharCounter()
vowel_counter("dog fish and cat fish", "aeiou")     # returns: 5
```

Two other text filters are provided, both of which are transformers: RunLength-Encode and RunLengthDecode. Here is how they are used:

```
rle_encoder = RunLengthEncode()
rle_text = rle_encoder(text)
...
rle_decoder = RunLengthDecode()
original_text = rle_decoder(rle_text)
```

The run length encoder converts a string into UTF-8 encoded bytes, and replaces 0x00 bytes with the sequence 0x00, 0x01, 0x00, and any sequence of three to 255 repeated bytes with the sequence 0x00, *count, byte*. If the string has lots of runs of four or more identical consecutive characters this can produce a shorter byte string than the raw UTF-8 encoded bytes. The run length decoder takes a run length encoded byte string and returns the original string. Here is the start of the RunLengthDecode class:

```
class RunLengthDecode(TextFilter):

    @property
    def is_transformer(self):
```

```
        return True

    def __call__(self, rle_bytes):
        ...
```

We have omitted the body of the `__call__()` method, although it is in the source that accompanies this book. The RunLengthEncode class has exactly the same structure.

The last ABC we will look at provides an Application Programming Interface (API) and a default implementation for an undo mechanism. Here is the complete ABC (from file Abstract.py):

```
class Undo(metaclass=abc.ABCMeta):


    @abc.abstractmethod
    def __init__(self):
        self.__undos = []

    @abc.abstractproperty
    def can_undo(self):
        return bool(self.__undos)

    @abc.abstractmethod
    def undo(self):
        assert self.__undos, "nothing left to undo"
        self.__undos.pop()(self)

    def add_undo(self, undo):
        self.__undos.append(undo)
```

The `__init__()` and undo() methods must be reimplemented since they are both abstract; and so must the read-only can_undo property. Subclasses don't have to reimplement the add_undo() method, although they are free to do so. The undo() method is slightly subtle. The self.__undos list is expected to hold object references to methods. Each method must cause the corresponding action to be undone if it is called—this will be clearer when we look at an Undo subclass in a moment. So to perform an undo we pop the last undo method off the self.__undos list, and then call the method as a function, passing self as an argument. (We must pass self because the method is being called as a function and not as a method.)

Here is the beginning of the Stack class; it inherits Undo, so any actions performed on it can be undone by calling Stack.undo() with no arguments:

```
class Stack(Undo):
```

```
    def __init__(self):
        super().__init__()
        self.__stack = []

    @property
    def can_undo(self):
        return super().can_undo

    def undo(self):
        super().undo()

    def push(self, item):
        self.__stack.append(item)
        self.add_undo(lambda self: self.__stack.pop())


    def pop(self):
        item = self.__stack.pop()
        self.add_undo(lambda self: self.__stack.append(item))
        return item
```

We have omitted Stack.top() and Stack.__str__() since neither adds anything new and neither interacts with the Undo base class. For the can_undo property and the undo() method, we simply pass on the work to the base class. If these two were not abstract we would not need to reimplement them at all and the same effect would be achieved; but in this case we wanted to force subclasses to reimplement them to encourage undo to be taken account of in the subclass. For push() and pop() we perform the operation and also add a function to the undo list which will undo the operation that has just been performed.

Abstract base classes are most useful in large-scale programs, libraries, and application frameworks, where they can help ensure that irrespective of implementation details or author, classes can work cooperatively together because they provide the APIs that their ABCs specify.

Multiple Inheritance

Multiple inheritance is where one class inherits from two or more other classes. Although Python (and, for example, C++) fully supports multiple inheritance, some languages—most notably, Java—don't allow it. One problem is that multiple inheritance can lead to the same class being inherited more than once (e.g., if two of the base classes inherit from the same class), and this means that the version of a method that is called, if it is not in the subclass but is in two or more of the base classes (or their base classes, etc.), depends on the method resolution order, which potentially makes classes that use multiple inheritance somewhat fragile.

Multiple inheritance can generally be avoided by using single inheritance (one base class), and setting a metaclass if we want to support an additional API, since as we will see in the next subsection, a metaclass can be used to give the promise of an API without actually inheriting any methods or data attributes. An alternative is to use multiple inheritance with one concrete class and one or more abstract base classes for additional APIs. And another alternative is to use single inheritance and aggregate instances of other classes.

Nonetheless, in some cases, multiple inheritance can provide a very convenient solution. For example, suppose we want to create a new version of the Stack class from the previous subsection, but want the class to support loading and saving using a pickle. We might well want to add the loading and saving functionality to several classes, so we will implement it in a class of its own:

```
class LoadSave:

    def __init__(self, filename, *attribute_names):
        self.filename = filename
        self.__attribute_names = []
        for name in attribute_names:
            if name.startswith("__"):
                name = "_" + self.__class__.__name__ + name
            self.__attribute_names.append(name)

    def save(self):
        with open(self.filename, "wb") as fh:
            data = []
            for name in self.__attribute_names:
                data.append(getattr(self, name))
            pickle.dump(data, fh, pickle.HIGHEST_PROTOCOL)

    def load(self):
        with open(self.filename, "rb") as fh:
            data = pickle.load(fh)
            for name, value in zip(self.__attribute_names, data):
                setattr(self, name, value)
```

The class has two attributes: filename, which is public and can be changed at any time, and __attribute_names, which is fixed and can be set only when the instance is created. The save() method iterates over all the attribute names and creates a list called data that holds the value of each attribute to be saved; it then saves the data into a pickle. The with statement ensures that the file is closed if it was successfully opened, and any file or pickle exceptions are passed up to the caller. The load() method iterates over the attribute names and the corresponding data items that have been loaded and sets each attribute to its loaded value.

Here is the start of the FileStack class that multiply-inherits the Undo class from the previous subsection and this subsection's LoadSave class:

```
class FileStack(Undo, LoadSave):

    def __init__(self, filename):
        Undo.__init__(self)
        LoadSave.__init__(self, filename, "__stack")
        self.__stack = []

    def load(self):
        super().load()
        self.clear()
```

The rest of the class is just the same as the Stack class, so we have not reproduced it here. Instead of using super() in the __init__() method we must specify the base classes that we initialize since super() cannot guess our intentions. For the LoadSave initialization we pass the filename to use and also the names of the attributes we want saved; in this case just one, the private __stack. (We don't want to save the __undos; and nor could we in this case since it is a list of methods and is therefore unpicklable.)

The FileStack class has all the Undo methods, and also the LoadSave class's save() and load() methods. We have not reimplemented save() since it works fine, but for load() we must clear the undo stack after loading. This is necessary because we might do a save, then do various changes, and then a load. The load wipes out what went before, so any undos no longer make sense. The original Undo class did not have a clear() method, so we had to add one:

```
    def clear(self):          # In class Undo
        self.__undos = []
```

In the Stack.load() method we have used super() to call LoadSave.load() because there is no Undo.load() method to cause ambiguity. If both base classes had had a load() method, the one that would get called would depend on Python's method resolution order. We prefer to use super() only when there is no ambiguity, and to use the appropriate base name otherwise, so we never rely on the method resolution order. For the self.clear() call, again there is no ambiguity since only the Undo class has a clear() method, and we don't need to use super() since (unlike load()) FileStack does not have a clear() method.

What would happen if, later on, a clear() method was added to the FileStack class? It would break the load() method. One solution would be to call super().clear() inside load() instead of plain self.clear(). This would result in the first super-class's clear() method that was found being used. To protect against such problems we could make it a policy to use hard-coded base classes when using multiple inheritance (in this example, calling Undo.clear(self)). Or we could avoid multiple inheritance altogether and use aggregation, for example, inheriting the Undo class and creating a LoadSave class designed for aggregation.

What multiple inheritance has given us here is a mixture of two rather different classes, without the need to implement any of the undo or the loading and saving ourselves, relying instead on the functionality provided by the base classes. This can be very convenient and works especially well when the inherited classes have no overlapping APIs.

Metaclasses

A metaclass is to a class what a class is to an instance; that is, a metaclass is used to create classes, just as classes are used to create instances. And just as we can ask whether an instance belongs to a class by using isinstance(), we can ask whether a class object (such as dict, int, or SortedList) inherits another class using issubclass().

The simplest use of metaclasses is to make custom classes fit into Python's standard ABC hierarchy. For example, to make SortedList a collections. Sequence, instead of inheriting the ABC (as we showed earlier), we can simply register the SortedList as a collections.Sequence:

```
class SortedList:
    ...
collections.Sequence.register(SortedList)
```

After the class is defined normally, we register it with the collections.Sequence ABC. Registering a class like this makes it a *virtual subclass*.* A virtual subclass reports that it is a subclass of the class or classes it is registered with (e.g., using isinstance() or issubclass()), but does not inherit any data or methods from any of the classes it is registered with.

Registering a class like this provides a promise that the class provides the API of the classes it is registered with, but does not provide any guarantee that it will honor its promise. One use of metaclasses is to provide both a promise and a guarantee about a class's API. Another use is to modify a class in some way (like a class decorator does). And of course, metaclasses can be used for both purposes at the same time.

Suppose we want to create a group of classes that all provide load() and save() methods. We can do this by creating a class that when used as a metaclass, checks that these methods are present:

```
class LoadableSaveable(type):
```

---

*In Python terminology, *virtual* does not mean the same thing as it does in C++ terminology.

```
        def __init__(cls, classname, bases, dictionary):
            super().__init__(classname, bases, dictionary)
            assert hasattr(cls, "load") and \
                    isinstance(getattr(cls, "load"),
                            collections.Callable), ("class '" +
                    classname + "' must provide a load() method")
            assert hasattr(cls, "save") and \
                    isinstance(getattr(cls, "save"),
                            collections.Callable), ("class '" +
                    classname + "' must provide a save() method")
```

Classes that are to serve as metaclasses must inherit from the ultimate metaclass base class, type, or one of its subclasses.

Note that this class is called when *classes* that use it are instantiated, in all probability not very often, so the runtime cost is extremely low. Notice also that we must perform the checks after the class has been created (using the super() call), since only then will the class's attributes be available in the class itself. (The attributes are in the dictionary, but we prefer to work on the actual initialized class when doing checks.)

col-
lections
ABCs

373 ☞

We could have checked that the load and save attributes are callable using hasattr() to check that they have the __call__ attribute, but we prefer to check whether they are instances of collections.Callable instead. The collections.Callable abstract base class provides the promise (but no guarantee) that instances of its subclasses (or virtual subclasses) are callable.

Once the class has been created (using type.__new__() or a reimplementation of __new__()), the metaclass is initialized by calling its __init__() method. The arguments given to __init__() are cls, the class that's just been created; classname, the class's name (also available from cls.__name__); bases, a list of the class's base classes (excluding object, and therefore possibly empty); and dictionary that holds the attributes that became class attributes when the cls class was created, unless we intervened in a reimplementation of the metaclass's __new__() method.

Here are a couple of interactive examples that show what happens when we create classes using the LoadableSaveable metaclass:

```
>>> class Bad(metaclass=Meta.LoadableSaveable):
...     def some_method(self): pass
Traceback (most recent call last):
...
AssertionError: class 'Bad' must provide a load() method
```

The metaclass specifies that classes using it must provide certain methods, and when they don't, as in this case, an AssertionError exception is raised.

```
>>> class Good(metaclass=Meta.LoadableSaveable):
...     def load(self): pass
...     def save(self): pass
>>> g = Good()
```

The Good class honors the metaclass's API requirements, even if it doesn't meet our informal expectations of how it should behave.

We can also use metaclasses to change the classes that use them. If the change involves the name, base classes, or dictionary of the class being created (e.g., its slots), then we need to reimplement the metaclass's __new__() method; but for other changes, such as adding methods or data attributes, reimplemeting __init__() is sufficient, although this can also be done in __new__(). We will now look at a metaclass that modifies the classes it is used with purely through its __new__() method.

As an alternative to using the @property and @*name*.setter decorators, we could create classes where we use a simple naming convention to identify properties. For example, if a class has methods of the form get_*name()* and set_*name()*, we would expect the class to have a private _*name* property accessed using *instance.name* for getting and setting. This can all be done using a metaclass. Here is an example of a class that uses this convention:

```
class Product(metaclass=AutoSlotProperties):

    def __init__(self, barcode, description):
        self.__barcode = barcode
        self.description = description

    def get_barcode(self):
        return self.__barcode

    def get_description(self):
        return self.__description

    def set_description(self, description):
        if description is None or len(description) < 3:
            self.__description = "<Invalid Description>"
        else:
            self.__description = description
```

We must assign to the private __barcode property in the initializer since there is no setter for it; another consequence of this is that barcode is a read-only property. On the other hand, description is a readable/writable property. Here are some examples of interactive use:

```
>>> product = Product("101110110", "8mm Stapler")
```

```
>>> product.barcode, product.description
('101110110', '8mm Stapler')
>>> product.description = "8mm Stapler (long)"
>>> product.barcode, product.description
('101110110', '8mm Stapler (long)')
```

If we attempt to assign to the bar code an AttributeError exception is raised with the error text "can't set attribute".

If we look at the Product class's attributes (e.g., using dir()), the only public ones to be found are barcode and description. The get_*name()* and set_*name()* methods are no longer there—they have been replaced with the *name* property. And the variables holding the bar code and description are also private (_barcode and _description), and have been added as slots to minimize the class's memory use. This is all done by the AutoSlotProperties metaclass which is implemented in a single method:

```
class AutoSlotProperties(type):

    def __new__(mcl, classname, bases, dictionary):
        slots = list(dictionary.get("__slots__", []))
        for getter_name in [key for key in dictionary
                            if key.startswith("get_")]:
            if isinstance(dictionary[getter_name],
                    collections.Callable):
                name = getter_name[4:]
                slots.append("__" + name)
                getter = dictionary.pop(getter_name)
                setter_name = "set_" + name
                setter = dictionary.get(setter_name, None)
                if (setter is not None and
                        isinstance(setter, collections.Callable)):
                    del dictionary[setter_name]
                dictionary[name] = property(getter, setter)
        dictionary["__slots__"] = tuple(slots)
        return super().__new__(mcl, classname, bases, dictionary)
```

A metaclass's __new__() class method is called with the metaclass, and the class name, base classes, and dictionary of the class that is to be created. We must use a reimplementation of __new__() rather than __init__() because we want to change the dictionary before the class is created.

We begin by copying the __slots__ collection, creating an empty one if none is present, and making sure we have a list rather than a tuple so that we can modify it. For every attribute in the dictionary we pick out those that begin with "get_" and that are callable, that is, those that are getter methods. For each getter we add a private name to the slots to store the corresponding data;

for example, given getter get_name() we add __name to the slots. We then take a reference to the getter and delete it from the dictionary under its original name (this is done in one go using dict.pop()). We do the same for the setter if one is present, and then we create a new dictionary item with the desired property name as its key; for example, if the getter is get_name() the property name is *name*. We set the item's value to be a property with the getter and setter (which might be None) that we have found and removed from the dictionary.

At the end we replace the original slots with the modified slots list which has a private slot for each property that was added, and call on the base class to actually create the class, but using our modified dictionary. Note that in this case we must pass the metaclass explicitly in the super() call; this is always the case for calls to __new__() because it is a class method and not an instance method.

For this example we didn't need to write an __init__() method because we have done all the work in __new__(), but it is perfectly possible to reimplement both __new__() and __init__() doing different work in each.

If we consider hand-cranked drills to be analogous to aggregation and inheritance and electric drills the analog of decorators and descriptors, then metaclasses are at the laser beam end of the scale when it comes to power and versatility. Metaclasses are the last tool to reach for rather than the first, except perhaps for application framework developers who need to provide powerful facilities to their users without making the users go through hoops to realize the benefits on offer.

Functional-Style Programming

Functional-style programming is an approach to programming where computations are built up from combining functions that don't modify their arguments and that don't refer to or change the program's state, and that provide their results as return values. One strong appeal of this kind of programming is that (in theory), it is much easier to develop functions in isolation and to debug functional programs. This is helped by the fact that functional programs don't have state changes, so it is possible to reason about their functions mathematically.

Three concepts that are strongly associated with functional programming are *mapping*, *filtering*, and *reducing*. Mapping involves taking a function and an iterable and producing a new iterable (or a list) where each item is the result of calling the function on the corresponding item in the original iterable. This is supported by the built-in map() function, for example:

```
list(map(lambda x: x ** 2, [1, 2, 3, 4]))      # returns: [1, 4, 9, 16]
```

The map() function takes a function and an iterable as its arguments and for efficiency it returns an iterator rather than a list. Here we forced a list to be created to make the result clearer:

```
[x ** 2 for x in [1, 2, 3, 4]]          # returns: [1, 4, 9, 16]
```

A generator expression can often be used in place of map(). Here we have used a list comprehension to avoid the need to use list(); to make it a generator we just have to change the outer brackets to parentheses.

Filtering involves taking a function and an iterable and producing a new iterable where each item is from the original iterable—providing the function returns True when called on the item. The built-in filter() function supports this:

```
list(filter(lambda x: x > 0, [1, -2, 3, -4])) # returns: [1, 3]
```

The filter() function takes a function and an iterable as its arguments and returns an iterator.

```
[x for x in [1, -2, 3, -4] if x > 0]          # returns: [1, 3]
```

The filter() function can always be replaced with a generator expression or with a list comprehension.

Reducing involves taking a function and an iterable and producing a single result value. The way this works is that the function is called on the iterable's first two values, then on the computed result and the third value, then on the computed result and the fourth value, and so on, until all the values have been used. The functools module's functools.reduce() function supports this. Here are two lines of code that do the same computation:

```
functools.reduce(lambda x, y: x * y, [1, 2, 3, 4])  # returns: 24
functools.reduce(operator.mul, [1, 2, 3, 4])         # returns: 24
```

The operator module has functions for all of Python's operators specifically to make functional-style programming easier. Here, in the second line, we have used the operator.mul() function rather than having to create a multiplication function using lambda as we did in the first line.

Python also provides some built-in reducing functions: all(), which given an iterable, returns True if all the iterable's items return True when bool() is applied to them; any(), which returns True if any of the iterable's items is True; max(), which returns the largest item in the iterable; min(), which returns the smallest item in the iterable; and sum(), which returns the sum of the iterable's items.

Now that we have covered the key concepts, let us look at a few more examples. We will start with a couple of ways to get the total size of all the files in list files:

```
functools.reduce(operator.add, (os.path.getsize(x) for x in files))
functools.reduce(operator.add, map(os.path.getsize, files))
```

Using map() is often shorter than the equivalent list comprehension or generator expression except where there is a condition. We've used operator.add() as
the addition function instead of lambda x, y: x + y.

If we only wanted to count the .py file sizes we can filter out non-Python files.
Here are three ways to do this:

```
functools.reduce(operator.add, map(os.path.getsize,
                   filter(lambda x: x.endswith(".py"), files)))
functools.reduce(operator.add, map(os.path.getsize,
                   (x for x in files if x.endswith(".py"))))
functools.reduce(operator.add, (os.path.getsize(x)
                   for x in files if x.endswith(".py")))
```

Arguably, the second and third versions are better because they don't require
us to create a lambda function, but the choice between using generator expressions (or list comprehensions) and map() and filter() is most often purely a
matter of personal programming style.

Using map(), filter(), and functools.reduce() often leads to the elimination
of loops, as the examples we have seen illustrate. These functions are useful
when converting code written in a functional language, but in Python we
can usually replace map() with a list comprehension and filter() with a list
comprehension with a condition, and many cases of functools.reduce() can be
eliminated by using one of Python's built-in functional functions such as all(),
any(), max(), min(), and sum(). For example:

```
sum(os.path.getsize(x) for x in files if x.endswith(".py"))
```

This achieves the same thing as the previous three examples, but is much
more compact.

op-
erator.
attrget-
ter()

359 🖙

In addition to providing functions for Python's operators, the operator module
also provides the operator.attrgetter() and operator.itemgetter() functions,
the first of which we briefly met earlier in this chapter. Both of these return
functions which can then be called to extract the specified attributes or items.

Whereas slicing can be used to extract a sequence of part of a list, and slicing
with striding can be used to extract a sequence of parts (say, every third item
with L[::3]), operator.itemgetter() can be used to extract a sequence of arbitrary parts, for example, operator.itemgetter(4, 5, 6, 11, 18)(L). The function
returned by operator.itemgetter() does not have to be called immediately and
thrown away as we have done here; it could be kept and passed as the function
argument to map(), filter(), or functools.reduce(), or used in a dictionary, list,
or set comprehension.

When we want to sort we can specify a key function. This function can be any function, for example, a lambda function, a built-in function or method (such as str.lower()), or a function returned by operator.attrgetter(). For example, assuming list L holds objects with a priority attribute, we can sort the list into priority order like this: L.sort(key=operator.attrgetter("priority")).

In addition to the functools and operator modules already mentioned, the iter-tools module can also be useful for functional-style programming. For example, although it is possible to iterate over two or more lists by concatenating them, an alternative is to use iertools.chain() like this:

```
for value in itertools.chain(data_list1, data_list2, data_list3):
    total += value
```

The itertools.chain() function returns an iterator that gives successive values from the first sequence it is given, then successive values from the second sequence, and so on until all the values from all the sequences are used. The itertools module has many other functions and its documentation gives many small yet useful examples and is well worth reading.

Partial Function Application

Partial function application is the creation of a function from an existing function and some arguments to produce a new function that does what the original function did, but with some arguments fixed so that callers don't have to pass them. Here's a very simple example:

```
enumerate1 = functools.partial(enumerate, start=1)
for lino, line in enumerate1(lines):
    process_line(i, line)
```

The first line creates a new function, enumerate1(), that wraps the given function (enumerate()) and a keyword argument (start=1) so that when enumerate1() is called it calls the original function with the fixed argument—and with any other arguments that are given at the time it is called, in this case lines. Here we have used the enumerate1() function to provide conventional line counting starting from line 1.

Using partial function application can simplify our code, especially when we want to call the same functions with the same arguments again and again. For example, instead of specifying the mode and encoding arguments every time we call open() to process UTF-8 encoded text files, we could create a couple of functions with these arguments fixed:

```
reader = functools.partial(open, mode="rt", encoding="utf8")
writer = functools.partial(open, mode="wt", encoding="utf8")
```

Now we can open text files for reading by calling reader(*filename*) and for writing by calling writer(*filename*).

One very common use case for partial function application is in GUI (Graphical User Interface) programming (covered in Chapter 13), where it is often convenient to have one particular function called when any one of a set of buttons is pressed. For example:

```
loadButton = tkinter.Button(frame, text="Load",
                        command=functools.partial(doAction, "load"))
saveButton = tkinter.Button(frame, text="Save",
                        command=functools.partial(doAction, "save"))
```

This example uses the tkinter GUI library that comes as standard with Python. The tkinter.Button class is used for buttons—here we have created two, both contained inside the same frame, and each with a text that indicates its purpose. Each button's command argument is set to the function that tkinter must call when the button is pressed, in this case the doAction() function. We have used partial function application to ensure that the first argument given to the doAction() function is a string that indicates which button called it so that doAction() is able to decide what action to perform.

Example: Valid.py

Descriptors

362 ☜

In this section we combine descriptors with class decorators to create a powerful mechanism for creating validated attributes.

Class decorators

367 ☜

Up to now if we wanted to ensure that an attribute was set to only a valid value we have relied on properties (or used getter and setter methods). The disadvantage of such approaches is that we must add validating code for every attribute in every class that needs it. What would be much more convenient and easier to maintain, is if we could add attributes to classes with the necessary validation built in. Here is an example of the syntax we would like to use:

```
@valid_string("name", empty_allowed=False)
@valid_string("productid", empty_allowed=False,
            regex=re.compile(r"[A-Z]{3}\d{4}"))
@valid_string("category", empty_allowed=False, acceptable=
        frozenset(["Consumables", "Hardware", "Software", "Media"]))
@valid_number("price", minimum=0, maximum=1e6)
@valid_number("quantity", minimum=1, maximum=1000)
class StockItem:

    def __init__(self, name, productid, category, price, quantity):
        self.name = name
        self.productid = productid
```

```
        self.category = category
        self.price = price
        self.quantity = quantity
```

The StockItem class's attributes are all validated. For example, the productid attribute can be set only to a nonempty string that starts with three uppercase letters and ends with four digits, the category attribute can be set only to a nonempty string that is one of the specified values, and the quantity attribute can be set only to a number between 1 and 1000 inclusive. If we try to set an invalid value an exception is raised.

Regular expressions ☞ 445

The validation is achieved by combining class decorators with descriptors. As we noted earlier, class decorators can take only a single argument—the class they are to decorate. So here we have used the technique shown when we first discussed class decorators, and have the valid_string() and valid_number() functions take whatever arguments we want, and then return a decorator, which in turn takes the class and returns a modified version of the class.

Class decorators 367 ☞

Let's now look at the valid_string() function:

```
def valid_string(attr_name, empty_allowed=True, regex=None,
                 acceptable=None):
    def decorator(cls):
        name = "__" + attr_name
        def getter(self):
            return getattr(self, name)
        def setter(self, value):
            assert isinstance(value, str), (attr_name +
                                    " must be a string")
            if not empty_allowed and not value:
                raise ValueError("{0} may not be empty".format(
                        attr_name))
            if ((acceptable is not None and value not in acceptable) or
                (regex is not None and not regex.match(value))):
                raise ValueError("{0} cannot be set to {1}".format(
                        attr_name, value))
            setattr(self, name, value)
        setattr(cls, attr_name, GenericDescriptor(getter, setter))
        return cls
    return decorator
```

The function starts by creating a class decorator function which takes a class as its sole argument. The decorator adds two attributes to the class it decorates: a private data attribute and a descriptor. For example, when the valid_string() function is called with the name "productid", the StockItem class gains the attribute __productid which holds the product ID's value, and the descriptor productid attribute which is used to access the value. For example, if we create an item using item = StockItem("TV", "TVA4312", "Electrical", 500, 1), we can get the product ID using item.productid and set it using, for example, item.productid = "TVB2100".

The getter function created by the decorator simply uses the global getattr() function to return the value of the private data attribute. The setter function incorporates the validation, and at the end, uses setattr() to set the private data attribute to the new (and valid) value. In fact, the private data attribute is only created the first time it is set.

Once the getter and setter functions have been created we use setattr() once again, this time to create a new class attribute with the given name (e.g., productid), and with its value set to be a descriptor of type GenericDescriptor. At the end, the decorator function returns the modified class, and the valid_string() function returns the decorator function.

The valid_number() function is structurally identical to the valid_string() function, only differing in the arguments it accepts and in the validation code in the setter, so we won't show it here. (The complete source code is in the Valid.py module.)

The last thing we need to cover is the GenericDescriptor, and that turns out to be the easiest part:

```python
class GenericDescriptor:

    def __init__(self, getter, setter):
        self.getter = getter
        self.setter = setter

    def __get__(self, instance, owner=None):
        if instance is None:
            return self
        return self.getter(instance)

    def __set__(self, instance, value):
        return self.setter(instance, value)
```

The descriptor is used to hold the getter and setter functions for each attribute and simply passes on the work of getting and setting to those functions.

Summary

In this chapter we learned a lot more about Python's support for procedural and object-oriented programming, and got a taste of Python's support for functional-style programming.

In the first section we learned how to create generator expressions, and covered generator functions in more depth. We also learned how to dynamically import modules and how to access functionality from such modules, as well as how to dynamically execute code. In this section we saw examples of how to create and use recursive functions and nonlocal variables. We also learned how to create custom function and method decorators, and how to write and make use of function annotations.

In the chapter's second section we studied a variety of different and more advanced aspects of object-oriented programming. First we learned more about attribute access, for example, using the __getattr__() special method. Then we learned about functors and saw how we could use them to provide functions with state—something that can also be achieved by adding properties to functions or using closures, both covered in this chapter. We learned how to use the with statement with context managers and how to create custom context managers. Since Python's file objects are also context managers, from now on we will do our file handling using try with ... except structures that ensure that opened files are closed without the need for finally blocks.

The second section continued with coverage of more advanced object-oriented features, starting with descriptors. These can be used in a wide variety of ways and are the technology that underlies many of Python's standard decorators such as @property and @classmethod. We learned how to create custom descriptors and saw three very different examples of their use. Next we studied class decorators and saw how we could modify a class in much the same way that a function decorator can modify a function.

In the last three subsections of the second section we learned about Python's support for ABCs (abstract base classes), multiple inheritance, and metaclasses. We learned how to make our own classes fit in with Python's standard ABCs and how to create our own ABCs. We also saw how to use multiple inheritance to unify the features of different classes together in a single class. And from the coverage of metaclasses we learned how to intervene when a class (as opposed to an instance of a class) is created and initialized.

The penultimate section introduced some of the functions and modules that Python provides to support functional-style programming. We learned how to use the common functional idioms of mapping, filtering, and reducing. We also learned how to create partial functions.

And the last section showed how to combine class decorators with descriptors to provide a powerful and flexible mechanism for creating validated attributes.

This chapter completes our coverage of the Python language itself. Not every feature of the language has been covered here and in the previous chapters, but those that have not are obscure and rarely used. None of the subsequent chapters introduces new language features, although all of them make use of modules from the standard library that have not been covered before, and some of them take techniques shown in this and earlier chapters further than we have seen so far. Furthermore, the programs shown in the following chapters have none of the constraints that have applied previously (i.e., to only use aspects of the language that had been covered up to the point they were introduced), so they are the book's most idiomatic examples.

Exercises

None of the three exercises described here requires writing a lot of code—and none of them are easy!

1. Copy the magic-numbers.py program and delete its get_function() functions, and all but one of its load_modules() functions. Add a GetFunction functor class that has two caches, one to hold functions that have been found and one to hold functions that could not be found (to avoid repeatedly looking for a function in a module that does not have the function). The only modifications to main() are to add get_function = GetFunction() before the loop, and to use a with statement to avoid the need for a finally block. Also, check that the module functions are callable using collections.Callable rather than using hasattr(). The class can be written in about twenty lines. A solution is in magic-numbers_ans.py.

2. Create a new module file and in it define three functions: is_ascii() that returns True if all the characters in the given string have code points less than 127; is_ascii_punctuation() that returns True if all the characters are in the string.punctuation string; and is_ascii_printable() that returns True if all the characters are in the string.printable string. The last two are structurally the same. Each function should be created using lambda and can be done in one or two lines using functional-style code. Be sure to add a docstring for each one with doctests and to make the module run the doctests. The functions require only three to five lines for all three of them, with the whole module fewer than 25 lines including doctests. A solution is given in Ascii.py.

3. Create a new module file and in it define the Atomic context manager class. This class should work like the AtomicList class shown in this chapter, except that instead of working only with lists it should work with any mutable collection type. The __init__() method should check the suitability of the container, and instead of storing a shallow/deep copy flag it should assign a suitable function to the self.copy attribute depending on the flag and call the copy function in the __enter__() method. The __exit__() method is slightly more involved because replacing the contents of lists is different than for sets and dictionaries—and we cannot use assignment because that would not affect the original container. The class itself can be written in about thirty lines, although you should also include doctests.

A solution is given in `Atomic.py` which is about one hundred fifty lines including doctests.

9

Processes and Threading

With the advent of multicore processors as the norm rather than the exception, it is more tempting and more practical than ever before to want to spread the processing load so as to get the most out of all the available cores. There are two main approaches to spreading the workload. One is to use multiple processes and the other is to use multiple threads. This chapter shows how to use both approaches.

Using multiple processes, that is, running separate programs, has the advantage that each process runs independently. This leaves all the burden of handling concurrency to the underlying operating system. The disadvantage is that communication and data sharing between the invoking program and the separate processes it invokes can be inconvenient. On Unix systems this can be solved by using the exec and fork paradigm, but for cross-platform programs other solutions must be used. The simplest, and the one shown here, is for the invoking program to feed data to the processes it runs and leave them to produce their output independently. A more flexible approach that greatly simplifies two-way communication is to use networking. Of course, in many situations such communication isn't needed—we just need to run one or more other programs from one orchestrating program.

An alternative to handing off work to independent processes is to create a threaded program that distributes work to independent threads of execution. This has the advantage that we can communicate simply by sharing data (providing we ensure that shared data is accessed only by one thread at a time), but leaves the burden of managing concurrency squarely with the programmer. Python provides good support for creating threaded programs, minimizing the work that we must do. Nonetheless, multithreaded programs are inherently more complex than single-threaded programs and require much more care in their creation and maintenance.

In this chapter's first section we will create two small programs. The first program is invoked by the user and the second program is invoked by the first program, with the second program invoked once for each separate process that is required. In the second section we will begin by giving a bare-bones introduction to threaded programming. Then we will create a threaded program that has the same functionality as the two programs from the first section combined so as to provide a contrast between the multiple processes and the multiple threads approaches. And then we will review another threaded program, more sophisticated than the first, that both hands off work and gathers together all the results.

Delegating Work to Processes

In some situations we already have programs that have the functionality we need but we want to automate their use. We can do this by using Python's subprocess module which provides facilities for running other programs, passing any command-line options we want, and if desired, communicating with them using pipes. We saw one very simple example of this in Chapter 5 when we used the subprocess.call() function to clear the console in a platform-specific way. But we can also use these facilities to create pairs of "parent–child" programs, where the parent program is run by the user and this in turn runs as many instances of the child program as necessary, each with different work to do. It is this approach that we will cover in this section.

In Chapter 3 we showed a very simple program, grepword.py, that searches for a word specified on the command line in the files listed after the word. In this section we will develop a more sophisticated version that can recurse into subdirectories to find files to read and that can delegate the work to as many separate child processes as we like. The output is just a list of filenames (with paths) for those files that contain the specified search word.

The parent program is grepword-p.py and the child program is grepword-p-child.py. The relationship between the two programs when they are being run is shown schematically in Figure 9.1.

The heart of grepword-p.py is encapsulated by its main() function, which we will look at in three parts:

```
def main():
    child = os.path.join(os.path.dirname(__file__),
                         "grepword-p-child.py")
    opts, word, args = parse_options()
    filelist = get_files(args, opts.recurse)
    files_per_process = len(filelist) // opts.count
    start, end = 0, files_per_process + (len(filelist) % opts.count)
    number = 1
```

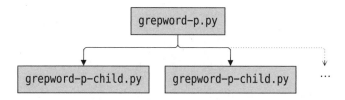

Figure 9.1 *Parent and child programs*

We begin by getting the name of the child program. Then we get the user's command-line options. The parse_options() function uses the optparse module. It returns the opts named tuple which indicates whether the program should recurse into subdirectories and the count of how many processes to use—the default is 7, and the program has an arbitrarily chosen maximum of 20. It also returns the word to search for and the list of names (filenames and directory names) given on the command line. The get_files() function returns a list of files to be read.

get_files()
333 ☞

Once we have the information necessary to perform the task we calculate how many files must be given to each process to work on. The start and end variables are used to specify the slice of the filelist that will be given to the next child process to work on. Usually the number of files won't be an exact multiple of the number of processes, so we increase the number of files the first process is given by the remainder. The number variable is used purely for debugging so that we can see which process produced each line of output.

```
pipes = []
while start < len(filelist):
    command = [sys.executable, child]
    if opts.debug:
        command.append(str(number))
    pipe = subprocess.Popen(command, stdin=subprocess.PIPE)
    pipes.append(pipe)
    pipe.stdin.write(word.encode("utf8") + b"\n")
    for filename in filelist[start:end]:
        pipe.stdin.write(filename.encode("utf8") + b"\n")
    pipe.stdin.close()
    number += 1
    start, end = end, end + files_per_process
```

For each start:end slice of the filelist we create a command list consisting of the Python interpreter (conveniently available in sys.executable), the child program we want Python to execute, and the command-line options—in this case just the child number if we are debugging. If the child program has a suitable shebang line or file association we could list it first and not bother including the Python interpreter, but we prefer this approach because it ensures that the child program uses the same Python interpreter as the parent program.

Once we have the command ready we create a subprocess.Popen object, specifying the command to execute (as a list of strings), and in this case requesting that we can write to the process's standard input. (It is also possible to read a process's standard output by setting a similar keyword argument.) We then write the search word followed by a newline and then every file in the relevant slice of the file list. The subprocess module reads and writes bytes, not strings, so we must encode the strings we write (and decode the bytes we read) using a suitable encoding, and for this we have chosen to use UTF-8. Once we have finished writing the list of files to the child process we close its standard input and move on.

It is not strictly necessary to keep a reference to each process (the pipe variable gets rebound to a new subprocess.Popen object each time through the loop), since each process runs independently, but we add each one to a list so that we can make them interruptible. Also, we don't gather the results together, but instead we let each process write its results to the console in its own time. This means that the output from different processes could be interleaved. (You will get the chance to avoid interleaving in the exercises.)

```
while pipes:
    pipe = pipes.pop()
    pipe.wait()
```

Once all the processes have started we wait for each child process to finish. This is not essential, but on Unix-like systems it ensures that we are returned to the console prompt when all the processes are done (otherwise, we must press Enter when they are all finished). Another benefit of waiting is that if we interrupt the program (e.g., by pressing Ctrl+C), all the processes that are still running will be interrupted and will terminate with an uncaught KeyboardInterrupt exception—if we did not wait the main program would finish (and therefore not be interruptible), and the child processes would continue (unless killed by a kill program or a task manager).

Apart from the comments and imports, here is the complete grepword-p-child.py program, split into two parts:

```
BLOCK_SIZE = 8000

number = "{0}: ".format(sys.argv[1]) if len(sys.argv) == 2 else ""
word = sys.stdin.readline().rstrip()
```

The program begins by setting the number string to the given number or to an empty string if we are not debugging. It then reads the first line since this contains the search word. This line and all the others are read as strings.

```
    for filename in sys.stdin:
        filename = filename.rstrip()
        previous = ""
        try:
            with open(filename, "rb") as fh:
                while True:
                    current = fh.read(BLOCK_SIZE)
                    if not current:
                        break
                    current = current.decode("utf8", "ignore")
                    if (word in current or
                        word in previous[-len(word):] +
                                current[:len(word)]):
                        print("{0}{1}".format(number, filename))
                        break
                    if len(current) != BLOCK_SIZE:
                        break
                    previous = current
        except EnvironmentError as err:
            print("{0}{1}".format(number, err))
```

All the lines after the first are filenames (with paths). For each one we open the relevant file, read it, and print its name if it contains the search word. It is possible that some of the files might be very large and this could be a problem, especially if there are 20 child processes running concurrently, all reading big files. We handle this by reading each file in blocks, keeping the previous block read to ensure that we don't miss cases when the only occurrence of the search word happens to fall across two blocks. Another benefit of reading in blocks is that if the search word appears early in the file we can finish with the file without having read everything, since all we care about is whether the word is in the file, not where it appears within the file.

The files are read in binary mode, so we must convert each block to a string before we can search it, since the search word is a string. We have assumed that all the files use the UTF-8 encoding, but this is most likely wrong in some cases. A more sophisticated program would try to determine the actual encoding and then close and reopen the file using the correct encoding. As we noted in Chapter 2, at least two Python packages for automatically detecting a file's encoding are available from the Python Package Index, `pypi.python.org/pypi`. (It might be tempting to decode the search word into a `bytes` object and compare `bytes` with `bytes`, but that approach is not reliable since some characters have more than one valid UTF-8 representation.)

Charac-
ter
encod-
ings

85 ☞

The `subprocess` module offers a lot more functionality than we have needed to use here, including the ability to provide equivalents to shell backquotes and shell pipelines, and to the `os.system()` and spawn functions.

In the next section we will see a threaded version of the grepword-p.py program so that we can compare it with the parent–child processes one. We will also look at a more sophisticated threaded program that delegates work and then gathers the results together to have more control over how they are output.

Delegating Work to Threads

Setting up two or more separate threads of execution in Python is quite straightforward. The complexity arises when we want separate threads to share data. Imagine that we have two threads sharing a list. One thread might start iterating over the list using for x in L and then somewhere in the middle another thread might delete some items in the list. At best this will lead to obscure crashes, at worst to incorrect results.

One common solution is to use some kind of locking mechanism. For example, one thread might acquire a lock and *then* start iterating over the list; any other thread will then be blocked by the lock. In fact, things are not quite as clean as this. The relationship between a lock and the data it is locking exists purely in our imagination. If one thread acquires a lock and a second thread tries to acquire the same lock, the second thread will be blocked until the first releases the lock. By putting access to shared data within the scope of acquired locks we can ensure that the shared data is accessed by only one thread at a time, even though the protection is indirect.

One problem with locking is the risk of deadlock. Suppose *thread #1* acquires lock *A* so that it can access shared data *a* and then within the scope of lock *A* tries to acquire lock *B* so that it can access shared data *b*—but it cannot acquire lock *B* because meanwhile, *thread #2* has acquired lock *B* so that it can access *b*, and is itself now trying to acquire lock *A* so that it can access *a*. So *thread #1* holds lock *A* and is trying to acquire lock *B*, while *thread #2* holds lock *B* and is trying to acquire lock *A*. As a result, both threads are blocked, so the program is deadlocked, as Figure 9.2 illustrates.

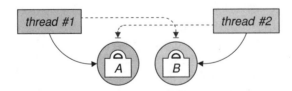

Figure 9.2 *Deadlock: two or more blocked threads trying to acquire each other's locks*

Although it is easy to visualize this particular deadlock, in practice deadlocks can be difficult to spot because they are not always so obvious. Some threading libraries are able to help with warnings about potential deadlocks, but it requires human care and attention to avoid them.

One simple yet effective way to avoid deadlocks is to have a policy that defines the order in which locks should be acquired. For example, if we had the policy that lock *A* must always be acquired before lock *B*, and we wanted to acquire lock *B*, the policy requires us to first acquire lock *A*. This would ensure that the deadlock described here would not occur—since both threads would begin by trying to acquire *A* and the first one that did would then go on to lock *B*—unless someone forgets to follow the policy.

Another problem with locking is that if multiple threads are waiting to acquire a lock, they are blocked and are not doing any useful work. We can mitigate this to a small extent with subtle changes to our coding style to minimize the amount of work we do within the context of a lock.

Every Python program has at least one thread, the main thread. To create multiple threads we must import the threading module and use that to create as many additional threads as we want. There are two ways to create threads: We can call threading.Thread() and pass it a callable object, or we can subclass the threading.Thread class—both approaches are shown in this chapter. Subclassing is the most flexible approach and is quite straightforward. Subclasses can reimplement __init__() (in which case they *must* call the base class implementation), and they *must* reimplement run()—it is in this method that the thread's work is done. The run() method must *never* be called by our code—threads are started by calling the start() method and that will call run() when it is ready. No other threading.Thread methods may be reimplemented, although adding additional methods is fine.

Example: A Threaded Find Word Program

In this subsection we will review the code for the grepword-t.py program. This program does the same job as grepword-p.py, only it delegates the work to multiple threads rather than to multiple processes. It is illustrated schematically in Figure 9.3.

One particularly interesting feature of the program is that it does not appear to use any locks at all. This is possible because the only shared data is a list of files, and for these we use the queue.Queue class. What makes queue.Queue special is that it handles all the locking itself internally, so whenever we access it to add or remove items, we can rely on the queue itself to *serialize* accesses. In the context of threading, serializing access to data means ensuring that only one thread at a time has access to the data. Another benefit of using queue.Queue is that we don't have to share out the work ourselves; we simply add items of work to the queue and leave the worker threads to pick up work whenever they are ready.

The queue.Queue class works on a first in, first out (FIFO) basis; the queue module also provides queue.LifoQueue for last in, first out (LIFO) access, and

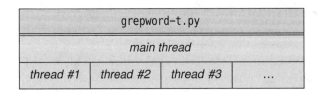

Figure 9.3 *A multithreaded program*

queue.PriorityQueue which is given tuples such as the 2-tuple (priority, item), with items with the lowest priority numbers being processed first. All the queues can be created with a maximum size set; if the maximum size is reached the queue will block further attempts to add items until items have been removed.

We will look at the grepword-t.py program in three parts, starting with the complete main() function:

```
def main():
    opts, word, args = parse_options()
    filelist = get_files(args, opts.recurse)
    work_queue = queue.Queue()
    for i in range(opts.count):
        number = "{0}: ".format(i + 1) if opts.debug else ""
        worker = Worker(work_queue, word, number)
        worker.daemon = True
        worker.start()
    for filename in filelist:
        work_queue.put(filename)
    work_queue.join()
```

Getting the user's options and the file list are the same as before. Once we have the necessary information we create a queue.Queue and then loop as many times as there are threads to be created; the default is 7. For each thread we prepare a number string for debugging (an empty string if we are not debugging) and then we create a Worker (a threading.Thread subclass) instance—we'll come back to setting the daemon property in a moment. Next we start off the thread, although at this point it has no work to do because the work queue is empty, so the thread will immediately be blocked trying to get some work.

With all the threads created and ready for work we iterate over all the files, adding each one to the work queue. As soon as the first file is added one of the threads could get it and start on it, and so on until all the threads have a file to work on. As soon as a thread finishes working on a file it can get another one, until all the files are processed.

Notice that this differs from grepword-p.py where we had to allocate slices of the file list to each child process, and the child processes were started and given their lists sequentially. Using threads is potentially more efficient in cases like this. For example, if the first five files are very large and the rest are small, because each thread takes on one job at a time each large file will be processed by a separate thread, nicely spreading the work. But with the multiple processes approach we took in the grepword-p.py program, all the large files would be given to the first process and the small files given to the others, so the first process would end up doing most of the work while the others might all finish quickly without having done much at all.

The program will not terminate while it has any threads running. This is a problem because once the worker threads have done their work, although they have finished they are technically still running. The solution is to turn the threads into daemons. The effect of this is that the program will terminate as soon as the program has no nondaemon threads running. The main thread is not a daemon, so once the main thread finishes, the program will cleanly terminate each daemon thread and then terminate itself. Of course, this can now create the opposite problem—once the threads are up and running we must ensure that the main thread does not finish until all the work is done. This is achieved by calling queue.Queue.join()—this method blocks until the queue is empty.

Here is the start of the Worker class:

```
class Worker(threading.Thread):

    def __init__(self, work_queue, word, number):
        super().__init__()
        self.work_queue = work_queue
        self.word = word
        self.number = number


    def run(self):
        while True:
            try:
                filename = self.work_queue.get()
                self.process(filename)
            finally:
                self.work_queue.task_done()
```

The __init__() method must call the base class __init__(). The work queue is the same queue.Queue shared by all the threads.

We have made the run() method an infinite loop. This is common for daemon threads, and makes sense here because we don't know how many files the thread must process. At each iteration we call queue.Queue.get() to get the next file to work on. This call will block if the queue is empty, and does not have to be protected by a lock because queue.Queue handles that automatically for us. Once we have a file we process it, and afterward we must tell the queue that we have done that particular job—calling queue.Queue.task_done() is essential to the correct working of queue.Queue.join().

We have not shown the process() function, because apart from the def line, the code is the same as the code used in grepword-p-child.py from the previous = "" line to the end (page 398).

One final point to note is that included with the book's examples is grepword-m.py, a program that is almost identical to the grepword-t.py program reviewed here, but which uses the multiprocessing module rather than the threading module. The code has just three differences: first, we import multiprocessing instead of queue and threading; second, the Worker class inherits multiprocessing.Process instead of threading.Thread; and third, the work queue is a multiprocessing.JoinableQueue instead of a queue.Queue.

The multiprocessing module provides thread-like functionality using forking on systems that support it (Unix), and child processes on those that don't (Windows), so locking mechanisms are not always required, and the processes will run on whatever processor cores the operating system has available. The package provides several ways of passing data between processes, including using a queue that can be used to provide work for processes just like queue.Queue can be used to provide work for threads.

The chief benefit of the multiprocessing version is that it can potentially run faster on multicore machines than the threaded version since it can run its processes on as many cores as are available. Compare this with the standard Python interpreter (written in C, sometimes called CPython) which has a GIL (Global Interpreter Lock) that means that only one thread can execute Python code at any one time. This restriction is an implementation detail and does not necessarily apply to other Python intepreters such as Jython.*

Example: A Threaded Find Duplicate Files Program

The second threading example has a similar structure to the first, but is more sophisticated in several ways. It uses two queues, one for work and one for results, and has a separate results processing thread to output results as soon as they are available. It also shows both a threading.Thread subclass and calling threading.Thread() with a function, and also uses a lock to serialize access to shared data (a dict).

The findduplicates-t.py program is a more advanced version of the finddup.py program from Chapter 5. It iterates over all the files in the current directory (or the specified path), recursively going into subdirectories. It compares

---

*For a brief explanation of why CPython uses a GIL see www.python.org/doc/faq/library/#can-t-we-get-rid-of-the-global-interpreter-lock and docs.python.org/api/threads.html.

the lengths of all the files with the same name (just like finddup.py), and for
those files that have the same name and the same size it then uses the MD5
(Message Digest) algorithm to check whether the files are the same, reporting
any that are.

We will start by looking at the main() function, split into four parts.

```
def main():
    opts, path = parse_options()
    data = collections.defaultdict(list)
    for root, dirs, files in os.walk(path):
        for filename in files:
            fullname = os.path.join(root, filename)
            try:
                key = (os.path.getsize(fullname), filename)
            except EnvironmentError:
                continue
            if key[0] == 0:
                continue
            data[key].append(fullname)
```

Each key of the data default dictionary is a 2-tuple of (size, filename), where
the filename does not include the path, and each value is a list of filenames
(which do include their paths). Any items whose value list has more than one
filename potentially has duplicates. The dictionary is populated by iterating
over all the files in the given path, but skipping any files we cannot get the size
of (perhaps due to permissions problems, or because they are not normal files),
and any that are of 0 size (since all zero length files are the same).

```
    work_queue = queue.PriorityQueue()
    results_queue = queue.Queue()
    md5_from_filename = {}
    for i in range(opts.count):
        number = "{0}: ".format(i + 1) if opts.debug else ""
        worker = Worker(work_queue, md5_from_filename, results_queue,
                        number)
        worker.daemon = True
        worker.start()
```

With all the data in place we are ready to create the worker threads. We begin
by creating a work queue and a results queue. The work queue is a priority
queue, so it will always return the lowest-priority items (in our case the
smallest files) first. We also create a dictionary where each key is a filename
(including its path) and where each value is the file's MD5 digest value. The
purpose of the dictionary is to ensure that we never compute the MD5 of the
same file more than once (since the computation is expensive).

With the shared data collections in place we loop as many times as there are threads to create (by default, seven times). The Worker subclass is similar to the one we created before, only this time we pass both queues and the MD5 dictionary. As before, we start each worker straight away and each will be blocked until a work item becomes available.

```
results_thread = threading.Thread(
                        target=lambda: print_results(results_queue))
results_thread.daemon = True
results_thread.start()
```

Rather than creating a threading.Thread subclass to process the results we have created a function and we pass that to threading.Thread(). The return value is a custom thread that will call the given function once the thread is started. We pass the results queue (which is, of course, empty), so the thread will block immediately.

At this point we have created all the worker threads and the results thread and they are all blocked waiting for work.

```
for size, filename in sorted(data):
    names = data[size, filename]
    if len(names) > 1:
        work_queue.put((size, names))
work_queue.join()
results_queue.join()
```

We now iterate over the data, and for each (size, filename) 2-tuple that has a list of two or more potentially duplicate files, we add the size and the filenames with paths as an item of work to the work queue. Since the queue is a class from the queue module we don't have to worry about locking.

Finally we join the work queue and results queue to block until they are empty. This ensures that the program runs until all the work is done and all the results have been output, and then terminates cleanly.

```
def print_results(results_queue):
    while True:
        try:
            results = results_queue.get()
            if results:
                print(results)
        finally:
            results_queue.task_done()
```

This function is passed as an argument to threading.Thread() and is called when the thread it is given to is started. It has an infinite loop because it is to be used as a daemon thread. All it does is get results (a multiline string), and if the string is nonempty, it prints it for as long as results are available.

The beginning of the Worker class is similar to what we had before:

```
class Worker(threading.Thread):

    Md5_lock = threading.Lock()

    def __init__(self, work_queue, md5_from_filename, results_queue,
                 number):
        super().__init__()
        self.work_queue = work_queue
        self.md5_from_filename = md5_from_filename
        self.results_queue = results_queue
        self.number = number

    def run(self):
        while True:
            try:
                size, names = self.work_queue.get()
                self.process(size, names)
            finally:
                self.work_queue.task_done()
```

The differences are that we have more shared data to keep track of and we call our custom process() function with different arguments. We don't have to worry about the queues since they ensure that accesses are serialized, but for other data items, in this case the md5_from_filename dictionary, we must handle the serialization ourselves by providing a lock. We have made the lock a class attribute because we want every Worker instance to use the same lock so that if one instance holds the lock, all the other instances are blocked if they try to acquire it.

We will review the process() function in two parts.

```
    def process(self, size, filenames):
        md5s = collections.defaultdict(set)
        for filename in filenames:
            with self.Md5_lock:
                md5 = self.md5_from_filename.get(filename, None)
            if md5 is not None:
                md5s[md5].add(filename)
            else:
                try:
                    md5 = hashlib.md5()
                    with open(filename, "rb") as fh:
                        md5.update(fh.read())
```

```
            md5 = md5.digest()
            md5s[md5].add(filename)
            with self.Md5_lock:
                self.md5_from_filename[filename] = md5
        except EnvironmentError:
            continue
```

We start out with an empty default dictionary where each key is to be an MD5 digest value and where each value is to be a set of the filenames of the files that have the corresponding MD5 value. We then iterate over all the files, and for each one we retrieve its MD5 if we have already calculated it, and calculate it otherwise.

Context
man-
agers

359 ☞

Whether we access the md5_from_filename dictionary to read it or to write to it, we put the access in the context of a lock. Instances of the threading.Lock() class are context managers that acquire the lock on entry and release the lock on exit. The with statements will block if another thread has the Md5_lock, until the lock is released. For the first with statement when we acquire the lock we get the MD5 from the dictionary (or None if it isn't there). If the MD5 is None we must compute it, in which case we store it in the md5_from_filename dictionary to avoid performing the computation more than once per file.

Notice that at all times we try to minimize the amount of work done within the scope of a lock to keep blocking to a minimum—in this case just one dictionary access each time.

GIL

404 ☞

Strictly speaking, we do not need to use a lock at all if we are using CPython, since the GIL effectively synchronizes dictionary accesses for us. However, we have chosen to program without relying on the GIL implementation detail, and so we use an explicit lock.

```
    for filenames in md5s.values():
        if len(filenames) == 1:
            continue
        self.results_queue.put("{0}Duplicate files ({1:n} bytes):"
                            "\n\t{2}".format(self.number, size,
                                "\n\t".join(sorted(filenames)))) 
```

At the end we loop over the local md5s default dictionary, and for each set of names that contains more than one name we add a multiline string to the results queue. The string contains the worker thread number (an empty string by default), the size of the file in bytes, and all the duplicate filenames. We don't need to use a lock to access the results queue since it is a queue.Queue which will automatically handle the locking behind the scenes.

The queue module's classes greatly simplify threaded applications, and when we need to use explicit locks the threading module offers many options. Here we used the simplest, threading.Lock, but others are available, including threading.RLock (a lock that can be acquired again by the thread that already holds it), threading.Semaphore (a lock that can be used to protect a specific number of resources), and threading.Condition that provides a wait condition.

Using multiple threads can often lead to cleaner solutions than using the subprocess module, but unfortunately, threaded Python programs do not necessarily achieve the best possible performance compared with using multiple processes. As noted earlier, the problem afflicts the standard implementation of Python, since the CPython interpreter can execute Python code on only one processor at a time, even when using multiple threads.

GIL
404 ☜

One package that tries to solve this problem is the multiprocessing module, and as we noted earlier, the grepword-m.py program is a multiprocessing version of the grepword-t.py program, with only three lines that are different. A similar transformation could be applied to the findduplicates-t.py program reviewed here, but in practice this is not recommended. Although the multiprocessing module offers an API (Application Programming Interface) that closely matches the threading module's API to ease conversion, the two APIs are not the same and have different trade-offs. Also, performing a mechanistic conversion from threading to multiprocessing is likely to be successful only on small, simple programs like grepword-t.py; it is too crude an approach to use for the findduplicates-t.py program, and in general it is best to design programs from the ground up with multiprocessing in mind. (The program findduplicates-m.py is provided with the book's examples; it does the same job as findduplicates-t.py but works in a very different way and uses the multiprocessing module.)

Another solution being developed is a threading-friendly version of the CPython interpreter; see www.code.google.com/p/python-threadsafe for the latest project status.

Summary

This chapter showed how to create programs that can execute other programs using the standard library's subprocess module. Programs that are run using subprocess can be given command-line data, can be fed data to their standard input, and can have their standard output (and standard error) read. Using child processes allows us to take maximum advantage of multicore processors and leaves concurrency issues to be handled by the operating system. The downside is that if we need to share data or synchronize processes we must devise some kind of communication mechanism, for example, shared memory (e.g., using the mmap module), shared files, or networking, and this can require care to get right.

The chapter also showed how to create multithreaded programs. Unfortunately, such programs cannot take full advantage of multiple cores (if run using the standard CPython interpreter), so for Python, using multiple processes is often a more practical solution where performance is concerned. Nonetheless, we saw that the queue module and Python's locking mechanisms, such as threading.Lock, make threaded programming as straightforward as possible—and that for simple programs that only need to use queue objects like queue.Queue and queue.PriorityQueue, we may be able to completely avoid using explicit locks.

Although multithreaded programming is undoubtedly fashionable, it can be much more demanding to write, maintain, and debug multithreaded programs than single-threaded ones. However, multithreaded programs allow for straightforward communication, for example, using shared data (providing we use a queue class or use locking), and make it much easier to synchronize (e.g., to gather results) than using child processes. Threading can also be very useful in GUI (Graphical User Interface) programs that must carry out long-running tasks while maintaining responsiveness, including the ability to cancel the task being worked on. But if a good communication mechanism between processes is used, such as shared memory, or the process-transparent queue offered by the multiprocessing package, using multiple processes can often be a viable alternative to multiple threads.

The following chapter shows another example of a threaded program; a server that handles each client request in a separate thread, and that uses locks to protect shared data.

Exercises

1. Copy and modify the grepword-p.py program so that instead of the child processes printing their output, the main program gathers the results, and after all the child processes have finished, sorts and prints the results. This only requires editing the main() function and changing three lines and adding three lines. The exercise does require some thought and care, and you will need to read the subprocess module's documentation. A solution is given in grepword-p_ans.py.

2. Write a multithreaded program that reads the files listed on the command line (and the files in any directories listed on the command line, recursively). For any file that is an XML file (i.e., it begins with the characters "<?xml"), parse the file using an XML parser and produce a list of the unique tags used by the file or an error message if a parsing error occurs. Here is a sample of the program's output from one particular run:

```
./data/dvds.xml is an XML file that uses the following tags:
    dvd
    dvds
./data/bad.aix is an XML file that has the following error:
    mismatched tag: line 7889, column 2
```

./data/incidents.aix is an XML file that uses the following tags:
    airport
    incident
    incidents
    narrative

The easiest way to write the program is to modify a copy of the findduplicates-t.py program, although you can of course write the program entirely from scratch. Small changes will need to be made to the Worker class's __init__() and run() methods, and the process() method will need to be rewritten entirely (but needs only around twenty lines). The program's main() function will need several simplifications and so will one line of the print_results() function. The usage message will also need to be modified to match the one shown here:

```
Usage: xmlsummary.py [options] [path]
outputs a summary of the XML files in path; path defaults to .

Options:
  -h, --help        show this help message and exit
  -t COUNT, --threads=COUNT
                    the number of threads to use (1..20) [default 7]
  -v, --verbose
  -d, --debug
```

Make sure you try running the program with the debug flag set so that you can check that the threads are started up and that each one does its share of the work. A solution is provided in xmlsummary.py, which is slightly more than 100 lines and uses no explicit locks.

10

- Creating a TCP Client
- Creating a TCP Server

Networking

Networking allows computer programs to communicate with each other, even if they are running on different machines. For programs such as web browsers, this is the essence of what they do, whereas for others networking adds additional dimensions to their functionality, for example, remote operation or logging, or the ability to retrieve or supply data to other machines. Most networking programs work on either a peer-to-peer basis (the same program runs on different machines), or more commonly, a client/server basis (client programs send requests to a server).

In this chapter we will create a basic client/server application. Such applications are normally implemented as two separate programs: a server that waits for and responds to requests, and one or more clients that send requests to the server and read back the server's response. For this to work, the clients must know where to connect to the server, that is, the server's IP (Internet Protocol) address and port number.[*] Also, both clients and server must send and receive data using an agreed-upon protocol using data formats that they both understand.

Python's low-level socket module (on which all of Python's higher-level networking modules are based) supports both IPv4 and IPv6 addresses. It also supports the most commonly used networking protocols, including UDP (User Datagram Protocol), a lightweight but unreliable connectionless protocol where data is sent as discrete packets (datagrams) but with no guarantee that they will arrive, and TCP (Transmission Control Protocol), a reliable connection- and stream-oriented protocol. With TCP, any amount of data can be sent and received—the socket is responsible for breaking the data into chunks that are small enough to send, and for reconstructing the data at the other end.

---

[*]Machines can also connect using service discovery, for example, using the bonjour API; suitable modules are available from the Python Package Index, pypi.python.org/pypi.

413

UDP is often used to monitor instruments that give continuous readings, and where the odd missed reading is not significant, and it is sometimes used for audio or video streaming in cases where the occasional missed frame is acceptable. Both the FTP and the HTTP protocols are built on top of TCP, and client/server applications normally use TCP because they need connection-oriented communication and the reliability that TCP provides. In this chapter we will develop a client/server program, so we use TCP.

Another decision that must be made is whether to send and receive data as lines of text or as blocks of binary data, and if the latter, in what form. In this chapter we use blocks of binary data where the first four bytes are the length of the following data (encoded as an unsigned integer using the struct module), and where the following data is a binary pickle. The advantage of this approach is that we can use the same sending and receiving code for *any* application since we can store almost any arbitrary data in a pickle. The disadvantage is that both client and server must understand pickles, so they must be written in Python or must be able to access Python, for example, using Jython in Java or Boost.Python in C++. And of course, the usual security considerations apply to the use of pickles.

Pickles
282 ☞

The example we will use is a car registration program. The server holds details of car registrations (license plate, seats, mileage, and owner). The client is used to retrieve car details, to change a car's mileage or owner, or to create a new car registration. Any number of clients can be used and they won't block each other, even if two access the server at the same time. This is because the server hands off each client's request to a separate thread. (We will also see that it is just as easy to use separate processes.)

For the sake of the example, we will run the server and clients on the same machine; this means that we can use "localhost" as the IP address (although if the server is on another machine the client can be given its IP address on the command line and this will work as long as there is no firewall in the way). We have also chosen an arbitrary port number of 9653. The port number should be greater than 1023 and is normally between 5001 and 32767, although port numbers up to 65535 are normally valid.

The server can accept five kinds of requests: GET_CAR_DETAILS, CHANGE_MILEAGE, CHANGE_OWNER, NEW_REGISTRATION, and SHUTDOWN, with a corresponding response for each. The response is the requested data or confirmation of the requested action, or an indication of an error.

Creating a TCP Client

The client program is car_registration.py. Here is an example of interaction (with the server already running, and with the menu edited slightly to fit on the page):

```
(C)ar  (M)ileage  (O)wner  (N)ew car  (S)top server  (Q)uit [c]:
License: 024 hyr
License: 024 HYR
Seats:   2
Mileage: 97543
Owner:   Jack Lemon
(C)ar  (M)ileage  (O)wner  (N)ew car  (S)top server  (Q)uit [c]: m
License [024 HYR]:
Mileage [97543]: 103491
Mileage successfully changed
```

The data entered by the user is shown in **bold**—where there is no visible input it means that the user pressed Enter to accept the default. Here the user has asked to see the details of a particular car and then updated its mileage.

As many clients as we like can be running, and when a user quits their particular client the server is unaffected. But if the server is stopped, the client it was stopped in will quit and all the other clients will get a "Connection refused" error and will terminate when they next attempt to access the server. In a more sophisticated application, the ability to stop the server would be available only to certain users, perhaps on only particular machines, but we have included it in the client to show how it is done.

We will now review the code, starting with the main() function and the handling of the user interface, and finishing with the networking code itself.

```
def main():
    if len(sys.argv) > 1:
        Address[0] = sys.argv[1]
    call = dict(c=get_car_details, m=change_mileage, o=change_owner,
                n=new_registration, s=stop_server, q=quit)
    menu = ("(C)ar  Edit (M)ileage  Edit (O)wner  (N)ew car  "
            "(S)top server  (Q)uit")
    valid = frozenset("cmonsq")
    previous_license = None
    while True:
        action = Console.get_menu_choice(menu, valid, "c", True)
        previous_license = call[action](previous_license)
```

Branch-
ing
using
dictio-
naries

330 ☞

The Address list is a global that holds the IP address and port number as a two-item list, ["localhost", 9653], with the IP address overridden if specified on the command line. The call dictionary maps menu options to functions.

The Console module is one supplied with this book and contains some useful functions for getting values from the user at the console, such as Console.get_string() and Console.get_integer(); these are similar to functions

developed in earlier chapters and have been put in a module to make them easy
to reuse in different programs.

As a convenience for users, we keep track of the last license they entered so
that it can be used as the default, since most commands start by asking for
the license of the relevant car. Once the user makes a choice we call the corresponding function passing in the previous license, and expecting each function
to return the license it used. Since the loop is infinite the program must be terminated by one of the functions; we will see this further on.

```
def get_car_details(previous_license):
    license, car = retrieve_car_details(previous_license)
    if car is not None:
        print("License: {0}\nSeats:   {1[0]}\nMileage: {1[1]}\n"
              "Owner:   {1[2]}".format(license, car))
    return license
```

This function is used to get information about a particular car. Since most
of the functions need to request a license from the user and often need some
car-related data to work on, we have factored out this functionality into the
retrieve_car_details() function—it returns a 2-tuple of the license entered
by the user and a named tuple, CarTuple, that holds the car's seats, mileage,
and owner (or the previous license and None if they entered an unrecognized
license). Here we just print the information retrieved and return the license
to be used as the default for the next function that is called and that needs
the license.

```
def retrieve_car_details(previous_license):
    license = Console.get_string("License", "license",
                                 previous_license)
    if not license:
        return previous_license, None
    license = license.upper()
    ok, *data = handle_request("GET_CAR_DETAILS", license)
    if not ok:
        print(data[0])
        return previous_license, None
    return license, CarTuple(*data)
```

This is the first function to make use of networking. It calls the handle_re-
quest() function that we review further on. The handle_request() function
takes whatever data it is given as arguments and sends it to the server, and
then returns whatever the server replies. The handle_request() function does
not know or care what data it sends or returns; it purely provides the networking service.

In the case of car registrations we have a protocol where we always send the name of the action we want the server to perform as the first argument, followed by any relevant parameters—in this case, just the license. The protocol for the reply is that the server always return a tuple whose first item is a Boolean success/failure flag. If the flag is False, we have a 2-tuple and the second item is an error message. If the flag is True, the tuple is either a 2-tuple with the second item being a confirmation message, or an n-tuple with the second and subsequent items holding the data that was requested.

So here, if the license is unrecognized, ok is False and we print the error message in data[0] and return the previous license unchanged. Otherwise, we return the license (which will now become the previous license), and a CarTuple made from the data list, (seats, mileage, owner).

```
def change_mileage(previous_license):
    license, car = retrieve_car_details(previous_license)
    if car is None:
        return previous_license
    mileage = Console.get_integer("Mileage", "mileage",
                                  car.mileage, 0)
    if mileage == 0:
        return license
    ok, *data = handle_request("CHANGE_MILEAGE", license, mileage)
    if not ok:
        print(data[0])
    else:
        print("Mileage successfully changed")
    return license
```

This function follows a similar pattern to get_car_details(), except that once we have the details we update one aspect of them. There are in fact two networking calls, since retrieve_car_details() calls handle_request() to get the car's details—we need to do this both to confirm that the license is valid and to get the current mileage to use as the default. Here the reply is always a 2-tuple, with either an error message or None as the second item.

We won't review the change_owner() function since it is structurally the same as change_mileage(), nor will we review new_registration() since it differs only in not retrieving car details at the start (since it is a new car being entered), and asking the user for all the details rather than just changing one detail, none of which is new to us or relevant to network programming.

```
def quit(*ignore):
    sys.exit()
```

```
def stop_server(*ignore):
    handle_request("SHUTDOWN", wait_for_reply=False)
    sys.exit()
```

If the user chooses to quit the program we do a clean termination by calling
sys.exit(). Every menu function is called with the previous license, but we
don't care about the argument in this particular case. We cannot write def
quit(): because that would create a function that expects no arguments and so
when the function was called with the previous license a TypeError exception
would be raised saying that no arguments were expected but that one was giv-
en. So instead we specify a parameter of *ignore which can take any number
of positional arguments. The name ignore has no significance to Python and is
used purely to indicate to maintainers that the arguments are ignored.

If the user chooses to stop the server we use handle_request() to inform the
server, and specify that we don't want a reply. Once the data is sent, han-
dle_request() returns without waiting for a reply, and we do a clean termination using sys.exit().

```
def handle_request(*items, wait_for_reply=True):
    SizeStruct = struct.Struct("!I")
    data = pickle.dumps(items, 3)

    try:
        with SocketManager(tuple(Address)) as sock:
            sock.sendall(SizeStruct.pack(len(data)))
            sock.sendall(data)
            if not wait_for_reply:
                return

            size_data = sock.recv(SizeStruct.size)
            size = SizeStruct.unpack(size_data)[0]
            result = bytearray()
            while True:
                data = sock.recv(4000)
                if not data:
                    break
                result.extend(data)
                if len(result) >= size:
                    break
        return pickle.loads(result)
    except socket.error as err:
        print("{0}: is the server running?".format(err))
        sys.exit(1)
```

This function provides all the client program's network handling. It begins
by creating a struct.Struct which holds one unsigned integer in network byte

order, and then it creates a pickle of whatever items it is passed. The function does not know or care what the items are. Notice that we have explicitly set the pickle protocol version to 3—this is to ensure that both clients and server use the same pickle version, even if a client or server is upgraded to run a different version of Python.

If we wanted our protocol to be more future proof, we could version it (just as we do with binary disk formats). This can be done either at the network level or at the data level. At the network level we can version by passing two unsigned integers instead of one, that is, length and a protocol version number. At the data level we could follow the convention that the pickle is always a list (or always a dictionary) whose first item (or "version" item) has a version number. (You will get the chance to version the protocol in the exercises.)

The SocketManager is a custom context manager that gives us a socket to use—we will review it shortly. The socket.socket.sendall() method sends all the data it is given—making multiple socket.socket.send() calls behind the scenes if necessary. We always send two items of data: the length of the pickle and the pickle itself. If the wait_for_reply argument is False we don't wait for a reply and return immediately—the context manager will ensure that the socket is closed before the function actually returns.

After sending the data (and when we want a reply), we call the socket.socket.recv() method to get the reply. This method blocks until it receives data. For the first call we request four bytes—the size of the integer that holds the size of the reply pickle to follow. We use the struct.Struct to unpack the bytes into the size integer. We then create an empty bytearray and try to retrieve the incoming pickle in blocks of up to 4 000 bytes. Once we have read in size bytes (or if the data has run out before then), we break out of the loop and unpickle the data using the pickle.loads() function (which takes a bytes or bytearray object), and return it. In this case we know that the data will always be a tuple since that is the protocol we have established with the car registration server, but the handle_request() function does not know or care about what the data is.

If something goes wrong with the network connection, for example, the server isn't running or the connection fails for some reason, a socket.error exception is raised. In such cases the exception is caught and the client program issues an error message and terminates.

```
class SocketManager:

    def __init__(self, address):
        self.address = address

    def __enter__(self):
        self.sock = socket.socket(socket.AF_INET, socket.SOCK_STREAM)
        self.sock.connect(self.address)
```

```
        return self.sock

    def __exit__(self, *ignore):
        self.sock.close()
```

The address object is a 2-tuple (IP address, port number) and is set when the context manager is created. Once the context manager is used in a with statement it creates a socket and tries to make a connection—blocking until a connection is established or until a socket exception is raised. The first argument to the socket.socket() initializer is the address family; here we have used socket.AF_INET (IPv4), but others are available, for example, socket.AF_INET6 (IPv6), socket.AF_UNIX, and socket.AF_NETLINK. The second argument is normally either socket.SOCK_STREAM (TCP) as we have used here, or socket.SOCK_DGRAM (UDP).

When the flow of control leaves the with statement's scope the context object's __exit__() method is called. We don't care whether an exception was raised or not (so we ignore the exception arguments), and just close the socket. Since the method returns None (in a Boolean context, False), any exceptions are propagated—this works well since we put a suitable except block in handle_request() to process any socket exceptions that occur.

Creating a TCP Server　　　　　　　　　　　　　　　　　　Ⅲ

Since the code for creating servers often follows the same design, rather than having to use the low-level socket module, we can use the high-level socketserver module which takes care of all the housekeeping for us. All we have to do is provide a request handler class with a handle() method which is used to read requests and write replies. The socketserver module handles the communications for us, servicing each connection request, either serially or by passing each request to its own separate thread or process—and it does all of this transparently so that we are insulated from the low-level details.

For this application the server is car_registration_server.py.* This program contains a very simple Car class that holds seats, mileage, and owner information as properties (the first one read-only). The class does not hold car licenses because the cars are stored in a dictionary and the licenses are used for the dicionary's keys.

We will begin by looking at the main() function, then briefly review how the server's data is loaded, then the creation of the custom server class, and finally the implementation of the request handler class that handles the client requests.

---

*The first time the server is run on Windows a firewall dialog might pop up saying that Python is blocked—click Unblock to allow the server to operate.

```
def main():
    filename = os.path.join(os.path.dirname(__file__),
                            "car_registrations.dat")
    cars = load(filename)
    print("Loaded {0} car registrations".format(len(cars)))
    RequestHandler.Cars = cars
    server = None
    try:
        server = CarRegistrationServer(("", 9653), RequestHandler)
        server.serve_forever()
    except Exception as err:
        print("ERROR", err)
    finally:
        if server is not None:
            server.shutdown()
            save(filename, cars)
            print("Saved {0} car registrations".format(len(cars)))
```

We have stored the car registration data in the same directory as the program. The cars object is set to a dictionary whose keys are license strings and whose values are Car objects. Normally servers do not print anything since they are typically started and stopped automatically and run in the background, so usually they report on their status by writing logs (e.g., using the logging module). Here we have chosen to print a message at start-up and shutdown to make testing and experimenting easier.

Our request handler class needs to be able to access the cars dictionary, but we cannot pass the dictionary to an instance because the server creates the instances for us—one to handle each request. So we set the dictionary to the RequestHandler.Cars class variable where it is accessible to all instances.

We create an instance of the server passing it the address and port it should operate on and the RequestHandler class object—not an instance. An empty string as the address indicates any accessible IPv4 address (including the current machine, localhost). Then we tell the server to serve requests forever. When the server shuts down (we will see how this happens further on), we save the cars dictionary since the data may have been changed by clients.

```
def load(filename):
    try:
        with contextlib.closing(gzip.open(filename, "rb")) as fh:
            return pickle.load(fh)
    except (EnvironmentError, pickle.UnpicklingError) as err:
        print("server cannot load data: {1}".format(err))
        sys.exit(1)
```

The code for loading is easy because we have used a context manager from the standard library's contextlib module to ensure that the file is closed irrespective of whether an exception occurs. Another way of achieving the same effect is to use a custom context manager. For example:

```
class GzipManager:

    def __init__(self, filename, mode):
        self.filename = filename
        self.mode = mode

    def __enter__(self):
        self.fh = gzip.open(self.filename, self.mode)
        return self.fh

    def __exit__(self, *ignore):
        self.fh.close()
```

From Python 3.1 the gzip.open() function supports the context manager protocol, so we can simply write:

with gzip.open(...) as fh.

Using the custom GzipManager, the with statement becomes:

```
with GzipManager(filename, "rb") as fh:
```

The save() function (not shown) is structurally the same as the load() function, only we open the file in write binary mode, use pickle.dump() to save the data, and don't return anything.

```
class CarRegistrationServer(socketserver.ThreadingMixIn,
                           socketserver.TCPServer): pass
```

This is the complete custom server class. If we wanted to create a server that used processes rather than threads, the only change would be to inherit the socketserver.ForkingMixIn class instead of the socketserver.ThreadingMixIn class. The term *mixin* is often used to describe classes that are specifically designed to be multiply-inherited. The socketserver module's classes can be used to create a variety of custom servers including UDP servers and Unix TCP and UDP servers, by inheriting the appropriate pair of base classes.

Multiple inheritance

377 ☜

Note that the socketserver mixin class we used must always be inherited first. This is to ensure that the mixin class's methods are used in preference to the second class's methods for those methods that are provided by both, since Python looks for methods in the base classes in the order in which the base classes are specified, and uses the first suitable method it finds.

The socket server creates a request handler (using the class it was given) to handle each request. Our custom RequestHandler class provides a method for each kind of request it can handle, plus the handle() method that it must have since that is the only method used by the socket server. But before looking at the methods we will look at the class declaration and the class's class variables.

```
class RequestHandler(socketserver.StreamRequestHandler):

    CarsLock = threading.Lock()
    CallLock = threading.Lock()
    Call = dict(
            GET_CAR_DETAILS=(
                    lambda self, *args: self.get_car_details(*args)),
            CHANGE_MILEAGE=(
                    lambda self, *args: self.change_mileage(*args)),
            CHANGE_OWNER=(
                    lambda self, *args: self.change_owner(*args)),
            NEW_REGISTRATION=(
                    lambda self, *args: self.new_registration(*args)),
            SHUTDOWN=lambda self, *args: self.shutdown(*args))
```

We have created a `socketserver.StreamRequestHandler` subclass since we are using a streaming (TCP) server. A corresponding `socketserver.Datagram-RequestHandler` is available for UDP servers, or we could inherit the `socketserver.BaseRequestHandler` class for lower-level access.

The `RequestHandler.Cars` dictionary is a class variable that was added in the `main()` function; it holds all the registration data. Adding additional attributes to objects (such as classes and instances) can be done outside the class (in this case in the `main()` function) without formality (as long as the object has a `__dict__`), and can be very convenient. Since we know that the class depends on this variable some programmers would have added `Cars = None` as a class variable to document the variable's existence.

Almost every request-handling method needs access to the `Cars` data, but we must ensure that the data is never accessed by two methods (from two different threads) at the same time; if it is, the dictionary may become corrupted, or the program might crash. To avoid this we have a lock class variable that we will use to ensure that only one thread at a time accesses the `Cars` dictionary.* (Threading, including the use of locks, is covered in Chapter 9.)

The `Call` dictionary is another class variable. Each key is the name of an action that the server can perform and each value is a function for performing the action. We cannot use the methods directly as we did with the functions in the client's menu dictionary because there is no `self` available at the class level. The solution we have used is to provide wrapper functions that will get `self` when they are called, and which in turn call the appropriate method with the given `self` and any other arguments. An alternative solution would be to

---

*The GIL (Global Interpreter Lock) ensures that accesses to the `Cars` dictionary are synchronized, but as noted earlier, we do not take advantage of this since it is a CPython implementation detail.

create the Call dictionary *after* all the methods. That would allow us to create entries such as GET_CAR_DETAILS=get_car_details, with Python able to find the get_car_details() method because the dictionary is created after the method is defined. We have used the first approach since it is more explicit and does not impose an order dependency on where the dictionary is created.

Although the Call dictionary is only ever read after the class is created, since it is mutable we have played it extra-safe and created a lock for it to ensure that no two threads access it at the same time. (Again, because of the GIL, the lock isn't really needed for CPython.)

GIL

404 ☞

```
def handle(self):
    SizeStruct = struct.Struct("!I")
    size_data = self.rfile.read(SizeStruct.size)
    .size = SizeStruct.unpack(size_data)[0]
    data = pickle.loads(self.rfile.read(size))

    try:
        with self.CallLock:
            function = self.Call[data[0]]
        reply = function(self, *data[1:])
    except Finish:
        return
    data = pickle.dumps(reply, 3)
    self.wfile.write(SizeStruct.pack(len(data)))
    self.wfile.write(data)
```

Whenever a client makes a request a new thread is created with a new instance of the RequestHandler class, and then the instance's handle() method is called. Inside this method the data coming from the client can be read from the self.rfile file object, and data can be sent back to the client by writing to the self.wfile object—both of these objects are provided by socketserver, opened and ready for use.

The struct.Struct is for the integer byte count that we need for the "length plus pickle" format we are using to exchange data between clients and the server.

We begin by reading four bytes and unpacking this as the size integer so that we know the size of the pickle we have been sent. Then we read size bytes and unpickle them into the data variable. The read will block until the data is read. In this case we know that data will always be a tuple, with the first item being the requested action and the other items being the parameters, because that is the protocol we have established with the car registration clients.

Inside the try block we get the lambda function that is appropriate to the requested action. We use a lock to protect access to the Call dictionary, although arguably we are being overly cautious. As always, we do as little as possible within the scope of the lock—in this case we just do a dictionary lookup to get a reference to a function. Once we have the function we call it, passing self as the first argument and the rest of the data tuple as the other arguments. Here we are doing a function call, so no self is passed by Python. This does not matter since we pass self in ourselves, and inside the lambda the passed-in self is used to call the method in the normal way. The outcome is that the call, self.*method*(*data[1:]), is made, where *method* is the method corresponding to the action given in data[0].

If the action is to shut down, a custom Finish exception is raised in the shutdown() method; in which case we know that the client cannot expect a reply, so we just return. But for any other action we pickle the result of calling the action's corresponding method (using pickle protocol version 3), and write the size of the pickle and then the pickled data itself.

```
def get_car_details(self, license):
    with self.CarsLock:
        car = copy.copy(self.Cars.get(license, None))
    if car is not None:
        return (True, car.seats, car.mileage, car.owner)
    return (False, "This license is not registered")
```

This method begins by trying to acquire the car data lock—and blocks until it gets the lock. It then uses the dict.get() method with a second argument of None to get the car with the given license—or to get None. The car is immediately copied and the with statement is finished. This ensures that the lock is in force for the shortest possible time. Although reading does not change the data being read, because we are dealing with a mutable collection it is possible that another method in another thread wants to change the dictionary at the same time as we want to read it—using a lock prevents this from happening. Outside the scope of the lock we now have a copy of the car object (or None) which we can deal with at our leisure without blocking any other threads.

Like all the car registration action-handling methods, we return a tuple whose first item is a Boolean success/failure flag and whose other items vary. None of these methods has to worry or even know how its data is returned to the client beyond the "tuple with a Boolean first item" since all the network interaction is encapsulated in the handle() method.

```
def change_mileage(self, license, mileage):
    if mileage < 0:
        return (False, "Cannot set a negative mileage")
    with self.CarsLock:
        car = self.Cars.get(license, None)
        if car is not None:
            if car.mileage < mileage:
                car.mileage = mileage
                return (True, None)
```

```
                    return (False, "Cannot wind the odometer back")
            return (False, "This license is not registered")
```

In this method we can do one check without acquiring a lock at all. But if the mileage is non-negative we must acquire a lock and get the relevant car, and if we have a car (i.e., if the license is valid), we must stay within the scope of the lock to change the mileage as requested—or to return an error tuple. If no car has the given license (car is None), we drop out of the with statement and return an error tuple.

It would seem that if we did the validation in the client we could avoid some network traffic entirely, for example, the client could give an error message (or simply prevent) negative mileages. Even though the client ought to do this, we must still have the check in the server since we cannot assume that the client is bug-free. And although the client gets the car's mileage to use as the default mileage we cannot assume that the mileage entered by the user (even if it is greater than the current mileage) is valid, because some other client could have increased the mileage in the meantime. So we can only do the definitive validation at the server, and only within the scope of a lock.

The change_owner() method is very similar, so we won't reproduce it here.

```
        def new_registration(self, license, seats, mileage, owner):
            if not license:
                return (False, "Cannot set an empty license")
            if seats not in {2, 4, 5, 6, 7, 8, 9}:
                return (False, "Cannot register car with invalid seats")
            if mileage < 0:
                return (False, "Cannot set a negative mileage")
            if not owner:
                return (False, "Cannot set an empty owner")
            with self.CarsLock:
                if license not in self.Cars:
                    self.Cars[license] = Car(seats, mileage, owner)
                    return (True, None)
            return (False, "Cannot register duplicate license")
```

Again we are able to do a lot of error checking before accessing the registration data, but if all the data is valid we acquire a lock. If the license is not in the RequestHandler.Cars dictionary (and it shouldn't be since a new registration should have an unused license), we create a new Car object and store it in the dictionary. This must all be done within the scope of the same lock because we must not allow any other client to add a car with this license in the time between the check for the license's existence in the RequestHandler.Cars dictionary and adding the new car to the dictionary.

```
def shutdown(self, *ignore):
    self.server.shutdown()
    raise Finish()
```

If the action is to shut down we call the server's shutdown() method—this will stop it from accepting any further requests, although it will continue running while it is still servicing any existing requests. We then raise a custom exception to notify the handler() that we are finished—this causes the handler() to return without sending any reply to the client.

Summary

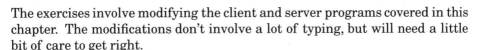

This chapter showed that creating network clients and servers can be quite straightforward in Python thanks to the standard library's networking modules, and the struct and pickle modules.

In the first section we developed a client program and gave it a single function, handle_request(), to send and receive arbitrary picklable data to and from a server using a generic data format of "length plus pickle". In the second section we saw how to create a server subclass using the classes from the socketserver module and how to implement a request handler class to service the server's client requests. Here the heart of the network interaction was confined to a single method, handle(), that can receive and send arbitrary picklable data from and to clients.

The socket and socketserver modules and many other modules in the standard library, such as asyncore, asynchat, and ssl, provide far more functionality than we have used here. But if the networking facilities provided by the standard library are not sufficient, or are not high-level enough, it is worth looking at the third-party Twisted networking framework (www.twistedmatrix.com) as a possible alternative.

Exercises

The exercises involve modifying the client and server programs covered in this chapter. The modifications don't involve a lot of typing, but will need a little bit of care to get right.

1. Copy car_registration_server.py and car_registration.py and modify them so that they exchange data using a protocol versioned at the network level. This could be done, for example, by passing two integers in the struct (length, protocol version) instead of one.

   This involves adding or modifying about ten lines in the client program's handle_request() function, and adding or modifying about sixteen lines in the server program's handle() method—including code to handle the case where the protocol version read does not match the one expected.

Solutions to this and to the following exercises are provided in car_reg-istration_ans.py and car_registration_server_ans.py.

2. Copy the car_registration_server.py program (or use the one developed in Exercise 1), and modify it so that it offers a new action, GET_LICENSES_ STARTING_WITH. The action should accept a single parameter, a string. The method implementing the action should always return a 2-tuple of (True, *list of licenses*); there is no error (False) case, since no matches is not an error and simply results in True and an empty list being returned.

   Retrieve the licenses (the RequestHandler.Cars dictionary's keys) within the scope of a lock, but do all the other work outside the lock to minimize blocking. One efficient way to find matching licenses is to sort the keys and then use the bisect module to find the first matching license and then iterate from there. Another possible approach is to iterate over the licenses, picking out those that start with the given string, perhaps using a list comprehension.

   Apart from the additional import, the Call dictionary will need an extra couple of lines for the action. The method to implement the action can be done in fewer than ten lines. This is not difficult, although care is required. A solution that uses the bisect module is provided in car_registration_server_ans.py.

3. Copy the car_registration.py program (or use the one developed in exercise 1), and modify it to take advantage of the new server (car_registration_server_ans.py). This means changing the retrieve_car_details() function so that if the user enters an invalid license they get prompted to enter the start of a license and then get a list to choose from. Here is a sample of interaction using the new function (with the server already running, with the menu edited slightly to fit on the page, and with what the user types shown in **bold**):

```
(C)ar  (M)ileage  (O)wner  (N)ew car  (S)top server  (Q)uit [c]:
License: da 4020
License: DA 4020
Seats:   2
Mileage: 97181
Owner:   Jonathan Lynn
(C)ar  (M)ileage  (O)wner  (N)ew car  (S)top server  (Q)uit [c]:
License [DA 4020]: z
This license is not registered
Start of license: z
No licence starts with Z
Start of license: a
```

```
(1) A04 4HE
(2) A37 4791
(3) ABK3035
Enter choice (0 to cancel): 3
License: ABK3035
Seats:   5
Mileage: 17719
Owner:   Anthony Jay
```

The change involves deleting one line and adding about twenty more lines. It is slightly tricky because the user must be allowed to get out or to go on at each stage. Make sure that you test the new functionality for all cases (no license starts with the given string, one licence starts with it, and two or more start with it). A solution is provided in car_registration_ans.py.

11

- DBM Databases
- SQL Databases

Database Programming

For most software developers the term *database* is usually taken to mean an RDBMS (Relational Database Management System). These systems use tables (spreadsheet-like grids) with rows equating to records and columns equating to fields. The tables and the data they hold are created and manipulated using statements written in SQL (Structured Query Language). Python provides an API (Application Programming Interface) for working with SQL databases and it is normally distributed with the SQLite 3 database as standard.

Another kind of database is a *DBM* (Database Manager) that stores any number of key–value items. Python's standard library comes with interfaces to several DBMs, including some that are Unix-specific. DBMs work just like Python dictionaries except that they are normally held on disk rather than in memory and their keys and values are always bytes objects and may be subject to length constraints. The shelve module covered in this chapter's first section provides a convenient DBM interface that allows us to use string keys and any (picklable) objects as values.

If the available DBMs and the SQLite database are insufficient, the Python Package Index, pypi.python.org/pypi, has a large number of database-related packages, including the bsddb DBM ("Berkeley DB"), object-relational mappers such as SQLAlchemy (www.sqlalchemy.org), and interfaces to popular client/server databases such as DB2, Informix, Ingres, MySQL, ODBC, and PostgreSQL.

In this chapter we will implement two versions of a program that maintains a list of DVDs, and keeps track of each DVD's title, year of release, length in minutes, and director. The first version uses a DBM (via the shelve module) to store its data, and the second version uses the SQLite database. Both programs can also load and save a simple XML format, making it possible, for example, to export DVD data from one program and import it into the other. The SQL-based version offers slightly more functionality than the DBM one, and has a slightly cleaner data design.

431

DBM Databases

bytes
286 ☜

The shelve module provides a wrapper around a DBM that allows us to interact with the DBM as though it were a dictionary, providing that we use only string keys and picklable values. Behind the scenes the shelve module converts the keys and values to and from bytes objects.

Since the shelve module uses the best underlying DBM that is available, it is possible that a DBM file saved on one machine won't be readable on another, if the other machine doesn't have the same DBM available. A common solution is to provide XML import and export for files that must be transportable between machines, and that is what we have done in this section's DVD program, dvds-dbm.py.

For the keys we use the DVDs' titles and for the values we use tuples holding the director, year, and duration. Thanks to the shelve module we don't have to perform any data conversion and can just treat the DBM object as a dictionary.

Since the structure of the program is similar to interactive menu-driven programs that we have seen before, we will focus just on those aspects that are specific to DBM programming. Here is an extract from the program's main() function, with the menu handling omitted:

```
db = None
try:
    db = shelve.open(filename, protocol=pickle.HIGHEST_PROTOCOL)
    ...
finally:
    if db is not None:
        db.close()
```

Here we have opened (or created if it does not exist) the specified DBM file for both reading and writing. Each item's value is saved as a pickle using the specified pickle protocol; existing items can be read even if they were saved using a lower protocol since Python can figure out the correct protocol to use for reading pickles. At the end the DBM is closed—this has the effect of clearing the DBM's internal cache and ensuring that the disk file reflects any changes that have been made, as well as closing the file.

The program offers options to add, edit, list, remove, import, and export DVD data. We will skip importing and exporting the data from and to XML format since it is very similar to what we have done in Chapter 7. And apart from adding, we will omit most of the user interface code, again because we have seen it before in other contexts.

```
def add_dvd(db):
    title = Console.get_string("Title", "title")
    if not title:
        return
    director = Console.get_string("Director", "director")
    if not director:
        return
    year = Console.get_integer("Year", "year", minimum=1896,
                               maximum=datetime.date.today().year)
    duration = Console.get_integer("Duration (minutes)", "minutes",
                               minimum=0, maximum=60*48)
    db[title] = (director, year, duration)
    db.sync()
```

This function, like all the functions called by the program's menu, is passed the DBM object (db) as its sole parameter. Most of the function is concerned with getting the DVD's details, and in the penultimate line we store the key–value item in the DBM file, with the DVD's title as the key and the director, year, and duration (pickled together by shelve) as the value.

In keeping with Python's usual consistency, DBMs provide the same API as dictionaries, so we don't have to learn any new syntax beyond the shelve.open() function that we saw earlier and the shelve.Shelf.sync() method that is used to clear the shelve's internal cache and synchronize the disk file's data with the changes that have been applied—in this case just adding a new item.

```
def edit_dvd(db):
    old_title = find_dvd(db, "edit")
    if old_title is None:
        return
    title = Console.get_string("Title", "title", old_title)
    if not title:
        return
    director, year, duration = db[old_title]
    ...
    db[title] = (director, year, duration)
    if title != old_title:
        del db[old_title]
    db.sync()
```

To be able to edit a DVD, the user must first choose the DVD to work on. This is just a matter of getting the title since titles are used as keys with the values holding the other data. Since the necessary functionality is needed elsewhere (e.g., when removing a DVD), we have factored it out into a separate find_dvd() function that we will look at next. If the DVD is found we get the user's changes, using the existing values as defaults to speed up the interaction. (We have omitted most of the user interface code for this function since it is almost the same as that used when adding a DVD.) At the end we store the data just as we did when adding. If the title is unchanged this will have the effect of overwriting the associated value, and if the title is different this has the effect of creating a new key–value item, in which case we delete the original item.

```
def find_dvd(db, message):
    message = "(Start of) title to " + message
    while True:
        matches = []
        start = Console.get_string(message, "title")
        if not start:
            return None
        for title in db:
            if title.lower().startswith(start.lower()):
                matches.append(title)
        if len(matches) == 0:
            print("There are no dvds starting with", start)
            continue
        elif len(matches) == 1:
            return matches[0]
        elif len(matches) > DISPLAY_LIMIT:
            print("Too many dvds start with {0}; try entering "
                    "more of the title".format(len(matches)))
            continue
        else:
            for i, match in enumerate(sorted(matches, key=str.lower)):
                print("{0}: {1}".format(i + 1, match))
            which = Console.get_integer("Number (or 0 to cancel)",
                            "number", minimum=1, maximum=len(matches))
            return matches[which - 1] if which != 0 else None
```

To make finding a DVD as quick and easy as possible we require the user to type in only one or the first few characters of its title. Once we have the start of the title we iterate over the DBM and create a list of matches. If there is one match we return it, and if there are several matches (but fewer than DISPLAY_LIMIT, an integer set elsewhere in the program) we display them all in case-insensitive order with a number beside each one so that the user can choose the title just by entering its number. (The Console.get_integer() function accepts 0 even if the minimum is greater than zero so that 0 can be used as a cancelation value. This behavior can be switched off by passing allow_zero=False. We can't use Enter, that is, nothing, to mean cancel, since entering nothing means accepting the default.)

```
def list_dvds(db):
    start = ""
    if len(db) > DISPLAY_LIMIT:
        start = Console.get_string("List those starting with "
                                  "[Enter=all]", "start")
    print()
    for title in sorted(db, key=str.lower):
        if not start or title.lower().startswith(start.lower()):
            director, year, duration = db[title]
            print("{0} ({1}) {2} minute{3}, by {4}".format(
                    title, year, duration, Util.s(duration), director))
```

Listing all the DVDs (or those whose title starts with a particular substring) is simply a matter of iterating over the DBM's items.

The Util.s() function is simply s = lambda x: "" if x == 1 else "s"; so here it returns an "s" if the duration is not one minute.

```
def remove_dvd(db):
    title = find_dvd(db, "remove")
    if title is None:
        return
    ans = Console.get_bool("Remove {0}?".format(title), "no")
    if ans:
        del db[title]
        db.sync()
```

Removing a DVD is a matter of finding the one the user wants to remove, asking for confirmation, and if we get it, deleting the item from the DBM.

We have now seen how to open (or create) a DBM file using the shelve module, and how to add items to it, edit its items, iterate over its items, and remove items.

Unfortunately, there is a flaw in our data design. Director names are duplicated, and this could easily lead to inconsistencies; for example, director Danny DeVito might be entered as "Danny De Vito" for one movie and "Danny deVito" for another. One solution would be to have two DBM files, the main DVD file with title keys and (year, duration, director ID) values, and a director file with director ID (i.e., integer) keys and director name values. We avoid this flaw in the next section's SQL database version of the program by using two tables, one for DVDs and another for directors.

SQL Databases

Interfaces to most popular SQL databases are available from third-party modules, and out of the box Python comes with the sqlite3 module (and with the SQLite 3 database), so database programming can be started right away. SQLite is a lightweight SQL database, lacking many of the features of, say, PostgreSQL, but it is very convenient for prototyping, and may prove sufficient in many cases.

To make it as easy as possible to switch between database backends, PEP 249 (Python Database API Specification v2.0) provides an API specification called DB-API 2.0 that database interfaces ought to honor—the sqlite3 module, for example, complies with the specification, but not all the third-party modules do. There are two major objects specified by the API, the connection object and the cursor object, and the APIs they must support are shown in Tables 11.1 and 11.2. In the case of the sqlite3 module, its connection and cursor objects both provide many additional attributes and methods beyond those required by the DB-API 2.0 specification.

The SQL version of the DVDs program is dvds-sql.py. The program stores directors separately from the DVD data to avoid duplication and offers one more menu option that lets the user list the directors. The two tables are shown in Figure 11.1. The program has slightly fewer than 300 lines, whereas the previous section's dvds-dbm.py program is slightly fewer than 200 lines, with most of the difference due to the fact that we must use SQL queries rather than perform simple dictionary-like operations, and because we must create the database's tables the first time the program runs.

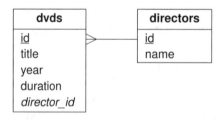

Figure 11.1 *The DVD program's database design*

The main() function is similar to before, only this time we call a custom connect() function to make the connection.

```
def connect(filename):
    create = not os.path.exists(filename)
    db = sqlite3.connect(filename)
    if create:
        cursor = db.cursor()
```

Table 11.1 *DB-API 2.0 Connection Object Methods*

Syntax	Description
db.close()	Closes the connection to the database (represented by the db object which is obtained by calling a connect() function)
db.commit()	Commits any pending transaction to the database; does nothing for databases that don't support transactions
db.cursor()	Returns a database cursor object through which queries can be executed
db.rollback()	Rolls back any pending transaction to the state that existed before the transaction began; does nothing for databases that don't support transactions

```
        cursor.execute("CREATE TABLE directors ("
            "id INTEGER PRIMARY KEY AUTOINCREMENT UNIQUE NOT NULL, "
            "name TEXT UNIQUE NOT NULL)")
        cursor.execute("CREATE TABLE dvds ("
            "id INTEGER PRIMARY KEY AUTOINCREMENT UNIQUE NOT NULL, "
            "title TEXT NOT NULL, "
            "year INTEGER NOT NULL, "
            "duration INTEGER NOT NULL, "
            "director_id INTEGER NOT NULL, "
            "FOREIGN KEY (director_id) REFERENCES directors)")
        db.commit()
    return db
```

The sqlite3.connect() function returns a database object, having opened the database file it is given and created an empty database file if the file did not exist. In view of this, prior to calling sqlite3.connect(), we note whether the database is going to be created from scratch, because if it is, we must create the tables that the program relies on. All queries are executed through a database cursor, available from the database object's cursor() method.

Notice that both tables are created with an ID field that has an AUTOINCREMENT constraint—this means that SQLite will automatically populate the IDs with unique numbers, so we can leave these fields to SQLite when inserting new records.

SQLite supports a limited range of data types—essentially just Booleans, numbers, and strings—but this can be extended using data "adaptors", either the predefined ones such as those for dates and datetimes, or custom ones that we can use to represent any data types we like. The DVDs program does not need this functionality, but if it were required, the sqlite3 module's documentation explains the details. The foreign key syntax we have used may not be the same as the syntax for other databases, and in any case it is merely documenting our intention, since SQLite, unlike many other databases, does enforce relational integrity. One other sqlite3-specific quirk is that its default behavior is to support implicit transactions, so there is no explicit "start transaction" method.

```
def add_dvd(db):
    title = Console.get_string("Title", "title")
    if not title:
        return
    director = Console.get_string("Director", "director")
    if not director:
        return
    year = Console.get_integer("Year", "year", minimum=1896,
                               maximum=datetime.date.today().year)
    duration = Console.get_integer("Duration (minutes)", "minutes",
                                   minimum=0, maximum=60*48)
    director_id = get_and_set_director(db, director)
    cursor = db.cursor()
    cursor.execute("INSERT INTO dvds "
                   "(title, year, duration, director_id) "
                   "VALUES (?, ?, ?, ?)",
                   (title, year, duration, director_id))
    db.commit()
```

This function starts with the same code as the equivalent function from the dvds-dbm.py program, but once we have gathered the data, it is quite different. The director the user entered may or may not be in the directors table, so we have a get_and_set_director() function that inserts the director if they are not already in the database, and in either case returns the director's ID ready for it to be inserted into the dvds table. With all the data available we execute an SQL INSERT statement. We don't need to specify a record ID since SQLite will automatically provide one for us.

In the query we have used question marks for placeholders. Each ? is replaced by the corresponding value in the sequence that follows the string containing the SQL statement. Named placeholders can also be used as we will see when we look at editing a record. Although it is possible to avoid using placeholders and simply format the SQL string with the data embedded into it, we recommend always using placeholders and leaving the burden of correctly encoding and escaping the data items to the database module. Another benefit of using placeholders is that they improve security since they prevent arbitrary SQL from being maliciously injected into a query.

```
def get_and_set_director(db, director):
    director_id = get_director_id(db, director)
    if director_id is not None:
```

Table 11.2 *DB-API 2.0 Cursor Object Attributes and Methods*

Syntax	Description
`c.arraysize`	The (readable/writable) number of rows that `fetch-many()` will return if no size is specified
`c.close()`	Closes the cursor, c; this is done automatically when the cursor goes out of scope
`c.description`	A read-only sequence of 7-tuples (`name`, `type_code`, `display_size`, `internal_size`, `precision`, `scale`, `null_ok`), describing each successive column of cursor c
`c.execute(sql,` `params)`	Executes the SQL query in string `sql`, replacing each placeholder with the corresponding parameter from the `params` sequence or mapping if given
`c.executemany(` `sql,` `seq_of_params)`	Executes the SQL query once for each item in the `seq_of_params` sequence of sequences or mappings; this method should not be used for operations that create result sets (such as `SELECT` statements)
`c.fetchall()`	Returns a sequence of all the rows that have not yet been fetched (which could be all of them)
`c.fetchmany(size)`	Returns a sequence of rows (each row itself being a sequence); `size` defaults to `c.arraysize`
`c.fetchone()`	Returns the next row of the query result set as a sequence, or `None` when the results are exhausted. Raises an exception if there is no result set.
`c.rowcount`	The read-only row count for the last operation (e.g., `SELECT`, `INSERT`, `UPDATE`, or `DELETE`) or -1 if not available or not applicable

```
        return director_id
    cursor = db.cursor()
    cursor.execute("INSERT INTO directors (name) VALUES (?)",
                   (director,))
    db.commit()
    return get_director_id(db, director)
```

This function returns the ID of the given director, inserting a new director record if necessary. If a record is inserted we retrieve its ID using the get_director_id() function we tried in the first place.

```
def get_director_id(db, director):
    cursor = db.cursor()
    cursor.execute("SELECT id FROM directors WHERE name=?",
                   (director,))
```

```
        fields = cursor.fetchone()
        return fields[0] if fields is not None else None
```

The get_director_id() function returns the ID of the given director or None if
there is no such director in the database. We use the fetchone() method because there is either zero or one matching record. (We know that there are
no duplicate directors because the directors table's name field has a UNIQUE constraint, and in any case we always check for the existence of a director before
adding a new one.) The fetch methods always return a sequence of fields (or
None if there are no more records), even if, as here, we have asked to retrieve
only a single field.

```
    def edit_dvd(db):
        title, identity = find_dvd(db, "edit")
        if title is None:
            return
        title = Console.get_string("Title", "title", title)
        if not title:
            return
        cursor = db.cursor()
        cursor.execute("SELECT dvds.year, dvds.duration, directors.name "
                        "FROM dvds, directors "
                        "WHERE dvds.director_id = directors.id AND "
                        "dvds.id=:id", dict(id=identity))
        year, duration, director = cursor.fetchone()
        director = Console.get_string("Director", "director", director)
        if not director:
            return
        year = Console.get_integer("Year", "year", year, 1896,
                                    datetime.date.today().year)
        duration = Console.get_integer("Duration (minutes)", "minutes",
                                        duration, minimum=0, maximum=60*48)
        director_id = get_and_set_director(db, director)
        cursor.execute("UPDATE dvds SET title=:title, year=:year, "
                        "duration=:duration, director_id=:director_id "
                        "WHERE id=:id", locals())
        db.commit()
```

To edit a DVD record we must first find the record the user wants to work on.
If a record is found we begin by giving the user the opportunity to change
the title. Then we retrieve the other fields so that we can provide the existing
values as defaults to minimize what the user must type since they can just
press Enter to accept a default. Here we have used named placeholders (of
the form :*name*), and must therefore provide the corresponding values using a
mapping. For the SELECT statement we have used a freshly created dictionary,
and for the UPDATE statement we have used the dictionary returned by locals().

We could use a fresh dictionary for both, in which case for the UPDATE we would pass dict(title=title, year=year, duration=duration, director_id=director_id, id=identity)) instead of locals().

Once we have all the fields and the user has entered any changes they want, we retrieve the corresponding director ID (inserting a new director record if necessary), and then update the database with the new data. We have taken the simplistic approach of updating all the record's fields rather than only those which have actually been changed.

When we used a DBM file the DVD title was used as the key, so if the title changed, we created a new key–value item and deleted the original. But here every DVD record has a unique ID which is set when the record is first inserted, so we are free to change the value of any other field with no further work necessary.

```
def find_dvd(db, message):
    message = "(Start of) title to " + message
    cursor = db.cursor()
    while True:
        start = Console.get_string(message, "title")
        if not start:
            return (None, None)
        cursor.execute("SELECT title, id FROM dvds "
                       "WHERE title LIKE ? ORDER BY title",
                       (start + "%"))
        records = cursor.fetchall()
        if len(records) == 0:
            print("There are no dvds starting with", start)
            continue
        elif len(records) == 1:
            return records[0]
        elif len(records) > DISPLAY_LIMIT:
            print("Too many dvds ({0}) start with {1}; try entering "
                  "more of the title".format(len(records), start))
            continue
        else:
            for i, record in enumerate(records):
                print("{0}: {1}".format(i + 1, record[0]))
            which = Console.get_integer("Number (or 0 to cancel)",
                                "number", minimum=1, maximum=len(records))
            return records[which - 1] if which != 0 else (None, None)
```

This function performs the same service as the find_dvd() function in the dvds-dbm.py program, and returns a 2-tuple (title, DVD ID), or (None, None) depending on whether a record was found. Instead of iterating over all the data we have used the SQL wildcard operator (%), so only the relevant records are retrieved.

And since we expect the number of matching records to be small, we fetch them all at once into a sequence of sequences. If there is more than one matching record and few enough to display, we print the records with a number beside each one so that the user can choose the one they want in much the same way as they could in the dvds-dbm.py program.

```
def list_dvds(db):
    cursor = db.cursor()
    sql = ("SELECT dvds.title, dvds.year, dvds.duration, "
            "directors.name FROM dvds, directors "
            "WHERE dvds.director_id = directors.id")
    start = None
    if dvd_count(db) > DISPLAY_LIMIT:
        start = Console.get_string("List those starting with "
                                   "[Enter=all]", "start")
        sql += " AND dvds.title LIKE ?"
    sql += " ORDER BY dvds.title"
    print()
    if start is None:
        cursor.execute(sql)
    else:
        cursor.execute(sql, (start + "%",))
    for record in cursor:
        print("{0[0]} ({0[1]}) {0[2]} minutes, by {0[3]}".format(
                record))
```

To list the details of each DVD we do a SELECT query that joins the two tables, adding a second element to the WHERE clause if there are more records (returned by our dvd_count() function) than the display limit. We then execute the query and iterate over the results. Each record is a sequence whose fields are those matching the SELECT query.

```
def dvd_count(db):
    cursor = db.cursor()
    cursor.execute("SELECT COUNT(*) FROM dvds")
    return cursor.fetchone()[0]
```

We factored these lines out into a separate function because we need them in several different functions.

We have omitted the code for the list_directors() function since it is structurally very similar to the list_dvds() function, only simpler because it lists only one field (name).

```
def remove_dvd(db):
    title, identity = find_dvd(db, "remove")
    if title is None:
```

```
            return
     ans = Console.get_bool("Remove {0}?".format(title), "no")
     if ans:
         cursor = db.cursor()
         cursor.execute("DELETE FROM dvds WHERE id=?", (identity,))
         db.commit()
```

This function is called when the user asks to delete a record, and it is very similar to the equivalent function in the dvds-dbm.py program.

We have now completed our review of the dvds-sql.py program and seen how to create database tables, select records, iterate over the selected records, and insert, update, and delete records. Using the execute() method we can execute any arbitrary SQL statement that the underlying database supports.

SQLite offers much more functionality than we needed here, including an auto-commit mode (and other kinds of transaction control), and the ability to create functions that can be executed inside SQL queries. It is also possible to provide a factory function to control what is returned for each fetched record (e.g., a dictionary or custom type instead of a sequence of fields). Additionally, it is possible to create in-memory SQLite databases by passing ":memory:" as the filename.

Summary ▐▌▌

Back in Chapter 7 we saw several different ways of saving and loading data from disk, and in this chapter we have seen how to interact with data types that hold their data on disk rather than in memory.

For DBM files the shelve module is very convenient since it stores string–object items. If we want complete control we can of course use any of the underlying DBMs directly. One nice feature of the shelve module and of the DBMs generally is that they use the dictionary API, making it easy to retrieve, add, edit, and remove items, and to convert programs that use dictionaries to use DBMs instead. One small inconvenience of DBMs is that for relational data we must use a separate DBM file for each key–value table, whereas SQLite stores all the data in a single file.

For SQL databases, SQLite is useful for prototyping, and in many cases in its own right, and it has the advantage of being supplied with Python as standard. We have seen how to obtain a database object using the connect() function and how to execute SQL queries (such as CREATE TABLE, SELECT, INSERT, UPDATE, and DELETE) using the database cursor's execute() method.

Python offers a complete range of choices for disk-based and in-memory data storage, from binary files, text files, XML files, and pickles, to DBMs and SQL databases, and this makes it possible to choose exactly the right approach for any given situation.

Exercise

Write an interactive console program to maintain a list of bookmarks. For each bookmark keep two pieces of information: the URL and a name. Here is an example of the program in action:

```
Bookmarks (bookmarks.dbm)
(1) Programming in Python 3........ http://www.qtrac.eu/py3book.html
(2) PyQt......................... http://www.riverbankcomputing.com
(3) Python....................... http://www.python.org
(4) Qtrac Ltd.................... http://www.qtrac.eu
(5) Scientific Tools for Python.... http://www.scipy.org

(A)dd  (E)dit  (L)ist  (R)emove  (Q)uit [l]: e
Number of bookmark to edit: 2
URL [http://www.riverbankcomputing.com]:
Name [PyQt]: PyQt (Python bindings for GUI library)
```

The program should allow the user to add, edit, list, and remove bookmarks. To make identifying a bookmark for editing or removing as easy as possible, list the bookmarks with numbers and ask the user to specify the number of the bookmark they want to edit or remove. Store the data in a DBM file using the shelve module and with names as keys and URLs as values. Structurally the program is very similar to dvds-dbm.py, except for the find_bookmark() function which is much simpler than find_dvd() since it only has to get an integer from the user and use that to find the corresponding bookmark's name.

As a courtesy to users, if no protocol is specified, prepend the URL the user adds or edits with http://.

The entire program can be written in fewer than 100 lines (assuming the use of the Console module for Console.get_string() and similar). A solution is provided in bookmarks.py.

12

- Python's Regular Expression Language
- The Regular Expression Module

Regular Expressions

A regular expression is a compact notation for representing a collection of strings. What makes regular expressions so powerful is that a single regular expression can represent an unlimited number of strings—providing they meet the regular expression's requirements. Regular expressions (which we will mostly call "regexes" from now on) are defined using a mini-language that is completely different from Python—but Python includes the re module through which we can seamlessly create and use regexes.[*]

Regexes are used for four main purposes:

- Validation: checking whether a piece of text meets some criteria, for example, contains a currency symbol followed by digits

- Searching: locating substrings that can have more than one form, for example, finding any of "pet.png", "pet.jpg", "pet.jpeg", or "pet.svg" while avoiding "carpet.png" and similar

- Searching and replacing: replacing everywhere the regex matches with a string, for example, finding "bicycle" or "human powered vehicle" and replacing either with "bike"

- Splitting strings: splitting a string at each place the regex matches, for example, splitting everywhere ": " or "=" is encountered

At its simplest a regular expression is an expression (e.g., a literal character), optionally followed by a quantifier. More complex regexes consist of any number of quantified expressions and may include assertions and may be influenced by flags.

---

[*] A good book on regular expressions is *Mastering Regular Expressions* by Jeffrey E. F. Friedl, ISBN 0596528124. It does not explicitly cover Python, but Python's re module offers very similar functionality to the Perl regular expression engine that the book covers in depth.

This chapter's first section introduces and explains all the key regular expression concepts and shows pure regular expression syntax—it makes minimal reference to Python itself. Then the second section shows how to use regular expressions in the context of Python programming, drawing on all the material covered in the earlier sections. Readers familiar with regular expressions who just want to learn how they work in Python could skip to the second section (starting on page 455). The chapter covers the complete regex language offered by the re module, including all the assertions and flags. We indicate regular expressions in the text using **bold**, show where they match using <u>underlining</u>, and show captures using <u>shading</u>.

Python's Regular Expression Language

In this section we look at the regular expression language in four subsections. The first subsection shows how to match individual characters or groups of characters, for example, match *a*, or match *b*, or match either *a* or *b*. The second subsection shows how to quantify matches, for example, match once, or match at least once, or match as many times as possible. The third subsection shows how to group subexpressions and how to capture matching text, and the final subsection shows how to use the language's assertions and flags to affect how regular expressions work.

Characters and Character Classes

The simplest expressions are just literal characters, such as **a** or **5**, and if no quantifier is explicitly given it is taken to be "match one occurrence". For example, the regex **tune** consists of four expressions, each implicitly quantified to match once, so it matches one *t* followed by one *u* followed by one *n* followed by one *e*, and hence matches the strings <u>tune</u> and at<u>tuned</u>.

Although most characters can be used as literals, some are "special characters"—these are symbols in the regex language and so must be escaped by preceding them with a backslash (\) to use them as literals. The special characters are \ . ^ $? + * { } [ ] ( ) |. Most of Python's standard string escapes can also be used within regexes, for example, \n for newline and \t for tab, as well as hexadecimal escapes for characters using the \x*HH*, \u*HHHH*, and \U*HHHHHHHH* syntaxes.

String escapes

62 ✎

In many cases, rather than matching one particular character we want to match any one of a set of characters. This can be achieved by using a *character class*—one or more characters enclosed in square brackets. (This has nothing to do with a Python class, and is simply the regex term for "set of characters".) A character class is an expression, and like any other expression, if not explicitly quantified it matches exactly one character (which can be any of the characters in the character class). For example, the regex **r[ea]d** matches both <u>red</u>

and r<u>ada</u>r, but not r<u>ea</u>d. Similarly, to match a single digit we can use the regex [**0123456789**]. For convenience we can specify a range of characters using a hyphen, so the regex [**0-9**] also matches a digit. It is possible to negate the meaning of a character class by following the opening bracket with a caret, so [**^0-9**] matches any character that is *not* a digit.

Note that inside a character class, apart from \, the special characters lose their special meaning, although in the case of ^ it acquires a new meaning (negation) if it is the first character in the character class, and otherwise is simply a literal caret. Also, – signifies a character range unless it is the first character, in which case it is a literal hyphen.

Since some sets of characters are required so frequently, several have shorthand forms—these are shown in Table 12.1. With one exception the shorthands can be used inside character sets, so for example, the regex [**\dA-Fa-f**] matches any hexadecimal digit. The exception is **.** which is a shorthand outside a character class but matches a literal **.** inside a character class.

Table 12.1 *Character Class Shorthands*

Symbol	Meaning
.	Matches any character except newline; or any character at all with the re.DOTALL flag; or inside a character class matches a literal .
\d	Matches a Unicode digit; or [**0-9**] with the re.ASCII flag
\D	Matches a Unicode nondigit; or [**^0-9**] with the re.ASCII flag
\s	Matches a Unicode whitespace; or [**\t\n\r\f\v**] with the re.ASCII flag
\S	Matches a Unicode nonwhitespace; or [**^ \t\n\r\f\v**] with the re.ASCII flag
\w	Matches a Unicode "word" character; or [**a-zA-Z0-9_**] with the re.ASCII flag
\W	Matches a Unicode non-"word" character; or [**^a-zA-Z0-9_**] with the re.ASCII flag

Meaning of the flags ☞ 451

Quantifiers

A quantifier has the form {*m,n*} where *m* and *n* are the minimum and maximum times the expression the quantifier applies to must match. For example, both **e{1,1}e{1,1}** and **e{2,2}** match f<u>ee</u>l, but neither matches felt.

Writing a quantifier after every expression would soon become tedious, and is certainly difficult to read. Fortunately, the regex language supports several convenient shorthands. If only one number is given in the quantifier it is taken to be both the minimum and the maximum, so **e{2}** is the same as **e{2,2}**. And as we noted in the preceding section, if no quantifier is explicitly given, it is assumed to be one (i.e., **{1,1}** or **{1}**); therefore, **ee** is the same as **e{1,1}e{1,1}** and **e{1}e{1}**, so both **e{2}** and **ee** match f<u>ee</u>l but not f<u>e</u>lt.

Having a different minimum and maximum is often convenient. For example, to match travelled and traveled (both legitimate spellings), we could use either **travel{1,2}ed** or **travell{0,1}ed**. The **{0,1}** quantification is so often used that it has its own shorthand form, **?**, so another way of writing the regex (and the one most likely to be used in practice) is **travell?ed**.

Two other quantification shorthands are provided: **+** which stands for **{1,**n**}** ("at least one") and ***** which stands for **{0,**n**}** ("any number of"); in both cases n is the maximum possible number allowed for a quantifier, usually at least 32767. All the quantifiers are shown in Table 12.2.

The **+** quantifier is very useful. For example, to match integers we could use **\d+** since this matches one or more digits. This regex could match in two places in the string 4588.91, for example, <u>4588</u>.91 and 4588.<u>91</u>. Sometimes typos are the result of pressing a key too long. We could use the regex **bevel+ed** to match the legitimate <u>beveled</u> and <u>bevelled</u>, and the incorrect <u>bevellled</u>. If we wanted to standardize on the one *l* spelling, and match only occurrences that had two or more *l*s, we could use **bevell+ed** to find them.

The ***** quantifier is less useful, simply because it can so often lead to unexpected results. For example, supposing that we want to find lines that contain comments in Python files, we might try searching for **#***. But this regex will match any line whatsoever, including blank lines because the meaning is "match any number of #s"—and that includes none. As a rule of thumb for those new to regexes, avoid using ***** at all, and if you do use it (or if you use **?**), make sure there is at least one other expression in the regex that has a non-zero quantifier—so at least one quantifier other than ***** or **?** since both of these can match their expression zero times.

It is often possible to convert ***** uses to **+** uses and vice versa. For example, we could match "tasselled" with at least one *l* using **tassel*ed** or **tassel+ed**, and match those with two or more *l*s using **tasselll*ed** or **tasselll+ed**.

If we use the regex **\d+** it will match <u>136</u>. But why does it match all the digits, rather than just the first one? By default, all quantifiers are *greedy*—they match as many characters as they can. We can make any quantifier nongreedy (also called *minimal*) by following it with a **?** symbol. (The question mark has two different meanings—on its own it is a shorthand for the **{0,1}** quantifier, and when it follows a quantifier it tells the quantifier to be nongreedy.) For example, **\d+?** can match the string 136 in three different places: <u>1</u>36, 1<u>3</u>6, and 13<u>6</u>. Here is another example: **\d??** matches zero or one digits, but prefers to match none since it is nongreedy—on its own it suffers the same problem as ***** in that it will match nothing, that is, any text at all.

Table 12.2 *Regular Expression Quantifiers*

Syntax	Meaning
e? or e{0,1}	Greedily match zero or one occurrence of expression e
e?? or e{0,1}?	Nongreedily match zero or one occurrence of expression e
e+ or e{1,}	Greedily match one or more occurrences of expression e
e+? or e{1,}?	Nongreedily match one or more occurrences of expression e
e* or e{0,}	Greedily match zero or more occurrences of expression e
e*? or e{0,}?	Nongreedily match zero or more occurrences of expression e
e{m}	Match exactly m occurrences of expression e
e{m,}	Greedily match at least m occurrences of expression e
e{m,}?	Nongreedily match at least m occurrences of expression e
e{,n}	Greedily match at most n occurrences of expression e
e{,n}?	Nongreedily match at most n occurrences of expression e
e{m,n}	Greedily match at least m and at most n occurrences of expression e
e{m,n}?	Nongreedily match at least m and at most n occurrences of expression e

Nongreedy quantifiers can be useful for quick and dirty XML and HTML parsing. For example, to match all the image tags, writing **<img.*>** (match one "<", then one "i", then one "m", then one "g", then zero or more of any character apart from newline, then one ">") will not work because the .* part is greedy and will match everything including the tag's closing >, and will keep going until it reaches the last > in the entire text.

Three solutions present themselves (apart from using a proper parser). One is **<img[^>]*>** (match <img, then any number of non-> characters and then the tag's closing > character), another is **<img.*?>** (match <img, then any number of characters, but nongreedily, so it will stop immediately before the tag's closing >, and then the >), and a third combines both, as in **<img[^>]*?>**. None of them is correct, though, since they can all match <u><img></u>, which is not valid. Since we know that an image tag must have a src attribute, a more accurate regex is **<img\s+[^>]*?src=\w+[^>]*?>**. This matches the literal characters <img, then one or more whitespace characters, then nongreedily zero or more of anything except > (to skip any other attributes such as alt), then the src attribute (the literal characters src= then at least one "word" character), and then any other non-> characters (including none) to account for any other attributes, and finally the closing >.

Grouping and Capturing

In practical applications we often need regexes that can match any one of two
or more alternatives, and we often need to capture the match or some part
of the match for further processing. Also, we sometimes want a quantifier to
apply to several expressions. All of these can be achieved by grouping with ( ),
and in the case of alternatives using alternation with |.

Alternation is especially useful when we want to match any one of several
quite different alternatives. For example, the regex `aircraft|airplane|jet`
will match any text that contains "aircraft" or "airplane" or "jet". The
same thing can be achieved using the regex `air(craft|plane)|jet`. Here, the
parentheses are used to group expressions, so we have two outer expres-
sions, `air(craft|plane)` and `jet`. The first of these has an inner expression,
`craft|plane`, and because this is preceded by `air` the first outer expression can
match only "aircraft" or "airplane".

Parentheses serve two different purposes—to group expressions and to capture
the text that matches an expression. We will use the term *group* to refer to a
grouped expression whether it captures or not, and *capture* and *capture group*
to refer to a captured group. If we used the regex `(aircraft|airplane|jet)` it
would not only match any of the three expressions, but would also capture
whichever one was matched for later reference. Compare this with the regex
`(air(craft|plane)|jet)` which has two captures if the first expression matches
("aircraft" or "airplane" as the first capture and "craft" or "plane" as the second
capture), and one capture if the second expression matches ("jet"). We can
switch off the capturing effect by following an opening parenthesis with `?:`, so
for example, `(air(?:craft|plane)|jet)` will have only one capture if it matches
("aircraft" or "airplane" or "jet").

A grouped expression is an expression and so can be quantified. Like any
other expression the quantity is assumed to be one unless explicitly given. For
example, if we have read a text file with lines of the form *key=value*, where
each *key* is alphanumeric, the regex `(\w+)=(.+)` will match every line that has a
nonempty key and a nonempty value. (Recall that . matches anything except
newlines.) And for every line that matches, two captures are made, the first
being the key and the second being the value.

For example, the *key=value* regular expression will match the entire line
`topic= physical geography` with the two captures shown shaded. Notice that
the second capture includes some whitespace, and that whitespace before the
= is not accepted. We could refine the regex to be more flexible in accepting
whitespace, and to strip off unwanted whitespace using a somewhat longer
version:

```
[ \t]*(\w+)[ \t]*=[ \t]*(.+)
```

This matches the same line as before and also lines that have whitespace around the = sign, but with the first capture having no leading or trailing whitespace, and the second capture having no leading whitespace. For example: ple: <u>topic = physical geography</u>.

We have been careful to keep the whitespace matching parts outside the capturing parentheses, and to allow for lines that have no whitespace at all. We did not use \s to match whitespace because that matches newlines (\n) which could lead to incorrect matches that span lines (e.g., if the re.MULTILINE flag is used). And for the value we did not use \S to match nonwhitespace because we want to allow for values that contain whitespace (e.g., English sentences). To avoid the second capture having trailing whitespace we would need a more sophisticated regex; we will see this in the next subsection.

Regex flags ☞ 460

Captures can be referred to using *backreferences*, that is, by referring back to an earlier capture group.* One syntax for backreferences inside regexes themselves is *i* where *i* is the capture number. Captures are numbered starting from one and increasing by one going from left to right as each new (capturing) left parenthesis is encountered. For example, to simplistically match duplicated words we can use the regex (\w+)\s+\1 which matches a "word", then at least one whitespace, and then the same word as was captured. (Capture number 0 is created automatically without the need for parentheses; it holds the entire match, that is, what we show underlined.) We will see a more sophisticated way to match duplicate words later.

In long or complicated regexes it is often more convenient to use names rather than numbers for captures. This can also make maintenance easier since adding or removing capturing parentheses may change the numbers but won't affect names. To name a capture we follow the opening parenthesis with (?P<*name*>. For example, (?P<key>\w+)=(?P<value>.+) has two captures called "key" and "value". The syntax for backreferences to named captures inside a regex is (?P=*name*). For example, (?P<word>\w+)\s+(?P=word) matches duplicate words using a capture called "word".

Assertions and Flags

One problem that affects many of the regexes we have looked at so far is that they can match more or different text than we intended. For example, the regex aircraft|airplane|jet will match "waterjet" and "jetski" as well as "jet". This kind of problem can be solved by using assertions. An assertion does not match any text, but instead says something about the text at the point where the assertion occurs.

---

*Note that backreferences cannot be used inside character classes, that is, inside [].

One assertion is **\b** (word boundary), which asserts that the character that precedes it must be a "word" (\w) and the character that follows it must be a non-"word" (\W), or vice versa. For example, although the regex **jet** can match twice in the text the jet and jetski are noisy, that is, the jet and jetski are noisy, the regex **\bjet\b** will match only once, the jet and jetski are noisy. In the context of the original regex, we could write it either as **\baircraft\b|\bairplane\b|\bjet\b** or more clearly as **\b(?:aircraft|airplane|jet)\b**, that is, word boundary, noncapturing expression, word boundary.

Many other assertions are supported, as shown in Table 12.3. We could use assertions to improve the clarity of a *key=value* regex, for example, by changing it to **^(\w+)=([^\n]+)** and setting the re.MULTILINE flag to ensure that each *key=value* is taken from a single line with no possibility of spanning lines. (The flags are shown in Table 12.5 on page 460, and the syntaxes for using them are described at the end of this subsection and are shown in the next section.) And if we also want to strip leading and trailing whitespace and use named captures, the full regex becomes:

```
^[ \t]*(?P<key>\w+)[ \t]*=[ \t]*(?P<value>[^\n]+)(?<![ \t])
```

Even though this regex is designed for a fairly simple task, it looks quite complicated. One way to make it more maintainable is to include comments in it. This can be done by adding inline comments using the syntax (?#*the comment*), but in practice comments like this can easily make the regex even more difficult to read. A much nicer solution is to use the re.VERBOSE flag—this allows us to freely use whitespace and normal Python comments in regexes, with the one constraint that if we need to match whitespace we must either use **\s** or a character class such as [ ]. Here's the *key=value* regex with comments:

Regex
flags

☞ 460

```
^[ \t]*                 # start of line and optional leading whitespace
(?P<key>\w+)            # the key text
[ \t]*=[ \t]*           # the equals with optional surrounding whitespace
(?P<value>[^\n]+)       # the value text
(?<![ \t])              # negative lookbehind to avoid trailing whitespace
```

Raw
strings

62 ☜

In the context of a Python program we would normally write a regex like this inside a raw triple quoted string—raw so that we don't have to double up the backslashes, and triple quoted so that we can spread it over multiple lines.

In addition to the assertions we have discussed so far, there are additional assertions which look at the text in front of (or behind) the assertion to see whether it matches (or does not match) an expression we specify. The expressions that can be used in lookbehind assertions must be of fixed length (so the quantifiers ?, +, and * cannot be used, and numeric quantifiers must be of a fixed size, for example, {3}).

Table 12.3 *Regular Expression Assertions*

Symbol	Meaning
^	Matches at the start; also matches after each newline with the re.MULTILINE flag
$	Matches at the end; also matches before each newline with the re.MULTILINE flag
\A	Matches at the start
\b	Matches at a "word" boundary; influenced by the re.ASCII flag—inside a character class this is the escape for the backspace character
\B	Matches at a non-"word" boundary; influenced by the re.ASCII flag
\Z	Matches at the end
(?=e)	Matches if the expression e matches at this assertion but does not advance over it—called *lookahead* or *positive lookahead*
(?!e)	Matches if the expression e does not match at this assertion and does not advance over it—called *negative lookahead*
(?<=e)	Matches if the expression e matches immediately before this assertion—called *positive lookbehind*
(?<!e)	Matches if the expression e does not match immediately before this assertion—called *negative lookbehind*

Regex flags

☞ 460

In the case of the *key=value* regex, the negative lookbehind assertion means that at the point it occurs the *preceding* character must not be a space or a tab. This has the effect of ensuring that the last character captured into the "value" capture group is not a space or tab (yet without preventing spaces or tabs from appearing inside the captured text).

Let's consider another example. Suppose we are reading a multiline text that contains the names "Helen Patricia Sharman", "Jim Sharman", "Sharman Joshi", "Helen Kelly", and so on, and we want to match "Helen Patricia", but only when referring to "Helen Patricia Sharman". The easiest way is to use the regex \b(Helen\s+Patricia)\s+Sharman\b. But we could also achieve the same thing using a lookahead assertion, for example, \b(Helen\s+Patricia)(?=\s+Sharman\b). This will match "Helen Patricia" only if it is preceded by a word boundary and followed by whitespace and "Sharman" ending at a word boundary.

To capture the particular variation of the forenames that is used ("Helen", "Helen P.", or "Helen Patricia"), we could make the regex slightly more sophisticated, for example, \b(Helen(?:\s+(?:P\.|Patricia))?)\s+(?=Sharman\b). This matches a word boundary followed by one of the forename forms—but only if this is followed by some whitespace and then "Sharman" and a word boundary.

Note that only two syntaxes perform capturing, (*e*) and (?P<*name*>*e*). None of the other parenthesized forms captures. This makes perfect sense for the lookahead and lookbehind assertions since they only make a statement about what follows or precedes them—they are not part of the match, but rather affect whether a match is made. It also makes sense for the last two parenthesized forms that we will now consider.

We saw earlier how we can backreference a capture inside a regex either by number (e.g., \1) or by name (e.g., (?P=*name*)). It is also possible to match conditionally depending on whether an earlier match occurred. The syntaxes are (?(*id*)*yes_exp*) and (?(*id*)*yes_exp*|*no_exp*). The *id* is the name or number of an earlier capture that we are referring to. If the capture succeeded the *yes_exp* will be matched here. If the capture failed the no_exp will be matched if it is given.

Let's consider an example. Suppose we want to extract the filenames referred to by the src attribute in HTML img tags. We will begin just by trying to match the src attribute, but unlike our earlier attempt we will account for the three forms that the attribute's value can take: single quoted, double quoted, and unquoted. Here is an initial attempt: src=(["'])([^"'>]+)\1. The ([^"'>]+) part captures a greedy match of at least one character that isn't a quote or >. This regex works fine for quoted filenames, and thanks to the \1 matches only when the opening and closing quotes are the same. But it does not allow for unquoted filenames. To fix this we must make the opening quote optional and therefore match only it if it is present. Here is the revised regex: src=(["'])?([^"'>]+)(?(1)\1). We did not provide a *no_exp* since there is nothing to match if no quote is given. Now we are ready to put the regex in context—here is the complete img tag regex using named groups and comments:

```
<img\s+               # start of the tag
[^>]*?                # any attributes that precede the src
src=                  # start of the src attribute
(?P<quote>["'])?      # optional opening quote
(?P<image>[^"'>]+)    # image filename
(?(quote)(?P=quote))  # closing quote (matches opening quote if given)
[^>]*?                # any attributes that follow the src
>                     # end of the tag
```

The filename capture is called "image" (which happens to be capture number 2).

Of course, there is a simpler but subtler alternative: src=(["']?)([^"'>]+)\1. Here, if there is a starting quote character it is captured into capture group 1 and matched after the nonquote characters. And if there is no starting quote character, group 1 will still match—an empty string since it is completely optional (its quantifier is zero or one), in which case the backreference will also match an empty string.

The final piece of regex syntax that Python's regular expression engine offers is a means of setting the flags. Usually the flags are set by passing them as additional parameters when calling the re.compile() function, but sometimes it is more convenient to set them as part of the regex itself. The syntax is simply (?*flags*) where *flags* is one or more of a (the same as passing re.ASCII), i (re.IGNORECASE), m (re.MULTILINE), s (re.DOTALL), and x (re.VERBOSE).* If the flags are set this way they should be put at the start of the regex; they match nothing, so their effect on the regex is only to set the flags.

Regex
flags
☞ 460

The Regular Expression Module ▐▐▐

The re module provides two ways of working with regexes. One is to use the functions listed in Table 12.4, where each function is given a regex as its first argument. Each function converts the regex into an internal format—a process called *compiling*—and then does its work. This is very convenient for one-off uses, but if we need to use the same regex repeatedly we can avoid the cost of compiling it at each use by compiling it once using the re.compile() function. We can then call methods on the compiled regex object as many times as we like. The compiled regex methods are listed in Table 12.6.

```
match = re.search(r"#[\dA-Fa-f]{6}\b", text)
```

This code snippet shows the use of an re module function. The regex matches HTML-style colors (such as #C0C0AB). If a match is found the re.search() function returns a match object; otherwise, it returns None. The methods provided by match objects are listed in Table 12.7

If we were going to use this regex repeatedly, we could compile it once and then use the compiled regex whenever we needed it:

```
color_re = re.compile(r"#[\dA-Fa-f]{6}\b")
match = color_re.search(text)
```

As we noted earlier, we use raw strings to avoid having to escape backslashes. Another way of writing this regex would be to use the character class **[\dA-F]** and pass the re.IGNORECASE flag as the last argument to the re.compile() call, or to use the regex **(?i)#[\dA-F]{6}\b** which starts with the ignore case flag.

---

*The letters used for the flags are the same as the ones used by Perl's regex engine, which is why s is used for re.DOTALL and x is used for re.VERBOSE.

If more than one flag is required they can be combined using the OR operator (|), for example, re.MULTILINE|re.DOTALL, or (?ms) if embedded in the regex itself.

We will round off this section by reviewing some examples, starting with some of the regexes shown in earlier sections, so as to illustrate the most commonly used functionality that the re module provides. Let's start with a regex to spot duplicate words:

```
double_word_re = re.compile(r"\b(?P<word>\w+)\s+(?P=word)(?!\w)",
                            re.IGNORECASE)
for match in double_word_re.finditer(text):
    print("{0} is duplicated".format(match.group("word")))
```

The regex is slightly more sophisticated than the version we made earlier. It starts at a word boundary (to ensure that each match starts at the beginning of a word), then greedily matches one or more "word" characters, then one or more whitespace characters, then the same word again—but only if the second occurrence of the word is not followed by a word character.

If the input text was "win in vain", *without* the first assertion there would be one match and two captures: win in vain. The use of the word boundary assertion ensures that the first word matched is a whole word, so we end up with no match or capture since there is no duplicate word. Similarly, if the input text was "one and and two let's say", *without* the last assertion there would be two matches and two captures: one and and two let's say. The use of the lookahead assertion means that the second word matched is a whole word, so we end up with one match and one capture: one and and two let's say.

The for loop iterates over every match object returned by the finditer() method and we use the match object's group() method to retrieve the captured group's text. We could just as easily (but less maintainably) have used group(1)—in which case we need not have named the capture group at all and just used the regex (\w+)\s+\1(?!\w). Another point to note is that we could have used a word boundary \b at the end, instead of (?!\w).

Another example we presented earlier was a regex for finding the filenames in HTML image tags. Here is how we would compile the regex, adding flags so that it is not case-sensitive, and allowing us to include comments:

```
image_re = re.compile(r"""
            <img\s+                  # start of tag
            [^>]*?                   # non-src attributes
            src=                     # start of src attribute
            (?P<quote>["'])?         # optional opening quote
            (?P<image>[^"'>]+)       # image filename
            (?(quote)(?P=quote))     # closing quote
            [^>]*?                   # non-src attributes
            >                        # end of the tag
```

```
                    """, re.IGNORECASE|re.VERBOSE)
    image_files = []
    for match in image_re.finditer(text):
        image_files.append(match.group("image"))
```

Again we use the finditer() method to retrieve each match and the match object's group() function to retrieve the captured texts. Since the case insensitivity applies only to **img** and **src**, we could drop the re.IGNORECASE flag and use **[Ii][Mm][Gg]** and **[Ss][Rr][Cc]** instead. Although this would make the regex less clear, it might make it faster since it would not require the text being matched to be set to upper- (or lower-) case—but it is likely to make a difference only if the regex was being used on a very large amount of text.

One common task is to take an HTML text and output just the plain text that it contains. Naturally we could do this using one of Python's parsers, but a simple tool can be created using regexes. There are three tasks that need to be done: delete any tags, replace entities with the characters they represent, and insert blank lines to separate paragraphs. Here is a function (taken from the html2text.py program) that does the job:

```
def html2text(html_text):
    def char_from_entity(match):
        code = html.entities.name2codepoint.get(match.group(1), 0xFFFD)
        return chr(code)

    text = re.sub(r"<!--(?:.|\n)*?-->", "", html_text)         #1
    text = re.sub(r"<[Pp][^>]*?(?!</)>", "\n\n", text)          #2
    text = re.sub(r"<[^>]*?>", "", text)                        #3
    text = re.sub(r"&#(\d+);", lambda m: chr(int(m.group(1))), text)
    text = re.sub(r"&([A-Za-z]+);", char_from_entity, text)     #5
    text = re.sub(r"\n(?:[ \xA0\t]+\n)+", "\n", text)           #6
    return re.sub(r"\n\n+", "\n\n", text.strip())               #7
```

The first regex, **<!--(?:.|\n)*?-->**, matches HTML comments, including those with other HTML tags nested inside them. The re.sub() function replaces as many matches as it finds with the replacement—deleting the matches if the replacement is an empty string, as it is here. (We can specify a maximum number of matches by giving an additional integer argument at the end.)

We are careful to use nongreedy (minimal) matching to ensure that we delete one comment for each match; if we did not do this we would delete from the start of the first comment to the end of the last comment.

The re.sub() function does not accept any flags as arguments, so . means "any character except newline", so we must look for . or \n. And we must look for these using alternation rather than a character class, since inside a character class . has its literal meaning, that is, period. An alternative would be to begin the regex with the flag embedded, for example, **(?s)<!--.*?-->**, or we could compile a regex object with the re.DOTALL flag, in which case the regex would simply be `<!--.*?-->`.

The second regex, `<[Pp][^>]*?(?!</)>`, matches opening paragraph tags (such as `<P>` or `<p align=center>`). It matches the opening `<p` (or `<P`), then any attributes (using nongreedy matching), and finally the closing `>`, providing it is not preceded by `/` (using a negative lookbehind assertion), since that would indicate a closing paragraph tag. The second call to the re.sub() function uses this regex to replace opening paragraph tags with two newline characters (the standard way to delimit a paragraph in a plain text file).

The third regex, `<[^>]*?>`, matches any tag and is used in the third re.sub() call to delete all the remaining tags.

HTML entities are a way of specifying non-ASCII characters using ASCII characters. They come in two forms: `&`*name*`;` where *name* is the name of the character—for example, `&copy;` for ©, and `&#`*digits*`;` where *digits* are decimal digits identifying the Unicode code point—for example, `&#165;` for ¥. The fourth call to re.sub() uses the regex `&#(\d+);`, which matches the digits form and captures the digits into capture group 1. Instead of a literal replacement text we have passed a lambda function. When a function is passed to re.sub() it calls the function once for each time it matches, passing the match object as the function's sole argument. Inside the lambda function we retrieve the digits (as a string), convert to an integer using the built-in int() function, and then use the built-in chr() function to obtain the Unicode character for the given code point. The function's return value (or in the case of a lambda expression, the result of the expression) is used as the replacement text.

The fifth re.sub() call uses the regex `&([A-Za-z]+);` to capture named entities. The standard library's html.entities module contains dictionaries of entities, including name2codepoint whose keys are entity names and whose values are integer code points. The re.sub() function calls the local char_from_entity() function every time it has a match. The char_from_entity() function uses dict.get() with a default argument of 0xFFFD (the code point of the standard Unicode replacement character—often depicted as). This ensures that a code point is always retrieved and it is used with the chr() function to return a suitable character to replace the named entity with—using the Unicode replacement character if the entity name is invalid.

The sixth re.sub() call's regex, `\n(?:[ \xA0\t]+\n)+`, is used to delete lines that contain only whitespace. The character class we have used contains a space, a nonbreaking space (which ` ` entities are replaced with in the preceding regex), and a tab. The regex matches a newline (the one at the end of a line that precedes one or more whitespace-only lines), then at least one (and as many as possible) lines that contain only whitespace. Since the match includes the newline, from the line preceding the whitespace-only lines we must replace the match with a single newline; otherwise, we would delete not just the whitespace-only lines but also the newline of the line that preceded them.

The result of the seventh and last re.sub() call is returned to the caller. This regex, \n\n+, is used to replace sequences of two or more newlines with exactly two newlines, that is, to ensure that each paragraph is separated by just one blank line.

In the HTML example none of the replacements were directly taken from the match (although HTML entity names and numbers were used), but in some situations the replacement might need to include all or some of the matching text. For example, if we have a list of names, each of the form *Forename Middlename1 ... MiddlenameN Surname*, where there may be any number of middle names (including none), and we want to produce a new version of the list with each item of the form *Surname, Forename Middlename1 ... MiddlenameN*, we can easily do so using a regex:

```
new_names = []
for name in names:
    name = re.sub(r"(\w+(?:\s+\w+)*)\s+(\w+)", r"\2, \1", name)
    new_names.append(name)
```

The first part of the regex, (\w+(?:\s+\w+)*), matches the forename with the first \w+ expression and zero or more middle names with the (?:\s+\w+)* expression. The middle name expression matches zero or more occurrences of whitespace followed by a word. The second part of the regex, \s+(\w+), matches the whitespace that follows the forename (and middle names) and the surname.

If the regex looks a bit too much like line noise, we can use named capture groups to improve legibility and make it more maintainable:

```
name = re.sub(r"(?P<forenames>\w+(?:\s+\w+)*)"
              r"\s+(?P<surname>\w+)",
              r"\g<surname>, \g<forenames>", name)
```

Captured text can be referred to in a sub() or subn() function or method by using the syntax *i* or \g<*id*> where *i* is the number of the capture group and *id* is the name or number of the capture group—so \1 is the same as \g<1>, and in this example, the same as \g<forenames>. This syntax can also be used in the string passed to a match object's expand() method.

Why doesn't the first part of the regex grab the entire name? After all, it is using greedy matching. In fact it will, but then the match will fail because although the middle names part can match zero or more times, the surname part must match exactly once, but the greedy middle names part has grabbed everything. Having failed, the regular expression engine will then backtrack, giving up the last "middle name" and thus allowing the surname to match.

Table 12.4 *The Regular Expression Module's Functions*

Syntax	Description
re.compile(r, f)	Returns compiled regex r with its flags set to f if specified
re.escape(s)	Returns string s with all nonalphanumeric characters backslash-escaped—therefore, the returned string has no special regex characters
re.findall(r, s, f)	Returns all nonoverlapping matches of regex r in string s (influenced by the flags f if given). If the regex has captures, each match is returned as a tuple of captures.
re.finditer(r, s, f)	Returns a match object for each nonoverlapping match of regex r in string s (influenced by the flags f if given)
re.match(r, s, f)	Returns a match object if the regex r matches at the start of string s (influenced by the flags f if given); otherwise, returns None
re.search(r, s, f)	Returns a match object if the regex r matches anywhere in string s (influenced by the flags f if given); otherwise, returns None
re.split(r, s, m, f)	Returns the list of strings that results from splitting string s on every occurrence of regex r doing up to m splits (or as many as possible if no m is given, and for Python 3.1 influenced by flags f if given). If the regex has captures, these are included in the list between the parts they split.
re.sub(r, x, s, m, f)	Returns a copy of string s with every (or up to m if given, and for Python 3.1 influenced by flags f if given) match of regex r replaced with x—this can be a string or a function; see text
re.subn(r, x, s m, f)	The same as re.sub() except that it returns a 2-tuple of the resultant string and the number of substitutions that were made—and for Python 3.1 influenced by flags f

Table 12.5 *The Regular Expression Module's Flags*

Flag	Meaning
re.A or re.ASCII	Makes \b, \B, \s, \S, \w, and \W assume that strings are ASCII; the default is for these character class shorthands to depend on the Unicode specification
re.I or re.IGNORECASE	Makes the regex match case-insensitively
re.M or re.MULTILINE	Makes ^ match at the start and after each newline and $ match before each newline and at the end
re.S or re.DOTALL	Makes . match every character including newlines
re.X or re.VERBOSE	Allows whitespace and comments to be included

Table 12.6 *Regular Expression Object Methods*

Syntax	Description
rx.findall(s start, end)	Returns all nonoverlapping matches of the regex in string s (or in the *start*:*end* slice of s). If the regex has captures, each match is returned as a tuple of captures.
rx.finditer(s start, end)	Returns a match object for each nonoverlapping match in string s (or in the *start*:*end* slice of s)
rx.flags	The flags that were set when the regex was compiled
rx.groupindex	A dictionary whose keys are capture group names and whose values are group numbers; empty if no names are used
rx.match(s, start, end)	Returns a match object if the regex matches at the start of string s (or at the start of the *start*:*end* slice of s); otherwise, returns None
rx.pattern	The string from which the regex was compiled
rx.search(s, start, end)	Returns a match object if the regex matches anywhere in string s (or in the *start*:*end* slice of s); otherwise, returns None
rx.split(s, m)	Returns the list of strings that results from splitting string s on every occurrence of the regex doing up to m splits (or as many as possible if no m is given). If the regex has captures, these are included in the list between the parts they split.
rx.sub(x, s, m)	Returns a copy of string s with every (or up to m if given) match replaced with x—this can be a string or a function; see text
rx.subn(x, s m)	The same as re.sub() except that it returns a 2-tuple of the resultant string and the number of substitutions that were made

Although greedy matches match as much as possible, they stop if matching more would make the match fail.

For example, if the name is "James W. Loewen", the regex will first match the entire name, that is, James W. Loewen. This satisfies the first part of the regex but leaves nothing for the surname part to match, and since the surname is mandatory (it has an implicit quantifier of 1), the regex has failed. Since the middle names part is quantified by *, it can match zero or more times (currently it is matching twice, " W." and " Loewen"), so the regular expression engine can make it give up some of its match without causing it to fail. Therefore, the regex backtracks, giving up the last \s+\w+ (i.e., " Loewen"), so the match becomes <u>James W. Loewen</u> with the match satisfying the whole regex and with the two match groups containing the correct texts.

When we use alternation (|) with two or more alternatives capturing, we don't know which alternative matched, so we don't know which capture group to retrieve the captured text from. We can of course iterate over all the groups to find the nonempty one, but quite often in this situation the match object's lastindex attribute can give us the number of the group we want. We will look at one last example to illustrate this and to give us a little bit more regex practice.

Suppose we want to find out what encoding an HTML, XML, or Python file is using. We could open the file in binary mode, and read, say, the first 1 000 bytes into a bytes object. We could then close the file, look for an encoding in the bytes, and reopen the file in text mode using the encoding we found or using a fallback encoding (such as UTF-8). The regex engine expects regexes to be supplied as strings, but the text the regex is applied to can be a str, bytes, or bytearray object, and when bytes or bytearray objects are used, all the functions and methods return bytes instead of strings, and the re.ASCII flag is implicitly switched on.

For HTML files the encoding is normally specified in a <meta> tag (if specified at all), for example, <meta http-equiv='Content-Type' content='text/html; charset=ISO-8859-1'/>. XML files are UTF-8 by default, but this can be overridden, for example, <?xml version="1.0" encoding="Shift_JIS"?>. Python 3 files are also UTF-8 by default, but again this can be overridden by including a line such as # encoding: latin1 or # -*- coding: latin1 -*- immediately after the shebang line.

Here is how we would find the encoding, assuming that the variable binary is a bytes object containing the first 1 000 bytes of an HTML, XML, or Python file:

```
match = re.search(r"""(?<![-\w])                    #1
                      (?:(?:en)?coding|charset)     #2
                      (?:=(["'])?([-\w]+)(?(1)\1)   #3
                      |:\s*([-\w]+))""".encode("utf8"),
                  binary, re.IGNORECASE|re.VERBOSE)
encoding = match.group(match.lastindex) if match else b"utf8"
```

To search a bytes object we must specify a pattern that is also a bytes object. In this case we want the convenience of using a raw string, so we use one and convert it to a bytes object as the re.search() function's first argument.

The first part of the regex itself is a lookbehind assertion that says that the match cannot be preceded by a hypen or a word character. The second part matches "encoding", "coding", or "charset" and could have been written as (?:encoding|coding|charset). We have made the third part span two lines to emphasise the fact that it has two alternating parts, =(["'])?([-\w]+)(?(1)\1)

Con-
ditional
match-
ing

454 ☜

Table 12.7 *Match Object Attributes and Methods*

Syntax	Description
`m.end(g)`	Returns the end position of the match in the text for group *g* if given (or for group 0, the whole match); returns -1 if the group did not participate in the match
`m.endpos`	The search's end position (the end of the text or the *end* given to `match()` or `search()`)
`m.expand(s)`	Returns string `s` with capture markers (\1, \2, \g<name>, and similar) replaced by the corresponding captures
`m.group(g, ...)`	Returns the numbered or named capture group *g*; if more than one is given a tuple of corresponding capture groups is returned (the whole match is group 0)
`m.groupdict( default)`	Returns a dictionary of all the named capture groups with the names as keys and the captures as values; if a *default* is given this is the value used for capture groups that did not participate in the match
`m.groups( default)`	Returns a tuple of all the capture groups starting from 1; if a *default* is given this is the value used for capture groups that did not participate in the match
`m.lastgroup`	The name of the highest numbered capturing group that matched or None if there isn't one or if no names are used
`m.lastindex`	The number of the highest capturing group that matched or None if there isn't one
`m.pos`	The start position to look from (the start of the text or the *start* given to `match()` or `search()`)
`m.re`	The regex object which produced this match object
`m.span(g)`	Returns the start and end positions of the match in the text for group *g* if given (or for group 0, the whole match); returns (-1, -1) if the group did not participate in the match
`m.start(g)`	Returns the start position of the match in the text for group *g* if given (or for group 0, the whole match); returns -1 if the group did not participate in the match
`m.string`	The string that was passed to `match()` or `search()`

and :\s*([-\w]+), only one of which can match. The first of these matches an equals sign followed by one or more word or hyphen characters (optionally enclosed in matching quotes using a conditional match), and the second matches a colon and then optional whitespace followed by one or more word or hyphen characters. (Recall that a hyphen inside a character class is taken to be a literal hyphen if it is the first character; otherwise, it means a range of characters, for example, [0-9].)

We have used the re.IGNORECASE flag to avoid having to write (?:(?:[Ee][Nn])?
[Cc][Oo][Dd][Ii][Nn][Gg]|[Cc][Hh][Aa][Rr][Ss][Ee][Tt]) and we have used the
re.VERBOSE flag so that we can lay out the regex neatly and include comments
(in this case just numbers to make the parts easy to refer to in this text).

There are three capturing match groups, all in the third part: (["']) which
captures the optional opening quote, ([-\w]+) which captures an encoding
that follows an equals sign, and the second ([-\w]+) (on the following line)
that captures an encoding that follows a colon. We are only interested in the
encoding, so we want to retrieve either the second or third capture group, only
one of which can match since they are alternatives. The lastindex attribute
holds the index of the last *matching* capture group (either 2 or 3 when a match
occurs in this example), so we retrieve whichever matched, or use a default
encoding if no match was made.

We have now seen all of the most frequently used re module functionality in
action, so we will conclude this section by mentioning one last function. The
re.split() function (or the regex object's split() method) can split strings
based on a regex. One common requirement is to split a text on whitespace
to get a list of words. This can be done using re.split(r"\s+", text) which returns a list of words (or more precisely a list of strings, each of which matches \S+). Regular expressions are very powerful and useful, and once they are
learned, it is easy to see all text problems as requiring a regex solution. But
sometimes using string methods is both sufficient and more appropriate. For
example, we can just as easily split on whitespace by using text.split() since
the str.split() method's default behavior (or with a first argument of None) is
to split on \s+.

Summary

Regular expressions offer a powerful way of searching texts for strings that
match a particular pattern, and for replacing such strings with other strings
which themselves can depend on what was matched.

In this chapter we saw that most characters are matched literally and
are implicitly quantified by {1}. We also learned how to specify character
classes—sets of characters to match—and how to negate such sets and include
ranges of characters in them without having to write each character individually.

We learned how to quantify expressions to match a specific number of times
or to match from a given minimum to a given maximum number of times, and
how to use greedy and nongreedy matching. We also learned how to group one
or more expressions together so that they can be quantified (and optionally
captured) as a unit.

The chapter also showed how what is matched can be affected by using various assertions, such as positive and negative lookahead and lookbehind, and by various flags, for example, to control the interpretation of the period and whether to use case-insensitive matching.

The final section showed how to put regexes to use within the context of Python programs. In this section we learned how to use the functions provided by the re module, and the methods available from compiled regexes and from match objects. We also learned how to replace matches with literal strings, with literal strings that contain backreferences, and with the results of function calls or lambda expressions, and how to make regexes more maintainable by using named captures and comments.

Exercises

1. In many contexts (e.g., in some web forms), users must enter a phone number, and some of these irritate users by accepting only a specific format. Write a program that reads U.S. phone numbers with the three-digit area and seven-digit local codes accepted as ten digits, or separated into blocks using hyphens or spaces, and with the area code optionally enclosed in parentheses. For example, all of these are valid: 555-555-5555, (555) 5555555, (555) 555 5555, and 5555555555. Read the phone numbers from sys.stdin and for each one echo the number in the form "(555) 555 5555" or report an error for any that are invalid.

   The regex to match these phone numbers is about eight lines long (in verbose mode) and is quite straightforward. A solution is provided in phone.py, which is about twenty-five lines long.

2. Write a small program that reads an XML or HTML file specified on the command line and for each tag that has attributes, outputs the name of the tag with its attributes shown underneath. For example, here is an extract from the program's output when given one of the Python documentation's index.html files:

   ```
   html
       xmlns = http://www.w3.org/1999/xhtml
   meta
       http-equiv = Content-Type
       content = text/html; charset=utf-8
   li
       class = right
       style = margin-right: 10px
   ```

   One approach is to use two regexes, one to capture tags with their attributes and another to extract the name and value of each attribute. Attribute values might be quoted using single or double quotes (in which case they may contain whitespace and the quotes that are not used to enclose them), or they may be unquoted (in which case they cannot contain whitespace or quotes). It is probably easiest to start by creating a regex to handle quoted and unquoted values separately, and then merging the two regexes into a single regex to cover both cases. It is best to use named groups to make the regex more readable. This is not easy, especially since backreferences cannot be used inside character classes.

A solution is provided in extract_tags.py, which is less than 35 lines long. The tag and attributes regex is just one line. The attribute name–value regex is half a dozen lines and uses alternation, conditional matching (twice, with one nested inside the other), and both greedy and nongreedy quantifiers.

Introduction to GUI Programming ||||

Python has no native support for GUI (Graphical User Interface) programming, but this isn't a problem since many GUI libraries written in other languages can be used by Python programmers. This is possible because many GUI libraries have Python *wrappers* or *bindings*—these are packages and modules that are imported and used like any other Python packages and modules but which access functionality that is in non-Python libraries under the hood.

Python's standard library includes Tcl/Tk—Tcl is an almost syntax-free scripting language and Tk is a GUI library written in Tcl and C. Python's tkinter module provides Python bindings for the Tk GUI library. Tk has three advantages compared with the other GUI libraries that are available for Python. First, it is installed as standard with Python, so it is always available; second, it is small (even including Tcl); and third, it comes with IDLE which is very useful for experimenting with Python and for editing and debugging Python programs.

Unfortunately, prior to Tk 8.5, Tk had a very dated look and a very limited set of widgets ("controls" or "containers" in Windows-speak). Although it is fairly easy to create custom widgets in Tk by composing other widgets together in a layout, Tk does not provide any direct way of creating custom widgets from scratch with the programmer able to draw whatever they want. Additional Tk-compatible widgets are available using the Tix library—this is also part of Python's standard library but it is not always provided on non-Windows platforms, most notably Ubuntu, which at the time of this writing offers it only as an unsupported add-on. Both Tk and Tix lack Python-oriented documentation—most of the documents are written for Tcl/Tk programmers and may not be easy for non-Tcl programmers to decipher.*

---

* The only Python/Tk book known to the author is *Python and Tkinter Programming* by John Grayson, ISBN 1884777813, published in 2000; it is out of date in some areas. A good Tcl/Tk book

467

For developing GUI programs that must run on any or all Python desktop platforms (e.g., Windows, Mac OS X, and Linux), using only a standard Python installation with no additional libraries, there is just one choice: Tk.

If it is possible to use third-party libraries the number of options opens up considerably. One route is to get the WCK (Widget Construction Kit, www.effbot.org/zone/wck.htm) which provides additional Tk-compatible functionality including the ability to create custom widgets whose contents are drawn in code.

The other choices don't use Tk and fall into two categories, those that are specific to a particular platform and those that are cross-platform. Platform-specific GUI libraries can give us access to platform-specific features, but at the price of locking us in to the platform. The three most well-established cross-platform GUI libraries with Python bindings are PyGtk (www.pygtk.org), PyQt (www.riverbankcomputing.com/software/pyqt), and wxPython (www.wxpython.org). All three of these offer far more widgets than Tk, produce better-looking GUIs (although the gap has narrowed with Tk 8.5), and make it possible to create custom widgets drawn in code. All of them are easier to learn and use than Tk and all have more and much better Python-oriented documentation than Tk. And in general, programs that use PyGtk, PyQt, or wxPython need less code and produce better results than programs written using Tk.

Yet despite its limitations and frustrations, Tk can be used to build useful GUI programs—IDLE being the most well known in the Python world. Furthermore, at the time of this writing, Tk development seems to have picked up, with Tk 8.5 offering theming which makes Tk programs look much more native, as well as the welcome addition of many new widgets.

The purpose of this chapter is to give just a flavor of Tk programming—for serious GUI development it is best to skip this chapter (since it shows the vintage Tk approach to GUI programming), and to use one of the alternative libraries. But if Tk is your only option, then realistically you will need to learn enough of the Tcl language to be able to read Tk's documentation.

In the following sections we will use Tk to create two GUI programs. The first is a very small dialog-style program that does compound interest calculations. The second is a more elaborate main-window-style program that manages a list of bookmarks (names and URLs). By using such simple data we can concentrate on the GUI programming aspects without distraction. In the coverage of the bookmarks program we will see how to create a custom dialog, and how to create a main window with menus and toolbars, as well as how to combine them all together to create a complete working program. But first we must review some of the basics of GUI programming since it is a bit different from writing console programs.

---

is *Practical Programming in Tcl and Tk* by Brent Welch and Ken Jones, ISBN 0130385603. All the Tcl/Tk documentation is online at www.tcl.tk.

Python console programs and module files always have a .py extension, but for Python GUI programs we use a .pyw extension (module files always use .py, though). Both .py and .pyw work fine on Linux, but on Windows, .pyw ensures that Windows uses the pythonw.exe interpreter instead of python.exe, and this in turn ensures that when we execute a Python GUI program, no unnecessary console window will appear. Mac OS X works similarly to Windows, using the .pyw extension for GUI programs.

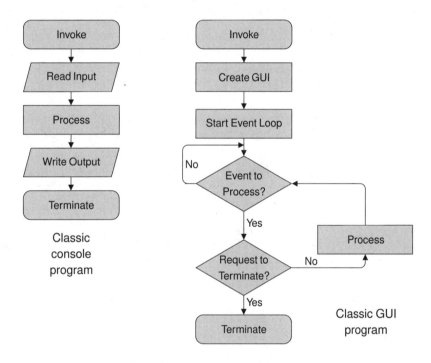

Figure 13.1 *Console programs versus GUI programs*

When a GUI program is run it normally begins by creating its main window and all of the main window's widgets, such as the menu bar, toolbars, the central area, and the status bar. Once the window has been created, like a server program, the GUI program simply waits. Whereas a server waits for client programs to connect to it, a GUI program waits for user interaction such as mouse clicks and key presses. This is illustrated in contrast to console programs in Figure 13.1. The GUI program does not wait passively; it runs an *event loop*, which in pseudocode looks like this:

```
while True:
    event = getNextEvent()
    if event:
        if event == Terminate:
```

```
            break
       processEvent(event)
```

When the user interacts with the program, or when certain other things occur, such as a timer timing out or the program's window being activated (maybe because another program was closed), an event is generated inside the GUI library and added to the event queue. The program's event loop continuously checks to see whether there is an event to process, and if there is, it processes it (or passes it on to the event's associated function or method for processing).

As GUI programmers we can rely on the GUI library to provide the event loop. Our responsibility is to create classes that represent the windows and widgets our program needs and to provide them with methods that respond appropriately to user interactions.

Dialog-Style Programs

The first program we will look at is the Interest program. This is a dialog-style program (i.e., it has no menus), which the user can use to perform compound interest calculations. The program is shown in Figure 13.2.

Figure 13.2 *The Interest program*

In most object-oriented GUI programs, a custom class is used to represent a single main window or dialog, with most of the widgets it contains being instances of standard widgets, such as buttons or checkboxes, supplied by the library. Like most cross-platform GUI libraries, Tk doesn't really make a distinction between a window and a widget—a window is simply a widget that has no widget parent (i.e., it is not contained inside another widget). Widgets that don't have a widget parent (windows) are automatically supplied with a frame and window decorations (such as a title bar and close button), and they usually contains other widgets.

Most widgets are created as children of another widget (and are contained inside their parent), whereas windows are created as children of the tkinter.Tk object—an object that conceptually represents the application, and something we will return to later on. In addition to distinguishing between widgets and windows (also called top-level widgets), the parent–child relationships help ensure that widgets are deleted in the right order and that child widgets are automatically deleted when their parent is deleted.

The initializer is where the user interface is created (the widgets added and laid out, the mouse and keyboard bindings made), and the other methods are used to respond to user interactions. Tk allows us to create custom widgets either by subclassing a predefined widget such as `tkinter.Frame`, or by creating an ordinary class and adding widgets to it as attributes. Here we have used subclassing—in the next example we will show both approaches.

Since the Interest program has just one main window it is implemented in a single class. We will start by looking at the class's initializer, broken into five parts since it is rather long.

```
class MainWindow(tkinter.Frame):

    def __init__(self, parent):
        super(MainWindow, self).__init__(parent)
        self.parent = parent
        self.grid(row=0, column=0)
```

We begin by initializing the base class. (Ideally we would like to write `super().__init__(parent)`, but at the time of this writing, this does not work, so we have called `super()` with the parent class and `self` object passed explicitly as arguments.) Then we keep a copy of the parent for later use. Rather than using absolute positions and sizes, widgets are laid out inside other widgets using layout managers. The call to `grid()` lays out the frame using the grid layout manager. Every widget that is shown must be laid out, even top-level ones. Tk has several layout managers but the grid is the easiest to understand and use, although for top-level layouts where there is only one widget to lay out we could use the packer layout manager by calling `pack()` instead of `grid(row=0, column=0)` to achieve the same effect.

```
        self.principal = tkinter.DoubleVar()
        self.principal.set(1000.0)
        self.rate = tkinter.DoubleVar()
        self.rate.set(5.0)
        self.years = tkinter.IntVar()
        self.amount = tkinter.StringVar()
```

Tk allows us to create variables that are associated with widgets. If a variable's value is changed programatically, the change is reflected in its associated widget, and similarly, if the user changes the value in the widget the associated variable's value is changed. Here we have created two "double" variables (these hold `float` values), an integer variable, and a string variable, and have set initial values for two of them.

```
principalLabel = tkinter.Label(self, text="Principal $:",
                                anchor=tkinter.W, underline=0)
principalScale = tkinter.Scale(self, variable=self.principal,
            command=self.updateUi, from_=100, to=10000000,
            resolution=100, orient=tkinter.HORIZONTAL)
rateLabel = tkinter.Label(self, text="Rate %:", underline=0,
                            anchor=tkinter.W)
rateScale = tkinter.Scale(self, variable=self.rate,
            command=self.updateUi, from_=1, to=100,
            resolution=0.25, digits=5, orient=tkinter.HORIZONTAL)
yearsLabel = tkinter.Label(self, text="Years:", underline=0,
                            anchor=tkinter.W)
yearsScale = tkinter.Scale(self, variable=self.years,
            command=self.updateUi, from_=1, to=50,
            orient=tkinter.HORIZONTAL)
amountLabel = tkinter.Label(self, text="Amount $",
                            anchor=tkinter.W)
actualAmountLabel = tkinter.Label(self,
            textvariable=self.amount, relief=tkinter.SUNKEN,
            anchor=tkinter.E)
```

This part of the initializer is where we create the widgets. The `tkinter.Label` widget is used to display read-only text to the user. Like all widgets it is created with a parent (in this case—and as usual—the parent is the containing widget), and then keyword arguments are used to set various other aspects of the widget's behavior and appearance. We have set the `principalLabel`'s text appropriately, and set its anchor to `tkinter.W`, which means that the label's text is aligned west (left). The underline parameter is used to specify which character in the label should be underlined to indicate a *keyboard accelerator* (e.g., Alt+P); further on we will see how to make the accelerator work. (A keyboard accelerator is a key sequence of the form Alt+*letter* where *letter* is an underlined letter and which results in the keyboard focus being switched to the widget associated with the accelerator, most commonly the widget to the right or below the label that has the accelerator.)

For the `tkinter.Scale` widgets we give them a parent of `self` as usual, and associate a variable with each one. In addition, we give a function (or in this case a method) object reference as their command—this method will be called automatically whenever the scale's value is changed, and set its minimum (`from_`, with a trailing underscore since plain `from` is a keyword) and maximum (`to`) values, and a horizontal orientation. For some of the scales we set a resolution (step size) and for the `rateScale` the number of digits it must be able to display.

The actualAmountLabel is also associated with a variable so that we can easily change the text the label displays later on. We have also given this label a sunken relief so that it fits in better visually with the scales.

```
principalLabel.grid(row=0, column=0, padx=2, pady=2,
                    sticky=tkinter.W)
principalScale.grid(row=0, column=1, padx=2, pady=2,
                    sticky=tkinter.EW)
rateLabel.grid(row=1, column=0, padx=2, pady=2,
                sticky=tkinter.W)
rateScale.grid(row=1, column=1, padx=2, pady=2,
                sticky=tkinter.EW)
yearsLabel.grid(row=2, column=0, padx=2, pady=2,
                sticky=tkinter.W)
yearsScale.grid(row=2, column=1, padx=2, pady=2,
                sticky=tkinter.EW)
amountLabel.grid(row=3, column=0, padx=2, pady=2,
                sticky=tkinter.W)
actualAmountLabel.grid(row=3, column=1, padx=2, pady=2,
                    sticky=tkinter.EW)
```

Having created the widgets, we must now lay them out. The grid layout we have used is illustrated in Figure 13.3.

principalLabel	principalScale
rateLabel	rateScale
yearsLabel	yearsScale
amountLabel	actualAmountLabel

Figure 13.3 *The Interest program's layout*

Every widget supports the grid() method (and some other layout methods such as pack()). Calling grid() lays out the widget within its parent, making it occupy the specified row and column. We can set widgets to span multiple columns and multiple rows using additional keyword arguments (rowspan and columnspan), and we can add some margin around them using the padx (left and right margin) and pady (top and bottom margin) keyword arguments giving integer pixel amounts as arguments. If a widget is allocated more space than it needs, the sticky option is used to determine what should be done with the space; if not specified the widget will occupy the middle of its allocated space. We have set all of the first column's labels to be sticky tkinter.W (west) and all of the second column's widgets to be sticky tkinter.EW (east and west), which makes them stretch to fill the entire width available to them.

All of the widgets are held in local variables, but they don't get scheduled for garbage collection because the parent–child relationships ensure that they are not deleted when they go out of scope at the end of the initializer, since all of them have the main window as their parent. Sometimes widgets are created as instance variables, for example, if we need to refer to them outside the initializer, but in this case we used instance variables for the variables associated with the widgets (self.principal, self.rate, and self.years), so it is these we will use outside the initializer.

```
principalScale.focus_set()
self.updateUi()
parent.bind("<Alt-p>", lambda *ignore: principalScale.focus_set())
parent.bind("<Alt-r>", lambda *ignore: rateScale.focus_set())
parent.bind("<Alt-y>", lambda *ignore: yearsScale.focus_set())
parent.bind("<Control-q>", self.quit)
parent.bind("<Escape>", self.quit)
```

At the end of the initializer we give the keyboard focus to the principalScale widget so that as soon as the program starts the user is able to set the initial amount of money. We then call the self.updateUi() method to calculate the initial amount.

Next, we set up a few key bindings. (Unfortunately, *binding* has three different meanings—variable binding is where a name, that is, an object reference, is bound to an object; a key binding is where a keyboard action such as a key press or release is associated with a function or method to call when the action occurs; and bindings for a library is the glue code that makes a library written in a language other than Python available to Python programmers through Python modules.) Key bindings are essential for some disabled users who have difficulty with or are unable to use the mouse, and they are a great convenience for fast typists who want to avoid using the mouse because it slows them down.

The first three key bindings are used to move the keyboard focus to a scale widget. For example, the principalLabel's text is set to Principal $: and its underline to 0, so the label appears as P̲rincipal $:, and with the first keyboard binding in place when the user types Alt+P the keyboard focus will switch to the principleScale widget. The same applies to the other two bindings. Note that we do not bind the focus_set() method directly. This is because when functions or methods are called as the result of an event binding they are given the event that invoked them as their first argument, and we don't want this event. So, we use a lambda function that accepts but ignores the event and calls the method without the unwanted argument.

We have also created two *keyboard shortcuts*—these are key combinations that invoke a particular action. Here we have set Ctrl+Q and Esc and bound them both to the self.quit() method that cleanly terminates the program.

It is possible to create keyboard bindings for individual widgets, but here we have set them all on the parent (the application), so they all work no matter where the keyboard focus is.

Tk's bind() method can be used to bind both mouse clicks and key presses, and also programmer-defined events. Special keys like Ctrl and Esc have Tk-specific names (Control and Escape), and ordinary letters stand for themselves. Key sequences are created by putting the parts in angle brackets and separating them with hyphens.

Having created and laid out the widgets, and set up the key bindings, the appearance and basic behavior of the program are in place. Now we will review the methods that respond to user actions to complete the implementation of the program's behavior.

```python
def updateUi(self, *ignore):
    amount = self.principal.get() * (
            (1 + (self.rate.get() / 100.0)) ** self.years.get())
    self.amount.set("{0:.2f}".format(amount))
```

This method is called whenever the user changes the principal, the rate, or the years since it is the command associated with each of the scales. All it does is retrieve the value from each scale's associated variable, perform the compound interest calculation, and store the result (as a string) in the variable associated with the actual amount label. As a result, the actual amount label always shows an up-to-date amount.

```python
def quit(self, event=None):
    self.parent.destroy()
```

If the user chooses to quit (by pressing Ctrl+Q or Esc, or by clicking the window's close button) this method is called. Since there is no data to save we just tell the parent (which is the application object) to destroy itself. The parent will destroy all of its children—all of the windows, which in turn will destroy all of their widgets—so a clean termination takes place.

```python
application = tkinter.Tk()
path = os.path.join(os.path.dirname(__file__), "images/")
if sys.platform.startswith("win"):
    icon = path + "interest.ico"
else:
    icon = "@" + path + "interest.xbm"
application.iconbitmap(icon)
application.title("Interest")
window = MainWindow(application)
application.protocol("WM_DELETE_WINDOW", window.quit)
application.mainloop()
```

After defining the class for the main (and in this case only) window, we have the
code that starts the program running. We begin by creating an object to represent the application as a whole. To give the program an icon on Windows we use
an `.ico` file and pass the name of the file (with its full path) to the `iconbitmap()`
method. But for Unix platforms we must provide a bitmap (i.e., a monochrome
image). Tk has several built-in bitmaps, so to distinguish one that comes from
the file system we must precede its name with an @ symbol. Next we give the
application a title (which will appear in the title bar), and then we create an instance of our `MainWindow` class giving the application object as its parent. At the
end we call the `protocol()` method to say what should happen if the user clicks
the close button—we have said that the `MainWindow.quit()` method should be
called, and finally we start the event loop—it is only when we reach this point
that the window is displayed and is able to respond to user interactions.

Main-Window-Style Programs

Although dialog-style programs are often sufficient for simple tasks, as the
range of functionality a program offers grows it often makes sense to create
a complete main-window-style application with menus and toolbars. Such
applications are usually easier to extend than dialog-style programs since we
can add extra menus or menu options and toolbar buttons without affecting the
main window's layout.

In this section we will review the `bookmarks-tk.pyw` program shown in Figure 13.4. The program maintains a set of bookmarks as pairs of (name, URL)
strings and has facilities for the user to add, edit, and remove bookmarks, and
to open their web browser at a particular bookmarked web page.

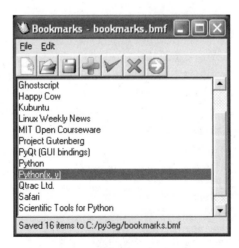

Figure 13.4 *The Bookmarks program*

The program has two windows: the main window with the menu bar, toolbar, list of bookmarks, and status bar; and a dialog window for adding or editing bookmarks.

Creating a Main Window

The main window is similar to a dialog in that it has widgets that must be created and laid out. And in addition we must add the menu bar, menus, toolbar, and status bar, as well as methods to perform the actions the user requests. The user interface is all set up in the main window's initializer, which we will review in five parts because it is fairly long.

```
class MainWindow:

    def __init__(self, parent):
        self.parent = parent

        self.filename = None
        self.dirty = False
        self.data = {}

        menubar = tkinter.Menu(self.parent)
        self.parent["menu"] = menubar
```

For this window, instead of inheriting a widget as we did in the preceding example, we have just created a normal Python class. If we inherit we can reimplement the methods of the class we have inherited, but if we don't need to do that we can simply use composition as we have done here. The appearance is provided by creating widget instance variables, all contained within a tkinter.Frame as we will see in a moment.

We need to keep track of four pieces of information: the parent (application) object, the name of the current bookmarks file, a dirty flag (if True this means that changes have been made to the data that have not been saved to disk), and the data itself, a dictionary whose keys are bookmark names and whose values are URLs.

To create a menu bar we must create a tkinter.Menu object whose parent is the window's parent, and we must tell the parent that it has a menu. (It may seem strange that a menu bar is a menu, but Tk has had a very long evolution which has left it with some odd corners.) Menu bars created like this do not need to be laid out; Tk will do that for us.

```
        fileMenu = tkinter.Menu(menubar)
        for label, command, shortcut_text, shortcut in (
                ("New...", self.fileNew, "Ctrl+N", "<Control-n>"),
                ("Open...", self.fileOpen, "Ctrl+O", "<Control-o>"),
                ("Save", self.fileSave, "Ctrl+S", "<Control-s>"),
```

```
                    (None, None, None, None),
                    ("Quit", self.fileQuit, "Ctrl+Q", "<Control-q>")):
            if label is None:
                fileMenu.add_separator()
            else:
                fileMenu.add_command(label=label, underline=0,
                        command=command, accelerator=shortcut_text)
                self.parent.bind(shortcut, command)
        menubar.add_cascade(label="File", menu=fileMenu, underline=0)
```

Each menu bar menu is created in the same way. First we create a tkinter.Menu object that is a child of the menu bar, and then we add separators or commands to the menu. (Note that an accelerator in Tk terminology is actually a keyboard shortcut, and that all the accelerator option sets is the text of the shortcut; it does not actually set up a key binding.) The underline indicates which character is underlined, in this case the first one of every menu option, and this letter becomes the menu option's keyboard accelerator. In addition to adding a menu option (called a command), we also provide a keyboard shortcut by binding a key sequence to the same command as that invoked when the corresponding menu option is chosen. At the end the menu is added to the menu bar using the add_cascade() method.

We have omitted the edit menu since it is structurally identical to the file menu's code.

```
        frame = tkinter.Frame(self.parent)
        self.toolbar_images = []
        toolbar = tkinter.Frame(frame)
        for image, command in (
                ("images/filenew.gif", self.fileNew),
                ("images/fileopen.gif", self.fileOpen),
                ("images/filesave.gif", self.fileSave),
                ("images/editadd.gif", self.editAdd),
                ("images/editedit.gif", self.editEdit),
                ("images/editdelete.gif", self.editDelete),
                ("images/editshowwebpage.gif", self.editShowWebPage)):
            image = os.path.join(os.path.dirname(__file__), image)
            try:
                image = tkinter.PhotoImage(file=image)
                self.toolbar_images.append(image)
                button = tkinter.Button(toolbar, image=image,
                                        command=command)
                button.grid(row=0, column=len(self.toolbar_images) -1)
            except tkinter.TclError as err:
                print(err)
        toolbar.grid(row=0, column=0, columnspan=2, sticky=tkinter.NW)
```

We begin by creating a frame in which all of the window's widgets will be contained. Then we create another frame, toolbar, to contain a horizontal row of buttons that have images instead of texts, to serve as toolbar buttons. We lay out each toolbar button one after the other in a grid that has one row and as many columns as there are buttons. At the end we lay out the toolbar frame itself as the main window frame's first row, making it north west sticky so that it will always cling to the top left of the window. (Tk automatically puts the menu bar above all the widgets laid out in the window.) The layout is illustrated in Figure 13.5, with the menu bar laid out by Tk shown with a white background, and our layouts shown with gray backgrounds.

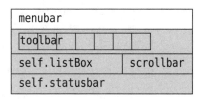

Figure 13.5 *The Bookmarks program's main window layouts*

When an image is added to a button it is added as a weak reference, so once the image goes out of scope it is scheduled for garbage collection. We must avoid this because we want the buttons to show their images after the initializer has finished, so we create an instance variable, self.toolbar_images, simply to hold references to the images to keep them alive for the program's lifetime.

Out of the box, Tk can read only a few image file formats, so we have had to use .gif images.* If any image is not found a tkinter.TclError exception is raised, so we must be careful to catch this to avoid the program terminating just because of a missing image.

Notice that we have not made all of the actions available from the menus available as toolbar buttons—this is common practice.

```
scrollbar = tkinter.Scrollbar(frame, orient=tkinter.VERTICAL)
self.listBox = tkinter.Listbox(frame,
                               yscrollcommand=scrollbar.set)
self.listBox.grid(row=1, column=0, sticky=tkinter.NSEW)
self.listBox.focus_set()
scrollbar["command"] = self.listBox.yview
scrollbar.grid(row=1, column=1, sticky=tkinter.NS)

self.statusbar = tkinter.Label(frame, text="Ready...",
                               anchor=tkinter.W)
self.statusbar.after(5000, self.clearStatusBar)
```

---

*If the Python Imaging Library's Tk extension is installed, all of the modern image formats become supported. See www.pythonware.com/products/pil/ for details.

```
self.statusbar.grid(row=2, column=0, columnspan=2,
                    sticky=tkinter.EW)
```

```
frame.grid(row=0, column=0, sticky=tkinter.NSEW)
```

The main window's central area (the area between the toolbar and the status bar) is occupied by a list box and an associated scrollbar. The list box is laid out to be sticky in all directions, and the scrollbar is sticky only north and south (vertically). Both widgets are added to the window frame's grid, side by side.

We must ensure that if the user scrolls the list box by tabbing into it and using the up and down arrow keys, or if they scroll the scrollbar, both widgets are kept in sync. This is achieved by setting the list box's yscrollcommand to the scrollbar's set() method (so that user navigation in the list box results in the scrollbar being moved if necessary), and by setting the scrollbar's command to the listbox's yview() method (so that scrollbar movements result in the list box being moved correspondingly).

The status bar is just a label. The after() method is a single shot timer (a timer that times out once after the given interval) whose first argument is a timeout in milliseconds and whose second argument is a function or method to call when the timeout is reached. This means that when the program starts up the status bar will show the text "Ready..." for five seconds, and then the status bar will be cleared. The status bar is laid out as the last row and is made sticky west and east (horizontally).

At the end we lay out the window's frame itself. We have now completed the creation and layout of the main window's widgets, but as things stand the widgets will assume a fixed default size, and if the window is resized the widgets will not change size to shrink or grow to fit. The next piece of code solves this problem and completes the initializer.

```
frame.columnconfigure(0, weight=999)
frame.columnconfigure(1, weight=1)
frame.rowconfigure(0, weight=1)
frame.rowconfigure(1, weight=999)
frame.rowconfigure(2, weight=1)

window = self.parent.winfo_toplevel()
window.columnconfigure(0, weight=1)
window.rowconfigure(0, weight=1)

self.parent.geometry("{0}x{1}+{2}+{3}".format(400, 500,
                                               0, 50))

self.parent.title("Bookmarks - Unnamed")
```

The columnconfigure() and rowconfigure() methods allow us to give weightings to a grid. We begin with the window frame, giving all the weight to the first column and the second row (which is occupied by the list box), so if the frame is resized any excess space is given to the list box. On its own this is not sufficient; we must also make the top-level window that contains the frame resizable, and we do this by getting a reference to the window using the wininfo_toplevel() method, and then making the window resizable by setting its row and column weights to 1.

At the end of the initializer we set an initial window size and position using a string of the form *widthxheight+x+y*. (If we wanted to set only the size we could use the form *widthxheight* instead.) Finally, we set the window's title, thereby completing the window's user interface.

If the user clicks a toolbar button or chooses a menu option a method is called to carry out the required action. And some of these methods rely on helper methods. We will now review all the methods in turn, starting with one that is called five seconds after the program starts.

```
def clearStatusBar(self):
    self.statusbar["text"] = ""
```

The status bar is a simple tkinter.Label. We could have used a lambda expression in the after() method call to clear it, but since we need to clear the status bar from more than one place we have created a method to do it.

```
def fileNew(self, *ignore):
    if not self.okayToContinue():
        return
    self.listBox.delete(0, tkinter.END)
    self.dirty = False
    self.filename = None
    self.data = {}
    self.parent.title("Bookmarks - Unnamed")
```

If the user wants to create a new bookmarks file we must first give them the chance to save any unsaved changes in the existing file if there is one. This is factored out into the MainWindow.okayToContinue() method since it is used in a few different places. The method returns True if it is okay to continue, and False otherwise. If continuing, we clear the list box by deleting all its entries from the first to the last—tkinter.END is a constant used to signify the last item in contexts where a widget can contain multiple items. Then we clear the dirty flag, filename, and data, since the file is new and unchanged, and we set the window title to reflect the fact that we have a new but unsaved file.

The ignore variable holds a sequence of zero or more positional arguments that we don't care about. In the case of methods invoked as a result of menu options choices or toolbar button presses there are no ignored arguments, but if a keyboard shortcut is used (e.g., Ctrl+N), then the invoking event is passed, and since we don't care how the user invoked the action, we ignore the event that requested it.

```
def okayToContinue(self):
    if not self.dirty:
        return True
    reply = tkinter.messagebox.askyesnocancel(
                    "Bookmarks - Unsaved Changes",
                    "Save unsaved changes?", parent=self.parent)
    if reply is None:
        return False
    if reply:
        return self.fileSave()
    return True
```

If the user wants to perform an action that will clear the list box (creating
or opening a new file, for example), we must give them a chance to save any
unsaved changes. If the file isn't dirty there are no changes to save, so we
return True right away. Otherwise, we pop up a standard message box with
Yes, No, and Cancel buttons. If the user cancels the reply is None; we take this to
mean that they don't want to continue the action they started and don't want
to save, so we just return False. If the user says yes, reply is True, so we give
them the chance to save and return True if they saved and False otherwise.
And if the user says no, reply is False, telling us not to save, but we still return
True because they want to continue the action they started, abandoning their
unsaved changes.

Tk's standard dialogs are not imported by import tkinter, so in addition to that
import we must do import tkinter.messagebox, and for the following method,
import tkinter.filedialog. On Windows and Mac OS X the standard native
dialogs are used, whereas on other platforms Tk-specific dialogs are used. We
always give the parent to standard dialogs since this ensures that they are
automatically centered over the parent window when they pop up.

All the standard dialogs are *modal*, which means that once one pops up, it is the
only window in the program that the user can interact with, so they must close
it (by clicking OK, Open, Cancel, or a similar button) before they can interact
with the rest of the program. Modal dialogs are easiest for programmers to
work with since the user cannot change the program's state behind the dialog's
back, and because they block until they are closed. The blocking means that
when we create or invoke a modal dialog the statement that follows will be
executed only when the dialog is closed.

```
def fileSave(self, *ignore):
    if self.filename is None:
        filename = tkinter.filedialog.asksaveasfilename(
                    title="Bookmarks - Save File",
                    initialdir=".",
                    filetypes=[("Bookmarks files", "*.bmf")],
                    defaultextension=".bmf",
```

```
                              parent=self.parent)
                  if not filename:
                      return False
                  self.filename = filename
                  if not self.filename.endswith(".bmf"):
                      self.filename += ".bmf"
          try:
              with open(self.filename, "wb") as fh:
                  pickle.dump(self.data, fh, pickle.HIGHEST_PROTOCOL)
              self.dirty = False
              self.setStatusBar("Saved {0} items to {1}".format(
                          len(self.data), self.filename))
              self.parent.title("Bookmarks - {0}".format(
                          os.path.basename(self.filename)))
          except (EnvironmentError, pickle.PickleError) as err:
              tkinter.messagebox.showwarning("Bookmarks - Error",
                      "Failed to save {0}:\n{1}".format(
                      self.filename, err), parent=self.parent)
          return True
```

If there is no current file we must ask the user to choose a filename. If they cancel we return False to indicate that the entire operation should be cancelled. Otherwise, we make sure that the given filename has the right extension. Using the existing or new filename we save the pickled self.data dictionary into the file. After saving the bookmarks we clear the dirty flag since there are now no unsaved changes, and put a message on the status bar (which will time out as we will see in a moment), and we update the window's title bar to include the filename (without the path). If we could not save the file, we pop up a warning message box (which will automatically have an OK button) to inform the user.

```
          def setStatusBar(self, text, timeout=5000):
              self.statusbar["text"] = text
              if timeout:
                  self.statusbar.after(timeout, self.clearStatusBar)
```

This method sets the status bar label's text, and if there is a timeout (a five-second timeout is the default), the method sets up a single shot timer to clear the status bar after the timeout period.

```
          def fileOpen(self, *ignore):
              if not self.okayToContinue():
                  return
              dir = (os.path.dirname(self.filename)
                      if self.filename is not None else ".")
              filename = tkinter.filedialog.askopenfilename(
```

```
                        title="Bookmarks - Open File",
                        initialdir=dir,
                        filetypes=[("Bookmarks files", "*.bmf")],
                        defaultextension=".bmf", parent=self.parent)
            if filename:
                self.loadFile(filename)
```

This method starts off the same as MainWindow.fileNew() to give the user the chance to save any unsaved changes or to cancel the file open action. If the user chooses to continue we want to give them a sensible starting directory, so we use the directory of the current file if there is one, and the current working directory otherwise. The filetypes argument is a list of (description, wildcard) 2-tuples that the file dialog should show. If the user chose a filename, we set the current filename to the one they chose and call the loadFile() method to do the actual file reading.

Separating out the loadFile() method is common practice to make it easier to load a file without having to prompt the user. For example, some programs load the last used file at start-up, and some programs have recently used files listed in a menu so that when the user chooses one the loadFile() method is called directly with the menu option's associated filename.

```
        def loadFile(self, filename):
            self.filename = filename
            self.listBox.delete(0, tkinter.END)
            self.dirty = False
            try:
                with open(self.filename, "rb") as fh:
                    self.data = pickle.load(fh)
                for name in sorted(self.data, key=str.lower):
                    self.listBox.insert(tkinter.END, name)
                self.setStatusBar("Loaded {0} bookmarks from {1}".format(
                            self.listBox.size(), self.filename))
                self.parent.title("Bookmarks - {0}".format(
                            os.path.basename(self.filename)))
            except (EnvironmentError, pickle.PickleError) as err:
                tkinter.messagebox.showwarning("Bookmarks - Error",
                        "Failed to load {0}:\n{1}".format(
                        self.filename, err), parent=self.parent)
```

When this method is called we know that any unsaved changes have been saved or abandoned, so we are free to clear the list box. We set the current filename to the one passed in, clear the list box and the dirty flag, and then attempt to open the file and unpickle it into the self.data dictionary. Once we have the data we iterate over all the bookmark names and append each one to the list box. Finally, we give an informative message in the status bar and update the window's title bar. If we could not read the file or if we couldn't unpickle it, we pop up a warning message box to inform the user.

```
def fileQuit(self, event=None):
    if self.okayToContinue():
        self.parent.destroy()
```

This is the last file menu option method. We give the user the chance to save any unsaved changes; if they cancel we do nothing and the program continues; otherwise, we tell the parent to destroy itself and this leads to a clean program termination. If we wanted to save user preferences we would do so here, just before the destroy() call.

```
def editAdd(self, *ignore):
    form = AddEditForm(self.parent)
    if form.accepted and form.name:
        self.data[form.name] = form.url
        self.listBox.delete(0, tkinter.END)
        for name in sorted(self.data, key=str.lower):
            self.listBox.insert(tkinter.END, name)
        self.dirty = True
```

If the user asks to add a new bookmark (by clicking Edit→Add, or by clicking the ✚ toolbar button, or by pressing the Ctrl+A keyboard shortcut), this method is called. The AddEditForm is a custom dialog covered in the next subsection; all that we need to know to use it is that it has an accepted flag which is set to True if the user clicked OK, and to False if they clicked Cancel, and two data attributes, name and url, that hold the name and URL of the bookmark the user has added or edited.

We create a new AddEditForm which immediately pops up as a modal dialog—and therefore blocks, so the if form.accepted ... statement is not executed until the dialog has closed.

If the user clicked OK in the AddEditForm dialog and they gave the bookmark a name, we add the new bookmark's name and URL to the self.data dictionary. Then we clear the list box and reinsert all the data in sorted order. It would be more efficient to simply insert the new bookmark in the right place, but even with hundreds of bookmarks the difference would hardly be noticeable on a modern machine. At the end we set the dirty flag since we now have an unsaved change.

```
def editEdit(self, *ignore):
    indexes = self.listBox.curselection()
    if not indexes or len(indexes) > 1:
        return
    index = indexes[0]
```

```
name = self.listBox.get(index)
form = AddEditForm(self.parent, name, self.data[name])
if form.accepted and form.name:
    self.data[form.name] = form.url
    if form.name != name:
        del self.data[name]
        self.listBox.delete(0, tkinter.END)
        for name in sorted(self.data, key=str.lower):
            self.listBox.insert(tkinter.END, name)
    self.dirty = True
```

Editing is slightly more involved than adding because first we must find the bookmark the user wants to edit. The curselection() method returns a (possibly empty) list of index positions for all its selected items. If exactly one item is selected we retrieve its text since that is the name of the bookmark the user wants to edit (and also the key to the self.data dictionary). We then create a new AddEditForm passing the name and URL of the bookmark the user wants to edit.

After the form has been closed, if the user clicked OK and set a nonempty bookmark name we update the self.data dictionary. If the new name and the old name are the same we can just set the dirty flag and we are finished (in this case presumably the user edited the URL), but if the bookmark's name has changed we delete the dictionary item whose key is the old name, clear the list box, and then repopulate the list box with the bookmarks just as we did after adding a bookmark.

```
def editDelete(self, *ignore):
    indexes = self.listBox.curselection()
    if not indexes or len(indexes) > 1:
        return
    index = indexes[0]
    name = self.listBox.get(index)
    if tkinter.messagebox.askyesno("Bookmarks - Delete",
                        "Delete '{0}'?".format(name)):
        self.listBox.delete(index)
        self.listBox.focus_set()
        del self.data[name]
        self.dirty = True
```

To delete a bookmark we must first find out which bookmark the user has chosen, so this method begins with the same lines that the MainWindow.editEdit() method starts with. If exactly one bookmark is selected we pop up a message box asking the user whether they really want to delete it. If they say yes the message box function returns True and we delete the bookmark from the list box and from the self.data dictionary, and set the dirty flag. We also set the keyboard focus back to the list box.

```
def editShowWebPage(self, *ignore):
    indexes = self.listBox.curselection()
    if not indexes or len(indexes) > 1:
        return
    index = indexes[0]
    url = self.data[self.listBox.get(index)]
    webbrowser.open_new_tab(url)
```

If the user invokes this method we find the bookmark they have selected and retrieve the corresponding URL from the self.data dictionary. Then we use the webbrowser module's webbrowser.open_new_tab() function to open the user's web browser with the given URL. If the web browser is not already running, it will be launched.

```
application = tkinter.Tk()
path = os.path.join(os.path.dirname(__file__), "images/")
if sys.platform.startswith("win"):
    icon = path + "bookmark.ico"
    application.iconbitmap(icon, default=icon)
else:
    application.iconbitmap("@" + path + "bookmark.xbm")
window = MainWindow(application)
application.protocol("WM_DELETE_WINDOW", window.fileQuit)
application.mainloop()
```

The last lines of the program are similar to those used for the interest-tk.pyw program we saw earlier, but with three differences. One difference is that if the user clicks the program window's close box a different method is called for the Bookmarks program than the one used for the Interest program. Another difference is that on Windows the iconbitmap() method has an additional argument which allows us to specify a default icon for all the program's windows—this is not needed on Unix platforms since this happens automatically. And the last difference is that we set the application's title (in the title bar) in the MainWindow class's methods rather than here. For the Interest program the title never changed, so it needed to be set only once, but for the Bookmarks program we change the title text to include the name of the bookmarks file being worked on.

Now that we have seen the implementation of the main window's class and the code that initializes the program and starts off the event loop, we can turn our attention to the AddEditForm dialog.

Creating a Custom Dialog

The AddEditForm dialog provides a means by which users can add and edit bookmark names and URLs. It is shown in Figure 13.6 where it is being used to edit an existing bookmark (hence the "Edit" in the title). The same dialog can also be used for adding bookmarks. We will begin by reviewing the dialog's initializer, broken into four parts.

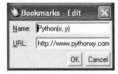

Figure 13.6 *The Bookmarks program's Add/Edit dialog*

```
class AddEditForm(tkinter.Toplevel):

    def __init__(self, parent, name=None, url=None):
        super(AddEditForm, self).__init__(parent)
        self.parent = parent
        self.accepted = False
        self.transient(self.parent)
        self.title("Bookmarks - " + (
                    "Edit" if name is not None else "Add"))

        self.nameVar = tkinter.StringVar()
        if name is not None:
            self.nameVar.set(name)
        self.urlVar = tkinter.StringVar()
        self.urlVar.set(url if url is not None else "http://")
```

We have chosen to inherit tkinter.TopLevel, a bare widget designed to serve as a base class for widgets used as top-level windows. (As noted earlier, we would like to write super().__init__(parent), but since this does not work we have called super() with the parent class and self object passed explicitly as arguments.) We keep a reference to the parent and create a self.accepted attribute and set it to False. The call to the transient() method is done to inform the parent window that this window must always appear on top of the parent. The title is set to indicate adding or editing depending on whether a name and URL have been passed in. Two tkinter.StringVars are created to keep track of the bookmark's name and URL, and both are initialized with the passed in values if the dialog is being used for editing.

```
        frame = tkinter.Frame(self)
        nameLabel = tkinter.Label(frame, text="Name:", underline=0)
        nameEntry = tkinter.Entry(frame, textvariable=self.nameVar)
```

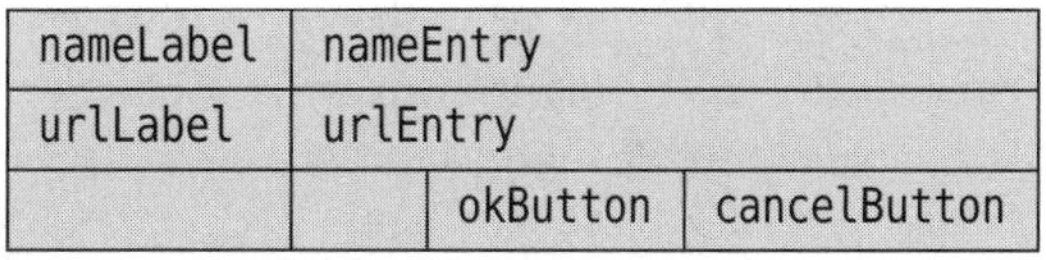

nameLabel	nameEntry		
urlLabel	urlEntry		
		okButton	cancelButton

Figure 13.7 *The Bookmarks program's Add/Edit dialog's layout*

```
nameEntry.focus_set()
urlLabel = tkinter.Label(frame, text="URL:", underline=0)
urlEntry = tkinter.Entry(frame, textvariable=self.urlVar)
okButton = tkinter.Button(frame, text="OK", command=self.ok)
cancelButton = tkinter.Button(frame, text="Cancel",
                                command=self.close)

nameLabel.grid(row=0, column=0, sticky=tkinter.W, pady=3,
            padx=3)
nameEntry.grid(row=0, column=1, columnspan=3,
            sticky=tkinter.EW, pady=3, padx=3)
urlLabel.grid(row=1, column=0, sticky=tkinter.W, pady=3,
            padx=3)
urlEntry.grid(row=1, column=1, columnspan=3,
            sticky=tkinter.EW, pady=3, padx=3)
okButton.grid(row=2, column=2, sticky=tkinter.EW, pady=3,
            padx=3)
cancelButton.grid(row=2, column=3, sticky=tkinter.EW, pady=3,
            padx=3)
```

The widgets are created and laid out in a grid, as illustrated in Figure 13.7. The name and URL text entry widgets are associated with the corresponding tkinter.StringVars and the two buttons are set to call the self.ok() and self.close() methods shown further on.

```
frame.grid(row=0, column=0, sticky=tkinter.NSEW)
frame.columnconfigure(1, weight=1)
window = self.winfo_toplevel()
window.columnconfigure(0, weight=1)
```

It only makes sense for the dialog to be resized horizontally, so we make the window frame's second column horizontally resizable by setting its column weight to 1—this means that if the frame is horizontally stretched the widgets in column 1 (the name and URL text entry widgets) will grow to take advantage of the extra space. Similarly, we make the window's column horizontally resizable by setting its weight to 1. If the user changes the dialog's height, the widgets will keep their relative positions and all of them will be centered within the window; but if the user changes the dialog's width, the name and URL text entry widgets will shrink or grow to fit the available horizontal space.

```
self.bind("<Alt-n>", lambda *ignore: nameEntry.focus_set())
self.bind("<Alt-u>", lambda *ignore: urlEntry.focus_set())
self.bind("<Return>", self.ok)
self.bind("<Escape>", self.close)

self.protocol("WM_DELETE_WINDOW", self.close)
self.grab_set()
self.wait_window(self)
```

We created two labels, Name: and URL:, which indicate that they have keyboard accelerators Alt+N and Alt+U, which when clicked will give the keyboard focus to their corresponding text entry widgets. To make this work we have provided the necessary keyboard bindings. We use lambda functions rather than pass the focus_set() methods directly so that we can ignore the event argument. We have also provided the standard keyboard bindings (Enter and Esc) for the OK and Cancel buttons.

We use the protocol() method to specify the method to call if the user closes the dialog by clicking the close button. The calls to grab_set() and wait_window() are both needed to turn the window into a modal dialog.

```
def ok(self, event=None):
    self.name = self.nameVar.get()
    self.url = self.urlVar.get()
    self.accepted = True
    self.close()
```

If the user clicks OK (or presses Enter), this method is called. The texts from the tkinter.StringVars are copied to correponding instance variables (which are only now created), the self.accepted variable is set to True, and we call self.close() to close the dialog.

```
def close(self, event=None):
    self.parent.focus_set()
    self.destroy()
```

This method is called from the self.ok() method, or if the user clicks the window's close box or if the user clicks Cancel (or presses Esc). It gives the keyboard focus back to the parent and makes the dialog destroy itself. In this context destroy just means that the window and its widgets are destroyed; the AddEditForm instance continues to exist because the caller has a reference to it.

After the dialog has been closed the caller checks the accepted variable, and if True, retrieves the name and URL that were added or edited. Then, once the MainWindow.editAdd() or MainWindow.editEdit() method has finished, the AddEditForm object goes out of scope and is scheduled for garbage collection.

Summary

This chapter gave you a flavor of GUI programming using the Tk GUI library. Tk's big advantage is that it comes as standard with Python. But it has many drawbacks, not the least of which is that it is a vintage library that works somewhat differently than most of the more modern alternatives.

If you are new to GUI programming, keep in mind that the major cross-platform competitors to Tk—PyGtk, PyQt, and wxPython—are all much easier to learn and use than Tk, and all can achieve better results using less code. Furthermore, these Tk competitors all have more and better Python-specific documentation, far more widgets, and a better look and feel, and allow us to create widgets from scratch with complete control over their appearance and behavior.

Although Tk is useful for creating very small programs or for situations where only Python's standard library is available, in all other circumstances any one of the other cross-platform libraries is a much better choice.

Exercises

The first exercise involves copying and modifying the Bookmarks program shown in this chapter; the second exercise involves creating a GUI program from scratch.

1. Copy the `bookmarks-tk.pyw` program and modify it so that it can import and export the DBM files that the `bookmarks.py` console program (created as an exercise in Chapter 11) uses. Provide two new menu options in the File menu, Import and Export. Make sure you provide keyboard shortcuts for both (keep in mind that Ctrl+E is already in use for Edit→Edit). Similarly, create two corresponding toolbar buttons. This involves adding about five lines of code to the main window's initializer.

   Two methods to provide the functionality will be required, `fileImport()` and `fileExport()`, between them fewer than 60 lines of code including error handling. For importing you can decide whether to merge imported bookmarks, or to replace the existing bookmarks with those imported. The code is not difficult, but does require quite a bit of care. A solution (that merges imported bookmarks) is provided in `bookmarks-tk_ans.py`.

2. In Chapter 12 we saw how to create and use regular expressions to match text. Create a dialog-style GUI program that can be used to enter and test regexes, as shown in Figure 13.8.

   You will need to read the `re` module's documentation since the program must behave correctly in the face of invalid regexes or when iterating over

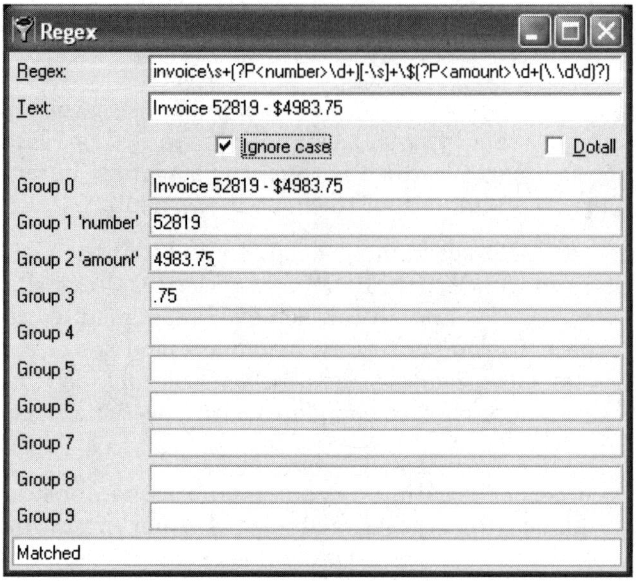

Figure 13.8 *The Regex program*

the match groups, since in most cases the regex won't have as many match groups as there are labels to show them. Make sure the program has full support for keyboard users—with navigation to the text entry widgets using Alt+R and Alt+T, control of the checkboxes with Alt+I and Alt+D, program termination on Ctrl+Q and Esc, and recalculation if the user presses and releases a key in either of the text entry widgets, and whenever a checkbox is checked or unchecked.

The program is not too difficult to write, although the code for displaying the matches and the group numbers (and names where specified) is a tiny bit tricky—a solution is provided in regex-tk.pyw, which is about one hundred forty lines.

Epilogue

If you've read at least the first six chapters and either done the exercises or written your own Python 3 programs independently, you should be in a good position to build up your experience and programming skills as far as you want to go—Python won't hold you back!

To improve and deepen your Python language skills, if you read only the first six chapters, make sure you are familiar with the material in Chapter 7, and that you read and experiment with at least some of the material in Chapter 8, and in particular the with statement and context managers.

Keep in mind, though, that apart from the pleasure and learning aspects of developing everything from scratch, doing so is rarely necessary in Python. We have already mentioned the standard library and the Python Package Index, pypi.python.org/pypi, both of which provide a huge amount of functionality. In addition, the online Python Cookbook at code.activestate.com/recipes/langs/python/ offers a large number of tricks, tips, and ideas, although it is Python 2-oriented at the time of this writing.

It is also possible to create modules for Python in other languages (any language that can export C functions, as most can). These can be developed to work cooperatively with Python using Python's C API. Shared libraries (DLLs on Windows), whether created by us or obtained from a third party, can be accessed from Python using the ctypes module, giving us virtually unlimited access to the vast amount of functionality available over the Internet thanks to the skill and generosity of open source programmers world wide.

And if you want to participate in the Python community, a good place to start is www.python.org/community where you will find Wikis and many general and special-interest mailing lists.

Index

All functions and methods are listed under their class or module, and in most cases also as top-level terms in their own right. For modules that contain classes, look under the class for its methods. Where a method or function name is close enough to a concept, the concept is not usually listed. For example, there is no entry for "splitting strings", but there are entries for the str.split() *method.*

Symbols

Q

R

Z

About the Author

Mark Summerfield

Mark is a computer science graduate with many years experience working in the software industry, primarily as a programmer. He also spent almost three years as Trolltech's documentation manager during which he founded and edited Trolltech's technical journal, *Qt Quarterly*. (Trolltech is now Nokia's Qt Software.) Mark is the coauthor of *C++ GUI Programming with Qt 4*, and author of *Rapid GUI Programming with Python and Qt: The Definitive Guide to PyQt Programming*. Mark owns Qtrac Ltd., www.qtrac.eu, where he works as an independent author, editor, trainer, and consultant, specializing in C++, Qt, Python, and PyQt.

Production

The text was written using the gvim text editor and marked up with the Lout typesetting language. All the diagrams were produced using Lout. The index was compiled by the author. Almost all of the code snippets were automatically extracted directly from the example programs and from test programs. The text and source code was version-controlled using Bazaar. The monospaced font used for code is derived from a condensed version of DejaVu Mono and was modified using FontForge. The marked-up text was previewed using kpdf, gv, and especially evince, and converted to PostScript by Lout, then to PDF by Ghostscript. The cover was provided by the publisher and features Kidwelly Castle.

All the editing and processing were done on Fedora and Kubuntu systems. All the example programs have been tested on Windows, Linux, and Mac OS X.

3.0

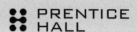

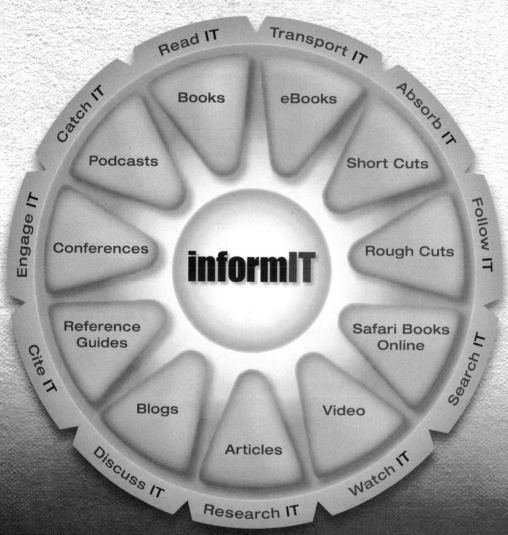

Try Safari Books Online FREE
Get online access to 5,000+ Books and Videos

 **FREE TRIAL—GET STARTED TODAY!**
www.informit.com/safaritrial

Find trusted answers, fast
Only Safari lets you search across thousands of best-selling books from the top technology publishers, including Addison-Wesley Professional, Cisco Press, O'Reilly, Prentice Hall, Que, and Sams.

Master the latest tools and techniques
In addition to gaining access to an incredible inventory of technical books, Safari's extensive collection of video tutorials lets you learn from the leading video training experts.

WAIT, THERE'S MORE!

Keep your competitive edge
With Rough Cuts, get access to the developing manuscript and be among the first to learn the newest technologies.

Stay current with emerging technologies
Short Cuts and Quick Reference Sheets are short, concise, focused content created to get you up-to-speed quickly on new and cutting-edge technologies.

FREE Online Edition

Your purchase of **Programming in Python 3** includes access to a free online edition for 45 days through the Safari Books Online subscription service. Nearly every Addison-Wesley Professional book is available online through Safari Books Online, along with more than 5,000 other technical books and videos from publishers such as Cisco Press, Exam Cram, IBM Press, O'Reilly, Prentice Hall, Que, and Sams.

SAFARI BOOKS ONLINE allows you to search for a specific answer, cut and paste code, download chapters, and stay current with emerging technologies.

Activate your FREE Online Edition at www.informit.com/safarifree

> **STEP 1:** Enter the coupon code: PGGSLZG.

> **STEP 2:** New Safari users, complete the brief registration form.
> Safari subscribers, just log in.

If you have difficulty registering on Safari or accessing the online edition, please e-mail customer-service@safaribooksonline.com